"*Fifty Key Figures in Cyberpunk Culture* is an excellent introduction to some of the writers, artists, theorists, and scientists whose influence has helped to shape today's technocultural imaginary. Readers will (re)discover cyberpunk culture's *makers*, from J.G. Ballard to Rosi Braidotti, from Marshall McLuhan to Richard K. Morgan, from Rudy Rucker to Joanna Russ, from Vernor Vinge to Norbert Wiener. *Fifty Key Figures* is both an exciting supplement to McFarlane Murphy, and Schmeink's recently published *The Routledge Companion to Cyberpunk Culture* and an important contribution to cyberculture studies in general."

— **Veronica Hollinger**, Editor of *Science Fiction Studies* and Professor Emerita of Cultural Studies at Trent University, Canada

"*Fifty Key Figures in Cyberpunk Culture* brings together a truly diverse and global array of entries that explodes the limits of cyberpunk's perceived 'monocromatism,' and heteronormative, masculine biases. The entries gathered here reveal cyberpunk to be a key cultural formation for investigating the racial, class, gender, and sexual intersections of our increasingly techno-saturated late-capitalist present. Your favorite 'deep-cut' author might be missing, but you'll discover far more than you'll miss."

— **Hugh Charles O'Connell**, Assistant Professor of English, University of Massachusetts Boston, USA

"From classic Movement sf writers like William Gibson, Bruce Sterling, and Pat Cadigan to key precursors like Samuel R. Delany, Joanna Russ, James Tiptree, Jr., and Philip K. Dick and contemporary practitioners like Charlie Brooker, Lana and Lilly Wachowski, Lauren Beukes, and Janelle Monáe—with a truly global collection of writers, filmmakers, scientists, and philosophers spanning every field of art and innovation over more than a century—McFarlane, Murphy, and Schmeink's *Fifty Key Figures* lays any possible doubt to rest: cyberpunk still rules our world."

— **Gerry Canavan**, President of the *Science Fiction Research Association* and Associate Professor of English, Marquette University, USA

FIFTY KEY FIGURES IN CYBERPUNK CULTURE

A collection of engaging essays on some of the most significant figures in cyberpunk culture, this outstanding guide charts the rich and varied landscape of cyberpunk from the 1970s to the present day.

The collection features key figures from a variety of disciplines, from novelists, critical and cultural theorists, philosophers, and scholars, to filmmakers, comic book artists, game creators, and television writers. Important and influential names discussed include J.G. Ballard, Jean Baudrillard, Rosi Braidotti, Charlie Brooker, Pat Cadigan, William Gibson, Donna J. Haraway, Nalo Hopkinson, Janelle Monáe, Annalee Newitz, Katsuhiro Ōtomo, Sadie Plant, Mike Pondsmith, Ridley Scott, Bruce Sterling, and the Wachowskis. The editors also include an afterword of 'Honorable Mentions' to highlight additional figures and groups of note that have played a role in shaping cyberpunk.

This accessible guide will be of interest to students and scholars of cultural studies, film studies, literature, media studies, as well as anyone with an interest in cyberpunk culture and science fiction.

Anna McFarlane is Lecturer in Medical Humanities at the University of Leeds, working on traumatic pregnancy and its expression in science fiction, horror, and fantasy. She is the co-editor of *The Routledge Companion to Cyberpunk Culture* (2020) and is co-editing *The Edinburgh Companion to Science Fiction and the Medical Humanities.* Her first monograph is a study of William Gibson's novels, *Cyberpunk Culture and Psychology: Seeing Through the Mirrorshades* (2021).

Graham J. Murphy is Professor with the School of English and Liberal Studies, Faculty of Arts, Seneca College. He is co-editor of *Beyond Cyberpunk: New Critical Perspectives* (2010), *Cyberpunk and Visual Culture* (2018), and *The Routledge Companion to Cyberpunk Culture* (2020). In addition to numerous book chapters and journal articles, he authored "Cyberpunk and Post-Cyberpunk" for *The Cambridge*

History of Science Fiction (2019) and a chapter on feminist cyberpunk for *The Routledge Companion to Gender and Science Fiction* (2022).

Lars Schmeink is Research Fellow at the Europa-Universität Flensburg and Lead Researcher of the "Science Fiction" subproject of "Future Work," a federally funded research project on labor in the 22nd century. He is also the author of *Biopunk Dystopias: Genetic Engineering, Society, and Science Fiction* (2016), and the co-editor of *Cyberpunk and Visual Culture* (2018), *The Routledge Companion to Cyberpunk Culture* (2020), and *New Perspectives on Contemporary German Science Fiction* (2022).

FIFTY KEY FIGURES IN CYBERPUNK CULTURE

Edited by
Anna McFarlane, Graham J. Murphy, and
Lars Schmeink

NEW YORK AND LONDON

Cover image: akinbostanci / Getty images

First published 2022
by Routledge
605 Third Avenue, New York, NY 10158

and by Routledge
4 Park Square, Milton Park, Abingdon, Oxon, OX14 4RN

Routledge is an imprint of the Taylor & Francis Group, an informa business

Library of Congress Cataloging-in-Publication Data
Names: McFarlane, Anna, editor. | Murphy, Graham J., 1970- editor. |
Schmeink, Lars, editor.
Title: Fifty key figures in cyberpunk culture / edited by Anna McFarlane, Graham
J. Murphy, and Lars Schmeink.
Description: New York, NY : Routledge, 2022. | Includes bibliographical
references and index.
Identifiers: LCCN 2021057710 (print) | LCCN 2021057711 (ebook) |
ISBN 9780367549176 (hbk) | ISBN 9780367549138 (pbk) |
ISBN 9781003091189 (ebk)
Subjects: LCSH: Cyberpunk culture.
Classification: LCC HM646 .F53 2022 (print) | LCC HM646 (ebook) |
DDC 306/.1—dc23/eng/20220104
LC record available at https://lccn.loc.gov/2021057710
LC ebook record available at https://lccn.loc.gov/2021057711

ISBN: 978-0-367-54917-6 (hbk)
ISBN: 978-0-367-54913-8 (pbk)
ISBN: 978-1-003-09118-9 (ebk)

DOI: 10.4324/9781003091189

Typeset in Bembo
by codeMantra

To Daniel
AM

To Steve, the best man
and
Jennifer and Declan, always
GJM

Once more with feeling …
LS

CONTENTS

ALPHABETICAL LIST
OF CONTENTS

CONTRIBUTORS

Stina Attebery is Lecturer at California Polytechnic State University, San Luis Obispo. She has published articles in the journals *American Quarterly*, *Medical Humanities*, *Extrapolation*, *Trace*, and *Humanimalia* and contributed to the collections *Gender and Environment in Science Fiction* (2018), *Cyberpunk and Visual Culture* (2018), and *The Routledge Companion to Cyberpunk Culture* (2020). She serves as the Division Head for Film and Television for the International Association for the Fantastic in the Arts and as an external editorial board member for *Studies in the Fantastic*.

Filip Boratyn is a Ph.D. student at the University of Warsaw. His dissertation project focuses on the cultural work of enchantment in the contemporary ecological imagination. He is the recipient of the 2020 David G. Hartwell Emerging Scholar Award from the International Association for the Fantastic in the Arts.

Mark Bould is Professor in Film and Literature at UWE Bristol, and a recipient of both the SFRA Award for Lifetime Contributions to SF Scholarship (2016) and the IAFA Distinguished Scholarship Award (2019). He co-edits the monograph series *Studies in Global Science Fiction*. His most recent books are *M. John Harrison: Critical Essays* (2019) and *The Anthropocene Unconscious* (2021).

Jędrzej Burszta holds a Ph.D. in Cultural Studies from the SWPS University in Warsaw (2019), and is Affiliated Faculty Member at the American Studies Center, University of Warsaw. His research interests include ethnography, queer theory, American speculative fiction, and popular culture. He recently co-edited (with Tomasz Basiuk) the volume *Queers in State Socialism: Cruising 1970s Poland* (2021), and is currently working on a monograph dedicated to queer science fiction literature. He is also a novelist and writes for the theater.

Willian Perpétuo Busch is a Brazilian Ph.D. candidate at Universidade Federal do Paraná, working on the history of science fiction in American academia.

Ritch Calvin teaches Women's, Gender, and Sexuality Studies at SUNY Stony Brook. He is the author of *Queering SF: Readings* (2022), *Feminist Science Fiction and Feminist Epistemology: Four Modes* (2016), and co-editor of *SF101: A Guide to Teaching and Studying Science Fiction* (2014); other work appears in *Science Fiction Studies*, *Extrapolation*, *Femspec*, *Utopian Studies*, *The Journal of the Fantastic in the Arts*, *Science Fiction Film and Television*, *The New York Review of Science Fiction*, and *The SFRA Review*.

Jeanne Cortiel is Professor of American Studies at the University of Bayreuth and the author of *Demand My Writing: Joanna Russ, Feminism and Science Fiction* (1999), *Passion für das Unmögliche* (2001), and *With a Barbarous Din: Race and Ethnic Encounter in Mid-Nineteenth-Century American Literature* (2016). Most recently, she has co-edited *Practices of Speculation: Modeling, Embodiment and Figuration* (2020). She is currently working on a project that explores global catastrophic risk in contemporary dystopian/utopian science fiction, film, and graphic narrative.

Doug Davis is Professor of English at Gordon State College in Barnesville, GA, where he teaches literature and writing. He is one of the authors of the OER American Literature textbook, *Writing the Nation* (2018), as well as the co-editor of the pedagogical ebook, *Science Fiction 101: Tools for Teaching SF in the Classroom* (2014), two special issues of the *Flannery O'Connor Review* on the topic of science and technology in O'Connor's fiction, and a special issue of *Configurations* on Kim Stanley Robinson. He has published essays on a range of topics, including the extinction of the dinosaurs, the cold war nuclear threat, science fiction pedagogy, and the fiction of Michael Bishop, James Dickey, Walker Percy, and Flannery O'Connor.

Sébastien Doubinsky is Associate Professor in the French Department of the University of Aarhus, Denmark. His research fields cover translation theory, reading theory and speculative fiction. He co-authored *Reading Literature Today* (2011) with Tabish Khair. He is also an established bilingual novelist and poet. His dystopian novel, *Missing Signal*, published by Meerkat Press, won the Bronze Foreword Reviews Award in the Best Science-Fiction Novel category in 2018.

Christophe Duret is Postdoctoral Fellow at the University of Montreal's Video Games Observation and Documentation University Lab, where he is conducting research on the representation of urban spaces in cyberpunk video games from the 2010s. He holds a doctorate in French Studies and a master's in Communication from the University of Sherbrooke, where he has been Lecturer since 2016. He has also co-edited a book on intertextuality in video games and has published several articles in journals such as *Sciences du Jeu, Communication & organisation, Itinéraires: Littérature, Textes, Cultures, Recherches en communication,* and *Intermédialités.* His research interests include mesocritics, videogame studies, transmediality, intermediality, and surveillance studies.

Adam Edwards is Ph.D. Researcher at the University of Birmingham, whose research is in cyberpunk literature in all its forms. His thesis connects earlier analysis of the genre to its modern iterations to reject a historicization of cyberpunk and emphasizes its continuing relevance. His research interests include science fiction, media studies, video games, and tabletop role-playing games.

Leighton Evans is an Associate Professor of Media Theory at Swansea University. He is the author of *Locative Social Media* (2015), *The Re-Emergence of Virtual Reality* (2018), and the co-author of *Location-Based Social Media: Space, Time and Identity* (2017), and *Intergenerational Locative Play: Augmenting Family* (2021).

Matthew Flisfeder is Associate Professor of Rhetoric and Communications at the University of Winnipeg. He is the author of *Algorithmic Desire: Toward a New Structuralist Theory of Social Media* (2021), *Postmodern Theory and Blade Runner* (2017), and *The Symbolic, The Sublime, and Slavoj Žižek's Theory of Film* (2012). He is the co-editor of *Žižek and Media Studies: A Reader* (2014).

Benjamin Franz is Coordinator of Cataloging and Metadata and Film Librarian at the Charles Evans Inniss Memorial Library for Medgar Evers College CUNY. A researcher with an interest in science fiction, cyberpunk, morality plays, horror, and surrealist cinema, he has been published in journals and books that include the BSFA journal *Vector, The Film and History Journal* and *The Simpsons Did It: Post Modernity in Yellow* (2014). His presentations have been a regular feature at the Film and History Center of Lawrence University's annual conference. He has chaired the Science Fiction area since 2017.

He currently serves as the chair of the American Library Association's (ALA) Film and Media Roundtable.

Paweł Frelik is Associate Professor and the Leader of Speculative Texts and Media Research Group at the American Studies Center, University of Warsaw. His teaching and research interests include science fiction, video games, and fantastic visualities. He has published widely in these fields and serves on the boards of *Science Fiction Studies, Extrapolation*, and *Journal of Gaming and Virtual Worlds*. In 2017, he was the first non-Anglophone recipient of the Thomas D. Clareson Award for Distinguished Service.

Francis Gene-Rowe teaches Science Fiction and Utopian Studies to English and History students at the University of Surrey and Royal Holloway, University of London. He writes on Philip K. Dick, William Blake, Ursula K. Le Guin, Walter Benjamin, tabletop gaming, anti-racism, petrocultures, ecology, speculative poetry and poetics, critical dystopia, situated knowledges, and goblin futures. He is a co-director of the London Science Fiction Research Community, Councillor of the British Science Fiction Association, and UK Representative for the Science Fiction Research Association.

María Goicoechea is Teacher and Researcher in the Department of English Studies at the Complutense University of Madrid. She has published extensively on cyberculture from the double perspective of science fiction and electronic literature. Her latest publications in English include the chapters "Bruce Sterling: Schismatrix Plus (Case Study)" in *The Routledge Companion to Cyberpunk Culture* (2020) and "The Dream of Interactivity in Children Literary Media" in *The Routledge Companion to Literary Media* (forthcoming).

Julia Grillmayr is a cultural studies scholar, broadcaster, journalist, and science communicator in Vienna and Linz, Austria. Her postdoctoral project at the University of Art and Design in Linz (funded by the Austrian Science Fund FWF) investigated the relationship between futurological 'scenario thinking' and contemporary science fiction literature.

Dan Hassler-Forest works as Assistant Professor of Media and Cultural Studies at Utrecht University. He has published books and articles on superhero movies, comics, transmedia storytelling, critical theory, and zombies. He has most recently completed two books on race and global media, focusing on the creative work of performing artist Janelle Monáe.

Anya Heise-von der Lippe teaches English Literature and Culture at the University of Tübingen. She holds an MA from the Technische Universität in Berlin and a Ph.D. in English Literature from the University of Tübingen. Publications include the edited collection *Posthuman Gothic* (2018) and the monograph *Monstrous Textualities* (2021), both published by the University of Wales Press. Her current research focuses on Romanticism and climate change. She is co-editor of the "Challenges for the Humanities" series with Narr Academic Publishers.

David M. Higgins is a Senior Editor for the *Los Angeles Review of Books*, and the Chair of the English Department at Inver Hills College in Minnesota, where he teaches classes on science fiction, graphic novels, and American literature. He is the author of *Reverse Colonization: Science Fiction, Imperial Fantasy, and Alt-Victimhood* (2021), and his article, "Toward a Cosmopolitan Science Fiction," won the 2012 SFRA Innovative Research Award. David's research has been published in *American Literature*, *Science Fiction Studies*, *Paradoxa*, and *Extrapolation*, and his work has appeared in *The Cambridge History of Science Fiction* and *The Cambridge Companion to American Science Fiction*. David has been a featured speaker on NPR's radio show *On Point*, and he serves as the Second Vice President for the International Association for the Fantastic in the Arts (IAFA).

Rebecca J. Holden is a fan and scholar of feminist, African American, and YA science fiction. She earned her Ph.D. in English Literature from the University of Wisconsin-Madison and is currently Principal Lecturer in the English Department at the University of Maryland, College Park. Holden has published essays, book chapters, and reviews on topics ranging from young adult Afrofuturism to feminist cyberpunk, and points in between, in *Foundation*, *Science Fiction Studies*, *Oxford Bibliographies in American Literature*, *Los Angeles Review of Books*, *Literary Afrofuturism in the Twenty-First Century*, *Luminescent Threads: Connections to Octavia Butler*, *Women of Other Worlds: Excursions through Science Fiction and Feminism* and others. With Nisi Shawl, Holden co-edited and contributed to the Locus-nominated *Strange Matings: Science Fiction, Feminism, African American Voices, and Octavia E. Butler* (2013).

Matthew Iung is Editorial Assistant for the *Los Angeles Review of Books*. He has a bachelor's degree in English (with minors in History and Journalism) from Concordia University in St. Paul, Minnesota. His publications have appeared in *The Routledge Companion to Cyberpunk Culture* as well as in Concordia's newspaper *The Sword*, and online in *Talking Comics* and *DM du Jour*. Matthew is an aspiring journalist with a lifelong love of comics, literature, and the arcane.

Agnieszka Kiejziewicz holds a Ph.D. in the Arts and Humanities and is author of *Japanese Cyberpunk: From Avant-Garde Transgressions to the Popular Cinema* (2018), *Japanese Avant-Garde and Experimental Film* (2020), and *Completed in Apparent Incompletion. The Sculpture Art of Wojciech Sęczawa* (2021). She works at the University of Gdańsk (Poland), where she teaches about new media, Asian cinema, and academic writing. Dr. Kiejziewicz also contributes to the development of The University of Gdańsk Film Center and cooperates with cultural institutions and art galleries. In her research activities, she focuses on the role of new technologies in society, body transgressions, and visual experiments following avant-garde aesthetics.

Christopher D. Kilgore has published on narrative theory, cyberpunk culture, and interdisciplinary writing support, and has taught college-level courses in literature and writing. He is currently Associate Director for the Scholarship of Teaching and Learning in the office of Teaching & Learning Innovation at the University of Tennessee, Knoxville.

Michał Kłosiński, Associate Professor at The Faculty of Humanities, University of Silesia, Poland, is an active member of Utopian Studies Society and The Society for Utopian Studies. During his doctoral studies, he participated in the Paris Program in Critical Theory. He published various articles on Polish literature, literary theory, and videogames in *Game Studies*, *International Journal of Baudrillard Studies*, *Pamiętnik Literacki*, *Teksty Drugie*, and *Wielogłos*. He is the author of *Świat pęknięty. O poemach naiwnych Czesława Miłosza* (2013), *Ratunkiem jest tylko poezja Baudrillard – Teoria – Literatura* (2015), and *Hermeneutyka gier wideo. Interpretacja immersja, utopia* (2018). He also co-edited *More After More. Essays Commemorating the Five-Hundredth Anniversary of Thomas More's Utopia* (2016), *Ekonomiczne teorie literatury* (2016), and *Dyskursy gier wideo* (2019). His current hermeneutical and post-phenomenological research can be placed at the intersection of literary theory, game studies, and utopian studies. His main interests are in critically oriented videogames, literary theory and philosophy of technology.

Lidia Kniaź-Hunek is a Ph.D. candidate at Maria Curie-Skłodowska University in Lublin, Poland. Her interests are primarily in Afrofuturism and Black futurity, as well as science fiction aesthetics in music video. She has published articles in *Extrapolation*, *Vector*, and *MOSF Journal of Science Fiction*. She serves as a co-editor for the *New Horizons in English Studies* and is a recipient of an EAAS Postgraduate Travel Grant, which funded her research visit at UC Riverside (Eaton Collection of Science Fiction & Fantasy). Kniaź-Hunek is currently working on her dissertation on Afrofuturist music videos while listening to Prince and Janelle Monáe.

Agnieszka Kotwasińska is an Assistant Professor at the American Studies Center, the University of Warsaw. She works in Gothic and horror studies, gender studies and queer theory, and feminist new materialism(s). Her research interests center on embodiment in the so-called low genres, death, illness, and mourning in horror, and schizoanalysis. She has published articles in *Somatechnics*, *Praktyka Teoretyczna*, and *Humanities*, among others. She is currently working on her first monograph exploring horror fiction by American women writers.

Anna Kurowicka works at the American Studies Center at the University of Warsaw. She was awarded the Kosciuszko Foundation grant to conduct research at Emory University. She has published on the representation of asexuality in popular culture and disability in science fiction in Polish and international journals. Her current research project is focused on representations of asexuality in popular culture and sexuality and gender in speculative fiction.

Nicolas Labarre is Assistant Lecturer at University Bordeaux Montaigne, France, where he teaches US Society and Culture, Comics and Video Games. His research focuses on genres and intermediality in comics. He is the author of *Heavy Metal, l'autre Métal Hurlant* (2017), *La bande dessinée contemporaine* (2018), and *Understanding Genres in Comics* (2020).

Rob Latham is the editor of *The Oxford Handbook of Science Fiction* (2014) and *Science Fiction Criticism: An Anthology of Essential Writings* (2017). He is a senior editor of *The Los Angeles Review of Books*.

Nicholas Laudadio is Associate Professor of English at the University of North Carolina Wilmington, where he teaches classes in science fiction, popular culture, and literary and critical theory. His research explores the cultural history of music and musical instruments with a particular focus on electronic music and science fiction in the 20th century.

Isiah Lavender III is Sterling-Goodman Professor of English at the University of Georgia, where he researches and teaches courses in African American literature and science fiction. His most recent book is *Afrofuturism Rising: The Literary Prehistory of a Movement* (2019) and the co-edited critical anthology *Literary Afrofuturism in the Twenty-First Century* (2020).

Anna McFarlane is Lecturer in Medical Humanities at the University of Leeds, working on traumatic pregnancy and its expression in science fiction, horror, and fantasy. She is the co-editor of *The Routledge Companion to Cyberpunk Culture* (2020) and is co-editing *The Edinburgh Companion to Science Fiction and the Medical Humanities*. Her first monograph is a study of William Gibson's novels, *Cyberpunk Culture and Psychology: Seeing Through the Mirrorshades* (2021).

Ania Malinowska is a writer, a cultural theorist, and Associate Professor in Media and Cultural Studies at the University of Silesia, Poland, and a former Senior Fulbright Fellow at the New School of Social Research in New York. Her research concentrates on cultural theory, emotion studies, digital humanities, and critical robotics—and specifically on the formation of cultural norms and the social, emotional and aesthetic codes in relation to digitalism. She has authored and edited several articles, chapters, special issues and books preoccupied with the posthuman condition and technologies of affect, including *Love in Contemporary Technoculture* (2022), *Data Dating. Love, Technology, Desire* (with V. Peri, 2021), *Technocultury miłości* (2019), *The Materiality of Love. Essays of Affection and Cultural Practice* (with M. Gratzke, 2018), *Media and Emotions. The New Frontiers of Affect in Digital Culture* (with T. Miller, 2017), and *Materiality and Popular Culture. The Popular Life of Things* (with K. Lebek, 2017).

Graham J. Murphy is Professor with the School of English and Liberal Studies (Faculty of Arts) at Seneca College. In addition to more than two dozen book chapters and articles published in a variety of edited collections and academic journals, he is also co-editor of *The*

Routledge Companion to Cyberpunk Culture (2020), *Cyberpunk and Visual Culture* (2018), and *Beyond Cyberpunk: New Critical Perspectives* (2010), and co-author of *Ursula K. Le Guin: A Critical Companion* (2006).

Sasha Myerson is finishing a Ph.D. at Birkbeck College, University of London. Her research focuses on the collective subjects and communities of 1990s feminist cyberpunk science fiction. Sasha is also a former co-director of the London Science Fiction Research Community and helps to organize the feminist research collective Beyond Gender.

Keren Omry is Senior Lecturer at the Department of English Language and Literature, at the University of Haifa. Her interests include speculative fiction, music and literature, and alternate histories, on which she has taught and published extensively. She is co-editor of the forthcoming *Routledge Companion to Gender and Science Fiction*, and of Palgrave's *Science Fiction: A New Canon* book series.

Wendy Gay Pearson is Associate Professor and Chair of the Department of Women's Studies and Feminist Research at the University of Western Ontario. She teaches sexuality studies, queer theory, queer and Indigenous cinema, and science fiction. She is the co-editor of *Reverse Shots: Indigenous Film and Media in an International Context* (2014) and the co-author of *Zero Patience* (2011). In addition, she is the co-editor of *Queer Universes: Sexualities in Science Fiction* (2008).

Mark Player is Lecturer in Film at the University of Reading, UK, whose research interests include DIY, punk and cyberpunk media from Japan. His research has been published in journals such as *Japan Forum*, *Punk & Post Punk*, and *Acta Universitatis Sapientiae Film and Media Studies*, and as chapters in books such as *Punk Identities, Punk Utopias: Global Punk and Media* (2021). He has also written more widely on Japanese and other East Asian cinemas for online outlets such as *Midnight Eye* and *Electric Sheep Magazine*.

Paul Graham Raven is Marie Skłodowska-Curie Postdoctoral Fellow at Lund University, Sweden, where he researches the narrative rhetorics of sociotechnical and climate imaginaries. His doctoral thesis proposed a novel model of sociotechnical change based on social practice theory, and a narrative prototyping methodology for infrastructure foresight. He is also an author and critic of science fiction, an occasional journalist and essayist, a collaborator with designers and artists, and a (gratefully) lapsed consulting critical futurist. He currently lives in Malmö with a cat, some guitars, and sufficient books to constitute an insurance-invalidating fire hazard.

Robin Anne Reid was Professor in the Department of Literature and Languages at Texas A&M University-Commerce for twenty-seven years before retiring in May 2020. Because of her disgust with the corporatization of university administration, she chose not to apply for emerita status but is enjoying scholarly pursuits as an independent scholar. She manages to write on feminist speculative fiction and J.R.R. Tolkien.

Brian Ruh has a Ph.D. in Communication and Culture from Indiana University, Bloomington. He is an independent scholar and is the author of *Stray Dog of Anime: The Films of Mamoru Oshii* (2004).

Lars Schmeink is Research Fellow at the Europa-Universität Flensburg and the project lead for the "Science Fiction" subproject of the "FutureWork" research network. In 2010, he inaugurated the Gesellschaft für Fantastikforschung, serving as President until 2019. He has published widely on popular culture, especially science fiction. His most important publications are *Biopunk Dystopias: Genetic Engineering, Society, and Science Fiction* (2016) and the co-edited volumes *Cyberpunk and Visual Culture* (2018), *The Routledge Companion to Cyberpunk Culture* (2020), and *New Perspectives on Contemporary German Science Fiction* (2022).

Simon Spiegel is Research Fellow and Lecturer at the Department of Film Studies at the University of Zurich and Privatdozent at the University of Bayreuth. He has published extensively on science fiction, utopian films, and the theory of the fantastic. Among his publications are *Utopias in Nonfiction Film* (2021) and *Utopia and Reality* (co-edited with Andrea Reiter and Marcy Goldberg, 2020).

Shige (CJ) Suzuki is Associate Professor of Modern Languages and Comparative Literature at Baruch College, The City University of New York (CUNY). His recent publications include *Manga: A Critical Guide* (co-authored with Ronald Stewart, forthcoming), the "Manga" entry for *The Routledge Companion to Cyberpunk Culture* (2020), "Reviving the Power of Storytelling: Post-3/11 Online 'Amateur' Manga" in *Women's Manga in Asia and Beyond: Uniting Different Cultures and Identities* (2019), "Yōkai Monsters at Large: Mizuki Shigeru's Manga, Transmedia Practices, and (Lack of) Cultural Politics" in *Transmedia Storytelling in East Asia: The Age of Digital Media* (2019).

Jonathan Thornton is studying for a Ph.D. in Science Fiction Literature at the University of Liverpool. His project is focused on the portrayal of insects in speculative fiction and fantastika. He has a master's degree in Science Fiction Literature and a master's in Medical Entomology, and works as an insectary technician at the Liverpool School of Tropical Medicine. He is a reviewer for Tor.com, and also writes criticism and reviews and conducts interviews for internet publications *Fantasy Faction*, *The Fantasy Hive*, and *Gingernuts of Horror*.

Jaak Tomberg is Senior Researcher of Contemporary Literature at the University of Tartu, Estonia. His research focuses on science fiction, realism, utopia, and the philosophy of literature. His two monographs focus on the poetics of science fiction, and his essay "On the 'Double Vision' of Realism and SF Estrangement in William Gibson's Bigend Trilogy" won the Science Fiction Research Association's Pioneer Award in 2014. Besides research, he regularly writes literary criticism.

Evan Torner is Associate Professor of German at the University of Cincinnati, where he also serves as undergraduate director of German studies and director of the UC Game Lab. His fields of expertise include East German genre cinema, German film history, critical race theory, science fiction, and role-playing games. He is finishing a monograph on the history of German science fiction cinema and co-editing a handbook on East German cinema.

Jo Lindsay Walton teaches and researches at the Sussex Humanities Lab, University of Sussex. With Polina Levontin he edits *Vector*, the critical journal of the British Science Fiction Association. His fiction appears in *Gross Ideas Tales of Tomorrow's Architecture* (2019), *Twelve Tomorrows* (2016), *Big Echo* (2019), and *Phase Change: New SF Energies* (2022). His website is jolindsaywalton.com, and he can be found on Twitter, @jolwalton.

D. Harlan Wilson is an award-winning novelist, critic, editor, playwright, and Professor of English at Wright State University-Lake

Campus. He is the author of over thirty book-length works of fiction and nonfiction, and hundreds of his stories, essays, reviews, and plays have appeared in magazines, journals, and anthologies throughout the world in multiple languages. For more information, visit www.dharlanwilson.com.

INTRODUCTION

Anna McFarlane, Graham J. Murphy, and Lars Schmeink

Although the term 'cyberpunk' was lifted from the Bruce Bethke short story "Cyberpunk" (1983) by editor Gardner Dozois and used to refer to a cadre of authors (loosely assembled under the name of the 'Movement') writing thematically, if not stylistically, similar stories in the early-1980s, it was famously codified by **Bruce Sterling** through his editorship of *Mirrorshades: The Cyberpunk Anthology* (1986). Sterling's Preface to the collection was a tour-de-force manifesto that celebrated, promoted, and, in some ways, created those elements that would be readily identified as key cyberpunk traits. "The theme of body invasion," Sterling wrote, "prosthetic limbs, implanted circuitry, cosmetic surgery, genetic alteration. The even more powerful theme of mind invasion: brain-computer interfaces, artificial intelligence, neurochemistry—techniques radically redefining the nature of humanity, the nature of the self" (xiii). Sterling's enthusiastic baptism of cyberpunk as a distinct subgenre that was revolutionizing science fiction and providing a definitive break from what he characterized as a stagnant genre culture, a characterization that is muted in the Preface but raging full-force in his *Cheap Truth* broadsheet/fanzine that he edited under the pseudonym 'Vincent Omniaveritas,' had two immediate, and ironically contradictory, effects. He simultaneously became the genre's midwife and its (attempted) murderer.

While it must be said that Sterling's efforts ensured literary cyberpunk's impact upon the sf landscape unmistakable, his attempt to bring together a handful of different writers and call the assemblage *the* cyberpunk anthology is in part the job of a PR agent, and Sterling rose to the occasion with aplomb. For example,

> Sterling brought an idea for a cyberpunk anthology to [David] Hartwell, who promptly told Sterling he didn't have enough authors

to assemble a collection. Sterling then went on a recruitment campaign to complete the project and the release of *Mirrorshades: The
Cyberpunk Anthology* (1986) effectively completed the rebranding
of the Movement into the easily marketable *cyberpunk*.

(Murphy 522)

At the same time, while Sterling professes the "'typical cyberpunk
writer' does not exist; this person is only a Platonic fiction" (ix), he
simultaneously locates cyberpunk's historical roots in the "sixty-year
tradition of modern popular SF [...] steeped in the lore and tradition of the SF field" (x) and provides the above-mentioned themes
common to cyberpunk; thus, in codifying cyberpunk and helping
popularize and anthologize it through the *Mirrorshades* collective,
Sterling (un)intentionally triggered a number of eulogies to lament
cyberpunk's demise, if not outright death, possibly beginning with
that of cyberpunk original member **Lewis Shiner**, but gradually
spreading outwards. Namely, just as cyberpunk truly gained widespread attention and started to infiltrate all levels of popular and
critical culture(s), some of its earliest practitioners began to distance
themselves accordingly.

While arguments over the health (or existence) of cyberpunk
simmered for some time, recent scholarship is less interested in the
question of cyberpunk's cybernetic heartbeat, preferring to shift and
consider the broader impact of these writers and their transmedia
fellow travelers in film, television, video games, comic books, artwork, fashion, even advertising. What emerges is an understanding
that cyberpunk has evolved beyond transmedial genre conventions
to become a more generalized cultural formation, or a cultural *mode*
as opposed to a distinct (and perhaps ossified) genre. *Fifty Key Figures
in Cyberpunk Culture* takes as its premise a central argument advanced
in Thomas Foster's *The Souls of Cyberfolk: Posthumanism as Vernacular
Theory*; namely, Foster, quoting Lawrence Grossberg, writes that
cyberpunk isn't so much a "genre, which is organized around 'the
existence of necessary formal elements,' [but] a cultural formation
[which is] a historical articulation of textual practices with a 'variety
of other cultural, social, economic, historical and political practices'"
(xvi). Thus, this collection is the latest entrant in a much larger critical arc—one that includes *Beyond Cyberpunk: New Critical Perspectives*
(eds. Murphy and Vint), *Cyberpunk and Visual Culture* (eds. Murphy
and Schmeink), and *The Routledge Companion to Cyberpunk Culture*
(eds. McFarlane, Murphy, and Schmeink)—that takes this 'cultural
formation' approach to show how cyberpunk motifs have moved

through various media, crossed geopolitical boundaries, and been made and remade by different groups at different times to express fundamental insights into our contemporary, globalized, interconnected societies.

Fifty Key Figures in Cyberpunk Culture is, arguably, the conclusion of its editors' respective explorations in cyberpunk culture, until some time and distance has occurred, at which point we'll likely return to see how our cyberpunk culture has evolved and possibly edit a new collection. In that vein, we don't assert that there is a singular cyberpunk culture; that is an erroneous, and entirely misleading, assertion because there is no monolithically singular cyberpunk culture. Instead, culture is diversified, pluralized, sometimes contradictory, and perpetually resistant to an all-too-easy encapsulation. In addition, while we are not suggesting that cyberpunk is the only lens through which to understand sf or our increasingly science-fictional realities, we are convinced it is the most productive and generative lens. For example, someone could rebut our cyberpunk focus and argue we live in a 'space opera' culture; after all, space opera narratives pre-date cyberpunk by numerous decades and the influence of space opera can be felt in everything from popular culture to the recent fad of billionaires funding their private ventures into the edge of space as 'space tourism,' often disingenuously promoted to the general public as somehow advancing the cause of humanity while these corporate giants engage in questionable (if not deplorable) employment practices vis-à-vis worker wages, the gig economy, and union busting. Nevertheless, such a rebuttal or comparison would be remarkably superficial and miss the entire point of framing cyberpunk as a cultural formation: space opera and its various spin-offs in both fiction and the 'real' world have been eclipsed since the 1980s by those intimate technologies that penetrate our bodies, or the inverted and everted cyberspatial realities that are increasingly seamless in our quotidian existences. This 'cyberpunk-as-cultural-formation' reality was shown in stark relief in the earliest days of the COVID-19 pandemic when businesses, schools, government, and just about every avenue of social life (at least in largely westernized nations with the infrastructure) transitioned to online delivery and our physical bodies became even more intimately connected to that cyberspatial realm popularized in many (but not all) quarters of cyberpunk. Many of us turned to our computer monitors to weather the pandemic storm, not our portable rocket packs or spaceships. To paraphrase the title to Sherryl Vint's Afterword to *Beyond Cyberpunk: New Critical*

Perspectives, we are living in the world cyberpunk made, but at the same time cyberpunk *continues* to make it as it evolves and prolif- erates into nearly every aspect of our lives. In this manner, *Fifty Key Figures in Cyberpunk Culture* is an extended appendix to *The Routledge Companion to Cyberpunk Culture* in its focus on those *makers* of our cyberpunk cultural formation.

In our focus on the fifty key *makers* of cyberpunk culture, we've chosen our entries with an eye to giving the reader a flavor for the diverse ways in which specific actors working with cyberpunk have helped shape our cyberpunk culture, even if their work may have pre-dated cyberpunk's official codification. We do, of course, offer a number of entries on those actors who were instrumental in the Movement's earliest days as it transitioned to cyberpunk, all of whom are included in Sterling's *Mirrorshades* anthology: Sterling, **Pat Cadigan**, **Rudy Rucker**, and **Lewis Shiner**, for exam- ple, all feature here, as well as **William Gibson**, whose novel *Neuromancer* (1984) is cyberpunk's ur-text, making him the hon- orary godfather of cyberpunk. We have also attempted to show the transmedia power of cyberpunk imagery, including figures from film (**Mamoru Oshii**), comic books (**Warren Ellis**), table- top role-playing games (**Mike Pondsmith**), video games (**Warren Spector**), and performance art (**Stelarc**). We also wanted to show- case the feedback between cyberpunk and critical theory because the former has engaged in conversations with the latter and acted as a form of theory in science-fictional form, evidenced in such texts as **J. G. Ballard**'s proto-cyberpunk *Crash* (1973) or **Lana and Lilly Wachowski**'s *The Matrix* (1999). In other words, cyberpunk has been inspired by futurologists like **Alvin and Heidi Toffler**, internet researchers and activists such as **Sadie Plant**, critical post- humanists like **Donna J. Haraway**, and transhumanists like **Ray Kurzweil**, and these close connections between (cyberpunk) fiction and (cyberpunk) theory are instrumental in understanding how the genre has evolved into a cultural mode.

While there is an understandable inclusion of cyberpunk's past, this collection is not (only) an exercise in nostalgia: we are also keen to show how cyberpunk is being created by today's cutting-edge figures, perhaps as a foreshadowing of how cyberpunk will continue to evolve. As a result, we have included a number of younger art- ists for whom cyberpunk is a central (but by no means the only) discourse: for example, **Janelle Monáe**'s music and 'emotion' pictures give cyberpunk the Afrofuturist and queer focus that has been lacking (or deliberately ignored) in yesterday's cyberpunk; or **Annalee Newitz**'s queer posthumanist twist on cyberpunk gives a flavor for the ways in which cyberpunk continues to engage our contemporary realities. In sum, these entries, authored by some of the foremost academics working in this transmedial mode today, draw out the ongoing importance of cyberpunk while never losing sight of the ways that the mode accretes and accumulates through the work of (post)human authors, filmmakers, musicians, illustrators, and/or critical theorists.

As we draw this introduction to a close, we also need to address the elephant in the room: this is not the definitive *Fifty Key Figures in Cyberpunk Culture*. If we believed this was the case, we'd have pushed Routledge to call it *The Fifty Key Figures in Cyberpunk Culture*, à la Sterling's *The Cyberpunk Anthology*. Nevertheless, we did dedicate some space to those who didn't 'make the cut' (however subjective that cut is) and offer an Honorable Mentions section that examines the ripples of cyberpunk beyond those whom we selected as central to its propagation. Nevertheless, we fully expect some readers to express dismay, frustration, or bewilderment that one figure or another somehow didn't survive into the final round; for example, while Sterling, Gibson, Shiner, and Rucker all make an appearance, the fifth cyberpunk *originateur*, John Shirley, is conspicuously absent, relegated to the Honorable Mentions section, and this has nothing to do with any ill-will toward Shirley or his work; the same can be said of Bruce Bethke, whose "Cyberpunk" gave the Movement its new name and whose award-winning novel *Headcrash* (1995) is one of the few examples of explicitly satirical cyberpunk. Similarly, an early list of possible entries included one focusing on the editors Gardner Dozois and Ellen Datlow, the latter instrumentally important in her tenure at *Omni* since she was singly responsible for getting Gibson's earliest work published and was also a driving force behind Cadigan's deserved success, but you'll notice that chapter never materialized; and so forth. In this vein, this collection is deliberately problematic right from the outset, at least in the sense that Carl Freedman (drawing on Louis Althusser) defines the term: "a conceptual framework within which further research and analysis can be conducted" (xx). Thus, while we hope our readers will for the most part enjoy the book and learn about those makers occupying the corners of cyberpunk 'culture' that they perhaps had never known, we're also hopeful that some readers will embrace its problematic nature—i.e., its opportunity for further research and analysis—and re-direct their energies away from online missives on Goodreads to propose to Routledge their own collection, perhaps *Fifty More Key Figures in Cyberpunk Culture* or *Fifty Key Figures in Cyberpunk Culture vol. 2* (reach out: we'll put you in touch with our contact at Routledge).

In conclusion, *Fifty Key Figures in Cyberpunk Culture* recognizes the complex relationships that have formed around cyberpunk and informed cyberpunk's evolution into a cultural formation. As we are living through a time that increasingly looks like a cyberpunk world, itself not necessarily a positive development given how dark cyberpunk can be, and we increasingly participate in moving our private behaviors into virtual realms that are subject to surveillance by the state, or by bad actors, or the monetization by corporate conglomerates (read the fine print of those Terms of Service agreements!), our hope is that this collection will contribute to our understanding of how cyberpunk makers have shaped (and continue to shape) our world(s), and how we might use the cyberpunk mode fostered by key figures in various proximities to cyberpunk as a critical tool for challenging these encroaching social, economic, and political structures.

Works Cited

Foster, Thomas. *The Souls of Cyberfolk: Posthumanism as Vernacular Theory.* U of Minnesota P, 2005.

Freedman, Carl. *Critical Theory and Science Fiction.* Wesleyan UP, 2013.

Murphy, Graham J. "Cyberpunk and Post-Cyberpunk." *The Cambridge History of Science Fiction*, edited by Gerry Canavan and Eric Carl Link, Cambridge UP, 2019, pp. 519–36.

Sterling, Bruce. Preface. *Mirrorshades: The Cyberpunk Anthology*, edited by Bruce Sterling, Ace, 1986, pp. ix–xvi.

FIFTY KEY FIGURES IN CYBERPUNK CULTURE

J.G. BALLARD (1930–2009)

British author.

J. G. Ballard was the author of nineteen novels and over a hundred short stories. A key figure of science fiction's (sf) New Wave of the 1960s, he wrote in a variety of genres, including natural disaster sf (*The Drowned World* [1962], *The Crystal World* [1966]), cultural disaster allegories (*The Atrocity Exhibition* [1970], *Crash* [1973]), fictional (auto)biographies (*Empire of the Sun* [1984]), and contemporary novels (*Cocaine Nights* [1996], *Super-Cannes* [2000]) that were written "from the stance that everything *had become* science fiction" (Wilson). The distinct literary quality of Ballard's fiction has led to the emergence of the adjective "Ballardian," defined by the *Collins English Dictionary* as "resembling or suggestive of the conditions described in J. G. Ballard's novels and stories, especially dystopian modernity, bleak man-made landscapes and the psychological effects of technological, social or environmental developments."

Ballard's deep influence on cyberpunk has been openly declared by many of the movement's main representatives, most notably by its chief impresario **Bruce Sterling**, who, in his Preface to *Mirrorshades: The Cyberpunk Anthology* (1986), listed Ballard as "an idolized role model to many cyberpunks" (xiv). In another key anthology, *Storming the Reality Studio: A* Casebook *of Cyberpunk and Postmodern Science Fiction* (1991), editor Larry McCaffery and author Richard Kadrey included Ballard's *The Atrocity Exhibition* and *Crash* in their "list of the cultural artifacts that helped to shape cyberpunks ideology and aesthetics" (17).

Aside from these accolades, Ballard's thematic and aesthetic influence on cyberpunk is inescapable in a myriad of ways. First, his depiction of contemporary reality in (especially) *The Atrocity Exhibition* and *Crash* as completely synthetic, thoroughly mediated, inescapably hyperreal, absolutely urban, and technologically saturated strongly foreshadows the ways that reality was *extrapolated to the future* by cyberpunk. All these qualities, in idiosyncratic form, are now perceived as quintessentially cyberpunk. For example, focusing on a community that has an intense and inescapable sexual fetish for car crashes, *Crash* works as an allegory that systematically and persistently explores the sinister and uncanny intrusion of technology into the body. In

DOI: 10.4324/9781003091189-3

cyberpunk, the explicitly negative overtones and the allegoric warning of such intrusions have been reduced, and the thorough technologization of bodies has become a common fact of its fictional worlds. Nevertheless, cyberpunk's treatment of the relationship between the natural and the artificial—embodied in the manifold prosthetic implants, supplements, and enhancements typical of its protagonists' bodies—owe a lot to the way Ballard initially staged the contemporary collision between technology and the body.

Ballard also took a frequent aesthetic and analytic interest in modern technological environments: the characters of *Crash* inhabit a seemingly endless web of suburban highways; the protagonist of *Concrete Island* (1974) finds himself stranded in a large area of derelict land created by several intersecting motorways; and *High Rise* (1975) follows the gradual disintegration of a micro-society in a self-sustaining 40-storey building from where no-one thinks of leaving. These were undoubtedly an inspiration to the various urban spaces and infinite cityscapes of cyberpunk, most notably The Sprawl of **William Gibson**'s first trilogy, and The Bridge of his second. Ballard's frequent focus on confined and totalized, endless or inescapable, urban spaces prefigure the fact that in cyberpunk we rarely—if ever—get out of them as well.

Ballard's interest in modern technological environments also extends to the inherently mediated nature of his techno-cultural present as well as society's increasing obsession with media celebrities and events at the time. *The Atrocity Exhibition*, Ballard's experimental and surreal collection of 'condensed novels,' explores the subversive impact of the mass media landscape on the private mind of the individual. Its protagonist tries to make sense of the status and meaning of the media-events happening around him—the death of Marilyn Monroe, Elizabeth Taylor's tracheotomy, the assassination of John F. Kennedy, and so on—and restages them as a personalized form of psychotherapy. The protagonist's name changes with each segment (Talbert, Traven, Travis, Talbot), symbolically indicating the effortless and/or schizophrenic mutability of mediatized subjectivity. This mutability prefigures the technological mutability of so many of cyberpunk's characters. Rob Latham, writing about New Wave sf's influence on cyberpunk, has noted that "[t]he fabrication and exploitation of synthetic celebrities, a key theme in cyberpunk texts ranging from **Pat Cadigan**'s 'Pretty Boy Crossover' (1986) to Gibson's *Idoru* (1996) to Richard Calder's *Cythera* (1998)" can be traced back, among other works, to the "media-based obsessions of Ballard" (8), and specifically to *The Atrocity Exhibition* (10). Nevertheless, Ballard's schizo-analytic approach has been replaced with a more playful one in cyberpunk.

The influence of Ballard's poetics upon cyberpunk cannot be understated. Brian McHale has argued that with such works as *Crash* and *The Atrocity Exhibition*, "Ballard developed a new style—dense, disjointed, and bristling with technical vocabularies," thus contributing to "shaping the poetics of [...] the cyberpunks" (24). Minute and microscopic attention to detail, scientific vocabulary instead of verbal slang, tonally flat accounts rather than emotional descriptions, showing rather than telling, and occasional but powerful metaphors that blur the borders between the natural and the artificial, the organic and the technic (see Tomberg, "Morality")—all of these added up to "a verbal equivalent of photographic hyperrealism" (Luckhurst 123) that is also deeply characteristic of cyberpunk, and "an unblinking, almost clinical objectivity" that Sterling explicitly related to Ballard as a generic precursor (xiv).

Ballard's influence on cyberpunk is thus evident even on the syntactic level where "science fiction's world-building processes" are folded "into the very texture of sentences, making implication (and its counterpart, active interference on the reader's part) do the work that exposition would do in more traditional types of science fiction" (McHale 88). While Istvan Csicsery-Ronay is a bit harsh when he says, pointing to Gibson, that "most of the literary cyberpunks bask in the glory of the one major writer who is original and gifted enough to make the whole movement seem original and gifted" (185), it might be true that there is ultimately no uniform poetics of cyberpunk common to all its authors,[1] and that the prevalent preconception of this poetics is based on the idiosyncratic sentences of Gibson. Nevertheless, many of the aforementioned Ballardian features, and especially the "rich thesaurus of metaphors linking the organic and the electronic" (Csicsery-Ronay 190), are definitely on show in the works of Sterling, Cadigan, **Neal Stephenson**, Alexander Besher, and others.

Ballard's prominent New Wave insistence upon inner space as the proper focus of sf found a not-too-distant descendant in cyberpunk's own most famous coinage and characteristic locus: cyberspace. In a manifesto-essay "Which Way to Inner Space?," originally published for *New Worlds* in 1962, Ballard suggested that "[t]he biggest developments of the immediate future will take place, not on the Moon or Mars, but on Earth, and it is inner space, not outer, that needs to be explored. The only truly alien planet is Earth" (197). With his statement, Ballard "wanted to marshal [science fiction] in

11

a new direction; instead of pointing it at the stars, he would point it at the human psyche and our intricate, uncanny technologies of desire" (Wilson). Following the publication of "Which Way to Inner Space?," "the very notion of inner space has gone through a series of transformations, including visual mapping, internal microscopic imagery, and of course cyberspace" (Seed 25). Arguably, "the 1960s obsession with 'inner space' is echoed in Gibson's famous evocation of cyberspace as a 'consensual hallucination'" (Latham 14); this impression is confirmed by cyberspace inhabiting "the nonspace of the mind" (Gibson 67). According to Csicsery-Ronay, New Wave sf (including Ballard) had even started to treat "hallucination as an object in the world," so that it became increasingly difficult to distinguish between "mystical truths and machine dreams" (190). By the time of cyberpunk, "reality ha[d] become a case of nerves—that is, the interfusion of the nervous system and computer-matrix, sensation and information" (Csicsery-Ronay 190). In this vein, cyberspace is the thoroughly technological materialization and modulation of the initially abstract, psychoanalytic, and surreal concept of inner space, of which Ballard was the chief proponent.

Finally, Ballard was the first writer who admittedly gave up writing sf because the technologically saturated reality around him had itself become science-fictional. After *The Atrocity Exhibition*, Ballard felt that "science fiction had expired; the futures it once envisioned had been ingested by the present" (Wilson). With *Crash*, Ballard started to map a present whose ceaseless functionality of technology, embodied in the automobile, the motorway systems, and the constant traffic, themselves felt futuristic. *Crash* emanates the same specific kind of technologically infused cognitive estrangement that sf usually does. Poetically, *Crash* inhabits a liminal space between realism and sf, establishing a space where these two generic tendencies converge. Almost three decades later, William Gibson's oeuvre took a similar ("realist") turn when he forfeited his usual future-oriented cyberpunk extrapolations with his Blue Ant trilogy[2] and started writing contemporary novels that were situated in the immediate present but nevertheless continued to *read like* science fiction. Gibson's reasoning was also similar: the present was over-accelerated, leaving no "place to stand from which to imagine a very elaborate future" (Nissley). The Blue Ant trilogy was an epitome of cyberpunk experiencing "a sea change into a more generalized cultural formation" (Foster xiv), of technological development catching up with cyberpunk and leading to the emergence of non-sf cyberpunk.[3] *Crash* was a distant generic precursor to these developments and, as Wilson correctly remarks, Ballard had "signaled the assimilation of the future by the present long before Gibson published his first science fiction story" (Wilson). Ballard's literary influence thus extends beyond the point where cyberpunk itself had started to transform into something else.

See also: **Pat Cadigan, Philip K. Dick, William Gibson, Neal Stephenson, Bruce Sterling**

Notes

Research for this chapter was supported by Estonian Research Council grant PRG 636.

1 Sterling did remark in his Preface to *Mirrorshades* that "the 'typical cyberpunk writer' does not exist; this person is only a Platonic fiction. For the rest of us, our label is an uneasy bed of Procrustes, where fiendish critics wait to lop and stretch us to fit" (ix), at least before Sterling lopped and stretched his retinue of authors to fit the *Mirrorshades* anthology.

2 *Pattern Recognition* (2003), *Spook Country* (2007), and *Zero History* (2010).

3 For details about non-sf cyberpunk, see Tomberg ("Non-SF"); Hollinger; McFarlane.

Works Cited

Ballard, J.G. "Which Way to Inner Space?" *A User's Guide to the Millennium: Essays and Reviews.* Flamingo, 1997, pp. 195–98.

Csicsery-Ronay, Jr., Istvan. "Cyberpunk and Neuromanticism." *Storming the Reality Studio*, edited by Larry McCaffery, Duke UP, 1991, pp. 182–93.

Foster, Thomas. *The Souls of Cyberfolk: Posthumanism as Vernacular Theory.* U of Minnesota P, 2005.

Gibson, William. *Neuromancer.* Ace, 1984.

Hollinger, Veronica. "Stories About the Future: From Recognizing Patterns to Pattern Recognition." *Science Fiction Studies*, vol. 33, no. 3, 2006, pp. 452–72.

Kadrey, Richard and Larry McCaffery. "Cyberpunk 101: A Schematic Guide to *Storming the Reality Studio.*" *Storming the Reality Studio: A Casebook of Cyberpunk and Postmodern Science Fiction*, edited by Larry McCaffery, Duke UP, 1991, pp. 17–32.

Latham, Rob. "Literary Precursors." *The Routledge Companion to Cyberpunk Culture*, edited by Anna McFarlane, Graham J. Murphy, and Lars Schmeink, Routledge, 2020, pp. 7–14.

Luckhurst, Roger. *"The Angle Between Two Walls": The Fiction of J.G. Ballard.* Liverpool UP, 1997.

McFarlane, Anna. "Cyberpunk and 'Science Fiction Realism' in Kathryn Bigelow's *Strange Days* and *Zero Dark Thirty.*" *Cyberpunk and Visual Culture*, edited by Graham J. Murphy and Lars Schmeink, Routledge, 2018, pp. 235–52.

McHale, Brian. *The Cambridge Introduction to Postmodernism.* Cambridge UP, 2015.

Nissley, Tom. "'Across the Border to Spook Country': An Interview with William Gibson." *Amazon.com*, 2007, amazon.com/Spook-Country-Blue-William-Gibson-ebook/dp/B000UVBSYQ.

Seed, David. *Science Fiction: A Very Short Introduction*. Oxford UP, 2011.

Sterling, Bruce. Preface. *Mirrorshades: The Cyberpunk Anthology*, edited by Bruce Sterling, Ace, 1988, pp. ix–xvi.

Tomberg, Jaak. "Morality and Amorality in Ba(udri)llard's *Crash*: A Poetic Perspective." *Science Fiction Studies*, vol. 47, no. 1, 2020, pp. 47–72.

Tomberg, Jaak. "Non-SF Cyberpunk." *The Routledge Companion to Cyberpunk Culture*, edited by Anna McFarlane, Graham J. Murphy, and Lars Schmeink, Routledge, 2020, pp. 81–90.

Wilson, D. Harlan. *J. G. Ballard*. U of Illinois P, 2017. (eBook)

Jaak Tomberg

STEVEN BARNES (1952–)

US author.

Steven Barnes's career has spanned forty years and he has written everything from novels and short stories to comic books and television scripts, covering science fiction, fantasy, and mystery. However, his contribution to cyberpunk culture has gone largely overlooked, in part because of the mode's monochromatism. While one of the critiques often leveled against cyberpunk, particularly its 1980s-era print version, is its almost total absence of women from the roster—the first wave of print cyberpunk was largely a guys-only club—it was also a *white* guys-only club at that. Cyberpunk's "unmistakable lack of diversity" (Murphy 21) resulted in a print canon "that overwhelmingly represents white male authors and characters to the exclusion of other groups" (Condis 7). Case in point: despite the presence of the Rastafarian Zion cluster or the gangster Kid Afrika in **William Gibson**'s *Neuromancer* (1984) and *Mona Lisa Overdrive* (1988), the mixed-race Hiro Protagonist in **Neal Stephenson**'s *Snow Crash* (1992), or Aech, a Black lesbian passing as a white male in Ernest Cline's *Ready Player One* (2012), these characters are written to add the requisite cool veneer to cyberspace adventures; they cannot mask the fact that cyberpunk protagonists are often "as comparably white as those" of the Pulp and Golden Age eras of sf (Brickler IV 152). Therefore, Barnes emerges not just as *the* only Black cyberpunk writer working in the heyday of this mode's first iteration, but as an unqualifiedly unique voice that expands our understanding of cyberpunk culture.

In his novel *Streetlethal* (1983), the first of a trilogy that includes *Gorgon Child* (1989) and *Firedance* (1994), Aubry Knight seeks revenge on his former employers—the Ortega drug cartel—after they set him up for murder. Barnes repeatedly deploys the noir imagery that made cyberpunk popular, notably in his description of Maxine Black, the prostitute that frames protagonist Aubry Knight for the murder: "Naked and transparent, the woman's smooth white body undulated slowly, beckoning to the empty streets. The streets were still slick from the afternoon rain; the hologram reflected back from the wet asphalt, an erotic mirage" (1). There is nothing more cyberpunk than a drug-addicted sex worker and her cyborgized john in a bleak and sleazy setting, and a fateful double-cross that sets the entire trilogy in motion.

The urban setting is a key feature of both *Streetlethal* and cyberpunk more broadly. As Lars Schmeink writes, "[o]ne of the most widely used images of cyberpunk is its placement in urban sprawls and far-reaching cityscapes" (277); or, as Claire Sponsler remarks, the "physical settings of most cyberpunk stories look strikingly like [...] blighted, rubble-strewn, broken-down cityscapes" (253). *Streetlethal* is no different: while it features aircars and entire libraries stored on information cubes, "The Great Quake" (113) has turned downtown Los Angeles (LA) into a maze-like wasteland. Furthermore, a "Thai-VI Spider" virus is slowly making waste of human bodies as the infected band together and attack everyone while their bodies rot. Meanwhile, another gang named the Scavengers sifts through the detritus searching for the "tremendous amount of wealth" buried "under the ruins of the Maze [...] Underground bank vaults with money—paper, securities, gold, Service Marks. Security tunnels for the jewelry exchange, some of which lead to diamond caches. Canned food. Equipment" (120). Neither the conglomerates nor the government care enough about what remains in the dystopian underbelly to risk going after it, thus leaving it for people crazy or desperate enough to salvage. As the series continues, Knight is pitted against Sterling Delacourte, a televangelist nut with grandeurs of delusion about becoming a God and returning slavery to America with his genetically engineered NewMen (*Gorgon Child*), and Phillipe Swarna, a Japanese-backed authoritarian president of Pan-Africa, the man Aubry is cloned from as spare parts meant to keep Swarna alive (*Firedance*).

Anyone familiar with William Gibson's *Neuromancer* will find uncanny parallels between Barnes's Aubry Knight and Gibson's hacker anti-hero Case, particularly when it comes to the latter's "certain relaxed contempt for the flesh" and "the bodiless exultation of cyberspace" that defines the body as meat (*Neuromancer* 6). Aubry's posthuman status as a clone and as a cyborg is not confirmed until the final book, but the character, described as "a statue carved from obsidian" (*Streetlethal* 15), has had physical enhancements evidenced in his speed, strength, coordination, and martial prowess. Aubry's physical body is "faster and stronger and has more energy than any body has the right to have" (*Firedance* 73), even if at one point in *Gorgon Child* he thinks of his body as "a ridiculous meat puppet. An automaton fiercely defending its absurd attachment to life" (276). Aubry receives cybernetic augmentation, jacked reflexes, and "linguistics implantation" where the US government "destroy[s] his face and rewire[s] his mind" to oust Swarna (*Firedance* 150, 138), but the primary difference here is that Aubry's mind and body are in perfect sync as opposed to the popular, if mischaracterized, image of the Cartesian mind-body separation that is often attributed to mainstream (read: white) cyberpunk writers. While Black people have always been reduced to their bodies by the white gaze, Barnes concentrates on the unification of the mind and body: Aubry is an image of a spiritually awakened cyborg capable of dismantling the existing racial stereotypes and producing what Kristen Lillvis has deemed as "posthuman blackness [...] boundary crossings" that "enable black subjects to make connections to diasporic history in the present and also imagine the future as a site of power" (8). As a cyborg clone, the Black American and Black African Aubry represents the fusion of these potent and competing identities across social time. Barnes therefore offers a racially informed vision of cyberpunk that moves beyond the amalgamation of human bodies with prosthetic technoscience. This is a techno-social-political racial assemblage that demonstrates what it means to be humanized in our hyper-globalized present (cf. Weheliye).

Hackers embody the global "high-tech [...] modern pop underground" (Sterling xi) embodied by cyberpunk, and Aubry Knight's "bifertile hermaphrodite" (*Firedance* 8) eight-year-old child Leslie is an unparalleled hacker cyborg. Leslie is described as conquering "the barrier erected by the computer system [...] phantasmal threats converted to their electronic analogues" until "a shadow-world of pure information" reveals itself and they can take whatever information they want (*Gorgon Child* 269). Leslie's unparalleled ability results from twin tragedies: Leslie is stolen from the womb of their mother, Promise, at the end of *Streetlethal* and then being experimented on by the NewMen in the Medusa project of *Gorgon Child*. As a result of these biological interventions, "all modifications performed upon" Leslie involve "implantation of preprogrammed fetal cortex. Some neural grooving of spinal tissue. And [...] nanotech, genetic, hormonal, cybernetic [...] to produce a perfect killing and infiltration machine" (*Firedance* 79). Just as he does with Aubry Knight, Barnes combines criminality and cyborgism in Leslie's characterization to flesh out his frightening future world.

Barnes also employs cyberpunk's vital hacker archetype in *Blood Brothers* (1996). Set in the wake of the 1992 LA Riots and spurred by the acquittal of the police officers who beat Rodney King, *Blood Brothers* features Derek Waites as Captain Africa, a notorious computer hacker who is now a reformed game designer. Waites must use his skills to save his ex-wife and daughter from a supernatural threat dating back to the antebellum era; he must free his distant cousin Austin Tucker (a white supremacist) from jail. Barnes's use of computer programming, the supernatural, and advanced genetics punctuates how a socially aware Black writer uses cyberpunk stylings to address the digital divide—the perceived, if not actual, uneven distribution and access to the internet and computers between racial groups in today's information age. In *Blood Brother*'s depiction of a Black hacker as his protagonist, Barnes dismantles a 21st-century stereotype by challenging the "self-fulfilling prophecy [that] people of color can't keep pace in a high-tech world that threatens to outstrip them" (Hines et al. 1–2).

The Aubry Knight series ends as Knight learns he is descended from the fictitious Ibandi tribe from the slopes of Mount Kilimanjaro, a tribe that stretches back thirty-thousand years. Barnes therefore mythically connects Knight to his later fantasy dualogy—*Great Sky Woman* (2006) and *Shadow Valley* (2009)—as these more recent novels focus on the Ibandi and their own trials and tribulations in the distant past. Therefore, in a manner that differentiates Barnes from other cyberpunk writers who use Africa as a prop, such as **Bruce Sterling**'s *Islands in the Net* (1988) that uses Africa "as the benchmark against which to measure the extent to which some other place has escaped disaster, barbarism, and backwardness, or risk falling into them" (Bould 215), Barnes's Aubry Knight trilogy not only sets up the Great Sky Woman series but also shares

> some of cyberpunk's concerns but none of its Young Turkism or yearning for the digital. Evoking Black power, Black pride, Afrotopianism, Afrocentricity, and Pan-Africanism, Barnes transforms his protagonist Aubry Knight [...] from a 'buck' stereotype into a property developer who rebuilds downtown Los Angeles [...] into a matter-of-fact multiracial future.
>
> (Bould 216)

More to the point, Barnes helps create an Afrocyberpunk that distorts the cyberpunk mode as "a deliberate means of expressing black discontent with the world, global capitalism, and the information age, acutely demonstrating that cyberpunk is not for whites only" (Lavender and Murphy 308).

Barnes lays down a marker for the next generation of Black sf writers by injecting Black cultural politics into a cyberpunk future that is (and has always been) racialized. By cross-cutting variables in his Afrocyberpunk storyworlds—NewMen, cyborgs, drug addicts, infected people, and street gangs as well as Black, brown, and yellow people—Barnes captures the textures of street life without falling into stereotypes. While Barnes's work still exists in the cultural vacuum created by authors and scholars who choose to largely exclude Black voices from a narrowly defined cyberpunk canon, the racial distinctiveness of his Aubry Knight trilogy stands out for countering racial oppression in a cultural mode that is still hampered by racial tokenism.

See also: **Samuel R. Delany, William Gibson, Janelle Monáe, Bruce Sterling**

Works Cited

Barnes, Steven. *Blood Brothers*. Tor, 1996.
———. *Firedance*. Tor, 1994.
———. *Gorgon Child*. Tor, 1989.
———. *Streetlethal*. Ace, 1983.
Bould, Mark. "Afrocyberpunk Cinema: The Postcolony Finds its Own Use for Things." *Cyberpunk and Visual Culture*, edited by Graham J. Murphy and Lars Schmeink, Routledge, 2018, pp. 213–34.
Brickler, Alexander Dumas J. IV. "Soul in the Shell: Steven Barnes's Aubry Knight Trilogy, Black Cyborgs, and Cyberpunk Investigations of Technological Black Bodies." *Black Bodies and Transhuman Realities: Scientifically Modifying the Black Body in Posthuman Literature and Culture*, edited by Melvin G. Hill, Lexington Books, 2019, pp. 151–176.
Condis, Megan A. "Playing the Game of Literature: *Ready Player One*, the Ludic Novel, and the Geeky 'Canon' of White Masculinity." *Journal of Modern Literature*, vol. 39, no. 2, 2016, pp. 1–19.
Gibson, William. *Neuromancer*. Ace, 1984.
Hines, Alicia H., et al., editors. "Introduction: Hidden Circuits." *Technicolor: Race, Technology, and Everyday Life*, NYU P, 2001, pp. 1–12.
Lavender III, Isiah and Graham J. Murphy. "Afrofuturism." *The Routledge Companion to Cyberpunk Culture*, edited by Anna McFarlane, Graham J. Murphy, and Lars Schmeink, Routledge, 2020, pp. 353–61.

Lillvis, Kristen. *Posthuman Blackness and the Black Female Imagination.* U of
Georgia P, 2017.
Murphy, Graham J. "The *Mirrorshades* Collective." *The Routledge Companion
to Cyberpunk Culture*, edited by Anna McFarlane, Graham J. Murphy, and
Lars Schmeink, Routledge, 2020, pp. 15–23.
Schmeink, Lars. "Afterthoughts: Cyberpunk's Engagement in Countervisuality."
Cyberpunk and Visual Culture, edited by Graham J. Murphy and Lars Schmeink,
Routledge, 2018, pp. 276–287.
Sponsler, Claire. "Beyond the Ruins: The Geopolitics of Urban Decay and
Cybernetic Play." *Science Fiction Studies*, vol. 20, no. 2, 1993, pp. 251–65.
Sterling, Bruce. Preface. *Mirrorshades: The Cyberpunk Anthology*, edited by
Bruce Sterling. Ace, 1986, pp. ix–xvi.
Weheliye, Alexander G. *Habeas Viscus: Racializing Assemblages, Biopolitics, and
Black Feminist Theories of the Human.* Duke UP, 2014.

Isiah Lavender III

JEAN BAUDRILLARD (1929–2007)

French sociologist and philosopher.

Cultural theorist, philosopher, and sociologist, Jean Baudrillard was a
central voice in theorizing cyberpunk culture. His visceral critiques of
consumer society, architecture, and media in such works as *Simulacra
and Simulation* make him a key figure for studying the correlations of
cyberpunk and neoliberalism thanks to his critique of consumer society as a new form of control, and his disillusionment with hyperreality
(McQueen 183). Baudrillard was first and foremost a critic of cyberpunk
culture, both fascinated and appalled by the development of cyberpunk
dystopian contemporaneity (Butler 31). Douglas Kellner maps cyberpunk ideas in Baudrillard's work (304), but stresses that Baudrillard
would never agree with cyberpunk's more affirmative aspects (315).
Baudrillard's work therefore acts as a bridge between cyberpunk in
popular culture and postmodern theory, an association reinforced by
cyberpunk itself.[1] The most notable example is Baudrillard's spectral
presence throughout **Lily and Lana Wachowski**'s *The Matrix* (1999):
Neo (Keanu Reeves) hides contraband in a hollowed-out edition of
Baudrillard's *Simulacra and Simulation*. Later, when Neo learns the truth
about the extensive virtual reality that has been pulled over his eyes and
the post-apocalyptic conditions of the 'real' world, Morpheus (Laurence
Fishburne) quotes Baudrillard, saying "welcome to the desert of the real."
Here, *The Matrix* touched upon the most thought-provoking image
associated with Baudrillard's theory, a Borgesian-inspired metaphor
evoking the disappearance of the real and symbolic impoverishment as

the effects of the overproduction of hyperreality (Butler 23–24). Finally, when Agent Smith (Hugo Weaving) likens humanity to a virus, astute audience members were likely reminded of Baudrillard's use of the virus as a metaphor for the economy, which gives insight into cyberpunk cultural production and its socio-economic framework (McQueen 219). Although Baudrillard criticized the Wachowskis' movie ("Matrix Decoded") for its naïve belief in the dualism of real/virtual, his work is part of a larger feedback loop: just as much as cyberpunk at-times borrows from Baudrillard, the French thinker was equally influenced by the literary philosophical musings of such cyberpunk precursors as **Philip K. Dick** and **J.G. Ballard** (Murphie and Potts 113–14).

Baudrillard's most important contribution to cyberpunk culture is his conceptualization of simulation and hyperreality. He popularized these ideas in *Simulacra and Simulation*, but they evolved from his critique of Marxism in *For a Critique of the Political Economy of the Sign*, and his earlier theoretical works: *Seduction*, *The Consumer Society: Myths and Structures*, and *Symbolic Exchange and Death*. It is from the discussion of the sign and signification that Baudrillard questions all systems of reference and deconstructs the relationship between signifier and signified, commodity and value, virtual and real, symbolic economy and political economy (Genosko 27, 41). Baudrillard initially described three orders of simulacra, but later added a fourth:

i. illusion: signs, images and objects are at play with reality, they seduce us (*trompe-l'oeil*);
ii. production: the relationship between copy and original is lost; signs, images, and objects become identical commodities; seduction falls prey to the system of needs (mass produced commodities);
iii. simulation: signs, images, and objects without origin are produced and consumed as globalized models of reality (IKEA lifestyle, reality TV) ruled by abstract codes (DNA, binary code);
iv. fractal: images, signs, and objects are produced, disseminated, and consumed at every level of social, economic, and political structure; they radiate, infect, and destabilize society and undermine reality (fake news, conspiracy theories).

(McQueen 218).

According to Baudrillard, all these orders coexist, but the latest incorporates and dominates the previous ones. The influence of the fourth level continues to resonate in today's critical theorists, such as

William Merrin, who claims that Baudrillard's hyperreality leads to 'hyporeality': a cascading deflation identified as a sense of loss or lack of reality as a believable point of reference for any kind of judgment (moral, esthetic, logical) (Merrin tbd).

Baudrillard's conceptualizations of simulation highlight the question of cyberpunk's countervisuality (Schmeink 285), namely the distortions which break the hyperreal and disclose the manipulations done to the fabric of reality. For example, in *The Gulf War Did Not Take Place*, a trinity of essays (published in *Libération* and *The Guardian* in 1991) focusing on the US-led coalition waging war in Iraq, Baudrillard depicts both the displacement and production of war as a form of spectacle and virtual reality, which turns conflict into reality TV and an ideological manipulation, best seen in its metaphors of intelligent missiles, clean war and surgical precision. Fascinated with the disappearance of objects, events, and reality (Shapiro 16–17), Baudrillard also claims that capitalism works better in simulations than it does in reality, as it introduces economies based on debt and entropy (transeconomy) and politics based on destabilization of society (transpolitics). He also observed and commented on the compression of future and present, which he attributed to a change in the structure of thinking caused by the immediacy, acceleration, and overabundance of information.[2]

Baudrillard's theoretical work provides innumerable access points for thinking through the complexities of cyberpunk culture. For example, his analysis of the relationship between seduction and production (*Seduction* 37), his critique of the reduction of sexuality to commodity, and fascination with "transsexuality," a new model of sexuality, indifferent to power and based in seductive play with sex and gender (*Screened* 9), provide an interesting framework for reading cyberpunk gender imaginary, sexual engineering, and machinic reproduction in terms of subversion of patriarchal power relations or rejection of binary divisions (Lavigne 139). As hyperreality and simulation quickly found their way into the cyberpunk theoretical vocabulary, these concepts overshadowed both seduction and the symbolic exchange, which Baudrillard posited as the counterpart of simulation, forming a pair of interrelated, opposing concepts. A radical alternative to the capitalist production of signs, the symbolic can be seen in the return of what political economy has repressed: death, terrorism, virus, system error, namely all that threatens media produced reality, its myths and its structures. "Virtual and viral go hand in hand," Baudrillard writes. "It is because the body itself has become a non-body, a virtual machine, that viruses are taking it over" (*Transparency*

63). He perceives biological and cybernetic viruses as a metaphor for the collapse that any system of total control (of body, society, virtuality) brings on itself. He also compares self-replication and viral proliferation to the logic of global capitalism. His immunological metaphors share similarities with biopunk and post-cyberpunk reimaginings of the virus as that which erodes boundaries between the digital and the corporeal (Kilgore 49).

If there is one idea that connects all Baudrillard's works, it is the logic of reversibility, which describes the innate ability of every system to undermine itself (Coulter 182). To explain it, he references Hölderlin: "Where there is danger some Salvation grows there too" (54). Baudrillard believes reversibility constitutes an alternative to the logic of binary divisions and the logic of linear progress: "Reversibility," he writes, "is simultaneously the reversibility of life and death, of good and evil, and of all that we have organized in terms of alternative values" (*Passwords* 15). With reversibility, Baudrillard explains how suicide, terrorism, or destruction of wealth incite autodestructive reactions from a capitalism fueled by the repression of death, the overproduction of the real, and the subjection of everything to the binary logic of digital code. In *The Spirit of Terrorism*, Baudrillard claims that terrorism is an inevitable effect of the asymmetry between good and evil, hegemonic globalization, economy, and politics. Terrorism hacked the system by turning media into platforms infecting populations with fear, and this caused governments to increase panoptic control over their own citizens. This asymmetry embroiders the very fabric of cyberpunk culture, evidenced in the conflicts playing out at the level of body, technology, economy, and power. Reversibility is at play in cyberpunk when viruses are used against the system; the AI goes rogue, the body rejects the implants, or a corporate mercenary turns terrorist. In addition, reversibility undermines the vision of neoliberalism as "realized utopia," a nihilistic moment in time—Baudrillard calls it "after the orgy" (*Transparency*)— in which all the expectations, desires, and needs are fulfilled. The orgy is proceeded by disillusionment, a sense of nothingness, emptiness, and void (*Transparency* 3–4). Finally, fascinated with photography, Las Vegas, and America but suspicious toward images, Disneyland, and capitalism, Baudrillard has highlighted the broken, deferred utopianism of contemporary cyberpunk cultural formations.[3] In the end, Baudrillard is perhaps more of an outcast from cyberpunk culture than its native inhabitant—his refusal to use digital cameras or a PC was arguably a punk gesture in its own right—but his philosophical work remains one of the most important access points to better understand or grasp the contours of our technocultural condition that is down-right Baudrillardian.

See also: **J.G. Ballard, Philip K. Dick, Lana and Lilly Wachowski**

Notes

1 See Lavigne's *Cyberpunk Women, Feminism, and Science Fiction* or Haar and McFarlane's "Simulation and Simulacra."
2 Scholars such as Veronica Hollinger and Jaak Tomberg have found this concept of the 'future present' useful in approaching realist cyberpunk texts in recent years. See Works Cited for details.
3 See Baudrillard's essay on the architecture of Centre Pompidou, the intimate journal *Cool Memories*, or his travel diary *America* for details.

Works Cited

Baudrillard, Jean. *America*. Translated by Chris Turner, Verso, 1989.
———. *Cool Memories V*. Translated by Chris Turner, Polity, 2006.
———. *Passwords*. Translated by Chris Turner, Verso, 2003.
———. *Seduction*. Translated by Brian Singer, New World Perspectives, 1990.
———. *Simulacra and Simulation*. Translated by Sheila Faria Glaser, U of Michigan P, 2006.
Baudrillard, Jean. *The Spirit of Terrorism*. Translated by Chris Turner, Verso, 2003.
———. "The Matrix Decoded: Le Nouvel Observateur Interview with Jean Baudrillard." Translated by Gary Genosko and Adam Bryx, *International Journal of Baudrillard Studies*, vol 1, no 2, 2004, https://baudrillardstudies.ubishops.ca/the-matrix-decoded-le-nouvel-observateur-interview-with-jean-baudrillard/.
———. *Symbolic Exchange and Death*. Translated by Iain Hamilton Grant, Sage, 2016.
———. *The Transparency of Evil. Essays on Extreme Phenomena*. Translated by James Benedict, Verso, 2002.
Butler, Rex. *Jean Baudrillard: The Defence of the Real*. Sage, 1999.
Coulter, Gerry. "Reversibility." *The Baudrillard Dictionary*, edited by Richard G. Smith, Edinburgh UP, 2010, pp. 181–83.
Genosko, Gary. *Baudrillard and Signs: Signification Ablaze*. Routledge, 1994.
Haar, Rebecca and Anna McFarlane. "Simulation and Simulacra." *The Routledge Companion to Cyberpunk Culture*, edited by Anna McFarlane, Graham J. Murphy, and Lars Schmeink, Routledge, 2020, pp. 255–63.
Hollinger, Veronica. "Stories about the Future: From Patterns of Expectation to Pattern Recognition." *Science Fiction Studies*, vol. 33, no. 3, 2006, pp. 452–72.
Hölderlin, Friedrich. *Selected Poems*. Translated by David Constantine, Bloodaxe Books, 1996.

Kellner, Douglas. *Media Culture*. Routledge, 1995.

Kilgore, Christopher D. "Post-Cyberpunk." *The Routledge Companion to Cyberpunk Culture*, edited by Anna McFarlane, Graham J. Murphy, and Lars Schmeink, Routledge, 2020, pp. 48–55.

Lavigne, Carlen. *Cyberpunk Women, Feminism and Science Fiction: A Critical Study*. McFarland & Company, Inc., 2013.

Merrin, William. "The Age of Hyporeality: Heteroclitic Empiricism and the Extinction Cascade of the Real." *Conspiracy Theories: Representations of the Political in the Age of Populism*, edited by Andrew Wilson, Routledge, forthcoming 2022.

McQueen, Sean. *Deleuze and Baudrillard: From Cyberpunk to Biopunk*. Edinburgh UP, 2016.

Murphie, Andrew, and John Potts. *Culture and Technology*. Palgrave Macmillan, 2003.

Schmeink, Lars. "Afterthoughts: Cyberpunk Engagements in Countervisuality." *Cyberpunk and Visual Culture*, edited by Graham J. Murphy and Lars Schmeink, Routledge, 2018, pp. 250–65.

Shapiro, Alan. *Star Trek: Technologies of Disappearance*. Avinus, 2004.

The Matrix. Directed by The Wachowskis, Warner Brothers, 1999.

Tomberg, Jaak. "On the 'Double Vision' of Realism and SF Estrangement in William Gibson's Bigend Trilogy." *Science Fiction Studies*, vol. 40, no. 2, 2013, pp. 263–85.

Michał Kłosiński

LAUREN BEUKES (1976–)

South African author and journalist.

Lauren Beukes started her career in journalism but branched out to become a prolific South African writer. In addition to numerous short stories and five novels, her work also includes writing for television, graphic novels, non-fiction, and popular history. Her second novel, *Zoo City* (2010), brought her international acclaim as a science fiction (sf) writer, winning the Arthur C. Clarke Award in 2011 and being nominated for the British Science Fiction Association award and the World Fantasy award. While her first novel, *Moxyland* (2008), and *Zoo City* explore many cyberpunk themes, Beukes's oeuvre resists easy categorization, instead playing with genre motifs and borders, challenging and blending tropes from noir to magical realism, from gritty horror to time travel, from post-apocalypse to road movie.

One of the cyberpunk themes uniting *Moxyland* and *Zoo City* is the relation of the human to the posthuman. *Moxyland* starts out with art school dropout and freelance photographer Kendra, one of the novel's four protagonists, selling herself to biotech company Inatec

Biologica to become a living advertisement for an energy drink. She is injected with nanotechnology, which makes her resistant to diseases, gives her perfect skin, and marks her with the brand's neon logo as a "Sponsor baby" (3). In Kendra, Beukes literalizes the idea of capitalist ownership of posthuman bodies, of claiming biopolitical control via technology. Kendra's life is precarious, both economically and medically (she wants to stave off hereditary cancer), and she believes the sponsorship deal to be her only chance of making it in the highly stratified society of Cape Town. However, the corporation uses the contract to shape Kendra the way they want, reducing her to an image (a model) and thus rejecting her "rightful ownership of her own body" (Barris 137). Although nanotech cures her of a weaponized virus that infects her at an illegal riot, "the technologised control mechanisms of [this] corporatised totalitarian society" (Barris 137) would rather keep the optics of the campaign intact: Inatec Biologica terminates her.

Whereas *Moxyland* explores a posthuman hybridity achieved via internalized technologies, *Zoo City* moves away from the tech-tropes of cyberpunk to stage Beukes's interrogation of a human–animal posthumanism, chiefly through the introduction of "aposymbiots" (or "zoos"). In the novel, humans that commit a violent crime become linked to an animal, "literally reconstitut[ing them] as human-animal unions" (Ericson 3) and branding them as Other. As a result, *Zoo City*'s characters mostly experience their aposymbiotic posthumanism as vulnerability and precarious Otherness. In both novels, Beukes showcases that the human is not a self-contained being, but a posthuman assemblage inextricably linked to a "political, cultural, and geographical landscape" (Ericson 9), always already connected to its surroundings, both via nature and technology.

Moxyland and *Zoo City* also reinforce socio-economic stratification and global inequality, notably in the South African cities Johannesburg and Cape Town. Beukes's characters—the "hustlers, journalists, recovering addicts (or those failing recovery), sex workers, squatters, police, criminals, and artists" (Spain 260)—are enmeshed with their technologized urban surroundings and move seamlessly through these spaces. For example, *Zoo City*'s Zinzi, "at once a street-hardened ex-convict, a formerly well-connected hipster, and the university-educated daughter of academic parents" (Sofianos 115), navigates both the seedy underbelly of Jo'burg and the gated communities of the wealthy. She echoes **William Gibson**'s now-famous epithet that the street finds its own uses for things, always adapting to the needs of her new situation and earning a living by finding lost things. Beukes's characters are drawn from the economically disenfranchised and those forgotten by society—the 'low-lifes' that **Bruce Sterling** famously claimed in his Preface to *Mirrorshades: The Cyberpunk Anthology* (1986) that defined cyberpunk's protagonists.

With her characters moving through the city spaces of both *Moxyland* and *Zoo City*, Beukes reveals South African urbanity as "simultaneously technological, mystical, cosmopolitan, futurist, and persistently haunted by both the occult and the past" (Dickson 67). The fictional versions of the cities represent our cyberpunk realities and highlight our techno-mediated connections with the political and cultural landscape. In *Moxyland*, life is determined by one's smartphone, which is used as a passport for movement in the city, as payment for public and private services, and even as biopolitical control through the police's ability to surveil every movement, to defuse protests by electro-shocking users, or even to disconnect citizens completely, thus restricting social and economic interactions. Central to the story of *Moxyland* is also the interdependence of virtual and material worlds: phones are not just entry points to the virtual world of information but are used to regulate material and geographical access as well. Similarly, the technologized world and African cosmologies become intermixed in *Zoo City*. For example, a *sangoma*, a shaman communicating with spirits, relies on his iPhone to commune with the other world: "The spirits find it easier with technology. It's not so logged as human minds [...] They still like rivers and oceans most of all, but data is like water—the spirits can move through it. That's why you get a prickly feeling around cellphone towers" (191)

Magic and technology are equated in *Zoo City*, both revealing a network of information, another world (virtual or spiritual) that is coextensive with the materiality of the city. In addition, part of what makes *Zoo City* work so well is Beukes's extension of this networked intermingling to the level of narrative structure. Zinzi works for a group of career criminals that organize advanced-fee frauds, writing emails from fake Nigerian heirs to gullible American marks. The details of one of these scams interlaces the narrative via email missives, structuring the novel into two different realities (the virtual scam and the material search for a missing singer) and showing how each impacts Zinzi's life.

While technology is an integral part of the lives of Beukes's protagonists, it is the ubiquity of media (especially in their digital form) that is the most defining cyberpunk feature of her early novels. As Phoenix Alexander writes, her use of digital media is "[a]lien but familiar, consumable and iconic, the digital medium as rendered in (and indeed structuring) Beukes' texts generates a sense of dystopian jouissance via an authorial dive into occidental late capitalism, camera held out before her as she plunges into the depths" (158)

This is true both for 'classical' reporting via media as it is for other networked digital realities—both functioning as focal points for the cyberpunk trope of parallel and virtual worlds. For example, in *Moxyland*, Toby streams everything he does via his "BabyStrange" (11) coat, which functions both as screen and camera system, thus presenting a highly manipulated reality of events like a subway riot and subsequent gassing of rioters and protestors by the police. Similarly, Tendeka is involved in an activist group that organizes anti-authoritarian protests via online video games, but ultimately realizes that this parallel world of activism is staged by the corporations to manipulate public opinion.

Although she dials down on the cyberpunk elements in her later fiction, *Moxyland* and *Zoo City* provide the foundation for understanding Beukes's crime and horror novels *Shining Girls* (2013) and *Broken Monsters* (2014). The former depicts a parallel world accessible not through technology but through the magic of the portal-house. While the Depression-era day-laborer Harper travels through time to kill women, Kirby Mazrachi, one of the shining girls—i.e., those girls shining with potential who must be killed to fuel Harper's travels—has survived Harper's attack and has now returned to hunt the hunter. The only information networks available to her circa 1993 are news-paper archives, and her archival research reveals Harper's actions in headlines of murder and images of anachronistically placed trophies, thus letting Kirby grasp the contours of Harper's atemporal world. Meanwhile, in *Broken Monsters*, digital and material representations are precariously perched on top of each other, several characters dealing with the dissonance of representing a different version of themselves in each reality. Layla, the daughter of police detective Versado, lives her life on social media; her parts of the narrative are interspersed with online chats, as well as full of references to media, viral hits, and inter-net jargon. She and her friend use a video chat app to lure pedophiles into a trap and expose them by using video grabs. Wanna-be journalist Jonno re-brands himself by moving from writing essays to becoming a video blogger desperate to find a new audience, receiving validation for his virtual representation, thus revealing socially problematic issues with self-styled representation and the anonymity of virtual realities. The same is true for Clayton, the failed artist turned serial killer, who transforms his victims into sculptures. The media attention that his 'art' receives validates his murders and allows him to slide deeper into psychosis. The mediated representation—i.e., being seen by other people and receiving attention—is Beukes's critique of our media-capitalized world: "We want to be seen; we want to be recognised as human. Social media offers us that affirmation through the likes; it's all about the eyeballs. It's about who is seen and who isn't, whose art is elevated and whose isn't, how you play the game – you know, the talent doesn't necessarily matter" (cited in Stobie 49)

Finally, Beukes's style is somewhat related to Gibson's: it is saturated with popular culture, brands and products, art and photography via "deliberately scattershot techno-cultural references that saturate her narratives" (Alexander 158). This is no accident. As Jennifer M. Schmidt writes, Beukes deliberately focuses on artists and journalists whose lives are strongly mediated, publicized, and influenced by the marketplace of attention, often exploring the impact of globalized capitalism on the vulnerable. Her prose therefore relies on a "pastiche of pop culture savvy and hyper-attunement to the mechanisms of power" (151). This merging of popular style with techno-dystopian political power makes Beukes's work an important comment on and depiction of our technologically saturated twenty-first-century reality, as well as part of the literary tradition that defines the cyberpunk mode.

See also: **Rosi Braidotti, William Gibson, Melissa Scott, Neil Stephenson, Bruce Sterling**

Works Cited

Alexander, Phoenix. "Spectacles of Dystopia: Lauren Beukes and the Geopolitics of Digital Space." *Safundi*, vol. 16, no. 2, 2015, pp. 156–72, doi: 10.1080/17533171.2015.1028181.

Barris, Ken. "Re/membering the Future? Speculative Fiction by Eben Venter and Lauren Beukes." *Current Writing*, vol. 29, no. 2, 2017, pp. 131–140. doi: 10.1080/1013929X.2017.1347428.

Beukes, Lauren. *Moxyland*. Mulholland, 2008.

———. *Zoo City*. Mulholland, 2010.

———. *Shining Girls*. Mulholland, 2013.

———. *Broken Monsters*. Mulholland, 2014.

Dickson, Jessica. "Reading the (Zoo) City: The Social Realities and Science Fiction of Johannesburg." *Johannesburg Salon,* vol. 7, 2014, pp. 67–78.

Ericson, Suzanne. "Thinking with Crocodiles, Thinking through Humans: Vulnerable, Entangled Selves in Lauren Beukes's *Zoo City*." *Scrutiny2: Issues in English Studies in Southern Africa*, vol. 23, no. 1, 2018, pp. 22–34, doi: 10.1080/18125441.2017.1408676.

Schmidt, Jennifer M. "The girls who don't die: Subversions of gender and genre in recent fiction by Lauren Beukes." *Safundi: The Journal of South*

African and American Studies, vol. 17, no. 2, 2016, pp. 137–155, doi: 10.1080/17533171.2016.1171474.

Sofianos, Konstantin. "Magical Nightmare Jo'burg." *Safundi: The Journal of South African and American Studies*, vol. 14, no. 1, 2013, pp. 111–20, doi: 10.1080/17533171.2012.760834.

Spain, Andrea. "Shining girls and forgotten men in Lauren Beukes' urban 'America.'" *Safundi: The Journal of South African and American Studies*, vol. 18, no. 3, 2017, pp. 258–278, doi: 10.1080/17533171.2017.1329855.

Lars Schmeink

ROSI BRAIDOTTI (1954–)

Italian philosopher and academic.

Over the last thirty years, Rosi Braidotti has been associated with several high-theory concepts: materialist feminism, nomadism, vitalist materialism, the posthuman, critical posthumanism—all of which have rippled not just through philosophy or gender studies departments but through all (post)humanities. While it is tempting to think of her career in terms of genealogical progression from a robust feminist inquiry, through Gilles Deleuze-inspired theories of nomadism and becomings, to the posthuman, Braidotti is, first and foremost, a *feminist* philosopher of embodiment, whose critical output is perhaps best understood as a product of "French poststructuralist philosophies of May 1968" and "transnational feminist theories" (Blaagaard and van der Tuin 3). In a true nomadic spirit, as a child Braidotti moved from Italy to Australia, then came to Paris as a recent graduate of the University of Canberra to study with French poststructuralist stars (such as Deleuze and Michel Foucault) and feminist philosophers (especially Luce Irigaray), and in the late 1980s settled in the Netherlands as a professor of women's studies at the University of Utrecht, where she is now a Distinguished University Professor. Thanks to the flows, flights, and intensities of nomadism, Braidotti has become a bona fide polyglot, speaking, writing, thinking, and publishing in several languages; she "has been aided, inspired, multiplied," as an author and a critical thinker (Deleuze and Guattari 2). As such, Braidotti has emerged at the forefront for thinking more critically (and in more complex ways) about the intricate wirings of cyberpunk culture.

Braidotti's most straightforward engagement with cyberpunk cultures can be traced back to her early work in the late 1990s and early 2000s. In *Transpositions: On Nomadic Ethics* (2006), Braidotti follows **Donna J. Haraway**'s figure of the cyborg, referring to marginal genres (such as cyberpunk) or technological others/Others (such as cyborgs and cyber-monsters) as very much capable of radically reconfiguring humanist subjectivity and "scrambl[ing] the established codes" (101). Or, in "Postface," Braidotti and Nina Lykke envision new "figurations of otherness," "hybrid, and yet 'woman-friendly': monsters, goddesses and cyborgs" that are "familiar, yet idiosyncratic and slightly disconcerting," which might prove to be effective sites of resistance against "the post-industrial epistemological haze" (Lykke 248). Finally, in "Cyberfeminism with a Difference," Braidotti calls for "a turn to 'minor' literary genres, such as science fiction and more specifically cyber-punk" (sic) to find non-nostalgic re-imaginings of the future, badly needed after the collapse of modernist dreams and ideals and the demise of classical humanism.[1] As Braidotti writes, "[s]ome of the most moral beings left in western postmodernity are the science-fiction writers who take the time to linger on the death of the humanist ideal of Man, thus inscribing this loss—and the ontological insecurity it entails—at the (dead) heart of contemporary cultural concerns" ("Cyberfeminism"). Patricia MacCormack argues that "Braidotti takes the celebration of difference in reference to human bodies and transgressive subjects to a political level where the very concept of 'human' and 'subject' are being problematized and manipulated by global capitalism, biology, science, and philosophy" (78). This perspective clearly informs Braidotti's 2002 book *Metamorphoses: Towards a Materialist Theory of Becoming*, an exploration of postmodern monsters not as fixed points but as processes that counter phallogocentric forms of subjectivity. Braidotti highlights the privileging of mutants and monsters over more traditionally conceptualized humans in such 'minor literatures' as horror and sf, especially cyberpunk (177–79) and, in so doing, she locates new forms of nomadic subjectivities.[2] In Braidotti's nomadism, subjectivity is seen as inherently relational, open-ended, and responsive, which makes a nomadic subjectivity an important alternative to the highly individualized closed-off self under advanced capitalism. Similarly, in *Transpositions*, Braidotti continues the exploration of subjectivity and argues compellingly that various "technological artefacts" such as, for instance, "Tamagochis and Pokemon [sic], as well as more advanced fictional figures from the twilight zone known as 'virtual reality'" are capable of destabilizing traditionally conceived subjectivity as much as "any traditional literary or cinematic character, or indeed any living human or companion species" (121). In sum, Braidotti's early work on nomadism, cyber-teratology, and 'minor literature' is founded upon a commitment to feminist reformulations of subjectivity, understood as embodied *and* embedded, and theorized outside of exclusionary humanist paradigms.

This commitment is at the core of Braidotti's dedication to exploring new forms of subjectivities in not only chapters, articles, lectures, and three co-edited collections on the posthuman and critical posthumanism, but also her books *The Posthuman* (2013), *Posthuman Knowledge* (2019), and *Posthuman Feminism* (2022). In Braidotti's formulation, the posthuman does not refer to transhumanist fantasies of *posthuman* superiority or technologically-assisted transcendence, both of which are heavily, if rather superficially, coated in cyberpunk aesthetics; rather, the posthuman is "a theoretical figuration," "a navigational tool," and "a working hypothesis about the kind of subject we are becoming" in a world shaped by ecological catastrophe, advanced capitalism, and ever-expanding technologies (*Posthuman Knowledge* 2). In a way, *The Posthuman* reads like a critical companion to a world seen through a decidedly cyberpunk lens: a world marked by biogenetic and biomedical capitalism, "necro-political modes of governance" (124), and "techno-scientific structure[s]" of the global economy (59). Stating simply that "[t]he Vitruvian Man has gone cybernetic," Braidotti points to the extensive cyborgization of everyday life, social fabric and cultural production, with cyborgs being not only "the glamorous bodies of high-tech, jet-fighter pilots, athletes or film stars, but also the anonymous masses of the underpaid, digital proletariat who fuel the technology-driven global economy without ever accessing it themselves" (*The Posthuman* 90).

While Braidotti admits that most mainstream cyberpunk texts seem to her "very sloppy" and "essentialistic" in their portrayal of sexual difference, she does point to feminist science fiction (sf) authors and artists such as Kathy Acker, Angela Carter, Trinh T. Minh-ha, and Cindy Sherman for powerful alternatives to mainstream nostalgia for the now defunct "humanistic certainties" ("Cyberfeminism"). As this cluster of artists (among others) demonstrates, it is up to the cyberfeminists, feminist fabulators, riot girls, and multi-media artists to push forward new utopias in which sexual difference is neither seemingly abolished through fantasies of male-centric disembodied transcendence nor fetishized through the monstrous feminine and fantasies of male-only reproduction. Braidotti insists that technology is the best tool for women to "disengage our collective imagination from the phallus and its accessory values: money, exclusion and domination, nationalism, iconic femininity and systematic violence," despite a widening gender gap and "polarization between the sexes" engendered by new media technologies, which she accurately predicted in the mid-1990s ("Cyberfeminism"), even before the advent of Web 2.0. Thus, for example, Laboria Cuboniks's *Xenofeminism: A Politics for Alienation* (2015), a manifesto for a cyber-feminist future, flatly rejects the supposed inviolability of the natural and pays close attention to how embodiment and power relations mesh with technology. At the same time, such fictions as **Richard K. Morgan**'s *Altered Carbon* trilogy,[3] Kameron Hurley's *The Stars are Legion* (2017), and Shane Carruth's movie *Upstream Color* (2013) all take up Braidotti's challenge of constructing radical thought experiments in which the body and its capacity for being affected and for affecting others (human and non-human subjects alike) remain central to the discussion of social hierarchies, race, gender, sex, and technology.

While shifting her research interests to the posthuman, Braidotti has not radically changed her critical focus; if anything, her recent work on the posthuman and critical posthumanism remains very much in dialogue with her earlier work on nomadic subjectivity and embodiment. Still, Braidotti's recent publications are more accessible to people without a philosophical background, and they function as *de facto* wide-sweeping handbooks to posthuman thought, processes, and subjects. Cyberpunk studies increasingly references Braidotti's recent work,[4] but I contend it is her earlier work on cyberfeminism, corporeal feminism, and cyber-teratology that most fundamentally engages with and informs cyberpunk and cyber-feminist research.[5] Ultimately, "Braidotti's teratology [understood] as an experiment in philosophies between women, abjection, alterity, alien, maternal, and machinic becomings" brings the monster (the anomalous human, the less-than-human, the non-human) in close (almost intimate) proximity to the posthuman (MacCormack 80–81). These figurations of (cyber-)otherness and the theorization of nomadic subjectivity help to see cyberpunk texts as thought experiments, neither intrinsically technophobic nor technophilic, and always looking to "push the [humanist] crisis to its innermost resolution" ("Cyberfeminism").

See also: **Donna J. Haraway, N. Katherine Hayles, Richard K. Morgan, Shoshanna Zuboff**

Notes

1 In this context, one heavily influenced by Gilles Deleuze and Félix Guattari, 'minor literature' refers to works written in a major language, which at the same time de-stratify and displace (deterritorialize) that said language (and its attendant discourses and imaginaries) and emphasize the political and collective potential of literature.

2 Braidotti recognizes that while it is possible to recover the monstrous or the anomalous for politically generative futures and for "transformative politics and processes of becoming," the cyber-teratological imaginary can also express "the fear and the anxieties of the Majority, embodied in the dominant subject-position of the male, white, heterosexual, urbanized property-owning speaker of a standard language" (*Metamorphoses* 213).

3 *Altered Carbon* (2002); *Broken Angels* (2003); *Woken Furies* (2005).

4 See also Murgia; Schmeink; selected essays in McFarlane, Murphy, and Schmeink; and Heise-von der Lippe.

5 Examples include Lavigne; du Preez; Melzer; and Kember.

Works Cited

Blaagaard, Bolette and Iris van der Tuin, editors. *The Subject of Rosi Braidotti: Politics and Concepts*. Bloomsbury, 2014.

Braidotti, Rosi. "Cyberfeminism with a Difference." *Disability Studies in Nederland*, 1996, pp. 1–12, disabilitystudies.nl/sites/disabilitystudies.nl/files/beeld/onderwijs/ cyberfeminism_with_a_difference.pdf.

———. *Metamorphoses: Towards a Materialist Theory of Becoming*. Polity, 2002.

———. *Nomadic Subjects: Embodiment and Sexual Difference in Contemporary Feminist Theory*. 2nd ed., Columbia UP, 2011.

———. *The Posthuman*. Polity, 2013.

———. *Posthuman Knowledge*. Polity, 2019.

———. *Transpositions: On Nomadic Ethics*. Polity, 2006.

Heise-von der Lippe, Anya, editor. *Posthuman Gothic*. U of Wales P, 2017.

Kember, Sarah. *Cyberfeminism and Artificial Life*. Routledge, 2003.

Lavigne, Carlen. *Cyberpunk Women, Feminism and Science Fiction: A Critical Study*. McFarland & Company, Inc., 2013.

Lykke, Nina, and Rosi Braidotti. "Postface." *Between Monsters, Goddesses and Cyborgs: Feminist Confrontations with Science, Medicine and Cyberspace*, edited by Nina Lykke and Rosi Braidotti, Zed Books, 1996, pp. 242–249.

MacCormack, Patricia. "Pro-Proteus: The Transpositional Teratology of Rosi Braidotti." *The Subject of Rosi Braidotti: Politics and Concepts*, edited by Bolette Blaagaard and Iris van der Tuin, Bloomsbury, 2014, pp. 78–86.

McFarlane, Anna, Graham J. Murphy, and Lars Schmeink, editors. *The Routledge Companion to Cyberpunk Culture*. Routledge, 2020.

Melzer, Patricia. *Alien Constructions: Science Fiction and Feminist Thought*. U of Texas P, 2006.

Murgia, Claudio. *(Beyond) Posthuman Violence: Epic Rewritings of Ethics in the Contemporary Novel*. Vernon P, 2019.

du Preez, Amanda. *Gendered Bodies and New Technologies: Rethinking Embodiment in a Cyber-era*. Cambridge Scholars, 2009.

Schmeink, Lars. *Biopunk Dystopias: Genetic Engineering, Society and Science Fiction*. Liverpool UP, 2016.

Agnieszka Kotwasińska

CHARLTON 'CHARLIE' BROOKER (1971–)

English television writer, presenter, and author.

Charlie Brooker's professional career includes work in a variety of media, including contributions to print magazines and newspapers (*PC Zone*; weekly TV review column "Screen Burn" in *The Guardian*, 2000–10), a popular satirical website *TVGoHome* (1999–2003), and work in radio (BBC Radio 4, *So Wrong It's Right* 2010–12). Much of his writing has been collected in book form, and he was awarded the 2009 Columnist of the Year award at the British Press Awards for his "Screen Burn" column. His most acclaimed and influential work, however, has appeared on television. Brooker was part of the thriving British comedy scene of the late 1990s and early 2000s, most notably having collaborated as a writer with boundary-pushing comedian Chris Morris on the controversial special episode of *Brass Eye* called "Paedogeddon" (2001), which satirized the sensationalist tone of how television news programs covered the issue of pedophilia.[1] After co-creating the one-series comedy shows *Spoons* and *Nathan Barley*, both in 2005 (the latter with Morris), he achieved wide popularity with *Charlie Brooker's Screenwipe* (2006–08), a show including television reviews and satirical commentary on the nature of the medium and its influence on British (and, to an extent, American) society. Brooker both created and presented the show, which, after its initial five-season run, has spawned many continuations,[2] was rewarded by the Royal Television Society (2010), and has received three British Comedy Awards (2009, 2011, 2012), as well as the BAFTA TV Award for Best Comedy and Comedy Entertainment Program (2017).

With his acclaimed 2008 zombie horror series *Dead Set* Brooker began to venture into narrative drama while maintaining the elements of social satire that had permeated his previous projects. Brooker's most popular and acclaimed work has been the science fiction anthology series *Black Mirror* (2011–). With its first two seasons and a special produced by Channel 4, the series was picked up by Netflix in 2015, which, at the time of writing, has released three more seasons and the interactive film *Black Mirror: Bandersnatch* (2018). Highly praised for its commentary on humanity's destructive reliance on modern technology, the show has altogether won 23 awards and has been nominated 78 times for its various episodes. Three of them ("San Junipero" [3.04], "USS Callister" [4.01], and *Bandersnatch*) have received the Primetime Emmy Award for Outstanding Television Movie (2017, 2018, 2019). In his *Guardian* column "The Dark Side," Brooker discussed being inspired by Rod Serling's *The Twilight Zone* (CBS, 1959–64) and *Black Mirror* has been called "*The Twilight Zone* of the twenty-first century" (Cirucci and Vacker vii). Terence McSweeney and Stuart Joy also give a specifically British lineage for Brooker's work, including *Tales of the Unexpected* (ITV, 1978–88) and *Hammer House of Horror* (Hammer films/ITC, 1980) as major points of reference (2–3).

Brooker's work occupies a paradoxical position of using the system of globalized media and taking advantage of technological advancements to critique contemporary, developed societies' reliance on mass media and technology. This paradox contributes to the dry, almost cynical, satirical irony of *Screenwipe* and the dramatic irony of *Black Mirror*, emphasized by the latter's trademark shock endings. The interchangeably bleak and grotesque lens through which Brooker looks at media and technology necessitates his consideration as a (post-)cyberpunk writer and creator, as his work highlights the ways cyberpunk has become a "cultural formation" (Foster xv) not only through shaping the thematic and aesthetic focus of cultural texts, but also through bringing into focus the many ways in which we are already living in a cyberpunk reality (cf. McFarlane, Murphy, and Schmeink). Much of Brooker's critique of contemporary television in *Screenwipe*—e.g., its appeal to the viewers' basest instincts and desires—closely resembles the grotesque media landscape of **Warren Ellis** and Darick Robertson's quintessential cyberpunk comic book series *Transmetropolitan* (Vertigo Comics, 1997–2002). Brooker's position in the show as an ironic commentator recalls the detached yet captivated outsider, Spider Jerusalem, even if *Screenwipe* does not openly reference cyberpunk aesthetics. Similarly, the quotidian near-future of the *Black Mirror* universe addresses many of cyberpunk's major themes without striving for an aesthetically detached impression of futurity. Among these themes, there are those identified by **Bruce Sterling** in his Preface to *Mirrorshades: The Cyberpunk Anthology* (1986) as "body invasion: prosthetic limbs, implanted circuitry, cosmetic surgery, genetic alteration" and "mind invasion: brain-computer interfaces, artificial intelligence, neurochemistry" (xiii), but *Black Mirror* constantly emphasizes the resemblance of its fictional technology to that of the present, always "visceral," "intimate," one that "sticks to the skin" and "responds to the touch" (Sterling xiii).

Black Mirror relies upon Brooker's two major, often interrelated, thematic interests: the corruptive yet addictive relationship contemporary societies have developed with media, and the inescapable appeal of the technological *novum*, which exercises detrimental influence on the characters' fates, often despite their realization that something is terribly wrong. *Black Mirror* highlights how both media and technological innovations are produced and imposed on consumers by multinational corporate capitalism and its critique of the media often introduces a political context. The (in)famous first episode of the show, "The National Anthem" (1.01), satirizes politics as a media spectacle in having the British Prime Minister forced to perform intercourse with a pig on live television. "The Waldo Moment" (2.03), which introduces a seemingly absurd plot in which a foul-mouthed animated teddy bear named Waldo runs for public office, had been one of the worst-reviewed episodes of the show at the time of its broadcast (2013) until it proved unexpectedly prescient when a vulgar reality television host was elected President of the United States three years later.[3] With the hindsight of a decade that saw populism assume its place at the center of the political discourse in several different places across the globe, "The Waldo Moment" seems attuned to the postmodern realization that any sense of reality in politics has been superseded by an alternative reality enabled by the media, in which the entertainment qualities of a political candidate are much more valuable than their moral integrity, or the extent to which their policies can be implemented within the framework of a liberal democracy.

Many of *Black Mirror*'s episodes rely on a technological *novum*, often resembling certain contemporary technological advancements, but with their features exaggerated *ad absurdum* or *ad horrendum*. Some of these *novums* are designed to enhance biological functions in a way characteristic of the frequent cyberpunk topics of critical posthumanism and transhumanism. "The Entire History of You"[4] (1.03) introduces a wearable device allowing its user to record whatever they hear or see with an option to replay these memories or have someone else display their memories for another person to see. As Henry Jenkins has pointed out, this recording device reflects a larger cultural turn (described by Bruce Sterling) in which "science fiction had shifted from a focus on 'the giant steam snorting wonders of the past' toward a focus on the 'utterly intimate' technologies of the current moment" (Jenkins 45). This turn is characteristic for much of cyberpunk, but also neatly conforms with Brooker's approach to modern technology. Technology acts as a prosthesis or an enhancer of interpersonal relationships, such as in "Be Right Back" (2.01), "USS Callister," or "Hang the DJ" (4.04).

"San Junipero," an uncharacteristic example of technological optimism, invites a closer analysis, as it is one of the most acclaimed episodes of the show, exploring the theme of virtually simulated life-after-death through a lesbian love story. "San Junipero" introduces the characters of Yorkie and Kelly, two young women who meet in a nightclub in the titular town of San Junipero in the 1980s. The episode's reveal, tying into the cyberpunk theme of posthuman simulations, is that both Yorkie and Kelly are elderly, and that San Junipero is a simulated virtual reality they visit as a form of escape. As San Junipero has the capability to host the consciousness of the deceased—a source of controversy in the story world as not everyone opts to have their existence extended *postmortem*—the two women reunite in the simulation after their death. The episode represents a utopian aspect of cyberpunk in Brooker's oeuvre and constitutes one of the best representations of *Black Mirror*'s approach to cyberpunk as a cultural formation. Even though "San Junipero" does not replicate cyberpunk aesthetics, it excitedly explores the existential possibilities offered by the introduction of a device that allows for uploading one's consciousness into a simulation, even if this posthuman *novum* is controversial in the story world. It engages with a cyberpunk transhumanist posthumanism, but it anchors it in the nostalgic aesthetics of the past, rather than introduce the futuristic imagery characteristic of classic cyberpunk texts. Breaking away from the show's predominant technophobia, episodes such as "San Junipero" present a more nuanced look at cyberpunk themes and complicate *Black Mirror*'s shared universe so that it is not exclusively presented as a horrific dystopia.

Brooker's *Black Mirror* is sometimes accused of an overly technophobic attitude, reinforced by what Conley and Burroughs call "the [show's] signature narrative tactic [... of] the traumatic twist" (139). They mention "Shut Up and Dance" (3.03) as the primary example, in which a teenager is blackmailed into participating in a bank robbery by somebody who hacked the teen's laptop video camera and recorded him masturbating to internet pornography. Throughout the episode, the easiness with which he agrees to the blackmailers' demands strains the limits of believability, but at the end of the episode it is revealed that the young man was viewing child pornography, which brutally shatters the viewer's sympathy for the boy. The show's technophobia is thus rooted in its pessimistic view of human nature, and the demands of its most frequent narrative device, the shock ending. *Black Mirror*'s fear of technology does not only register as a distillation of Brooker's personal anxiety but is "intrinsically connected to the fears and anxieties of the decade in which it was produced" (McSweeney and Joy 1). In exploring these fears and anxieties, Brooker (and *Black*

Mirror in particular) provides opportunities for all of us to explore the less comfortable corners of cyberpunk culture.

See also: **Warren Ellis, Richard K. Morgan**

Notes

1 The episode provoked so many complaints and so much tabloid-fueled controversy that Channel 4 was forced to apologize for its broadcast.
2 *Charlie Brooker's Gameswipe* (2009), *Newswipe with Charlie Brooker* (2009–10), *Charlie Brooker's Weekly Wipe* (2013–15), and a number of specials and annual year-in-review episodes.
3 Charlie Brooker revealed in an interview that he had also been initially unsatisfied with the episode, until the 2016 elections proved it to be unexpectedly predictive (Ritman).
4 Written by Jesse Armstrong, "The Entire History of You" is one of the few episodes for which Brooker has no writing, co-writing, or story credit.

Works Cited

Brooker, Charlie. "The Dark Side of Our Gadget Addiction." *The Guardian*, December 1, 2011.
Cirucci, Angela M., and Barry Vacker, editors. *Black Mirror and Critical Media Theory*. Lexington Books, 2018.
Conley, Donovan, and Benjamin Burroughs. "*Black Mirror*, Mediated Affect and the Political." *Culture, Theory and Critique*, vol. 60, no. 2, 2019, pp. 139–53.
Foster, Thomas. *The Souls of Cyberfolk: Posthumanism as Vernacular Theory*. U of Minnesota P, 2005.
Jenkins, Henry. "Enhanced Memory: 'The Entire History of You.'" *Through the Black Mirror: Deconstructing the Side Effects of the Digital Age*, edited by Terence McSweeney and Stuart Joy, Palgrave Macmillan, 2019, pp. 43–54.
McFarlane, Anna, Graham J. Murphy, and Lars Schmeink, editors. *The Routledge Companion to Cyberpunk Culture*. Routledge, 2020.
McSweeney, Terence and Stuart Joy. "Introduction: Read that Back to Yourself and Ask If You Live in a Sane Society." *Through the Black Mirror: Deconstructing the Side Effects of the Digital Age*, edited by Terence McSweeney and Stuart Joy, Palgrave Macmillan, 2019, pp. 1–16.
Ritman, Alex. "*Black Mirror* Creator on How He (Unknowingly) Predicted the Rise of Donald Trump, Season 3." *The Hollywood Reporter*, October 21, 2016, https://www.hollywoodreporter.com/live-feed/black-mirror-creator-charlie-brooker-season-3-donald-trump-940324.
Sterling, Bruce. Preface. *Mirrorshades: The Cyberpunk Anthology*, edited by Bruce Sterling, Ace, 1988, pp. ix–xvi.

Filip Boratyn

PAT[RICIA] CADIGAN (1953–)

US novelist and short story writer.

Ever since the first wave of print cyberpunk first appeared in the 1980s, Pat Cadigan has proven instrumental to the evolution of cyberpunk and cyberpunk culture. She holds a Bachelor of Arts from the University of Kansas (1975), where she met and studied with the late American science fiction (sf) writer and scholar James Gunn. During her studies, she became active in sf fandom, participated in sf conventions, and began editing 'zines. Her first publication was "Death from Exposure" (1978), and she has since published over one hundred short stories in sf, fantasy, and horror, many of which are collected in *Patterns* (1989), *Home by the Sea* (1992), and *Dirty Work* (1993). Her longer fiction includes *Mindplayers* (1987)—a cut-up novel assembling the stories "The Pathosfinder" (1981), "Nearly Departed" (1983), "Variation on a Man" (1984), and "Lunatic Bridge" 1987—*Synners* (1991), *Fools* (1992), *Tea from an Empty Cup* (1998)—adapted from "Death in the Promised Land" (1995) and "Tea from an Empty Cup" (1997)—and the pseudo-sequel *Dervish Is Digital* (2000). She has increasingly turned to television and film novelizations and tie-ins, including *The Making of Lost in Space* (1998), *Lost in Space: Promised Land* (1998), *The Twilight Zone: Upgrade/Sensuous Cindy* (2004), *Jason X* (2005), *Iron City* (*Alita: Battle Angel*) (2018), *Alita: Battle Angel* (2019), and *Harley Quinn: Mad Love* (with Paul Dini) (2018). Her most recent novel (at the time of publication) is the novelization of **William Gibson**'s unused screenplay for the film *Alien 3*, appropriately titled *Alien 3: The Unproduced Screenplay* (2021). Cadigan has earned numerous awards, including the Arthur C. Clarke Award (*Synners*, 1992; *Fools*, 1995), the Locus Readers' Award ("Angel," 1988; *Patterns*, 1990; "The Girl-Thing Who Went Out for Sushi," 2013), the Hugo Award ("The Girl-Thing Who Went Out for Sushi"), the Seiun Award ("The Girl-Thing Who Went Out for Sushi"), and the 2020 Scribe Award for Best Adapted Novel (*Alita: Battle Angel*). Finally, Cadigan has participated in conferences and symposia on future technology, including lectures at MIT's International Space University (1992), the Whitney Museum's series on Performing Bodies and Smart Machines (1992), a conference on virtual reality (VR) at the London Institute for Contemporary Arts (1994), and a Virtual Futures conference at the University of Warwick (1994).

Although her work spans many modes and genres, Cadigan is frequently referred to as the "Queen of Cyberpunk" (Gillis 49), in part because her short story "Rock On" (1984) was the only cyberpunk story written by a woman to appear in **Bruce Sterling**'s groundbreaking *Mirrorshades: The Cyberpunk Anthology* (1986). Cadigan immediately embraced the moniker—she admits that she allows (or compels) her "publishers to use the blurb 'the Queen of Cyberpunk,' bestowed upon me by the *London Guardian* back in the mid-1990s. I like it; it makes me feel good" ("Manifesto" xiii)—and helped expand the definition of cyberpunk and broaden the canon in her edited collection *The Ultimate Cyberpunk* (2002). In several interviews, Cadigan has—somewhat unconvincingly—attributed the gender disparity to a "statistical anomaly" and somewhat dismissively remarks that cyberpunk "was never concerned with the biology of the writers involved" so forcing "the issue of how many women there are [in cyberpunk] is simply another way to begin from an improper assumption" ("Manifesto," xiii). More substantively, Cadigan's cyberpunk was generally more attuned to issues of gender and race and embodiment than her male counterparts; for example, **Sadie Plant** writes that "[if] Gibson began to explore the complexities of the matrix, Cadigan's fictions perplex reality and identity to the point of irrelevance" (334).

Cadigan's near-future sf is set largely on Earth (often in California) and is routinely "interested in technology of all kinds" (Cyberpunks Staff), but what interests her more than the machinery are the implications and consequences of those technologies. For example, in *Synners*, the Dr. Fish virus and the Artie Fish/Visual Mark fusion that takes place when the hacker Visual Mark uploads his consciousness into cyberspace were unexpected consequences of technology. Similarly, in both *Mindplayers* and *Fools* Cadigan foregrounds the personal and social implications of a technology that allows a person to enter the mind of another, or that allows the sharing and selling of personal memories, including such negative effects as memory addiction, mindcrimes, and a fragmented sense of identity, the latter a narrative trope Cadigan returns to in *Tea from an Empty Cup*. None of these by-products were the intended applications of mindsharing technology but are consequences that are seemingly unavoidable when (to borrow an aphorism by William Gibson) "the street finds its own uses for things" (186).

Similarly, in "Virtual Reality: As Real As You Want It to Be," Cadigan suggests that we have always had VR, but that we have only just now begun to develop the technology to make it a reality and a boon for education, training, and experimentation; but, as with any other technology, VR is and will be a "mixed blessing" ("Virtual Reality" xii). For example, in "Pretty Boy Crossover," VR feeds our (often narcissistic) need to see and be seen when Pretty Boys and Girls trade their corporeal selves for the opportunity to be dancing simulations projected 24/7 into real-time nightclubs. Or *Fools* demonstrates that VR can push the boundaries of the technique of method acting while also demonstrating that virtual reality is "inextricably intertwined with identity" (cited in Heuser 131). Finally, as the police procedurals *Tea from an Empty Cup* and *Dervish Is Digital* show, VR can both facilitate and complicate police work.

While many cyberpunk texts address questions of identity and (dis) embodiment, Cadigan takes a more nuanced and critical stance. As Lisa Yaszek remarks, Cadigan casts women as "resourceful heroines who oppose the exploitative practices of an inherently masculinist capitalism" and, in so doing, she "sharply criticizes the technological manipulation of bodies, identities, and histories by the entertainment industry" (34). Therefore, while many male cyberpunk writers seem to embrace (albeit problematically) a digital existence at the expense of an embodied one, Cadigan takes a more critical perspective. *Synners*, for example, focuses on the complicated relationship between mind (identity) and body. As I have argued elsewhere, each of the four primary characters—Gina, Gabe, Visual Mark, and Artie Fish—represent different attitudes toward embodiment, and what emerges is a rupturing of "the simple (and simplified) binary of mind and body" and a foregrounding of "embodiment as a place of experience and knowledge" (Calvin 46).

Cadigan has suggested that her attitude toward embodiment might have been shaped by her own gendered experiences; as a result, she has not been quite so willing to abandon the corporeal body for cyberspatial disembodiment. *Tea from an Empty Cup* drives that message home: Dore Konstantin, the detective-protagonist who reappears in *Dervish Is Digital*, recognizes advantages and disadvantages of the cyberbody but eschews the virtual in favor of the real. In fact, Cadigan undercuts some of the foundational tropes of cyberpunk; for example, Graham J. Murphy observes that Konstantin is no expert hacker but a relative novice in artificial reality (AR), largely blundering her way through AR and being repeatedly tagged as a novice netwalker by the other avatars she frustratingly encounters in her investigations (147).

Cadigan's cyberpunk focuses on questions of human identity: Where does it reside? Who can access it? How does it change when disembodied or digitized? Can identity be commodified? And for how much? She has repeatedly thematized these questions, particularly around gender, race, and sexuality. In "Pretty Boy Crossover," for example, Pretty Boy dreams of a posthuman existence, of being a "blip on a chip," while Bobby is happy to be "Self-Aware Data" (136), or S-A-D. But Pretty Boy, increasingly dismayed by the implications of a corporate-sponsored posthuman transcendence, ultimately opts out, remaining flesh and bone and embracing his corporeality at the end of the story. In *Mindplayers*, Deadpan Allie, compelled by law into mindplayer training and fearing contact with other minds, finds that over time, "she discovers that each mind-to-mind episode leaves traces in her mind which increasingly dilute her sense of self" (Heuser 129). Finally, *Fools* offers the most thorough examination of personal identity: three persons with three distinct identities—Marva, Marceline, and Mercine—occupy the same body, and they are all in search of their original body. Are they, in fact, three people? Three bodies? Are they all aspects of one person? And how does each of the three influence—mentally, emotionally, and physically—the other two? The narrative structure and shifting point-of-view, signaled by changes in font style, deny a unified authority and a single consciousness, positioning the character(s) as an exploration of the possibilities (or a set of possibilities) of virtual reality and as a means to use technology to explore fractured identity, often the result of technology.

Cadigan's cyberpunk is also suffused with a palpable nostalgia, despite her fascination with scientific and technological innovation. In *Tea from an Empty Cup*, Dore Konstantin enters artificial reality and sees her own body from above, quickly followed by a sense of "nostalgia" (Mitchell 121), while Yuki, the other protagonist of the novel, experiences nostalgia via old-fashioned office décor. In "Rock On," Gina is the last bastion against the loss of rock'n'roll, an authentic form of genuine music played by real musicians and not the synthesized bilge that is beamed to the masses. Similarly, *Synners* teems with references to Bob Dylan, Neil Young, Lou Reed, and the Rolling Stones. Perhaps most tellingly, *Synners* concludes with Gabe living modestly in a small house near the ocean—with no dataline—as he returns to an idyllic, pastoral past. Even Gina's electronic clone admits that only the embodied can "*really* boogie" (433), while Gabe believes that all the socketed people should be "banned" (435). Finally, Sabine Heuser draws our attention to Deadpan Allie's techno-removable eyes that remain the windows to the soul, a nostalgic view of the location of the self (127). In the end, if Cadigan's cyberpunk can be encapsulated in an admittedly trite summary, it is that technological innovations bring change, but that change is often at an unanticipated cost: addiction, dislocation, and fractured identity. And, at the same time, this change often brings about a reflection on the past, one steeped in nostalgia for the sensation of corporeality. If we are increasingly living in cyberpunk's posthuman futures (as is popularly claimed), Cadigan's work offers vitally important interrogations into the complexities of that state.

See also: **William Gibson, N. Katherine Hayles, Sadie Plant, Melissa Scott, Bruce Sterling**

Works Cited

Cadigan, Pat. "Foreword: Virtual Reality: As Real As You Want It to Be." *Virtual Reality: Applications and Explorations*, edited by Alan Wexelblat, Academic, 1993, pp. xi–xii.

———. "Not a Manifesto." *The Ultimate Cyberpunk*, edited by Pat Cadigan, ibooks, 2002, pp. vii–xiv.

———. "Pretty Boy Crossover." *Patterns*. Tor, 1989, pp. 129–38.

———. "Rock On." *Mirrorshades: The Cyberpunk Anthology*, edited by Bruce Sterling, Arbor House, 1986, pp. 35–43.

———. *Synners*. Four Walls Eight Windows, 1991.

———. *Tea from an Empty Cup*. Tor, 1998.

———. *Dervish Is Digital*. Tor, 2000.

Calvin, Ritch. "Pat Cadigan: *Synners* (Case Study)." *The Routledge Companion to Cyberpunk Culture*, edited by Anna McFarlane, Graham J. Murphy, and Lars Schmeink, Routledge, 2020, pp. 41–7.

Cyberpunks Staff. "An Interview with Cyberpunk Legend Pat Cadigan." *Cyberpunks*. August 8, 2019. https://www.cyberpunks.com/an-interview-with-cyperpunk-great-pat-cadigan/.

Gibson, William. "Burning Chrome." *Burning Chrome*. Ace, 1986, pp. 168–91.

Gillis, Stacy. "Cadigan, Pat (1953–)." *Women in Science Fiction and Fantasy. Volume 2. Entries*, edited by Robin Anne Reid, Greenwood, 2009, pp. 49.

Heuser, Sabine. *Virtual Geographies: Cyberpunk at the Intersection of the Postmodern and Science Fiction*. Rodopi, 2003.

Mitchell, Kaye. "Bodies That Matter: Science Fiction, Technoculture, and the Gendered Body." *Science Fiction Studies*, vol. 33, no.1, 2006, pp. 109–28.

Murphy, Graham J. "Imaginable Futures: *Tea from an Empty Cup* and the Notion of Nation." *Extrapolation*, vol. 45, no. 2, 2004, pp. 145–61.

Plant, Sadie. "On the Matrix: Cyberfeminist Simulations." *The Cybercultures Reader*, edited by David Bell and Barbara M. Kennedy, Routledge, 2000, pp. 325–36.

Yaszek, Lisa. "Feminist Cyberpunk." *The Routledge Companion to Cyberpunk Culture*, edited by Anna McFarlane, Graham J. Murphy, and Lars Schmeink, Routledge, 2020, pp. 32–40.

Ritch Calvin

DAVID CRONENBERG (1942–)

Canadian filmmaker and actor.

Toronto-born David Cronenberg is recognized globally as an iconic Canadian filmmaker and sometimes actor. Although he was seen early on as an outlier in the Canadian industry, which had been grounded historically in realism and documentary (Handling), Cronenberg's influence on the Canadian scene—one that also cultivated the pioneering work of other science fiction (sf) directors, like James Cameron and Ivan Reitman—has helped to pave the way for future arthouse directors in Canada (e.g., Atom Egoyan) and directors known for their work in cyberpunk culture (e.g., Denis Villeneuve and Brandon Cronenberg). Cronenberg was the subject of "Evolution," one of the first exhibitions at the TIFF (Toronto International Film Festival) Bell Lightbox Theatre in 2014, where many of the props used in his films were put on display, including some well-known to fans of cyberpunk culture, such as the Accumicon Spectacular Optometry International helmet used to brainwash Max Renn (James Woods) in *Videodrome* (1983), and Allegra Geller's (Jennifer Jason Leigh) MetaFlesh Game-Pods from *eXistenZ* (1999). In an article accompanying the online, virtual exhibition, Caroline Seck Langill writes that Cronenberg's films portray a science aesthetic that early on predicted our contemporary "reliance on and interaction with technology and its commingled objects." Through his attention to technological, as well as biological objects, Cronenberg's explorations of the intersection between media, the body, and the posthuman have become recognized as his signature traits in cyberpunk film and culture.

Cronenberg has directed over twenty films (including popular psychological horror and sf cyberpunk films), such as *Shivers* (1975), *Scanners* (1981), *The Dead Zone* (1983), *The Fly* (1986), *Dead Ringers* (1988), *Naked Lunch* (1991), *Crash* (1996), *A History of Violence* (2005), *A Dangerous Method* (2011), and *Cosmopolis* (2012). Many of Cronenberg's films have been produced in Canada, eschewing much of the high gloss aesthetics of the typical Hollywood blockbuster. Asked about his preference, Cronenberg has said that he sees his work as being closer to the arthouse cinema of the European industry than to the high budget glitz of American movies, despite admitting to being influenced by a range of American sf, horror, and psychological thrillers (Vanderburgh 87). His self-reflexive attitude toward the film and media industries comes across and is portrayed in films like *Videodrome* and *eXistenZ* where he demonstrates an awareness of the conditions of power and control in production. These are themes evoked generally in cyberpunk culture, of which Cronenberg is deemed to be an early pioneer thanks to his cult classic, *Videodrome*.

Similar themes come across in recent films, like his adaptation of Don DeLillo's *Cosmopolis* (2006), where Cronenberg builds an awareness of the ties between global networks of finance capital, corporate power, integrated networks of media simulation and spectacle, and the hyper-consumerism of techno-simulated urban environments that have become staples of sf and cyberpunk culture and aesthetics. Cronenberg's films have therefore become sources of intrigue for critical and cultural theorists interested in the intersections between media, materiality, embodiment, hyperreality, biopolitical capital, and the postmodern. Writers focusing on these themes and topics often mix Cronenberg's work with the writings of cultural and media philosophers and theories, such as the schizoanalytic methodologies of Gilles Deleuze and Félix Guattari, the simulation theories of **Jean Baudrillard**, theories of spectacle from Guy Debord, Fredric Jameson's historical materialist analysis of postmodernism, and the media theory of **Marshall McLuhan**. It is not surprising to see references to Cronenberg in early studies of virtual reality, such as Scott Bukatman's *Terminal Identity: The Virtual Subject in Postmodern Science Fiction* or Mark Fisher's *Flatline Constructs*. Because his films reflect mediations of the body, often portraying fluidity between the biological and the technological, Cronenberg's films also correspond with cyberpunk's intrigue with **Donna J. Haraway**'s cyborg theory, as well as theories of the posthuman (Hayles 33).

While his work is well placed at the origins of cyberpunk, Cronenberg's films depart somewhat from common tropes associated with the mode, such as depictions of cyberspace's informational networks portrayed in films like *TRON* (Lisberger 1982) or *The Matrix* (Wachowskis 1999). Instead, Cronenberg's films envision capital as a material, if not necessarily tangible, embodiment of time and space (Vint and Bould 227). *Videodrome* and *eXistenZ* portray the materiality of the body immersed in new media spaces, and planes of corporate control. While still parlaying the corporate and networked aspects of late capitalism, Cronenberg gives us a closer, more grounded depiction of the reality of these networks, portraying the business models of media systems and cultural industries (cable television, the porn industry, the videogames industry) embedded in the urban and commercial landscapes of late-twentieth-century capitalism. In *eXistenZ*, for instance, the titular video game sees the front end of digital capitalist culture (including interfaces, storefronts, and commercial retailers) fold into its back end in sites of production and manufacture, where technologies are built and programmed. Here we get to see the various layers of the video games industry's vertical structures of ownership and control, moving from spaces of exhibition (represented by a church) to that of distribution (a games store inside the game), to spaces of manufacturing—both at a game plant/farm, as well as a cabin in the woods where a games console, or 'pod,' is surgically repaired. Instead of fantasies of disembodied transcendence, where users enter imaginary spaces of virtual reality, or where characters metaphorically personify bits of information, as in *TRON* or *The Lawnmower Man* (Leonard 1992), Cronenberg presents us with direct transhumanist and bodily-infected representations of new media, where the human body connects to technological devices, and where bodies and technologies are seen both as productions and as ways for living experienced realities. Regarding the latter, the interconnectivity of media networks portrayed in Cronenberg's films, mixed with dimensions of power, authority, and desire, encourages viewers to call into question our lived perceptions of ordinary, non-mediated human reality.

This interrogation of our 'lived perceptions' comes across in *Videodrome* when Max wears the VR Accumicon helmet, or when his hand becomes fused with a gun; or, in *eXistenZ*, through the depiction of the game bioports, where players hook directly into the game console through a biocord that links into their spines. However, aspects of embodiment and the organic are also flipped in cases where technologies are represented as animate and living. The videocassette that Convex (Leslie Carlson) inserts into Max's (James Woods) body in *Videodrome* to brainwash him comes to life and is animated to appear to be more biological than technological. Similarly, the game console in *eXistenZ* is represented as a kind of biological organism, and when the console is damaged, games designer Allegra Geller brings it to her former mentor, Kiri Vinokur (Ian Holm), who performs surgery on the pod to rescue it. As Mark Fisher points out, often it is the machines in Cronenberg's films that "turn out to be anything but inert, just as human subjects end up behaving like passive automata" ("Work and Play" 72). Other examples of animated technology persist in Cronenberg's films, such as the typewriter in *Naked Lunch*, which transforms into a giant insect, or in *The Fly* when Seth Brundle's (Jeff Goldblum) DNA is technologically altered and mixed with a housefly, and they slowly transform into a posthuman hybrid. As he transforms into Brundlefly, the former scientist's rational humanistic identity is increasingly merged with the raw instincts of the fly.

Cronenberg's films in general navigate a biological–technological nexus that differs from other cyberpunk narratives. Specifically, while cyberpunk often relies upon the *metaphor* of fluid and mutable bodies surfing virtual realities and fulfilling cyberspatial fantasies, Cronenberg's films show technologies mediating our reflections about embodiment; our posthuman bodies are tethered to a corporeal reality dominated by proliferating new media. Although these depictions reflect the paranoid horror of corporate control common to cyberpunk culture, Cronenberg draws these themes out in ways evidently aroused by media theory, particularly with thinkers like the Canadian media studies pioneer Marshall McLuhan, who is recognized as the inspiration for the character of Dr. Brian O'Blivion (Jack Creley) in *Videodrome*. As we see in this film and elsewhere in Cronenberg's oeuvre, McLuhan's concept of media as "extensions of man" spills into the kinds of posthumanist theories that his own work is known to inspire within cyberpunk culture. For example, Scott Bukatman writes that "Cronenberg's spatialization of both bodily and viral forces presents a collision between McLuhan's extension of the body beyond its biological boundaries and Baudrillard's vision of the usurpation and dissolution of individual power" (83).

Loss of control portrayed by the characters in both *Videodrome* and *eXistenZ* adds to feelings of paranoia present throughout cyberculture, depicting conspiracy and espionage intersecting with struggles over power, usually between tech corporations and resistance movements. In *Videodrome*, Max is driven automatically to carry out the programming of Convex's brainwashing, killing colleagues at the TV station where he works, as well as attempting to assassinate O'Blivion's daughter, Bianca (Sonja Smits). In *eXistenZ*, characters inside the virtual world of the game act out pre-programmed behaviors automatically as part of the ludic elements needed to move the game along. These struggles are often depicted at the subterranean level and involve the dark decay of subculture in the urban environment, rather than in the overt visible spaces high above the ground. This contributes to a feeling of flatness in the films, brought on by a loss of identity that raises questions about the surface level of appearances versus the stability of ontological reality. *Videodrome* in particular "presents a destabilized reality in which image, reality, hallucination, and psychosis become indissolubly melded [… as] image addiction and viral invasion" (Bukatman 85).

Cronenberg's interest in the mutual evolution and the hybridity of the human–machine marks his distinct appeal for cyberpunk culture. Bodily invasion and loss of control are themes that permeate his world, often showing instances where subjectivity is arrested and replaced with the automatic. Cronenberg's films emphasize structures of external control by media systems, instead of those of internal emotion and the individual. Media as systems, and less as screens, are shown to break down our assumed sense of interiority. Everything, beyond an overt paranoia, exists at the surface level of the body; and, in fact, the body becomes the locale of signification and connection to the real in his films, and a site of psychosexual, social, and political conflict, made evident with the battle cry from *Videodrome*, "long live the new flesh!"

See also: **Jean Baudrillard, Donna J. Haraway, Marshall McLuhan**

Works Cited

Bukatman, Scott. *Terminal Identity: The Virtual Subject in Post-Modern Science Fiction.* Duke UP, 1993.

eXistenZ. Directed by David Cronenberg, performances by Jennifer Jason Leigh, Jude Law, Ian Holm, and Willem Dafoe, Dimension Films, 1999.

Fisher, Mark. "Work and Play in *eXistenZ.*" *Film Quarterly*, vol. 65, no. 3, 2012, pp. 70–73.

———. *Flatline Constructs: Gothic Materialism and Cybernetic Theory-Fiction.* Exmiliary, 2018.

Handling, Piers. "A Canadian Cronenberg." *The Shape of Rage: The Films of David Cronenberg*, edited by Piers Handling, Academy of Canadian Cinema/General Publishing, 1983.

Hayles, N. Katherine. *How We Became Posthuman: Virtual Bodies in Cybernetics, Literature and Informatics.* U of Chicago P, 1999.

Jameson, Fredric. "Postmodernism, Or The Cultural Logic of Late Capitalism." *New Left Review*, no. 146, 1984, pp. 53–92.

Seck Langill, Caroline. "The Menace of Things: David Cronenberg's Vibrant Objects." *David Cronenberg: Virtual Exhibition*, 2014, http://cronenbergmuseum.tiff.net/artefacts-artifacts-eng.html.

Vanderburgh, Jennifer. "GHOSTBUSTED! Popular Perceptions of English-Canadian Cinema." *Canadian Journal of Film Studies*, vol. 12, no. 2, 2003, pp. 81–98.

Videodrome. Directed by David Cronenberg, performances by James Woods, Sonja Smits, Debbie Harry, Peter Dvorsky, and Jack Creley, Universal Pictures, 1983.

Vint, Sheryl and Mark Bould. "All That Melts Into Air is Solid: Rematerialising Capital in *Cube* and *Videodrome.*" *Socialism and Democracy*, vol. 20, no. 3, 2006, pp. 217–43.

Matthew Flisfeder

SAMUEL R. DELANY (1942–)

Author, queer theorist, and professor of literature.

A towering figure in American twentieth-century speculative fiction, Samuel R. Delany has published over twenty novels and twenty-four short stories. He won the Nebula Award for the novels *Babel-17* (1966), *The Einstein Intersection* (1967), and the short story "Aye, and Gomorrah" (1967), and both the Nebula and the Hugo Award for "Time Considered as a Helix of Semi-Precious Stones" (1968). Most recently, he received the Locus Award for the short story "The Hermit of Houston" (2017). In his long career, Delany has experimented with various sf subgenres (space opera, dystopia, sword-and-sorcery), and later published gay erotica novels, as well as more than a dozen non-fiction works, including memoirs (*The Motion of Light in Water*, 1988), sf criticism (*The Jewel-Hinged Jaw*, 1977), and queer theory (*Times Square Red, Times Square Blue*, 1999).

Beginning with the publication of *The Jewels of Aptor* (1962), Delany was recognized as a rising star of American sf and became associated with a generation of counterculture-era writers who wished to redefine and revitalize the genre—sometimes referred to as the New Wave, although Delany at times distanced himself from the informal movement (Luckhurst 162). A prolific author, erudite intellectual, and stylistic innovator, Delany transgressed the generic limitations of sf, creating a rich and ambitious body of work that boldly rearticulated the thematic impulses of science-fictional worldbuilding to critically explore mythology, linguistics, racial difference, non-normative sexualities, and bodily pleasures, and envisioned "entire societies in order to depict those at the society's margins. Outlaw, artist, the sexually unconstrained—these embody that revolutionary impulse at the heart of much of Delany's work" (Sallis xiii).

Delany's influence on cyberpunk is arguably a testament to his position as a prominent "postmodernist" experimenter, especially in relation to the impact of his writing on the two leading "father figures" of the first wave of print cyberpunk, **William Gibson** and **Bruce Sterling**. Gibson expresses his admiration for Delany's fiction, acknowledging the lasting impression it left on him as an adolescent reader of sf (McCaffrey 279), and Sterling listed Delany as one of "the older writers [of] ancestral cyberpunk," in his Preface to *Mirrorshades: The Cyberpunk Anthology* (1986). Regarded as a literary precursor to the postmodern turn in sf that was so energetically embraced by the cyberpunk practitioners of the 1980s, Delany's influence can be traced not only in his estranging and self-reflexive experimental fiction, but also to his role as a critic and theoretician of the mode who actively took part in the discursive formation of the cyberpunk literary movement.

The Hugo-nominated *Nova* (1968) is widely regarded as proto-cyberpunk, and it was an inventive and highly influential achievement in Delany's early career. A dazzling, galaxy-spinning quest narrative that leads its characters (and readers) into the center of an explod-ing nova, it continued Delany's ambitious explorations of the space opera subgenre while simultaneously establishing a blueprint for several cyberpunk tropes: cyborgized lifestyles, prosthetic limbs, holographic avatars, and mass media evolved into a visual form of broadcasting "sent out across the galaxy on psychoramics" (Delany, *Nova* 99). *Nova* is set in a far-future galaxy politically and economically divided between two rival mega-corporations (Von Ray and Red Shift Limited). The protagonist Mouse, a musical artist, criminal, and outcast, is one of many cyborg-like figures inhabiting the far-future who directly con-nect with starships and computers through bioengineered "studs" and "sockets" installed at the base of the spinal cord. The dense narra-tive is interwoven with highly rhetorical 'info dumps' presenting the sociocultural transformations that have taken place in the interplan-etary society, explained with the use of the metaphor of the web, "the matrix in which history happens today" (Delany, *Nova* 121). Delany's vision brilliantly extrapolates the accelerating processes of globalization, characterized by "communication explosion, movements of people, movements of information, the development of movies, radio, and television" (107), to create a thought-provoking vision of a futuristic society inhabited by "plugged-in," alienated laborers whose lives—despite the colorful, baroque setting of the novel—nonetheless remain defined by the interlocking powers of capital and mass media.

Perhaps equally influential for literary cyberpunk was Delany's fiction from the 1970s and 1980s—a period that brought him the well-deserved acclaim of literary critics and academics, but at the same time signaled his growing reluctance to cater to the expectations of genre enthusiasts. The monumental *Dhalgren* (1975), his labyrinthine masterpiece set in the decaying surreal city of Bellona, featured a cast of streetwise adolescent dropouts—urban drifters of diverse ethnicities and sexualities, wander-ing in commune-like gangs through the metropolitan ruins. Alienated from society, but no longer confined to its margins, the protagonists of *Dhalgren* can be read as representing a 'punk' sensibility that would later become a defining characteristic of the cyberpunk ethos. In a 1996 fore-word to the novel, Gibson acknowledged the importance of its allegori-cal depiction of the unrest experienced in American cities in the 1960s, noting the duality of existence in the metaphorical "prose-city" which "had no specific locale, and [whose] internal geography was mainly fluid. Its inhabitants nonetheless knew, at any given instant, whether they were in the city or in America" (804). Although evoking a radically different feeling than the hyperreal sensory overload that came to define the neon-lit, corporate-controlled, metropolitan nightmares of literary cyberpunk's first wave, Delany's portrayal of a deserted city left on its own, displaced both temporally and spatially, in a future that has already become its own past, provided a new sense of how sf could critically engage with the sociopolitical realities of late capitalism.

Trouble on Triton (1976), a Foucault-inspired "ambiguous heterotopia" (as declares the novel's subtitle), interrogated the fluidity and plasticity of gender identity and sexual practices together with the flexibilities of capital, presenting a postmodernist critique of commodity culture taken to its limits. However, contrary to the transhuman disembodied sexualities preferred by many cyberpunk writers, for Delany the corporeality of the body always remains at the fore, and his queer explorations of non-normative sexual fantasies are founded on the principle "that bodily autonomy and desire are not always clean, sanitary, or polite" (Lothian 147). Some critics have insisted that *Stars in My Pocket Like Grains of Sand* (1984), another complex queer sf novel exploring gay male sexual cultures extrapolated into the distant future, published in the same year as Gibson's *Neuromancer*, should have been considered part of the first wave of cyberpunk as "it also provides an alternate model for the internet to Gibson's matrix" (Lavender and Murphy 355). Meanwhile, the short story "Among the Blobs" (1988), later reprinted in Larry McCaffery's cyberpunk anthology *Storming the Reality Studio* (1991), exemplifies Delany's penchant for meshing diverse generic conventions and stylistic elements in a densely written story of an unemployed gay man cruising in a subway restroom while also struggling to fight off the titular alien Blob assaulting him seemingly on another plane of existence. The story consists of two interweaving, parallel narratives that finally reveal the Blob to be more of a sensation of sexual desire than a formless organic alien, a terrifying and orgasmic force of queer monstrosity whose descriptions twist the story's meaning, turning it into a tale of urban male same-sex fantasy.

In the essay "Racism and Science Fiction," Delany acknowledged his influence on first wave cyberpunk authors as both writer and critic, while also noting a certain reluctance on the part of the sf community to identify him as something other than "the black sf writer," although elsewhere he humorously asserts his status as cyberpunk's "favorite 'faggot' uncle who [...] showed the kids some magic tricks" (Tatsumi

177). Perhaps the most crucial intervention to cyberpunk came from Delany's insistence on the failure of its early advocates to acknowledge their literary debt to the feminist sf of the 1970s. Poking fun at the "cyberpunk patriarchal nervousness" indicated by Sterling's exclusion in the Preface to *Mirrorshades* of feminist sf writers like **Joanna Russ**, Vonda McIntyre, or Ursula K. Le Guin, Delany argued that

> the feminist explosion—which obviously infiltrates the cyberpunk writers so much—is the one they seem to be the least comfortable with, even though it's one that, much more than the New Wave, has influenced them most strongly, both in progressive and in reactionary ways—progressive in its political cynicism, reactionary to the extent that cynicism can only be expressed through a return to a certain kind of macho rhetoric that was dated by 1960.
> (Tatsumi 176)

Delany pointed to the character of Molly Millions from Gibson's Sprawl trilogy (and "Johnny Mnemonic") as strikingly reminiscent of one of the four protagonists from Joanna Russ's *The Female Man* (1975)—the militant Alice "Jael" Reasoner, engaged in a literal battle between sexes whose modifications include surgical claws and steel teeth—an inspiration which Gibson would only later acknowledge himself (cf. Wolmark 116). Delany's criticism was aimed primarily at the revolutionary rhetoric accompanying the cyberpunk's revolt against the sf written in the previous decade, and by emphasizing the ignorant disavowal of any intertextual dialogue with the subversive feminist sf that preceded it, he was one of the first to challenge cyberpunk's white, masculinist heteronormativity, a statement later echoed by other sf scholars (Nixon; Lavigne 23–30). Finally, Delany also voiced skepticism about the validity of cyberpunk's claim to represent the urban sprawl of technologized late modernity, which for him amounted to "what any astute critic has got to admit was finally a pervasive misreading of an interim period of urban technoculture" (Dery 193).

In addition to the postmodern stylistic texture and the imaginative worldbuilding of his experimental, speculative fictions, Delany's influence on cyberpunk as a literary formation is inherently linked to his reflections on sf as a 'paraliterary' mode of literature. His influential essay "About 5,750 Words," written in 1968 and later reprinted in *The Jewel-Hinged Jaw*, juxtaposes the genre with what he calls "mundane fiction," which can be roughly equated with 'literary' fiction, and argues that sf is essentially *another language*: "A distinct level of subjunctivity informs all the words in an sf story at a level that is different from that which informs naturalistic fiction, fantasy, or reportage" (10). Delany's formalist deconstruction of the semiotics of *science fiction reading* disregards the division between "content" and "style" and reformulates sf as a form of "paraliterature," which engages in world-building on the level of language, requiring the reader to actively interact with the text sentence-by-sentence in order to identify new possible (and potentially multiple) meanings (Broderick 65–75). This mode of writing/reading sf corresponds to the intensity of cyberpunk poetics, as expressed in narratives that attempt to translate both the virtual densities of cyberspace and the artificial urban landscapes of technocultural late modernity into sophisticated literary prose that toys with readers' expectations and takes them on intensive visual journeys, as the best sf has always done, "for not only does it throw us worlds away, it specifies how we got there" (12).

See also: **Steven Barnes, William Gibson, Janelle Monáe, Joanna Russ, Bruce Sterling**

Works Cited

Broderick, Damien. *Reading by Starlight: Postmodern Science Fiction*. Routledge, 1995.

Delany, Samuel R. "About 5,570 Words." *The Jewel-Hinged Jaw: Notes on the Language of Science Fiction*. 1977. Wesleyan UP, 2009, pp. 1–16.

———. "Among the Blobs." *Storming the Reality Studio: A Casebook of Cyberpunk and Postmodern Science Fiction*, edited by Larry McCaffery, Duke UP, 1992, pp. 56–62.

———. *Dhalgren*. Bantam Books, 1975

———. *Nova*. 1968. Open Road Media, 2014.

———. *Stars in My Pocket Like Grains of Sand*. 1984. Wesleyan UP, 2004.

———. "Racism and Science Fiction." *Dark Matter: A Century of Speculative Fiction from the African Diaspora*, edited by Sheree R. Thomas. 1998. Warner, 2000, pp. 383–97.

———. *Trouble on Triton: An Ambiguous Heterotopia*. 1976. Wesleyan UP, 1996.

Dery, Mark. "Black to the Future: Interviews with Samuel R. Delany, Greg Tate, and Tricia Rose." *Flame Wars: The Discourse of Cyberculture*, edited by Mark Dery, Duke UP, 1994, pp. 179–222.

Gibson, William. "The Recombinant City." Samuel R. Delany, *Dhalgren*. Golancz, 2010, pp. 803–05.

Lavender, Isiah III and Graham J. Murphy "Afrofuturism." *The Routledge Companion to Cyberpunk*, edited by Anna McFarlane, Graham J. Murphy, and Lars Schmeink, Routledge, 2020, pp. 353–61.

Lavigne, Carlen. *Cyberpunk Women, Feminism, and Science Fiction: A Critical Study*. McFarland & Company, Inc., 2013.

Lothian, Alexis. *Old Futures: Speculative Fiction and Queer Possibility*. New York UP, 2018.

Luckhurst, Roger. *Science Fiction*. Polity, 2005.

McCaffrey, Larry. "An Interview with William Gibson." *Storming the Reality Studio: A Casebook of Cyberpunk and Postmodern Science Fiction*, edited by Larry McCaffery, Duke UP, 1991, pp. 263–85.

Nixon, Nicola. "Cyberpunk: Preparing the Ground for a Revolution or Keeping the Boys Satisfied?" *Science Fiction Studies*, vol. 19, no. 2, 1992, pp. 219–35.

Sallis, James. Introduction. *Ash of Stars: On the Writing of Samuel R. Delany*, edited by James Sallis, UP of Mississippi, 1996.

Sterling, Bruce. Preface. *Mirrorshades: The Cyberpunk Anthology*, edited by Bruce Sterling, 1986. Ace, 1988, pp. ix–xvi.

Tatsumi, Takayuki. "Some *Real* Mothers … The *SF Eye* Interview." *Silent Interviews on Language, Race, Sex, Science Fiction, and Some Comics*, Wesleyan UP, 1994, pp. 164–85.

Wolmark, Jenny. *Aliens and Others: Science Fiction, Feminism, and Postmodernism*, U of Iowa P, 1994.

Jędrzej Burszta

PHILIP K[INDRED] DICK (1928–1982)

US author.

Philip K. Dick has published forty-four novels and over one hundred and twenty short stories, with notable collections of the latter including *The Golden Man* (1980) and the five-volume *The Collected Stories of Philip K. Dick* (1987). While most of his published output was science fiction (sf), he also wrote nine realist novels between 1950 and 1960. Dick won the Hugo Award for *The Man in the High Castle* (1962), the John W. Campbell Memorial Award for *Flow My Tears, the Policeman Said* (1974), the British Science Fiction Association Award for *A Scanner Darkly* (1977), and the Kurd Laßwitz Award for *VALIS* (1981). A major figure of the sf canon, Dick was inducted into the Science Fiction Hall of Fame in 2005, and in 2007 became the first sf author to have their work published by the Library of America.

Dick's influence on cyberpunk (and sf more widely) has been profound. His work has been adapted across a variety of media, with prominent film and television adaptations including Paul Verhoeven's *Total Recall* (1990), Steven Spielberg's *Minority Report* (2002), Richard Linklater's *A Scanner Darkly* (2006), Frank Spotnitz's *The Man in the High Castle* (2015–19), and Ronald D. Moore and Michael Dinner's *Philip K. Dick's Electric Dreams* (2017). The adaptation towering above these all—in terms of its cultural impact and impact upon cyberpunk more specifically—is **Ridley Scott**'s *Blade Runner* (1982), the cinematic adaptation of Dick's *Do Androids Dream of Electric Sheep?* (1968). Bringing to screen many of the ideas that obsessed Dick in *Androids* (and his larger oeuvre), Scott's *Blade Runner*, a film whose "*mise-en-scène* [is] widely copied but rarely bettered" (Butler 70), spawned a range of spinoffs, responses, and sequels, including K. W. Jeter's authorized *Blade Runner* sequels and Denis Villeneuve's *Blade Runner 2049* (2017). Dick's influence can also be found in films and series that populate cyberpunk culture, including **David Cronenberg**'s *Videodrome* (1983) and *eXistenZ* (1999), Satoshi Kon's *Perfect Blue* (1997), Andrew Niccol's *Gattaca* (1997), Alex Proyas's *Dark City* (1998), **Lana and Lilly Wachowski**'s Matrix franchise (1999–), Michel Gondry's *Eternal Sunshine of the Spotless Mind* (2004), Christopher Nolan's *Inception* (2010), and **Charlie Brooker**'s *Black Mirror* (2011–19). Dick's work has also proven significant for several philosophers and cultural theorists, including **Jean Baudrillard**, Fredric Jameson, and Slavoj Žižek.

Dick's work is thematically consistent. As Dick put it, his two perennial themes are "What is reality?" and "What constitutes the authentic human being?" ("How to Build a Universe" 265), themes that are common to later cyberpunk narratives. At the same time, we can add such themes as the alienation of the subject, the opposition between empathy and entropy, systems of control and paranoia, salvation arriving from another world (extraterrestrial and/or metaphysical), and doubles and dichotomies. Dick touches upon these themes in an interlacing fashion, such that phenomena that might usually be treated as subjective experiences or concerns are shown to bear implications at the level of society, culture, or even the world. Although there are some shifts in his writing style over the course of his career—most notably after 1970, when he stopped taking amphetamines while writing and battled through several years of writer's block—the writing typically preoccupies itself with dystopian systems and vistas of experience and society. Dick's work—particularly his incisive explorations of paranoia[1]—is exemplary of Michel Foucault's characterization of "permanent, exhaustive, omnipresent surveillance, capable of making all visible, as long as it could itself remain invisible" (214), of "the cyborg-system gaze of large institutions" that dominate our "Veillance Society" (Gray 364). Control of advanced technology in Dick's fiction—typically media technologies, but also experimental drugs (*Now Wait for Last Year* [1966]), interstellar teleportation (*Lies, Inc* [1984]), and holographic "scramble suits" used by narcotics police in *A Scanner Darkly*—typically resides with an oppressive state and/or the cutthroat corporations that would become the antagonist of choice for cyberpunk. Other themes include urban decay (*Do Androids Dream of Electric Sheep?*), climate change (*The Three Stigmata of Palmer Eldritch* [1965]), corporate espionage and industrial sabotage (*Ubik* [1969]), state surveillance and carceral networks (*The Man in the High* Castle), seemingly permanent states of (cold) war (*Time Out of Joint* [1959]), and heterotopian enclaves (*Counter-Clock World* [1967]) that can be compromised from within and/or manipulated from without (*The Simulacra* [1964]), such that all factions operate within the power games of control.

Dick is one of the great(est) writers of simulated realities and media's ability to influence and control culture, or what Guy Debord called "the society of the spectacle" and **Marshall McLuhan** glossed as "the medium is the message." Keenly aware of the power of television and other media to control both words and images, media manipulation is a regular theme in Dick's work, perhaps epitomized in *Flow My Tears, the Policeman Said*, which portrays celebrity as constituting a reality principle unto itself. Individual memories can prove to be simulations ("We Can Remember It for You Wholesale" [1966]), as can whole societies and worlds (*A Maze of Death* [1970]), or even an entire universe can prove to be a hologram (*VALIS*). Psychotropic drugs are often at the heart of such pseudo-realities, but it is just as likely to arise from electronic means deployed on a systematic basis ("How to Build a Universe" 262). Rather than doomy prognostications of a future yet to arrive, the societies and worlds of Dick's oeuvre are trenchant examinations of our own cyberpunk present. As Steven Shaviro puts it: "our world, too, is organized by money, ubiquitously commodified, penetrated by electronic media, and saturated with advertising messages" (98).

As evidenced by his 1972 address "The Android and the Human," Dick's lectures and fiction display an awareness of and interest in cybernetics and related systems thinking: *Solar Lottery* (1955) borrows concepts from game theory and *VALIS* includes a theory of living, autonomous information.[2] Consumerism and commodities are also tied closely to simulation in Dick's work: robotic neighbors incentivize emigration to Mars in *We Can Build You* (1972) and *The Simulacra*, while *Ubik* and *The Three Stigmata of Palmer Eldritch* investigate the relationship between animacy and commodity objects. A fundamental uncertainty about phenomena and experience underpins much of Dick's work, born in part of a blurring of the categories of human and machine, outlined by Dick in one of his lectures: "The greatest change growing across our world these days is probably the momentum of the living toward reification, and at the same time a reciprocal entry into animation by the mechanical" ("Man, Android and Machine" 212). The resonance with **Donna J. Haraway**'s punchier articulation that "[o]ur machines are disturbingly lively, and we ourselves frighteningly inert" (152), first published some nine years after Dick's pronouncement, is striking.

Ultimately, Dick's work asks, "What are the actual qualities of [our] virtual existence?" (Shaviro 94), with the answer seeming to be a deadlock, wherein the alienated subject is unable to formulate or believe in alternative possibilities. This impasse, however, does not survive unscathed, as Dick's writing instigates a breakdown of cognitive structures and categories, such that it becomes impossible to understand world, experience, or subjecthood in terms of Eurocentric Enlightenment-derived thought. While Dick's fiction and non-fiction lionize what he refers to as "human" qualities—usually described in terms of empathy, kinship, and balking at evildoing—his so-called "human" subjects often do not fulfill the criteria for the anthropically-privileged, liberal humanist subject. Those who appear to be human often prove to be cruel and untrustworthy, while the most compassionate individuals may be non-anthropomorphic aliens (*Clans of the Alphane Moon* [1964]), robots (*We Can Build You*), or both (*Now Wait for Last Year*). In his lecture "Man, Android and Machine" (1976), Dick breaks down the discontinuity between human and machine (and human and alien), instead labeling morally authentic subjecthood "human" (independently of Homo Sapiens status) and the empathy-lacking, simulated type of being "android." This ambiguity is perhaps most extensively explored in *Do Androids Dream of Electric Sheep?*, in which the relative "humanity" of androids and humans becomes nigh-impossible to distinguish at times, a motif Scott capitalized upon in his *Blade Runner* adaptation. The novel also explores forms of kinship with animals (see Vint), and interspecies relationality arises throughout Dick's work (*Dr Bloodmoney* [1965]). In a significant break from the cyberpunk that would soon follow, Dick may decouple human-ness from both the biologically human and western anthropocentric thought, but his biological humans tend not to receive bionic modifications to their bodies; instead, their cyborgism arises in the form of mutations, strange powers, or the somatic effects of experimental drug consumption. In purely aesthetic terms, Dick is not the most typical of (proto)cyberpunks, but his treatments of experience, subject, and object, as well as his enduring influence across a range of media, make his work one of the mode's foundation stones and continues to prove instrumental in navigating the complexities of our cyberpunk culture(s).

See also: **Jean Baudrillard, Charlton 'Charlie' Brooker, David Cronenberg, Donna J. Haraway, Marshall McLuhan, Syd Mead, Ridley Scott, Lana and Lilly Wachowski, Norbert Wiener**

Notes

1 For details, see Freedman 1984.
2 For more on Dick and cybernetics, see Warrick 1984, 1987.

Works Cited

Butler, Andrew M. "Philip K. Dick." *Fifty Key Figures in Science Fiction*, edited by Mark Bould, Andrew M. Butler, Adam Roberts, and Sherryl Vint, Routledge, 2010, pp. 66–70.

Dick, Philip K. "The Android and the Human." *The Shifting Realities of Philip K. Dick: Selected Literary and Philosophical Writings*, edited by Lawrence Sutin, Vintage, 1995, pp. 183–210.

———. "How to Build a Universe That Doesn't Fall Apart Two Days Later." *The Shifting Realities of Philip K. Dick: Selected Literary and Philosophical Writings*, edited by Lawrence Sutin, Vintage, 1995, pp. 259–80.

———. "Man, Android and Machine." *The Shifting Realities of Philip K. Dick: Selected Literary and Philosophical Writings*, edited by Lawrence Sutin, Vintage, 1995, pp. 211–32.

Freedman, Carl. "Towards a Theory of Paranoia: The Science Fiction of Philip K. Dick." *Science Fiction Studies*, vol. 11, no. 1, 1984, pp. 15–24.

Foucault, Michel. *Discipline & Punish: The Birth of the Prison*. Vintage, 1979

Gray, Chris Hables. "Veillance Society." *The Routledge Companion to Cyberpunk Culture*, edited by Anna McFarlane, Graham J. Murphy, and Lars Schmeink, Routledge, 2020, pp. 362–72.

Haraway, Donna J. "A Cyborg Manifesto: Science, Technology, and Socialist-Feminism in the Late Twentieth Century." *Simians, Cyborgs and Women: The Reinvention of Nature*. Routledge, 1991, pp. 149–82.

Shaviro, Steven. *Connected: Or What It Means to Live in the Network Society*. U of Minnesota P, 2003.

Vint, Sherryl. "Speciesism and Species Being in 'Do Androids Dream of Electric Sheep?'" *Mosaic: An Interdisciplinary Critical Journal*, vol. 40, no. 1, 2007, pp. 111–26.

Warrick, Patricia. *Robots, Androids, and Mechanical Oddities: The Science Fiction of Philip K. Dick*. Southern Illinois UP, 1984.

———. *Mind in Motion: The Science Fiction of Philip K. Dick*. Southern Illinois UP, 1987.

Francis Gene-Rowe

CORY DOCTOROW (1971–)

Canadian-British writer, journalist, blogger, and social commentator.

Cory Doctorow is a prolific author and co-author of novels, graphic novels, short story collections, and non-fiction. He served as the co-editor of BoingBoing.net (2000–2020) and maintains Craphound. com, an archival repository of his works, which he publishes under Creative Common licenses and which are free to share, and Pluralistic. net, which serves to post links and trivia. He has won a number of important science fiction awards, among them the John W. Campbell Award for Best New Writer (since renamed the Astounding Award) in 2000, the Locus Award for Best First Novel (*Down and Out in the Magic Kingdom,* 2004), Sunburst Awards (*A Place So Foreign and 8 More,* 2004; *Little Brother,* 2008), Locus awards ("I, Robot," 2006; "When Sysadmins Ruled The Earth," 2007), as well as Prometheus Awards for *Little Brother, Pirate Cinema* (2012), and *Homeland* (2013), the sequel to *Little Brother.*

Doctorow's writing, both fictional and journalistic, deals with current information technologies and their impact on society and personal rights, making him one of the most important cyberpunk authors of the twenty-first century. As Colin Milburn argues, Doctorow uses "the tropes of cyberpunk for immediate political interventions" (378), highlighting cyberpunk's political potential and its relevance for our digitized world. In his work, Doctorow advocates for a free and decentralized internet and has been vocal about a socialist approach to the next economy, which prioritizes people over profits, file sharing rights for all, and a post-scarcity economy (Cranbury). His fictional works, Milburn argues, are "themselves exercises in cyberpunk activism" (378) and have been put into practice by activists. More than the original 1980s cyberpunks, Doctorow is concerned with providing a utopian vision of a post-scarcity economy and the transformative potential of digital technologies to counter his avid criticism of current developments in global surveillance capitalism, a vision perhaps most fully realized in *Walkaway* (2017), a sprawling novel that unfolds the potential of 3D printing for realizing this post-scarcity, potentially transhuman future that, in a manner reminiscent of his 3D printing stories "Printcrime" (2006) and "After the Siege" (2007), is met with violent resistance by centralized, dystopian, power brokers. Doctorow argues, for example, that every human being is entitled to the full scope of human knowledge available in our post-scarcity net economy, to access the full breadth and depth of human inquiry without charge.

Doctorow is opposed to pay-to-play databases, and views social networking sites where the individual receives free content in exchange for the site monetizing their personal information as unethical; he has likened Facebook, for example, to a "surveillance system" (Knowles 14). In this vein, Doctorow has spoken in opposition to intellectual property, which he sees as a destructive and pervasive trend: the ownership of knowledge. Consequently, Doctorow takes a dim view in both his fiction and non-fiction of copyright law: "Copyright—with all its quirks, exceptions and carve-outs—was, for centuries, a legal regime that attempted to address the unique characteristics of knowledge, rather than pretending to be just another set of rules for the governance of property" ("World Intellectual Property" 24). In his short story "Craphound," for example, Doctorow comments on intellectual property (IP) by having an alien species collect human material culture, devoid of its original function or corporate added value. Similarly, "Unauthorized Bread" (2019) satirically critiques the increasing ubiquity of 'smart' technologies and their proliferation of socio-economic disenfranchisement when the most precarious citizens are unable (or unwilling) to afford updated software apps or sponsored grocery items. His first novel, *Down and Out in the Magic Kingdom*, lays the foundations for these thematic pursuits by depicting a world that does not need to rely on industrial production and in which people can live for hundreds of years. The novel's 100-year-old protagonist, Jules has his adventures in a Disney World populated with clones, interface connections for humans to enter cyberspace, and an expanded bounty of plenty for all. Putting his politics into action, Doctorow's novel (and almost all of his subsequent work) was made freely available online with a Creative Commons license "on the same day it was released in bookstores" (Lessig 2004), a mechanism to both provide online copies of all creative material in an open and free manner and to generate promotion. As Doctorow has famously remarked, "[a]n artist's enemy is obscurity, not piracy" (Bethune).

Alternative uses for technology and the free expression of human creativity—a thought similar to **William Gibson**'s oft-cited maxim that the street finds its own uses for things (215)—are at the heart of his fictions, particularly those aimed at a young adult (YA) audience. These books celebrate youth techno-defiance and include *Little Brother* and its in-universe sequels "Lawful Interception" (2013), *Homeland*, and *Attack Surface* (2020), as well as *Pirate Cinema* and "Anda's Game" (2004), the latter story paving the way to *For the Win* (2010), a novel as much about massively multiplayer online role-playing games and the

Bildungsroman format common to YA as labor rights and the exploitation of the virtual economy. Doctorow's award-winning *Little Brother* is a retro-tech exploration of youth culture (Bernick) that focuses on a hacker named Marcus Yallow who anonymizes himself with the online identity "w1n5t0n," a reference to George Orwell's protagonist from *Nineteen Eighty-Four* (1949). Over the arc of the story, w1n5t0n has several encounters with the security state in the San Francisco Bay Area and involves himself with the counter-culture group UAW/MF, or "Up Against the Wall MotherF—kers." *Little Brother* therefore permits Doctorow to provide his critiques on the effects that the 'War on Terror' and the ensuing security state have had on North American youth culture (Bernick), while its sequels evolve w1n5t0n's narrative arc, with *Homeland* in particular focusing on the Obama administration's hunt for the editors of Wikileaks and the persecution of whistleblowers Edward Snowden and Chelsea Manning. The tension between trying to work in the surveillance state and possessing an *a priori* ethical obligation to resist the state and demand intellectual property be free dominates *Homeland* and speaks to the core conflict in the western world: intellectual property cannot be regulated and still be free and accessible information. The only response, as Doctorow frames it, is to resist the surveillance state. Finally, *Attack Surface* focuses on the exploits of Marcus Yallow's former 'frenemy' and crush Masha Maximow, as she combats a mass surveillance program in the dying post-Soviet nation of Slavstakia. When the fledgling revolutionaries Masha is supporting take over the mass surveillance program her employer, Xoth, had her install, Masha must stop them from becoming the very fascist monsters they are fighting. This novel focuses on Doctorow's antipathy to mass surveillance, and our ethical need to resist any state or other power that would employ it.

Doctorow's homage to George Orwell's *Nineteen Eighty-Four* is not restricted to "w1n5t0n" and the titular *Little Brother*; Orwell's imprint is found throughout Doctorow's fiction, as befits an author Doctorow describes as "in that kind of Gibsonian sense, a radical presentist" ("Riding" 60). Aside from the obvious influences on "Printcrime" or the *Little Brother* sequence, Orwell is mashed up with Isaac Asimov in "I, Robot" (2005), a post-Singularity narrative organized around Police Detective (Third Grade) Arturo Icaza de Arana-Goldberg's struggles with his wayward daughter, his newly appointed robot partner, and the return of his estranged wife. As Graham J. Murphy writes, "Doctorow locates the world of 'I, Robot' in Orwell's classic dystopia: UNATS [United North American Trading Sphere] is allied with Oceania in a war against Eurasia" and "agents from Social Harmony are hyper-vigilant in their pursuit of all perceived threats to UNATS's social fabric" (258). Tellingly, Doctorow contrasts the dystopian UNATS with Eurasia, a decidedly transhuman utopian alternative organized around Asimovian positronic brains and transhuman bodies. As a result, Doctorow's "repeated return to the utopia/dystopia chassis [...] is the leverage he needs to create allegories 'about [today's] digital rights management technology'" (Murphy 259). More recently, *Makers* (2009) depicts the rise-and-fall-and-rise of a new economic system organized around micro-communities and 3D printing, helping lay the foundations for the post-scarcity utopia of *Walkaway*.

Finally, one of Doctorow's most cyberpunk efforts is *Pirate Cinema*. The novel focuses on the exploits of Trent McCauley, a young Londoner who actively pirates scenes and dialogue shots from movies to remix into his own work. Such wanton theft of intellectual property is anathema to the UK legal system and, after three copyright infractions, the government denies his family access to the internet for a year. While Trent lives as a squatter, providing his pirate cinema efforts in the sewer system, creative freedom faces a bigger threat in the proposed TIP Act, which would severely punish any theft of intellectual property, no matter how small. In the novel, Doctorow demonstrates why intellectual property should not be controlled or constrained by government. The book's conclusion pushes a strong version of Doctorow's philosophy pitting Trent and his devotees in a protest against the TIP Act.

In sum, there is nothing more valuable to Doctorow than free, high-quality access to information. As such, his "novels and short stories explore the places where cultural value is measured by access to information, where property is traded for forms of common ownership, where networks are both the catalyst for, and the object of, social intervention, and where the human becomes an indefinable category" (Leonard). Reflecting a cyberpunk sensibility updated for the twenty-first century, Doctorow continues to support hacker and protest groups who resist a surveillance state seemingly inspired by Orwellian government and corporate interests. His sociological and political commitments continue to fuel his writings on the topics of freely available intellectual property, the value of Creative Commons licenses and open-source materials, and removing the notion of commodity from all content shared across the World Wide Web.

See also: **William Gibson, Shoshana Zuboff**

Works Cited

Bernick, Steele. "Interview with Cory Doctorow About 'Little Brother.'" *Journal of Adolescent & Adult Literacy*, vol. 53, no.5, 2010, pp. 434–39.

Cranbury, Sean. "*Makers*: The Cory Doctorow Interview (Built from Scratch)." *Books on the Radio*, November 18, 2009, https://booksontheradio. org/2009/11/18/makers-the-cory-doctorow-interview-built-from-scratch/.

Doctorow, Cory. *Attack Surface*. Tor, 2020.

———. *Down and Out in the Magic Kingdom*. Tor, 2003.

———. *Little Brother*. Tor Teen, 2008.

———. *Pirate Cinema*. Tor Teen, 2012.

———. "World Intellectual Property Organization in Shambolic Chaos." *Boing Boing*, 2014, https://bbs.boingboing.net/t/world-intellectual-property-organization-in-shambolic-chaos/42115.

Gibson, William. *Burning Chrome*. HarperCollins, 1995.

Knowles, David. "Facebook is a surveillance system Author Cory Doctorow Says." *Yahoo News*, August 15, 2018. https://news.yahoo.com/facebook-surveillance-system-sci-fi-author-cory-doctorow-says-090028574. html.

Lessig, Lawrence. *Free culture: How Big Media Uses Technology and the Law to Lock Down Culture and Control Creativity*. Penguin, 2004.

Leonard, P. "Open Networks, Distributed Identities: Cory Doctorow and the Literature of Free Culture." *Junctures: The Journal for Thematic Dialogue*, no. 15, 2012, https://junctures.org/index.php/junctures/article/view/220/306.

Milburn, Colin. "Activism." *The Routledge Companion to Cyberpunk Culture*, edited by Anna McFarlane, Graham J. Murphy, and Lars Schmeink, Routledge, 2020, pp. 373–81.

Murphy, Graham J. "'Predicting the Present': Overclocking Doctorow's *Overclocked*." *Science Fiction and Computing: Essays on Interlinked Domains*, edited by David L. Ferro and Eric G. Swedin, McFarland & Company, Inc., 2011, pp. 249–63.

Benjamin Aleksandr Franz

WARREN ELLIS (1968–)

British comic-book writer, novelist, and screenwriter.

Warren Ellis has emerged as one of the most prolific and influential comic-book authors of the late twentieth and early twenty-first centuries. He began writing for comics in the early 1990s with contributions to British magazines such as *Blast!*, *Deadline*, *Doctor Who Magazine*, *Speakeasy*, and *Judge Dredd* (Allred). Soon after, he started writing for DC Comics, Marvel Comics, and WildStorm Productions, where his groundbreaking work on *Stormwatch* (1993–98) and *The Authority* (1999–2000) won him widespread popular acclaim. Ellis's work is often characterized by a deflationary cynicism concerning possibilities for utopian advancement through cybernetic or transhumanist augmentation; he frequently explores how technological advancements serve the narrow interests of powerful elites. In addition, although the bulk of Ellis's creative production has been writing for comics, he has authored the novels *Crooked Little Vein* (2007) and *Gun Machine* (2013), as well as writing popular video games, television screenplays, and nonfiction essays for email newsletters, blogs, websites, and internet magazines.

Ellis's longest and arguably most notable comic series, *Transmetropolitan* (1997–2002),[1] is a dark transhumanist-cyberpunk comedy that "was the first series to take the settings and sensibility of cyberpunk and weld them onto the newfound freedom of long-form creator-owned comics" during the 1990s (Moore). The story follows Spider Jerusalem, a jaded gonzo journalist (modeled on Hunter S. Thompson) who uses his writing to expose various problems in the City, a violent and hypersexualized urban megascape where even household appliances suffer from drug addictions. *Transmetropolitian* draws barbed critical attention to the role of the media in society, the unsettling power of advertising and consumer culture, the racist politics of police violence, and the dark appeal of reactionary fascism within American politics. The series also anticipates how the rise of social media might create a culture of shallow online "influencers" who broadcast every aspect of their lives to become vehicles for predatory advertising memes, all while exploring Spider's efforts to cut through the damaging noise created by junk media to draw people's attention to the disturbing undercurrents of power shaping their lives. *Transmetropolitan* explores cyberpunk themes, including the power of media technologies to shape society, the perverse influences of advertising and consumer culture, and the sociopathic tendencies inherent to neoliberalism and late capitalism.

Transmetropolitian also offers a cynical view of transhumanism, suggesting that any optimism surrounding progressive possibilities for technological transcendence will be undermined by human greed, corruption, and shortsightedness.[2] For example, Spider uses a live internet news broadcast to interrupt a police attack on the Transient movement, a largely harmless cult-like group of utopian dreamers that have modified their own genetic structures with alien DNA. After the Transients begin pirating power from the City and publicizing themselves as an oppressed minority, the City government pays a few Transients to initiate acts of vandalism, which provides the police with the excuse to attack and subdue the Transient population. "It's an election year for a law-and-order president," Spider warns: "They'll come in and stamp on your bones." Spider's comment embodies Ellis's critique of 'law-and-order' political discourse in the United States, which emerges as a coded language of racism in the decades following the midcentury successes of the civil rights movement.[3] Ellis therefore expresses the deflationary view that all sides in such conflicts are inevitably corrupt, but the City's governmental monopoly on violence makes the state much more dangerous and reprehensible.

At the same time, one of *Transmetropolitan*'s most troubling aspects is its unapologetic misogyny: Spider, for example, throws his ex-wife's frozen head off a building, and the women toward whom he is not actively violent are often relentlessly sexualized and objectified: Channon Yarrow is a former stripper, Yelena, is a daughter-figure with whom he has a one-night stand, and Spider allows Indira Ataturk to be drugged into participating in a public orgy, which results in her becoming the central figure in a popular porn video called "Kali in Heat." Ellis explicitly frames Spider as morally reprehensible, and his casual dismissal of the Indira Ataturk incident is intended to disturb readers; yet, while artists are under no obligation to make their protagonists admirable, *Transmetropolitan*'s treatment of women is highly problematic: Spider is a profoundly flawed and misogynistic character, but readers are still invited to somehow regard him as a darkly charming anti-hero fighting against even uglier villains.

Ellis explicitly draws on cyberpunk elements throughout his work in superhero comics, such as the sixteen issues (plus a one-shot special) of *Doom 2099*, which was part of Marvel's larger series of future-oriented cyberpunk titles. His most significant work in early mainstream superhero comics, however, was his writing for *Stormwatch*, *The Authority*, and *DV8* (WildStorm/Image Comics/DC Comics; 1996–99). *Stormwatch* follows the adventures of a super-powered crisis intervention team sanctioned by the United Nations to address worldwide threats under the leadership of Henry Bendix/the Weatherman, a powerful cyborg director whose technological implants enable him to constantly assess global information flows from Skywatch, the team's orbiting satellite headquarters. Similar to other 1990s-era comic-book characters (e.g., DC's Batman and Maxwell Lord) who exercise agency by conducting advanced panoptical surveillance and information analysis, Bendix embodies what Joshua Pearson describes as the neoliberal fantasy of "power management," or the dream that "a cultivated awareness of complexity" can enable one to "leverage the smallest investment of resources for the greatest effect" (158–59). Ellis, however, exposes the sociopathic tendencies at the heart of power management fantasies, revealing Bendix to be an authoritarian figure bent on utilizing his masterful information resources to re-make the world according to his own perverse whims.[4]

In the aftermath of Bendix's defeat and the collapse of both the Stormwatch team in Ellis's *WildC.A.T.s/Aliens* (1998) one-shot crossover between Image Comics and Dark Horse Comics and the absorption by DC Comics of WildStorm Productions in 1999, Ellis launched a new comic, *The Authority*, chronicling the adventures of a super team formed from Stormwatch's remnants. Several members of Stormwatch/the Authority have powers based on cyberpunk themes: Midnighter is a Batman-style power manager capable of analyzing information about his opponents' abilities so quickly that he can strategically win most of his fights before they begin; the Engineer, Angela Spica, replaces her blood with nanotechnology that enables her to manifest cybernetic armor and weaponry; and Jack Hawksmoor enjoys a symbiotic connection with cities because of his transhuman biogenetic augmentations. Cyberpunk themes recur throughout many of Ellis's other works, which often reveal the extent to which cyberpunk expanded to become "a more generalized cultural formation" (rather than a discreet subcultural movement) in the late 1990s and beyond (Foster xiv). For example, his webcomic *Superidol* (2002) follows a young journalist as he reports on a computer-generated J-pop Idol Singer who has become self-aware. *Mek* (2003) draws on real-world inspirations to explore speculative cultures of technological body modification. *Tokyo Storm Warning* (2003), a homage to the Japanese anime *Neon Genesis Evangelion* (1995–96), depicts giant cybernetically-piloted robots battling kaiju monsters in an alternate-reality Japan. Ellis also provided the "groundwork, backstory, and structure" for the dark cyber-horror video game *Dead Space* (2008; cf. Snow), where humanity has exhausted Earth's natural resources and launched giant mining spacecraft to colonize the stars, only to encounter a horrifying alien influence that animates the dead while causing nightmarish paranoid hallucinations.

Perhaps unsurprisingly, given the tendencies toward misogyny and the fetishistic objectification of women's bodies in his early work, particularly *Transmetropolitan*, Ellis's personal life came under scrutiny when the #MeToo movement exposed widespread sexual misconduct in the comics industry. In 2020, more than sixty women joined to launch the website *So Many of Us*, which documents multiple instances when Ellis leveraged his celebrity to manipulate female fans and creators into sexual relationships under deceitful circumstances. Although no allegations of illegal behavior were made, one woman notes that Ellis's dishonesty in pursuit of sexual relations made full and informed consent "impossible," and another articulates her hope that Ellis and others will "see how negatively this behavior affects those that are targeted, and not repeat it" (Thielman). *So Many of Us* draws attention to the fact that an early cyberpunk culture that has often been critiqued for its widespread masculinism (cf. Nixon, Cadora, Yaszek, Melzer) must be held accountable for its shortcomings in order for contemporary cyberpunk to move toward its most worthwhile aspirations.

See also: **Moebius [Jean Giraud]**

Notes

1 For an extended consideration of cyberpunk and *Transmetropolitan*, see Higgins and Iung (2020).
2 Ellis arguably adopts the role of Spider Jerusalem in *Bad World* (2001) and *Bad Signal* (2003), writing furiously and sardonically about the darkest and weirdest corners of late-capitalist technomodernity and offering illustrated collections of his nonfiction email newsletters that explore bizarre-but-true subjects, such as serial killers, UFO cultists, cannibalism, urine therapy, and other strange human obsessions.
3 Ellis may have written the first arc of *Transmetropolitan* in response to the police beating of Rodney King in 1991 and the death of Wayne Douglas in police custody in 1995—similar instances of police brutality that led to highly-publicized civil uprisings.
4 A more beneficent vision of power management is depicted in *Global Frequency*, where Miranda Zero and her information specialist, Aleph, deploy tactical teams of unique specialists around the world at a moment's notice to confront unusual threats.

Works Cited

Allred, Will. "Ellis, Warren (1968–)." *Encyclopedia of Comic Books and Graphic Novels*, edited by M. Keith Booker, vol. 1, Greenwood Press, 2010, pp. 174–75.
Ellis, Warren and Darick Robertson. *Absolute Transmetropolitan Volume One.* DC Comics, 2015 (no pagination).
Ellis, Warren et al. *Doom 2099: The Complete Collection by Warren Ellis.* Marvel Comics, 2013 (no pagination).
Ellis, Warren, Tom Raney, and Jim Lee. *Stormwatch: Vol. 1.* DC Comics, 2012 (no pagination).
Ellis, Warren et al. *Stormwatch: Vol. 2.* DC Comics, 2013 (no pagination).

Ellis, Warren, Bryan Hitch, and Paul Neary. *The Authority: Vol. 1.* DC Comics, 2014 (no pagination).

Higgins, David M. and Matthew Iung. "Comic Books." *The Routledge Companion to Cyberpunk Culture,* edited by Anna McFarlane, Graham J. Murphy, and Lars Schmeink, Routledge, 2020, pp. 91–100.

Moore, Stuart. "Up A Goddamn Mountain: *Transmetropolitan* and the Future." *Absolute Transmetropolitan Volume One.* DC Comics, 2015 (no pagination).

Pearson, Joshua. "Frank Herbert's *Dune* and the Financialization of Heroic Masculinity." *CR: The New Centennial Review,* vol. 19, no. 1, 2019, pp. 155–180.

Snow, Jean. "Warren Ellis Gives *Dead Space* Its Creepy Narrative." *Wired,* August 8, 2008, https://www.wired.com/2008/08/warren-ellis-gi/.

Thielman, Sam. "Women speak out about Warren Ellis: 'Full and informed consent was impossible.'" *The Guardian,* July 13, 2020, www.theguardian.com/books/2020/jul/13/women-speak-out-about-warren-ellis-transmetropolitan.

David M. Higgins and Matthew Iung

WILLIAM GIBSON (1948–)

US-born, Canadian author.

William Gibson has published twelve novels, twenty-three short stories, two graphic novels, three screenplays, an array of non-fiction essays and articles, a blog, and a rich smattering of inter-media collaborations. His groundbreaking novel *Neuromancer* (1984) accomplished that rare hat trick, earning the Hugo, the Nebula, and the Philip K. Dick awards, as well as being nominated or shortlisted for nearly every other significant prize in the field. With his growing popularity and recognized prestige, Gibson's later works earned countless nominations and, in 2008, he was inducted into the Science Fiction Hall of Fame. In addition to virtually inventing many of the themes associated with cyberpunk, Gibson is celebrated for what Larry McCaffery has called his "stunning technopoetic prose" (217), and **Samuel R. Delany** described as a "wonderful, almost hypnotic, surface hardness" (197). Gibson's oeuvre abounds with rich metaphors, astounding in their acuteness and biting in their hard-boiled wit, that have often become synonymous with cyberpunk.

It is impossible to overstate Gibson's impact on cyberpunk culture. Writing in the Preface to Gibson's *Burning Chrome* (1986) collection, **Bruce Sterling** describes the galvanic effect of Gibson's writing: "Roused from its hibernation, SF is lurching from its cave into the bright sunlight of the modern zeitgeist. And we are lean and hungry and not in the best of tempers. From now on things are going to be different" (9). And they *were* different. Gibson's Sprawl trilogy—*Neuromancer, Count Zero* (1986), and *Mona Lisa Overdrive* (1988)—and the affiliated stories ("Fragments of a Hologram Rose" [1977], "Johnny Mnemonic" [1981], "Burning Chrome" [1982], "New Rose Hotel" [1985]), spawned an entire cultural industry with writers, filmmakers, musicians, visual artists, fashion designers, to say nothing of game-designers, all tapping in to the politics and aesthetics of Gibson's "consensual hallucination that was the matrix" (*Neuromancer* 5).

Gibson was not the first nor the only writer concerned with the growing intimacy between humankind and technology but, through his early publications, his friendships and collaborations with pioneering cyberpunk writers **Lewis Shiner**, John Shirley, **Rudy Rucker**, and Bruce Sterling, and, ultimately, with his groundbreaking debut novel, Gibson had managed to tap into this wellspring of 1980s technofetishism and create an entire cultural vocabulary still in use today. Set in an urban dystopian future with only loosely related plotlines, the Sprawl texts portray (typically male) protagonists who *jack in* (i.e., physically connect computer hardware into a bioport grafted onto the *meat*, that is, the body), break *ICE* (or, hack through cyber-security barriers called Intrusion Countermeasures Electronics), and travel through *cyberspace*, a seemingly infinite, virtual world described as "[l]ines of light ranged in the nonspace of the mind, clusters and constellations of data" (*Neuromancer* 51). Gibson's cyberpunk terminology has become so ubiquitous that it not only returns without explication in later Gibson worlds, but is also found in general parlance.

In the late-1980s to early-1990s, Gibson's cyberpunk impulses moved him beyond the text and into several collaborative and intermedial performance projects, which all further explore the interface of the body and society with the technological. During these years, Gibson worked with *La Fura Dels Baus*, a provocative, multidisciplinary and immersive Catalan theater group; with ArtFutura, a performed spectacle accompanied by a cycle of conferences; and with **Stelarc**, a performance artist who tests the boundaries between machine and man. Writing of the latter, Gibson describes each Stelarc performance as a moment "of the purest technologically induced cognitive disjunction" (*Distrust* 189). In this celebration of the *purity* of technology and a disjointed cognition that is manifested in bodily performances, Gibson conceptualizes the pillars of cyberpunk.

These Gibsonian cyberpunk parameters include a prescient fascination with technology alongside a meticulously critical consideration of the price to individuals and societies for its advancement; a bleak, often dystopian, urban, corporate-controlled setting; a globalist geography that breaks past the US-centered pull of much early sf and is, at best, an almost naive globalism alongside a romantic fascination with the East that is, at worst, full-blown orientalism; a plethora of non-heroic characters descended from the hard-boiled tradition (flawed, isolated, often drug-dependent); and, coloring it all, a pervasive patina of burning chrome, that is a (now-retrofuturistic) metonym for the glitter and gloss of The Future.

Having carved out cyberspace, Gibson keeps exploring it, as he returns to the themes of his early classically cyberpunk trilogy, gradually updating them but, as Graham J. Murphy explains, in a "slower, more deliberate fashion [...] offering a subtly complex engagement with the post/human tapestry of presence, pattern, simulation, virtuality, and digital/corporeal embodiment" (72). The narrative premise of Gibson's Bridge trilogy (*Virtual Light* [1993], *Idoru* [1996], *All Tomorrow's Parties* [1999]) rests on socio-economic—as well as physical—precarity in a dystopian, near-future San Francisco-Oakland Bay Bridge. Home to a veritable shantytown, the Bridge recalls the suspended hideout of the Lo Teks in "Johnny Mnemonic," not only in its dizzying heights and ramshackle construction but in the kinds of marginalized yet resilient communities that live there.

Throughout Gibson's broader cyberpunk aesthetic, spatiality—most often, verticality—is linked to a pervasive critique of the excesses of capitalism that is evident from his first forays into cyberspace in "Fragments of a Hologram Rose." In that story, the protagonist describes his first experience with an ASP ("Apparent Sensory Perception") deck: "A ten-dollar bill fed into the slot bought you five minutes of free-fall gymnastics in a Swiss orbital spa, trampolining through twenty-meter perihelions with a sixteen-year-old *Vogue* model" (52). The link between verticality and technology, within a critique of capitalism, is here explicit as the character pays an exorbitant sum to immerse himself in an arguably coveted but ultimately decadent and inadequate experience. These themes culminate in The Jackpot sequence—*The Peripheral* (2014), *Agency* (2020), and an unnamed (at time of writing) third novel—and the ominous bio-tech high-rise buildings that tower throughout the novels. Built by Assemblers, a runaway nano-technology that conflates the organic with the technological in the novels, skyrises in Tokyo and San Francisco (*Virtual Light*), and in a future London (*The Peripheral*), serve as the ominous settings for sinister plans—aggressive gentrification in the former; murder and a politics of greed in the latter—that threaten to destabilize the structures of society.

Indeed, the game-changing wealth of *Count Zero*'s Josef Virek, the sinister manipulations of the Blue Ant series' Hubertus Bigend,[1] the monied self-indulgence of *The Peripheral* and *Agency*'s kleptocracy, or simply 'Klept,' and the violent political ambitions of US Vice-President Junior Henderson in the comic series *Archangel* (2016–17) are further instances where corrupted wealth and power seek to change the very order of Time: Virek's search for immortality, Bigend's marketing goal of prescience, and both the Klept's and Henderson's manipulations of the Time Stubs. Gibson has famously quipped that "the future is already here, just not very evenly distributed" (NPR), making clear his biting critique of capitalist greed. And yet, Gibson offers some relief with an oeuvre rich in moments of near-sublime aesthetic creation. The emotionally charged Cornell-like boxes that spark the action in *Count Zero* and Nora's ephemeral film fragments in *Pattern Recognition* are examples of semi-autonomous creativity that produces distilled time-stopping, awe-inspiring beauty as a counter to the excesses of overdetermined corporate production.

Gibson's Blue Ant trilogy signals his departure from the explicitly science fictional, turning instead to a present-day timeframe. And yet, the realism of the Blue Ant novels is one which reveals that "cyberspace has colonized our everyday life and continues to colonize everyday life. It's no longer 'the other place'" (Gibson, cit. in Holstein). While all three novels are grounded in historical events—9/11, the 2003 invasion of Iraq, the stock market crash of 2008—their plots are propelled by a "growing connectivity" within "networked societies" and the "thoroughly mediatized nature of the cityscapes [that] makes it difficult to establish a clear-cut boundary between the real and the imagined, the strange and the familiar, the authentic and the manufactured" (Krawczyk-Łaskarzewska 1–2). Bigend uses nearly unlimited means of surveillance to translate every action, encounter, and event into a network of information that can be analyzed, manipulated, and commodified. The characters roam the texts, trying to either encrypt or decode, in keeping with the hard-boiled detective traditions. Like Cayce Pollard or *Idoru*'s Colin Laney, who identifies nodal patterns of syncretic complexity, characters—and with them readers—are always searching for the titular *pattern* across fragments that link the material with the virtual.

A pervasive theme in Gibson's writing locates this link at the interface between the "meat" of the body and the virtual, a theme that becomes central in Gibson's Jackpot Trilogy. The peripherals are embodied avatars, veritable meat-puppets for hire, which can be inhabited and remotely activated. Thus, the Cartesian metaphor dividing the subject from the meat, the mind from the body, becomes literal as characters from a near-future US-backwater visit an alternate far-future-post-apocalyptic London by inhabiting these peripherals. This is the matrix taken to a new level as the very experience of reality within the novels is overlaid with cyberpunk possibilities. As Anna McFarlane writes, "Gibson's use of realism with a contemporary setting to express science-fictional impulses while at the same time elevating the haptic over the optic has the combined effect of bringing the needs of the future into focus" (121). Indeed, time itself becomes malleable when characters gain access to a technology that lets them splinter off the very path of time into multiple alternate "time stubs," a narrative conceit central to Bruce Sterling and Lewis Shiner's "Mozart in Mirrorshades" (1985), a story Gibson explicitly acknowledges in the "Acknowledgements and Thanks" section for *The Peripheral* but has also influenced his writing of *Archangel*.

Furthermore, *Agency* depicts an alternate 2017 in which Hillary Clinton has won the Presidential election, hinting that our own lived timeline is simply one of many temporal "stubs," manipulated by the petty machinations of corrupt futural wealth. Gibson cycles back to his earliest cyberpunk interests: cyberspace, technofetishism, dystopian critique of capitalism, extrapolating them to new horizons, with new risks and new threats. And yet, as Gary Westfahl reminds us, despite the uncompromising and unabated critique, "despite the stylishly cynical attitude said to characterize cyberpunk, Gibson has shown himself to be unfashionably optimistic" (164). *Agency*, a novel about both personhood and mediation through technology, has at its center Verity Jane, a talented "app whisperer" who is hired to beta test Eunice, a cutting-edge AI who gradually grows more autonomous and more powerful. Thus, with the aptly named Verity, *truth*, in an age riddled with fake news and QAnon conspiracy theories openly promoted by some political leaders, Gibson seeks a *good victory*, Eunice, to map out a cautious triumph along the road of obstacles that is our contemporary moment.

See also: **Pat Cadigan, Rudy Rucker, Melissa Scott, Lewis Shiner, Bruce Sterling**

Note

1 *Pattern Recognition* (2003), *Spook Country* (2007), and *Zero History* (2010).

Works Cited

Delany, Samuel R. and Mark Dery. "Black to the Future: Interviews with Samuel R. Delany, Greg Tate, and Tricia Rose." *Flame Wars: The Discourse of Cyberculture*, edited by Mark Dery, Duke UP, 1994, pp. 179–222.

Gibson, William. "Fragments of a Hologram Rose." *Burning Chrome*. Grafton, 1988, pp. 51–58.

———. *Neuromancer*. Ace, 1984.

———. "The Science in Science Fiction" on *Talk of the Nation*, NPR. November 30, 1999. http://www.npr.org/templates/story/story.php?storyId=1067220; Timecode 11:55.

———. *Distrust That Particular Flavor*. Penguin, 2012.

Holstein, Eric, Raoul Abdaloff, and William Gibson. "Interview de William Gibson VO." *ActuSF.com*. October 31, 2017. https://www.actusf.com/detail-d-un-article/article-5710.

Krawczyk-Łaskarzewska, Anna. "Space Over Time: The Urban Space in William Gibson's Techno-thriller Novels." *European Journal of American Studies*, vol. 10, no. 3, 2015, pp. 1–20. http://journals.openedition.org/ejas/11373.

McCaffery, Larry and William Gibson. "An Interview with William Gibson." *Mississippi Review*, vol. 16, no. 2/3, 1988, pp. 217–36.

McFarlane, Anna. "'Anthropomorphic Drones' and Colonized Bodies: William Gibson's *The Peripheral*." *English Studies in Canada*, vol. 42, no. 1–2, 2016, pp. 115–32.

Murphy, Graham J. "Post/Humanity and the Interstitial: A Glorification of Possibility in Gibson's Bridge Sequence." *Science Fiction Studies*, vol. 30, no. 1, 2003, pp. 72–89.

Sterling, Bruce. Preface. *Burning Chrome*, by William Gibson. Grafton, 1988, pp. 9–13.

Westfahl, Gary. *William Gibson*. U of Illinois P, 2013.

Keren Omry

DONNA J. HARAWAY (1944–)

US academic and cultural critic.

Donna J. Haraway is best known for her famous "Manifesto for Cyborgs," published in the journal *Socialist Review* in 1985, less than a year after **William Gibson**'s *Neuromancer* (1984). Haraway's "Manifesto" has had a tremendous influence on the conception and portrayal of cyborg figures in theory, art, and popular culture. In addition, science fiction (sf) plays a crucial role in Haraway's critical thinking more generally. The historian of science relies on sf and proto-cyberpunk authors like **Joanna Russ**, **Samuel R. Delany**, **James Tiptree, Jr.**, Octavia Butler, and Vonda McIntyre to think about

"Science, Technology, and Socialist-Feminism in the Late Twentieth Century." As she writes in the republished and slightly updated version of the manifesto for *Simians, Cyborgs, and Woman: The Reinvention of Science* (1991), "[t]hese are our story-tellers exploring what it means to be embodied in high-tech worlds. They are theorists for cyborgs" (173). Haraway views the cyborg as both "a hybrid of machine and organism" and a "creature of social reality as well as a creature of fiction" (*Simians* 149). She gives a prominent role to irony—"humour and serious play"—as a critical tool: "Irony is about contradictions that do not resolve into larger wholes, even dialectically, about the tension of holding incompatible things together because both or all are necessary and true" (*Simians* 149). Together with shared motives, this stance is what makes Haraway's work especially significant for cyberpunk culture. After all, many cyberpunk narratives similarly manage to make serious propositions and claims about real-world socio-politics without taking themselves dead serious or being self-righteous.

Haraway approaches her areas of research—for example, the history of primatology in *Primate Visions: Gender, Race and Nature in the World of Modern Science* (1989), or the promises of genetic engineering in *Modest_Witness@Second_Millennium.FemaleMan©_Meets_OncoMouse™: Feminism and Technoscience* (1997)—with often painstakingly small steps and intentional, circular arguments. Race, gender, and the definition and construction of 'nature' are categories of analysis, but instead of dissecting these matters and explaining the tensions away, she makes "a critical and joyful fuss" about them (*Staying* 31). Her work is dedicated to creating epistemologies that are continuously interrogated to accommodate the "ontologically dirty" (*Modest* 127), those who are not on one side of the subject/object, human/non-human, living/non-living, organic/machinic divide.

In her feminist interrogations of technoscience narratives, Haraway acknowledges that like-minded feminists, "prefer our science fiction to be a bit more utopic" (*Simians* 186). For example, Haraway spotlights **Marge Piercy**'s *Woman on the Edge of Time* (1976), a novel whose protagonist is at the crossroads between a future feminist utopia and a technocratic-totalitarian dystopia. Piercy's Connie, a Chicana woman who is involuntarily held in a mental hospital, has access to both versions of the future and struggles against her powerlessness to influence the course of events. Haraway uses Piercy's novel to underscore the importance of "staying with the trouble"; sticking with difficult and ambiguous situations to avoid escapist or easy ways out.

Piercy's cyberpunk novel *He, She, and It* (or *Body of Glass*, 1991) was inspired by both Gibson's *Neuromancer* and Haraway's "Manifesto" and, in a feedback loop, Haraway quotes *He, She and It* at the very beginning of *Modest_Witness*, highlighting that Piercy's cyborgs live "without innocence in the regime of technobiopower, where literacy is about the joining of informatics, biologics, and economics" (2). *Modest_Witness* is Haraway's most cyberpunk monograph, in its style and particularly in its reliance upon Joanna Russ's feminist proto-cyberpunk novel *The Female Man* (1975). Haraway's main critique regarding the discourse of biotechnology is the "mystification of kind and purity" and the "unintended tones of fear of the alien and suspicion of the mixed," ideas that are rooted in "doctrines of white racial hegemony" (61). In her assessment of the technoscientific world, sf serves a crucial function because of its multi-layered portrait of this world, but even more so because it helps to grasp the fact that the material and the semiotic are intrinsically interwoven. Haraway continuously points to elements of storytelling inside scientific practices and, at the same time, draws attention to the fact that "(o)ne story is not as good as another" (*Primate Visions* 331). It is important to cultivate *some* stories and be wary of others: "It matters what stories make worlds, what worlds make stories" (*Staying* 12).

The absence of the cyberpunk "boys' club" (Cadora 158) from Haraway's bibliography is not surprising; after all, it also matters *who* tells the stories and who, at least traditionally, was excluded from the discourse. Haraway explicitly wants "feminists to be enrolled more tightly in the meaning-making processes of technoscientific world-building" (*Modest* 127), and as critics such as Karen Cadora or, more recently, Lisa Yaszek and Patricia Melzer have shown, even though some powerful texts of feminist sf were written at the time, what is considered "the original 1980s cyberpunk movement" consists of mostly male authors and did little for feminist empowerment. Engaging feminist and female writers and scientists is important to Haraway, since she repeatedly observed how they were excluded from citation indexes, unlike their male contemporaries. Furthermore, "cyborg writing," with its potential to displace hierarchical dualisms and naturalized or gendered identities, clearly has a feminist, anti-racist and anti-speciesist agenda (*Simians* 175).

In this context, Haraway turns to Octavia Butler's *Dawn* (1987), a novel about, as she pointedly sums up, "the transformation of humanity through genetic exchange with extra-terrestrial lovers/rescuers/destroyers/genetic engineers" (*Simians* 179). *Dawn* is an impressive exercise in "staying with the trouble" and of bearing with contradictions. Butler's extra-terrestrial Oankali are ambiguous and never-innocent figures. Their main strategy for reproduction and evolution is hybridization, which creates a powerful contrast to the "discourses of natural harmony, the nonalien, purity" that Haraway criticizes in *Modest_Witness*. These ideas are not only racist, but "unsalvageable for understanding our genealogy" in what she describes (in a very cyberpunk manner) as "the New World Order, Inc." (*Modest* 62). Finally, the Oankali's technology is not outside of them, but "they are complexly webbed into a universe of living machines" (379). The Oankali thus help us understand our own cyborg world, where the "machine is not an *it* to be animated, worshipped, and dominated. The machine is us, our processes, an aspect of our embodiment" (*Simians* 180).[1]

In this respect, Haraway turns to Anne McCaffrey's *The Ship Who Sang* (1969). Drawing inspiration from the story about Helva, a girl who has her brain placed into a spaceship computer and body (a.k.a. 'brainship'), Haraway thinks about how "machines can be prosthetic devices, intimate components, friendly selves" (*Simians* 178). Helva not only steers her metal body particularly well, but fully embodies the ship and develops a distinct cyborg personality with its own needs and interests. The novel therefore provides an interesting framework to think about what Haraway calls "women in the integrated circuit"; "their integration/exploitation into a world system of production/reproduction and communication called the informatics of domination" (*Simians* 163). In contrast, the novel does little for "the utopian dream of the hope for a monstrous world without gender" (181). Even though Helva's brainship body lacks sex organs, it is never questioned that the ship could be anything but heterosexual. Nevertheless, sentient ships, gender, and agency have been successfully revised in recent feminist cyberpunk (or cyberpunk-adjacent) novels, including Anne Leckie's Ancillary space opera (*Ancillary Justice* [2013]; *Ancillary Sword* [2014]; *Ancillary Mercy* [2015]), or Martha Wells's Murderbot Diaries series (2017–20). In these recent instances, the non-binary cyborg figures further complicate gender identities and, more generally, a narrow anthropomorphism that presupposes that sentience must come with heterosexuality, or any kind of sexual orientation at all.

Finally, Vonda McIntyre's *Superluminal* (1983), a novel "where no character is 'simply' human" (*Simians* 179), features prominently in Haraway's "Manifesto." In line with such proto-cyberpunk stories as Samuel Delany's "Aye, and Gomorrah" (1967) and James Tiptree, Jr.'s "The Girl Who Was Plugged In" (1973), McIntyre's novel links sex and physical attraction to the cyborgization of bodies, bringing forth a queering of sexualities and gender identities. *Superluminal* also explores the potential of body modifications for multispecies living through the protagonist Orca and her family who, as "divers," are genetically altered so they can live underwater and communicate with killer whales. In a comparable fashion, Sam J. Miller's recent *Blackfish City* (2018) tells the story of an almost extinct people of "nanobonders" whose descendants engage in a fight for their own survival as well as against socio-economic injustice. In this community, "[e]very animal serves a purpose, brings a different kind of skill or resource" (Miller 228). The humans harvest these skills, but also take responsibility for what Haraway might call "multispecies flourishing."

Haraway explored human-involved multispecies communities in her own speculative fiction the "Camille Stories," a feminist fabulation that concludes *Staying with the Trouble*. It follows five generations of the non-binary protagonist Camille. By means of genetic modification, every Camille gets more and more features of a monarch butterfly. Their task is to connect the human community to this endangered species, and finally to mourn its extinction. In her most recent work, Haraway seems more interested in utopic stories of human–plant–animal–alien interactions than in the often dystopic explorations of cybernetic futures in the more classic cyberpunk tradition.[2] For example, she recommends N.K. Jemisin's Broken Earth trilogy (2015–2017) and Sue Burke's *Semiosis* (2018) which, in very different ways, give voice to non-humans and planetary forces. Furthermore, Haraway points to the figure of the Coyote or Trickster of American Southwest Indian accounts, as a particularly useful myth for science, helping us to grasp "our situation when we give up mastery but keep searching for fidelity, knowing all the while we will be hoodwinked" (*Simians* 199). Therefore, it comes as no surprise that she recommends Rebecca Roanhorse, who explores this figure in her novels *Trail of Lightning* (2018) and *Storm of Locusts* (2019) in new, fascinating ways.

Looking at cyberpunk through the lens of Haraway's work, we can become aware of elements that call for a critical distance to the genre, like lazy techno-pessimisms or inappropriate macho aesthetics. However, this lens can also magnify elements that make cyberpunk particularly contemporary and rich for cultural analyses, like its appreciation of more-than-human entities of all sorts, its ongoing fascination for hybridity and, in the best case, an irony that is playful and funny, serious and engaging, at the same time.

See also: **Rosi Braidotti, Samuel R. Delany, N. Katherine Hayes, Marge Piercy, Joanna Russ, James Tiptree, Jr.**

Notes

1 On this point, Nnedi Okorafor offers fascinating organic spaceships and tentacular beings in her *Binti* novella series (2015–17), recently collected in omnibus format as *Binti: The Complete Trilogy* (2020).
2 Haraway talked about her favorite recent sf at Experimental Engagements, the annual conference of the Society for Literature, Science, and the Arts, at UC Irvine on November 9, 2019, as well as at "Warum wir alle Familie sind" at Belvedere 21 in Vienna (via Skype), on November 30, 2019.

Works Cited

Cadora, Karen "Feminist Cyberpunk." *Beyond Cyberpunk: New Critical Perspectives*, edited by Graham J. Murphy and Sherryl Vint, Routledge, 2010, pp. 157–72.
Haraway, Donna J. *Modest_WitnessSecond_Millennium. FemaleMan©_Meets_OncoMouseTM: Feminism and Techno–science*. Routledge, 1997.
———. *Primate Visions: Gender, Race, and Nature in the World of Modern Science*. Routledge, 1989.
———. *Simians, Cyborgs, and Women: The Reinvention of Nature*. Routledge, 1991.
———. *Staying with the Trouble: Making Kin in the Chthulucene*. Duke UP, 2016.
Melzer, Patricia. "Cyborg Feminism." *The Routledge Companion to Cyberpunk Culture*, edited by Anna McFarlane, Graham J. Murphy, and Lars Schmeink. Routledge, 2020, pp. 291–99.
Miller, Sam J. *Blackfish City*. Ecco, 2018.
Yaszek, Lisa. "Feminist Cyberpunk." *The Routledge Companion to Cyberpunk Culture*, edited by Anna McFarlane, Graham J. Murphy, and Lars Schmeink, Routledge, 2020, pp. 32–40.

Julia Grillmayr

N[ANCY] KATHERINE HAYLES (1943–)

US literary theorist and critic.

N. Katherine Hayles is a renowned literary theorist and critic, greatly appreciated for pulling together the discourses of the humanities and the sciences in productive ways. She has bridged this gap herself, first receiving a BSc and an MSc in Chemistry and, after some years working as a research chemist, receiving an MA in English Literature from Michigan State University in 1970, and her Ph.D. in English Literature from the University of Rochester in 1977. Since 2017, she has been Distinguished Research Professor at the University of California and, as of 2018, James B. Duke Professor of Literature Emerita at Duke

University, two universities with which she has been involved as a teacher and researcher for three decades. Her main fields of research are literature, science and technology of the twentieth and twenty-first centuries, electronic textuality, modern and postmodern American and British fiction, critical theory, and science fiction (sf).

Her first book, *The Cosmic Web: Scientific Field Models and Literary Strategies in the Twentieth Century* (1984), unites the humanities and the sciences by singling out the *field concept*—i.e., a mutually interconnective field whose individual parts form an interactive whole—as the technological, mathematical, and philosophical heart of twentieth-century physics, mathematics, linguistics, and literature. In this vein, literature is "an imaginative response to complexities and ambiguities that are implicit in the [scientific field] models but that are often not explicitly recognized" (10). The monograph features readings of Robert M. Pirsig, D.H. Lawrence, Vladimir Nabokov, Jorge Luis Borges, and Thomas Pynchon, all the while exploring science and literature's mutual influence.

In the edited collection *Chaos and Order: Complex Dynamics in Literature and Science* (1991), Hayles uses the concept of chaos to open an interdisciplinary plane of discussion and continue her exploration of the interconnectedness between the humanities and the sciences. In her introduction, Hayles exposes the forces of cultural configurations (e.g., postmodernism) as they surreptitiously impinge on scientific frames. She argues that literary critics would benefit from studying scientific concepts rather than using them as mere tropes, to trace the convergences between the science of chaos and postmodern critical theory and literature, and to expose how both fields are embedded in culture. "[B]oth the literary and scientific manifestations [of chaos]," Hayles writes, "are involved in feedback loops with the culture. They help to create the context that energizes the questions they ask; at the same time, they also ask questions energized by the context" (7). The collection therefore includes essays informed by natural philosophy, metafiction, mathematics, postmodernity, and theology that explore figures including Ilya Prigogine, whose work on dissipative structures influenced cyberpunk auteurs **Bruce Sterling** (*Schismatrix*, 1985) and **Lewis Shiner** (*Deserted Cities of the Heart*, 1988).

The cross-fertilization between science, postmodernism, and literature became particularly productive in her criticism of the "dematerialization of embodiment" characteristic of postmodern ideology and present in both literary and information theory ("The Materiality of Informatics" [1993]), her analyses of cyberpunk and cyborg narratives ("Virtual Bodies and Flickering Signifiers" and "The Life Cycle of

Cyborgs" [both 1993]), and her gendered revision of corporeal habitus in cyberspace ("Embodied Virtuality" [1995]). Her embodied, female gaze inscribes the body back into the matrix, underscoring in the process the binary sets (man/woman, mind/body) implicit in conceptualizations of information theory, and the importance of embodied learning, which redefines the relevance of context and nonconscious processes to human cognition.

Many of these ideas were included in *How We Became Posthuman: Virtual Bodies in Cybernetics, Literature, and Informatics* (1999), which is undoubtedly Hayles's most emblematic work, especially for cyberpunk criticism. Hayles argues that the interpenetration of technology and human life has transformed our understanding of the subject and its boundaries. She does so by intertwining the history of cybernetics and informatics with analyses of literary texts that illustrate various articulations of the posthuman. Her main thesis deconstructs the transhumanist articulation of the posthuman (epitomized by Hans Moravec) that posits human identity as "essentially an informational pattern rather than embodied enaction" (xii) and posits that in the near future human consciousness will be transferable to a computer—a belief that has been fruitfully developed, and critiqued, in cyberpunk. "Information, like humanity," Hayles asserts, "cannot exist apart from the embodiment that brings it into being as a material entity in the world; and embodiment is always instantiated, local and specific. Embodiment can be destroyed, but it cannot be replicated. Once the specific form constituting it is gone, no amount of massaging data will bring it back" (*How We Became* 49).

Hayles revises the birth of cybernetics and its various waves, underscoring the conceptual evolution and the elisions necessary to deprive information of its body and construct a posthuman version of the self. In so doing, she establishes a dialogue between the postulates held by scientific researchers and theorists, such as Claude Shannon, Warren Weaver, Hans Wiener, Heinz von Foerster, Margaret Mead, Humberto Maturana, and Francisco Varela, as well as the literary representations of virtuality and cyborgic entities found in sf works by cyberpunk and cyberpunk-adjacent luminaries, including **Philip K. Dick**, **William Gibson**, Greg Bear, and **Neal Stephenson**. For example, Gibson's *Neuromancer* (1984) and Stephenson's *Snow Crash* (1992) foresaw the tensions implicit in the mutation experienced by subjectivity and its coupling with information technologies through cybernetic circuits. In particular, Hayles posits that Gibson's Sprawl trilogy[1] "presents a vision of the posthuman future that is already upon us" and signals "the posthuman is experienced as an everyday, lived reality as well as an intellectual proposition" (39). Meanwhile, *Snow Crash* "reinforces the equation of humans with computers through the tangled loops it creates between material signifiers and signifying materialities" (278); thus, *Snow Crash* teaches us that "[w]e should value the late evolutionary add-ons of consciousness and reason not because they are foundational but because they allow the human to emerge out of the posthumans we have always already been" (279). Hayles also explores Cole Perriman's *Terminal Games* (1994), Richard Powers's *Galatea 2.2* (1995), and Bear's *Blood Music* (1985) to articulate a semiosis of virtuality that stages the tensions between materiality and immateriality. Finally, *How We Became Posthuman* offers more questions than answers as to what exactly can be made of our posthuman condition, but its great value resides in its ability to convincingly argue that

> [t]he posthuman need not be recuperated back into liberal humanism, nor need it be construed as anti-human. Located within the dialectic of pattern/randomness and grounded in embodied actuality rather than disembodied information, the posthuman offers resources for rethinking the articulation of humans with intelligent machines.
>
> (287)

Hayles's next two books—*Writing Machines* (2002) and *My Mother Was a Computer: Digital Subjects and Literary Texts* (2005)—combine with *How We Became Posthuman* to form a triptych dedicated to exploring a more nuanced understanding of embodiment through the study of the text's materiality and the modes of 'intermediation'—i.e., those complex interactions between language and the regime of computation— that take place in a digital age. While *Writing Machines* is devoted to that special type of literary work that "interrogates the inscription technology that produces it"—i.e., the "technotext"[2] (25)—*My Mother Was a Computer* explores the social and cultural processes in which the interpenetration of language and code, old and new technologies, show their complexity. Sf texts, such as **James Tiptree, Jr.**'s "The Girl Who Was Plugged In" (1973), Neal Stephenson's *Cryptonomicon* (1999), Stanislaw Lem's "The Mask" (1976), and Greg Egan's *Quarantine* (1992)*, Permutation City* (1994), and *Distress* (1995), provide perfect examples of print texts that nevertheless bear the mark of digitalization, attend to the complex feedback loops between the economy of information and subjectivity, and can be used to test the limits of what Hayles calls the regime of computation; namely, "is computation

[...] to be considered a metaphor appropriated from information technologies or an accurate description of psychic processes?" (172).

In *How We Think: Digital Media and Contemporary Technogenesis* (2012), Hayles develops the implications of contemporary technogenesis—the coevolution of humans and technics—for research in the humanities, trying to bridge the gap between digital humanists and print-based scholars, and setting the basis for an approach that encompasses both regimes of knowledge, which she calls Comparative Media Studies. This need for "a theory of embodied cognition encompassing conscious, unconscious, and nonconscious processes" (*How We Think* 55) gains momentum in *Unthought: The Power of the Cognitive Nonconscious* (2017), whose central premise is a rethinking of our previous understanding of cognition to expand it beyond consciousness and hence to include all the processes that provide the basis for intelligence, including the operations performed by other living beings, machines, and human-technical cognitive assemblages. Hayles resorts to sf that "interrogate[s] the consequences of consciousness far beyond what the science reveals, probing specially its phenomenological and cultural dimensions [...] and the crucial importance of nonconscious cognition" (87), including Tom McCarthy's *Remainder* (2005), Peter Watts's *Blindsight* (2006), and Colson Whitehead's *The Intuitionist* (1999).

Hayles has found in sf a *locus classicus* to probe contemporary theories of posthumanism, virtuality, and technogenesis, and cyberpunk has a central role in these explorations, especially in her earlier work. Through her insightful analyses, she has recursively demonstrated sf's ability to provide "deep, rich, and challenging contextualizations" (Hayles, "H-") in which to problematize the hidden assumptions of technoromantic utopias, explore their social-ethical implications, and posit the unforeseeable corollaries of humanity's evolution as it links its destiny to ever-more-complex technological extensions. Ultimately, Hayles's importance and critical influence is undeniable and, alongside **Donna J. Haraway** and **Rosi Braidotti**, she is at the forefront of critical posthumanism. Her work is founded upon exploring narratives that provide fertile ground for discussing the changes that our potent fusion with technology is forging in the way we think and in human identity, particularly as our sense of self disseminates in multiple assemblages with other humans, non-human animals, and machines in our cyberpunk environs. Hayles's explorations of the posthuman problematize its boundaries in virtual spaces and alternative dimensions and reflect the tensions and anxieties which are ubiquitous in a cyberpunk polarized between a disembodied, liberalist, and masculinist fantasy of self-sufficient autonomy and a situated, ecologically and ethically committed, non-binary positionality toward post-human embodiment.

See also: **Rosi Braidotti, William Gibson, Donna J. Haraway, Lewis Shiner, Bruce Sterling, James Tiptree, Jr.**

Notes

1 The Sprawl trilogy consists of *Neuromancer* (1984), *Count Zero* (1986), and *Mona Lisa Overdrive* (1989)
2 Hayles has become electronic literature's honorary ambassador through the publication of *Electronic Literature: New Horizons for the Literary* (2008), a pioneer work which contributes to establish the field of electronic literature in academia by providing the first systematic survey of its most important creations and a close-reading of canonic works.

Works Cited

Hayles, N. Katherine. *The Cosmic Web: Scientific Field Models and Literary Strategies in the Twentieth Century*. Cornell UP, 1984.
———. "Introduction: Complex dynamics in literature and science." *Chaos and Order: Complex Dynamics in Literature and Science*, edited by N. Katherine Hayles, U of Chicago P, 1991.
———. "The Materiality of Informatics." *Configurations: A Journal of Literature, Science and Technology*, vol. 1, no. 1, 1993, pp. 147–70.
———. "The Life Cycle of Cyborgs: Writing the Posthuman." *The Cyborg Handbook*, edited by Chris Hables Gray, Routledge, 1995, pp. 321–35.
———. "Embodied Virtuality: Or How to Put Bodies Back into the Picture." *Immersed in Technology: Art and Virtual Environments*, edited by Diana Augaitis, Douglas MacLeod, and Mary Anne Moser, The MIT P, 1995, pp. 1–28.
———. *How We Became Posthuman: Virtual Bodies in Cybernetics, Literature and Informatics*. U of Chicago P, 1999.
———. *Writing Machines*. The MIT P, 2002.
———. *My Mother was a Computer: Digital Subjects and Literary Texts*. U of Chicago P, 2005.
———. *Electronic Literature: New Horizons for the Literary*. U of Notre Dame P, 2008.
———. "H-: Wrestling with Transhumanism." *Transhumanism and Its Critics*, Metanexus, 2011, https://www.metanexus.net/h-wrestling-transhumanism/.
———. *How We Think: Digital Media and Contemporary Technogenesis*. U of Chicago P, 2012.
———. *Unthought: The Power of the Cognitive Nonconscious*. U of Chicago P, 2017.

María Goicoechea

NALO HOPKINSON (1960–)

Canadian-Jamaican author and professor of creative writing

Nalo Hopkinson is a speculative fiction writer who has published six novels, two volumes of short stories, a chapbook, and two graphic novels in Neil Gaiman's Sandman universe (Vertigo/DC Comics). She has edited three fiction anthologies, co-edited two additional anthologies, and co-edited *Lightspeed Magazine's People of Colo(u)r Destroy Science Fiction!* Special Issue. Sometimes described as an Afro-Caribbean Canadian author of science fiction (sf) and fantasy, Hopkinson grew up in Jamaica, Guyana, and Trinidad—with a short stint in the US. She moved to Canada when she was 16, where she lived until 2011 when she moved to Riverside, CA, where she was a Professor of Creative Writing at the University of California-Riverside ("Nalo Hopkinson Brief Biography"), before accepting a position in 2021 as a Professor with the University of British Columbia's School of Creative Writing. Her awards and nominations are too numerous to list here, but her 2021 induction as the 37th Damon Knight Grand Master clearly demonstrates Hopkinson's ongoing impact on sf.

Hopkinson is not typically identified as a cyberpunk author, in part because throughout her fiction she explicitly "use[s] Afro-Caribbean spirituality, culture, and language [in] the idioms and settings of contemporary speculative fiction" as a means of "subverting the genre, which speaks so much about the experience of being alienated, but contains so little written by alienated people themselves" (*Brown Girl*, cover copy). For example, in *Midnight Robber* (2000), the protagonist Tan-Tan is a girl of Afro-Caribbean descent born on the planet Toussaint. Two hundred years prior, the Marryshow Corporation had brought Tan-Tan's ancestors, the "Taino Carib and Arawak; African; Asian, Indian; even the Euro" (18), to Toussaint after the Grande Nanotech Sentient Interface (known as Granny Nanny and her web) seeded the planet with nanomites (10), killing the "indigenous fauna [...] [t]o make Toussaint safe for those from the nation ships" (33). Despite the mixed heritage of its inhabitants, the festivals, music, and all culture on Toussaint can trace its origins to Afro-Caribbean roots, including the "artificial intelligence that safeguards all the people"— Granny Nanny—which is "named after the revolutionary and magic worker who won independent rule in Jamaica for the Maroons who had run away from slavery" ("A Conversation"). The novel is also replete with house operating systems called *eshus*, "named after the West African deity who can be in all places at once, who is the ghost in the machine" ("A Conversation"). Through her narrative depiction of networked people and embedded advanced technology—all children are injected with nanomites that form an embedded earbud connecting them to Granny Nanny's web—artificial intelligence, nanotechnology, and corporate states, Hopkinson works with cyberpunk's central motifs, and more recently, scholars have described her fiction as cyberpunk (see McFarlane, Yaszek). However, Hopkinson moves the genre in new and exciting directions by imagining "what technologies a largely African diasporic culture might build" ("A Conversation"). Finally, unlike the technologically supported oppression that is common in much cyberpunk, *Midnight Robber*'s advanced technologies mean that no one must do physical labor: characters repeatedly remark that "back-break ain't for people" (8) and "*Nobody higher than a next somebody*" (121).

Hopkinson's Toussaint—a planet run by a corporation, overrun by AIs, and where people become addicted to their implanted interfaces—echoes other cyberpunk worlds, such as **William Gibson**'s Sprawl or the far-future universe depicted in **Bruce Sterling**'s Shaper/Mechanist series;[1] but, compared to cyberpunk more broadly, particularly with its blend of interchangeable posthuman bodies, corporate greed, and at-times gruesome violence, Toussaint is downright utopian: "[M]ost of the way through creating the world I needed to tell the story," Hopkinson explains, "I realized [...] that I had created a utopia" ("A Conversation"). As scholars have noted, Hopkinson's resulting Afrofuturist perspective "expand[s] cyberpunk's seemingly unilateral vision of carnivorous corporate machines bent on annihilating humans and human practices" (Enteen 276); and "[b]y making a cyberspace network into the technological agent of a postcolonial future, *Midnight Robber* appropriates white visions of a utopian future in cyberspace" (Thaler 108).

Still, Toussaint is no untainted world where all is celebratory and whose inhabitants use their freedom from hard labor ('back-break'), racism, and inequity for everyone's benefit. While Granny Nanny has a "sense of love, care, and duty" to her people, being connected to her "really does feel like mothering, and sometimes that's a good thing, sometimes it's a smothering thing" ("A Conversation"). Also, as others have highlighted, Toussaint's utopia hides "genocide on a scale that equals the European extirpation of the Caribbean's native cultures" (Clemente 14). In creating their utopia, the Marryshevites destroy anything that might upset the balance they hope to create, which includes removing the indigenous life and then exiling the people who do not fit into that utopia to New Half-Way Tree, the prison planet where Toussaint's killers, rapists, and "people we don't know what to do with" (72) are exiled. As the "dark version of the real thing" (2), New Half-Way Tree is characterized as Toussaint's "dub side,"[2] a world without advanced technology, full of 'back-break' and 'alien' lifeforms. When Tan-Tan was seven, she was kidnapped by her father (who was awaiting trial for murder), brought to New Half-Way Tree, and sexually abused by him for years. Tan-Tan kills him when he rapes her a final time on her sixteenth birthday. She escapes into the bush with her friend, one of the Douen (New Half-Way Tree's intelligent, lizard-like natives), and lives with them, learning Douen culture and secrets. Pregnant with her father's child and hunted by her stepmother, Tan-Tan goes from one human settlement to another—meting out justice as the 'Robber Queen' and triggering new folk tales about her adventures. At the novel's end, Tan-Tan gives birth to her child—a boy she names Tubman—and we learn Granny Nanny had directed Tan-Tan's nanomites into the fetus's growing tissue, making Tubman's "whole body [...] one living connection with the Grande Anansi Nanotech Interface" (326). Clearly, Granny Nanny's utopia (Toussaint) has shortchanged its inhabitants by hiding its dub side, but when the "dub side" unites with its "A" side, the "monstrous" baby becomes the true hope in Hopkinson's cyberpunk narrative.

While many scholars and critics initially failed to connect *Midnight Robber* to cyberpunk, going so far as to dismiss its depictions of cyberspace and nanotechnology as window dressing,[3] others unpack how it significantly reworks cyberpunk tropes. Jillana Enteen, for example, notes how Hopkinson "hacks" the Western-based language, individualism, and masculine technology of cyberpunk; specifically, she "render[s] visible current socioeconomic inequities, suggest[s] [an] alternative formulation of the relationship between humans and technology, and increase[s] the cultural repository of ideas that inspire technological and social development" (263). Similarly, Lisa Yaszek argues Hopkinson "replaces conventional representations of cyberspace as a feminine space to be penetrated by male heroes with Granny Nanny, a still-feminine but decidedly active network that intervenes into the physical world to guide her human children toward socially-just futures" (35).[4] At the same time, *Midnight Robber* is more than a simple repudiation of the original cyberpunk: it expands upon 1990s-era feminist cyberpunk and the feminist cyborg consciousness developed by posthumanism scholar **Donna J. Haraway** (among others) that has become central to understanding our cyberpunk culture. In Haraway's theory, "cyborg unities are monstrous and illegitimate" (154)—such as Tan-Tan and her baby Tubman—and can teach us how not to be "Man" (173), but to find new, more hopeful unions. *Midnight Robber* therefore gives life to Haraway's utopian cyborg[5] and is thus aligned with the feminist cyberpunk of **Pat Cadigan** (*Synners* [1991]), Kathleen Ann Goonan (the Nanotech Quartert[6]), Laura J. Mixon (*Glass Houses* [1992]; *Proxies* [1998]), **Marge Piercy** (*He, She and It/Body of Glass* [1991]) and **Melissa Scott** (*Trouble and Her Friends* [1994]), fiction that uses the Harawayian feminist cyborg figure (to greater or lesser degrees) to offer (at-times utopian) reworkings of masculinist cyberpunk. Specifically, feminist cyberpunk's protagonists are women who use their considerable expertise to remake their worlds rather than simply survive them. Hopkinson's feminist cyborgs, however, differ from other feminist cyberpunk protagonists, in that they are not expert users of technology who chose to plug in for political progress; instead, they become expert storytellers, not only masterfully "introducing black myths and blending them with [...] familiar cyberpunk motifs" (Lavender 314), but also insisting that in changing the stories we tell, people may change themselves and their worlds beyond current understandings.

In sum, Hopkinson's subversion of cyberpunk's motifs in *Midnight Robber* showcases how Afro-Caribbean people can successfully repurpose cyberpunk motifs and technologies. By exposing the dub side of that utopian cyberpunk world, *Midnight Robber* also points to a necessary co-evolution of humans, advanced technology, and native life. Not primarily focused on technological expertise common to cyberpunk, Hopkinson instead creates a cyberpunk in which the ways stories are imagined, created, and retold have discernable effects on the biological bodies and worlds in which her characters live, thus leaving an indelible mark on how the genre looks, sounds, and feels, a mark that will hopefully inspire future generations of authors, filmmakers, and artists to think about and explore cyberpunk stories, bodies, and cyberpunk culture in 'dub side' ways.

See also: **Steven Barnes, William Gibson, Samuel R. Delany, Donna J. Haraway, Janelle Monáe, Marge Piercy, Melissa Scott, Bruce Sterling**

Notes

1 Gibson's Sprawl trilogy includes *Neuromancer* (1984), *Count Zero* (1986), and *Mona Lisa Overdrive* (1988). Sterling's Shaper/Mechanist series consists of "Swarm" (1982), "Spider-Rose" (1982), "Cicada Queen" (1983), "Sunken Gardens" (1984), "Twenty Evocations" (1984), and *Schismatrix* (1985).

2 The dub side of a reggae record refers to its 'B' side, usually a remixed, instrumental version of the 'A' side single.

3 See Anatol; Boyle; Collier; Johnston; Smith; Soyka; and others.

4 See also Grace L. Dillon, who ties Hopkinson's reworking of cyberpunk motifs
to "indigenous scientific literacies" (25).

5 See Clemente; Braithwaite; Fehskens; Sorenson; and Thaler.

6 Goonan's Nanotech Quartet includes *Queen City Jazz* (1994); *Mississippi Blues*
(1997); *Crescent City Rhapsody* (2000); and *Light Music* (2002).

Works Cited

Anatol, Giselle. "Maternal Discourses in Nalo Hopkinson's *Midnight Robber.*"
African American Review, vol. 40, no. 1, 2006, pp. 111–24.

Braithwaite, Alisa K. "Connecting to a Future Community: Storytelling, the
Database, and Nalo Hopkinson's *Midnight Robber.*" *The Black Imagination:
Science Fiction, Futurism and the Speculative*, edited by Sandra Jackson and
Julie E. Moody-Freeman, Peter Lang Publishing, Inc., 2011, pp. 81–99.

Boyle, Elizabeth. "Vanishing Bodies: 'Race' and Technology in Nalo
Hopkinson's *Midnight Robber.*" *African Identities*, vol. 7, no. 2, 2009,
pp. 177–91.

Clemente, Bill. "Tan-Tan's Exile and Odyssey in Nalo Hopkinson's *Midnight
Robber.*" *Foundation: The International Review of Science Fiction*, vol. 33, no.
91, 2004, pp. 10–24.

Collier, Gordon. "Spaceship Creole: Nalo Hopkinson, Canadian-Caribbean
Fabulist Fiction, and Linguistic/Cultural Syncretism." *Matatu: Journal for
African Culture and Society*, vol. 27–28, 2003, pp. 443–56.

Dillon, Grace L. "Indigenous Scientific Literacies in Nalo Hopkinson's
Ceremonial Worlds." *Journal of the Fantastic in the Arts*, vol. 18, no. 1,
2007, pp. 23–41.

Enteen, Jillana. "'On the Receiving End of the Colonization': Nalo Hopkinson's
'Nansi Web." *Science Fiction Studies*, vol. 34, no. 2, 2007, pp. 262–82.

Fehskens, Erin M. "The Matter of Bodies: Materiality on Nalo Hopkinson's
Cybernetic Planet." *The Global South*, vol. 4, no. 2, 2010, pp. 136–156.

Haraway, Donna J. *Simians, Cyborgs, and Women: The Reinvention of Nature.*
Routledge, 1991.

Hopkinson, Nalo. *Brown Girl in the Ring.* Warner, 1998.

———. "A Conversation with Nalo Hopkinson." *SF Site* April 27, 2006,
http://www.sfsite.com/03b/nh77.htm.

———. *Midnight Robber.* Warner, 2000.

———. "Nalo Hopkinson Brief Biography." *NALO HOPKINSON,
AUTHOR*, http://nalohopkinson.com/brief-biography.html.

Johnston, Nancy. "On Planet Caribbean." *The Globe and Mail*, April
22, 2000, https://www.theglobeandmail.com/arts/on-planet-caribbean/
article767295/.

Lavender III, Isiah. "Critical Race Theory." *The Routledge Companion to
Cyberpunk Culture*, edited by Anna McFarlane, Graham J. Murphy, and
Lars Schmeink, Routledge, 2020, pp. 308–16.

McFarlane, Anna. "AI and Cyberpunk Networks." *AI Narratives: A History of Imaginative Thinking About Intelligent Machines*, edited by Stephen Cave, Kanta Dihal, and Sarah Dillon, Oxford UP, 2020, pp. 284–308.

"Nalo Hopkinson." *The Internet Speculative Fiction Database*, n.d., http://www.isfdb.org/cgi-bin/ea.cgi?Nalo_Hopkinson.

Review of *Brown Girl in the Ring* by Nalo Hopkinson. *Publishers Weekly*, n.d., https://www.publishersweekly.com/978-0-446-674331.

Smith, Eric D. "'The Only Way Out Is Through': Space, Narrative, and Utopia in Nalo Hopkinson's *Midnight Robber*." *Genre: Forms of Discourse and Culture*, vol. 42, no. 1–2, 2009, pp. 135–63.

Sorenson, Leif. "Dubwise into the Future: Versioning Modernity into Nalo Hopkinson." *African American Review*, vol. 47, no. 2–3, 2014, pp. 267–83.

Soyka, David. "The SF Site Featured Review: *Midnight Robber*." *SF Site*, 2000, https://www.sfsite.com/05b/mr81.htm.

Thaler, Ingrid. *Black Atlantic Speculative Fictions: Octavia E. Butler, Jewelle Gomez, and Nalo Hopkinson*. Routledge, 2010.

Yaszek, Lisa. "Feminist Cyberpunk." *The Routledge Companion to Cyberpunk Culture*, edited by Anna McFarlane, Graham J. Murphy, and Lars Schmeink, Routledge, 2020, pp. 32–40.

Rebecca J. Holden

GAKURYU ISHII (1957–)

Japanese film director.

Within the broader web of global cyberpunk, Japanese cyberpunk forms a particularly thick and branching node. This Japanese movement has its own history independent of American cyberpunk, but there have also been moments of interconnection and encounter between the two. Japanese cyberpunk features its own visual aesthetics and subject matter, embodied by filmmakers such as Shigeru Izumiya (*Death Powder* [1986]), **Shinya Tsukamoto** (*Tetsuo: The Iron Man* [1989]), and Shozin Fukui (✓ *964 Pinocchio* [1991]; *Rubber's Lover* [1996]). One of the most influential figures in this loose movement, however, is Gakuryu Ishii, formerly known as Sogo Ishii before changing his name in 2010. Ishii is a prolific director in Japan, having directed several feature films and numerous shorts, music videos, and TV episodes, and his work, particularly his early independent films, is integral to the development of cyberpunk in Japan and connects punk music and politics with a broader history of cyberpunk science fiction and cyberpunk culture.

Ishii grew up in Fukuoka, a city on Kyushu, one of Japan's southernmost islands. As a teenager in the 1970s, Ishii became involved in the city's local heterogeneous proto-punk rock scene, known as *mentai* (Player, "Anarchy" 105), and was a sometime singer and guitarist (Mes and Sharp 67). Moving to Tokyo in 1977 to study at Nihon University, Ishii borrowed equipment from the university and began directing his first 8mm and 16mm films. From the late 1970s until the mid-1980s, Ishii tapped into his history with the *mentai* rock scene as his work developed alongside Japan's burgeoning punk scene. He worked closely with several bands from the period, producing music videos such as *Anarchy 80 Ishin* (1981) and *Stop Jap* (1982). During this period, Ishii was also central to the emerging *jishu seisaku eiga* movement—a wave of "autonomously produced films" with similar values to punk's "do-it-yourself" ethos in the west (Player, "Anarchy" 99). With TV sets becoming more common across Japan, and with the price of cinema tickets remaining high, revenues for Japan's major film studios began to plummet. As a result, fewer assistant director positions were made available and opportunities for new and emerging directors shrank. However, as the Japanese electronics industry boomed, the 8mm camera became increasingly affordable, leading to an explosion of independently made films by young artists and students.

In the context of the autonomous film movement, youth rebellion is a common theme in Ishii's early punk films. In 1977's independently produced short *Panic High School*, a high school student brings a shotgun to school and shoots his teacher in the middle of a lesson. In a series of chaotic sequences, accompanied by a sharp electronic-rock soundtrack, the student runs between school buildings, evading riot police, until he is finally arrested. Japanese entertainment company Nikkatsu showed interest in the film, and a year later the short was remade into a feature film, with Ishii working as co-director alongside Yukihiro Sawada. While it is unclear how much input Ishii had in the remake—he later criticized Nikkatsu for "pushing me out of my own film" (Player, "Anarchy" 107)—Ishii's punk style remains visible. For instance, the shooter's rebellion against the rigorous and relentless examination system in Japanese schools is emphasized as the film's protagonist, Jono, seeks to avenge his classmate who commits suicide under the pressure of university entrance exams. In striking crowd scenes, teachers and riot police shout and trip over each other in uncoordinated panic. In one of the film's most visually interesting shots, Jono runs up a staircase crammed with students all running in the opposite direction. The sheer mass of bodies on screen at once, the camera placed right in among them, and Jono's struggle to get past them literalize his rebellion and desire for identity against the pressures of the education system.

Youth rebellion, massed bodies, and chaotic crowds also feature heavily in Ishii's next two feature films as he worked to develop a visual style that is recognizably cyberpunk. His second feature, *Crazy Thunder Road* (1980), focuses on a violent clash between two biker gangs. The film's visual style prefigures **Katsuhiro Ōtomo**'s *Akira* (1988) as leather-clad bikers race through the outskirts of a city at night in a blur of light trails. *Crazy Thunder Road* was filmed on 16mm while Ishii was still at university and is described by Tom Mes and Jasper Sharp as a "tour de force of automotive eroticism" (74), which evokes the Mechanophilia of J.G. Ballard's *Crash* (1973). While the film was produced independently, the film studio Toei showed an interest and gave it a 35mm theatrical release.

Crazy Thunder Road's success helped Ishii to secure funding from Toei for his next feature film, *Burst City* (1982). One of Ishii's most significant films, Mes and Sharp describe *Burst City* as the "defining statement" of Japanese punk film (76). Mark Player considers it to be crucial "in the evolution of Japanese punk aesthetics into Japanese cyberpunk aesthetics" ("Anarchy" 109), an aesthetic that is more horror-tinged than North American cyberpunk and often "suggesting that anxieties over rapid modernity are not some far-off venture but something that should be worried about now" (Player, "Post-Human"). Filmed on the outskirts of Tokyo in the decaying, post-industrial landscape of Kawaguchi, punk bands traveled from across Japan to appear in the film, including appearances by The Rockers, The Roosters, and The Stalin. The film is set in a dystopian near-future and follows three main narrative threads. In the first, a sub-culture of punks lives in the ruins of abandoned factories by day; by night they street race, hold punk concerts, and clash with riot police. The second thread follows a sex worker who wishes to escape the city, but who is being used by a yakuza gang to bribe officials. In the third, a man with a metal hand and a man who cannot stop scream-ing fall in with a group of homeless outcasts who are being pressed by the yakuza and city officials into building a nuclear power plant. At the film's finale, these threads converge as workers and punks battle against (and defeat) the yakuza and the police. During these climactic scenes, the camera is placed right inside the crowd; a punk soundtrack accompanies the action as "the camera blurs the rioting and dancing bodies into one mass" (Toohey 214). *Burst City* defiantly unites an emerging cyberpunk visual style with punk music and politics as the film "provides visualization of how people at the bottom of Japanese social and political hierarchies" can "survive rebellion against oppres-sive government" (Toohey 214).

Following *Burst City*, Ishii directed a short film titled *Asia Strikes Back* (1983) to accompany his band Sogo Ishii and the Bacillus Army while on tour. Filmed in a non-linear, fragmented style, cyberpunk imagery is prominent in the film as a group of psychic soldiers trains in an underground bunker; they are connected with each other and share thoughts through a network of wires plugged into their brains. At the film's climax, one of the soldiers breaks free from the collective, only to discover that the long-awaited war they've been training for has already happened, leaving the outside world a nuclear wasteland. Keeping with the 'nuclear' theme, Ishii then turned his lens in *Crazy Family* (1984) to a nuclear family who, driven insane by atomized suburban life, destroy their home as they try to kill each other. The final film of Ishii's (cyber)punk phase is another short, *Halber Mensch* (1986), made in collaboration with Einstürzende Neubauten, a German industrial band whose songs explore "the cyborgian confluence of the human with media technology" (Torner 418). Set in an abandoned industrial building, Ishii's previous fast-paced style is tempered by a degree of sensuality, as he films the band playing a variety of industrial equipment—including saws, grinders, metal pipes, power drills, and shopping trolleys—as musical instruments. In a mix of slow, circling shots and intense close-ups, the lines between human and machine, instrument and tool, and music and industrial noise begin to destabilize and blur.

By the late 1980s, Ishii's cinematic output became more sporadic, largely because he struggled to find financing. During this time, he "spent a lot of time reading books," especially the work of cyberpunk precursors **Philip K. Dick** and **J.G. Ballard** (Mes and Sharp 72). By the mid-1990s Ishii's film career evolved into "a more conceptual and meditative style" (Mes and Sharp 72), and both Dick's and Ballard's influences are seen in the abstract and dream-like *August in the Water* and *Labyrinth of Dreams* (1997). A coming-of-age film, *August in the Water* returns to Fukuoka (a setting he explores in many of his films, beginning with *Panic High School*), and incorporates elements of mysticism as a meteor strike causes a series of strange events to unfold in the town, including a plague that turns people's organs into stone. There is a similar sense of slowly unfolding dread in *Labyrinth of Dreams*, a period drama that focuses on the fatal relationship of a bus conductor with a serial killer.

Ishii's twenty-first-century output begins with *Gojoe* (2000), a *jidaigeki*, or historical action film, set in medieval Japan. Like *Burst City*, *Gojoe* focuses on those who live on the margins of society, with large portions of the film set in an impoverished hamlet at the border of a river across which demons invade the world at night. An interest in monsters recurs in Ishii's return to Japanese cyberpunk: the protagonist of *Electric Dragon 80.000 V* (2001) is a private investigator who tracks down lost lizards with electric superpowers. Another of Ishii's bands, Mach 1.67, provide an industrial rock soundtrack as Dragon Eye, the film's protagonist, channels his aggressive electrical powers into playing an electric guitar. Punk sentiments also return in Ishii's most recent *jidaigeki* film *Punk Samurai Slash Down* (2018), based on a novel by punk singer Ko Machida who also starred in *Burst City*. Not coincidentally, many filmmakers of the *jishu seisaku eiga* movement and, later, Japanese cyberpunk worked with punk musicians: Shozin Fukui reminisces, "many directors had their own bands. They were all influenced by Sogo Ishii, I think" (cited in, Player 105).

In sum, while Ishii's films remain obscure in the west, his influence on North American cyberpunk is notable. In a 2006 blog post, **William Gibson** acknowledges Ishii as an influence on his novel *Idoru* (1996) and states that "nobody, but nobody, ever put the punk in cyberpunk the way he did" (n.p.). In fact, on a visit to Japan, Gibson and Ishii met and discussed collaborating together on an unrealized film project to be set in the Walled City of Kowloon in Hong Kong, a setting which features heavily in both *Idoru* and *All Tomorrow's Parties* (1999). Ishii's work is sorely overdue for reissue and wider distribution in the west so that new generations of scholars and artists can engage with his films.

See also: **J.G. Ballard, Philip K. Dick, William Gibson, Katsuhiro Ōtomo, Shinya Tsukamoto**

Works Cited

Gibson, William. "Burst City Trailer." *William Gibson Books*, July 21, 2006, https://web.archive.org/web/20071121223044/http://www.william gibsonbooks.com/blog/2006_07_01_archive.asp#115354123358489417.

Mes, Tom, and Jasper Sharp. *The Midnight Eye Guide to New Japanese Film*. Stone Bridge P, 2005.

Player, Mark. "Anarchy in Japan's Film Industry: How Punk Rescued Japanese Cinema." *Punk & Post Punk*, vol. 6, no. 1, March 2017, pp. 97–121.

———. "Post-Human Nightmares: The World of Japanese Cyberpunk Cinema." *Midnight Eye*, May 13, 2011, http://www.midnighteye.com/features/post-human-nightmares-the-world-of-japanese-cyberpunk-cinema/.

Toohey, David. "From Music to Revolution: The Semiotics of Punk and Cinematic Symbolism in Sôgo Ishii's Burst City." *Punk & Post Punk*, vol. 7, no. 2, 2018, pp. 203–18.

Torner, Evan. "Germany." *The Routledge Companion to Cyberpunk Culture*, edited by Anna McFarlane, Graham J. Murphy, and Lars Schmeink, Routledge, 2020, pp. 415–22.

Sasha Myerson

RAYMOND (RAY) KURZWEIL (1948–)

US inventor, author, and futurist.

Ray Kurzweil is an inventor, scientist, futurist, and author of one novel and seven books of nonfiction, including three *New York Times* bestsellers. Throughout his decades-long career, he has developed a broad range of products and software, including assistive technologies such as optical character recognition software (OCR), the flatbed scanner, and text-to-speech synthesis. He is also responsible for significant advancements in digital musical instruments, medical education technologies, digital finance, and artificial intelligence (AI) deployment. An MIT graduate who studied with AI pioneer and computer scientist Marvin Minsky, Kurzweil emerged as one of the foremost techno-optimists of the late 20th century and received such awards as the US National Medal of Technology in 1999 and the Lemelson-MIT prize in 2001.

As a child growing up in New York City (Queens), Kurzweil was determined to become an inventor. He eventually became deeply interested in computers and found himself at fifteen on *I've Got a Secret* with Steve Allen playing a piano piece composed by his own software. After high school, he went to MIT to study computer science and literature and, after some early successes selling companies based on his software development, Kurzweil began to work in assistive technologies. He started a company that developed optical character recognition technology that he later sold to Xerox and continued work on assistive technologies, including reading machines and speech and pattern recognition systems. After a meeting with Stevie Wonder (one of the first users of Kurzweil's reading machine) in the early 1980s, during which the performer explained the limitations he felt plagued the current generation of synthesizers, Kurzweil set out to make a synthesizer that was more realistic in its timbres and more responsive to the performer, per Wonder's specifications. The resulting instrument, the Kurzweil K250, was featured on countless hit records, Wonder served as Kurzweil Music Systems' musical advisor, and Kurzweil won a 2015 Grammy Award for his lifetime contributions to music.

Kurzweil's relevance to cyberpunk culture comes not from his science fiction (sf)—represented by a single 2019 illustrated novel about a young scientist, entitled *Danielle*—but from his many predictions about humanity's future. His best-selling nonfiction work—*The Age of Intelligent Machines* (1990), *The Age of Spiritual Machines: When Computers Exceed Human Intelligence* (1999), and *The Singularity is Near: When Humans Transcend Biology* (2005)—outline and expand upon central components of Kurzweil's fascination with "the Singularity," the moment when technological evolution and AI surpass their biological counterparts, pass the Turing Test, and effectively become sentient. Kurzweil also writes extensively about the transhumanist idea that human consciousness will someday be uploadable to a digital substrate. He has also advanced the idea that humans, if they live long enough to witness the singularity, could then live on forever in a computer network, an idea that is central to numerous works in the cyberpunk canon and the spark that seems to drive much of Kurzweil's varied output.

Kurzweil's work in the 1990s specified a timeline for the emergence of the singularity. He posited an exponential rate of technological evolution that, within 20 years of publication, would surpass that of biological development, leading to a future of highly intelligent, largely beneficent AI and immortal, digital humans all interacting on a worldwide computer network in real time. One of Kurzweil's central ideas from *Spiritual Machines*, his law of accelerating returns, argues that change is exponential, and that the singularity is coming faster than we think. The consequences will be tremendous: "Before 2030," Kurzweil writes, "we will have machines proclaiming Descartes's dictum. And it won't seem like a programmed response. The machines will be earnest and convincing. Should we believe them when they claim to be conscious entities with their own volition?" (60). But this is just one in a whole host of predictions about the effects such advanced computing power will have on day-to-day life—Kurzweil's predictions are so numerous that they have a dedicated (and extensive) Wikipedia page.[1]

After *Spiritual Machines*, *The Singularity is Near* further clarified and expanded on these earlier notions, changing the dates and adding new predictions, such as suggesting that by 2010 there would be a supercomputer powerful enough to mimic human intelligence, and that by 2020 you would be able to purchase such a powerful computer for a thousand US dollars. Despite the popularity of his work and the large cultural footprint his predictions have claimed over the decades—PBS called him one of "16 revolutionaries who made America" and *Inc*

Magazine called him "Edison's Rightful Heir"—other critics suggest his prognostications rely on an accelerated timeline that is more optimistic than timelines proposed by other leading AI researchers. As recently as 2019, Rodney Brooks cited Kurzweil's predictions about autonomous tech as being too optimistic, warning against "belief in magic" when "predicting the future of AI." It is John Rennie, former editor of *Scientific American*, who gives voice to these concerns most plainly in his 2010 essay "Ray Kurzweil's Slippery Future." While Kurzweil's "genius is beyond dispute," Rennie argues his reputation as the premier tech oracle is somewhat undeserved, observing that "scoring Kurzweil's prophecies turns out to be a difficult and contentious exercise." Specifically, Kurzweil's "clearest and most successful predictions often lack originality or profundity. And most of his predictions come with so many loopholes that they border on the unfalsifiable" (Rennie). Inverting the typical narrative that Kurzweil, an avid reader of Golden Age sf as a child, drew from those early works as he invented his own path, Rennie suggests that the famed inventor was drawing from pre-existing ideas found in key cyberpunk texts of the 1980s, including such canonical entries like **Masamune Shirow**'s *Ghost in the Shell* (1989), **Ridley Scott**'s *Blade Runner* (1982), **William Gibson**'s *Neuromancer* (1984), and **Bruce Sterling**'s *Islands in the Net* (1988); as a result, "the fact that many sources anticipated Kurzweil's prediction of a vigorous online society does not discredit it. But the praise that congratulates him for the originality of the idea implicitly obscures all those others who did it before him" (Rennie). But ultimately, Rennie's argument is that Kurzweil's brand of 'tech punditry' is as much about commanding large speaking fees as it is about making accurate assessments of technology's future.

Whether or not one agrees with Rennie's assessment of Kurzweil and his work, the explicit leashing of Kurzweil to cyberpunk illustrates not only how intertwined he and his world view are with this broader cultural formation but also how Rennie considers Kurzweil's predictions to be more akin to popular fiction than evidence-based expectation. It likewise reveals a complex interaction between capitalism and futurism that can be summed up in a line from an interview Kurzweil gave to trade magazine *Computerworld* in 1993: "[W]hat turns me on is to create technology that impacts people's lives." The article's focus was Kurzweil's transition from musical instruments and assistive technologies to AI, but what stands out is Kurzweil describing his enthusiasm for the human side of tech development as 'turning him on.'

Like Timothy Leary before him, Kurzweil often finds himself at the border of legitimate academic and corporate endeavors: while focused on helping people, his visionary prognostications are perhaps undercut by a pseudo-new age 'turned on' vibe that befits a self-styled tech guru or oracle; in fact, he often uses Leary-influenced 'turn on, tune in, drop out' aesthetics in his interviews, once observing in a commencement speech that "inventing is a lot like surfing" (Akron). And his interest in the question of uploading consciousness and sentient AI dovetails nicely with his lifelong interest in 'solving' aging. Shortly after writing *Intelligent Machines*, Kurzweil wrote a diet book called *10% Solution for a Healthy Life* (1993), which argues for a low-fat diet, and later two books on aging: *Fantastic Voyage: Live Long Enough to Live Forever* (2005) and *Transcend: Nine Steps to Living Well Forever* (2009). These books, along with his significant investment in cryogenic technology, paints a portrait of a person who, between cutting edge research, global lecturing, and hawking dietary supplements on his Transcend website,[2] is trying to outwit his own mortality.

In the end, Kurzweil's AI evangelism comes across as the latest in a line of immortality promises that humans have long been chasing. If we can reverse engineer a brain, we can recreate it and arguably recreate the person in digital form after their physical death, or so the transhumanist 'logic' goes. The philosophical concerns are many, and many texts have explored and debated the moral and ethical components of AI and sentient software and breaching the human/machine consciousness divide. But for Kurzweil, it is more straightforward: newer technologies like neural networks and nanobots offer a way to help humanity deal with its own physical limitations in the shape of assistive technologies like OCR and speech to text for the visually impaired and the deaf, as well as in the shape of fighting off death. On the one hand, Kurzweil's work feels like that of the everyman genius who genuinely wants to use technology to help all people deal with modern life. On the other, a less generous reading might suggest that he wants to be the one who solved death (especially for the wealthy who can afford his solution). Nevertheless, Kurzweil's genius is undeniable. His work has deeply affected and helped and entertained people with a broad range of needs and abilities from across the world and his understanding of how technology and culture are intertwined can be inspiring, in part because it often asks us to consider and value humanity's best intentions for technology. His influence on cyberpunk culture is as significant as its influence on him, and the impact of Kurzweil's life's work is central to a better understanding of the shifting borders between the human mind and the machines we make with it.

See also: **William Gibson, Jaron Lanier, Ridley Scott, Masamune Shirow, Bruce Sterling, Vernor Vinge**

Notes

1 https://en.wikipedia.org/wiki/Predictions_made_by_Ray_Kurzweil
2 https://transcend.me/

Works Cited

Brooks, Rodney. "AGI Has Been Delayed." *RodneyBrooks.com*. May 17, 2019, https://rodneybrooks.com/agi-has-been-delayed/.
Kurzweil, Ray. *The Age of Intelligent Machines*. Viking, 1990.
———. *The Age of Spiritual Machines*. Penguin Books, 2000.
———. *The Singularity is Near: When Humans Transcend Biology*. Viking, 2005.
———. "The Future Ain't What it Used to Be." Commencement Speech, University of Akron, 2012, https://www.uakron.edu/president/speeches_statements/?id=c6856afc-067b-40d5-bfc1-ac93f118e3f5.
———. "Interview with Ray Kurzweil." *Computerworld*, March 19, 1993.
Kurzweil, Ray and Terry Grossman. *Fantastic Voyage: Live Long Enough to Live Forever*. Rodale, 2004.
———. *Transcend: Nine Steps to Living Well Forever*. Rodale, 2010.
Kurzweil, Raymond. *The 10% Solution for a Healthy Life*. Three Rivers P, 1993.
Rennie, John. "Ray Kurzweil's Slippery Futurism." *IEEE Spectrum*. November 29, 2010, https://spectrum.ieee.org/computing/software/ray-kurzweils-slippery-futurism.
"26 Most Fascinating Entrepreneurs: Raymond Kurzweil." *Inc Magazine*. November 29, 2010, https://www.inc.com/magazine/20050401/26-kurzweil.html.

Nicholas Laudadio

JARON LANIER (1960–)

US computer scientist and social commentator.

Jaron Lanier is a significant figure in cyberpunk culture, primarily for his pioneering work in virtual reality (VR) during the 1980s and early 1990s. These halcyon days of VR in popular culture were an articulation of **William Gibson**'s 'consensual hallucination,' which aimed to redefine how we might use computers. He has also articulated an influential critique of contemporary online culture and social media, and the economic and political underpinnings of this culture, marking

Lanier as an important commentator on the perils and promises of cyberculture.

Lanier was a leader in the initial wave of commercial VR, which emerged in the late-1980s through the Virtual Programming Languages company (VPL) in San Francisco. VPL was instrumental in developing the first instances of surgical simulations, vehicle interior prototyping, and multi-person virtual worlds using a head-mounted display called the EyePhone alongside haptic components called Data Gloves (Lanier, *Gadget* 128). These technologies were significant early attempts at bringing cyberspace, as envisaged by Gibson in *Neuromancer* (1984) and other cyberpunk works, to realization as an embodied, experiential space. Lanier has argued that the intention of VPL was to create spontaneous new worlds through VR, which would be sensitive, empathetic, and "express the stuff of the mind" (Lanier, *Dawn* 114), believing that with the seemingly infinite abundance of everything in virtual worlds, creativity would become especially valuable (Lanier, *Gadget* 25). The goal of VPL was to bring VR to a mass audience while developing and producing these spaces for interaction (Evans).

One of the most important aspects of the work of VPL was to fix the material form of VR in popular consciousness through the image of goggles and gloves (LaValle 30). With headsets like the EyePhone or HRX and Data Gloves, VPL established a visual motif for using VR that would become the *de facto* model for the VR aesthetic as equipment and would influence (as well as directly shape) the 'look' of VR for films of the time—e.g., *The Lawnmower Man* (Leonard 1992), *Strange Days* (Bigelow 1995), and *Hackers* (Softley 1995)—while working directly with Steven Spielberg as an advisor on *Minority Report* (2002). More important than the physical aesthetic was the notion of VR, as it was conceived by Lanier, as not only a way of simulating the real world but a way of building new worlds for consciousness where the constraints of the physical world would be cast away. This idealistic notion of VR and experimentation with multi-person virtual worlds in the 1980s envisaged that cyberspace could transcend the privileges and prejudices of economic power, station of birth, and race by providing a world where all people could express their beliefs freely. Lanier's vision was an attempt to design environments that corresponded to the cyber-utopian dream of a more open world with the help of interconnected, immersive, and interactive technologies. The idea that VR could afford a new kind of freedom to the user, and to human beings in general, fueled predictions of VR's near-future dominance in the 1990s thanks to Lanier's vision.

These early discourses of VR were part of the wider discourses on technology in early 1990s technoculture that promised social, as well as technological, progress. At the time, technologists, novelists, pundits, and visionaries converged on the idea of VR as a transcendent technology of the near future (Lister et al. 106). This discourse was encoded across contemporary culture; VR was new, and the ideas of VR at the time of Lanier's work drew on values, ideologies, and myths that positioned the medium as a natural conclusion to the history of media technologies and a projection into a utopian future (Chesher 15–16). Lanier's vision of VR was of a medium that facilitated shared spaces and cooperation through the interface and in a computer-generated environment; it was a means to not only transcend the barriers of space and time but also to co-exist in a meaningful manner in cyberspace. This notion informs the Metaverse of **Neal Stephenson**'s *Snow Crash* (1992) and Bruce Bethke's *Headcrash* (1995), two key cyberpunk works of the 1990s. Lanier's VR was not just for vision, but to touch, ultimately offering a deeply human way of co-existing socially with others. The transformation of the human–computer interface into a human–computer–human interface through physical integration illustrates a twisting of technology and cybernetics to blur the lines between the virtual and physical that is quintessentially cyberpunk. Lanier continues to research avatar embodiment, hologram integration and homuncular flexibility in VR as a researcher at Microsoft, continuing to bring these visions to the re-emerging field of VR.

As well as this pioneering work in computer science, Lanier has become a key critic of contemporary internet culture and the effect that major digital companies such as Facebook, Google, and Twitter have on society and on the individual psyche. This skeptical approach to technology may seem at odds with the techno-utopianism of Lanier's work in VR and his work for Microsoft, but the arguments that Lanier makes are entirely compatible with his view of technology as a potentially liberating force. The apparent juxtaposition is in reality a product of a nuanced analysis of the political economy, embedded politics, and social effects of the contemporary digital giants, whose desire to commoditize and control sits in contrast with the view of cyberculture expressed in the discourses on VR in the 1980s and 1990s. Lanier's *You Are Not a Gadget* (2010) develops an analysis of online culture that is predicated on a view of the contemporary user as a kind of "digital peasant" (48), with our relationship to platform providers being akin to feudalism. Lanier argues that to know what is occurring with society or ideology, we must "follow the money"

(52). Within contemporary digital culture, money is flowing to advertising instead of to musicians, journalists, and artists. The content of social and digital media is worthless beyond what can be realized from advertisers, and culture itself will become empty.

Lanier's argument is that the combination of a collective social consciousness through social media and advertising has resulted in a new kind of social contract. The basic idea of this contract is that creative people (with space for creativity being so critical in early VR) are encouraged to treat their work as fragments to be given without pay over social media. Lanier describes this emergent culture as "computationalism" (*Gadget* 97), a term usually used to describe a philosophy of mind. In this context it describes a philosophy underpinned by an understanding of the world as a computational process, with people as subprocesses. The effect of this is a decrease in stylistic variety in culture as cultural artifacts become fragmented and subject to the economic logic of advertising.

The argument from *You Are Not a Gadget* is largely concerned with this lacuna of creativity in contemporary culture, but the notions of computationalism and the underlying logic of the political economy of contemporary online culture are developed further in *Who Owns the Future?* Lanier makes a series of arguments that begin to describe what **Shoshana Zuboff** would later call "surveillance capitalism." For example, Lanier argues that it is unfair to demand that people cease sharing and pirating copyrighted files when those same people are not paid for their participation in very lucrative network schemes such as Facebook. These people are spied on and not compensated for the data they produce for sale. While everyone should pay for music, there should be reciprocity in the wider culture in which that music is experienced. Lanier argues that the structure of networks distorts our ability to see such contradictions. Google and Facebook present the contract to the user in a manner that makes them feel they have the advantage, without seeing the wider cultural or social effects of the contract.

Lanier illustrates this feudalism with several examples, such as the eBook (*Future* 297). If you buy a physical book, you can resell it at will, or continue to enjoy it no matter where you decide to buy other books. Every purchase of an old-fashioned book opens an opportunity to earn money by enhancing provenance. An author signature can make it more meaningful to you and increase its value. The eBook affords only tenuous rights within the company store it was purchased in. We cannot resell, nor can we do anything else to realize the purchase as an investment. Using a different reading device will in most

101

cases lose rights to the text. The feudalism of the digital economy is to limit choice and options as a consumer, and therefore to be beholden to the platform that we have purchased from and must continue to use.

Lanier's solution to this is to realize that, while creative and cultural products should be paid for, they should be balanced with payments for our data. While it could be seen as draconian to charge for access to information and material we have come to expect for free, it would feel very different if companies were also paying us for information services we contribute to, and which form the fundamental basis of their business model. If Lanier's argument is correct, then a lot of people will end up with money due to them for their activity while the companies involved could still realize their profits from advertising (at a reduced rate). However, Lanier is honest that his suggestion is unlikely to be adopted. He rightly observes that the digital world has become remarkably consolidated, dominated by a small number of companies. The solution to this is to turn away from these behemoths. Lanier characterizes Facebook as a "BUMMER" (*Ten Arguments* 25), as are Google, Instagram, Twitter, Snapchat, and even WhatsApp. All these enterprises are all based on the BUMMER system, in which "Behaviors of Users are Modified, and Made into an Empire for Rent" (*Ten Arguments* 25–26). When someone uses social media in general, they are not a customer; they are the product. People are paying to manipulate their behavior based on statistical probabilities that they cannot see or understand. Nobody needs to know *why* someone is more likely to buy X or vote Y if they have just seen a cat video, or a news item that makes them feel sad, but mathematically speaking they are, so that is what the system will show. This is what makes these systems very different from traditional marketing, in which companies try to persuade the consumer to buy X or vote Y because it will make them safer, cooler, richer, sexier, etc. Facebook and Google work by manipulating our emotions, information networks, friendship communication, awareness of news, social behavior, etc., to make us more statistically likely to buy X or Y.

In characterizing contemporary online culture as deadening to creativity, fundamentally exploitative, anathema to creativity and cooperation outside of commercial manipulation, and something that should be rejected for the good of our own souls, Lanier's cyberpunk credentials are again affirmed; antipathy and rejection of hyper-consumerist social media in favor of a free relationship to cyberculture.

See also: **Pat Cadigan, William Gibson, Neal Stephenson, Bruce Sterling, Shoshanna Zuboff**

Works Cited

Chesher, Chris. "Colonizing Virtual Reality: Construction of the Discourse of Virtual Reality." *Cultronix*, no. 1, 1994, pp. 15–28.

Evans, Leighton. *The Re-Emergence of Virtual Reality*. Routledge, 2018.

Lanier, Jaron. *Dawn of the New Everything: Encounters with Reality and Virtual Reality*. Holt, 2017.

———. *Ten Arguments for Deleting Your Social Media Accounts Right Now.* Random House, 2018.

———. *Who Owns the Future?* Simon and Schuster, 2014.

———. *You Are Not a Gadget: A Manifesto.* Vintage, 2010.

Lister, Martin et al. *New Media: A Critical Introduction.* 2nd ed., Routledge, 2009.

LaValle, Steven M. *Virtual Reality.* Cambridge UP, 2017.

Zuboff, Shoshana. *The Age of Surveillance Capitalism.* Profile, 2019.

Leighton Evans

MARSHALL McLUHAN (1911–80)

Canadian academic and scholar.

Marshall McLuhan was a revolutionary Canadian theorist who spearheaded the study of electronic media. Subverting literary and scholarly conventions, his analyses of the technological landscape brought him fame and scorn. Although "cyberpunk" is not a term that has been frequently associated with his name—he died in 1980 before the movement had taken off—he was as much a cyberpunk as any science fiction (sf) author, filmmaker, or artist that followed after him, constructing a pop philosophy about the cultural maelstrom that would come to dominate the cyberpunk zeitgeist. Above all, he depicted (and predicted) how technology invaded, influenced, and transformed consciousness. "[M]y own approach to media study has always been to report the subliminal effects of our own technologies upon our psyches," he wrote in 1972, "to report not the program, but the impact of the medium upon the human user" ("The End" 202).

McLuhan was at once an old school literary critic and a new age techno-fetishist. His ideas about the history and future of electronic media hinge on the development of art and literature. The purpose of studying technology, as he saw it, was "nothing less than ensuring the survival of literature" (Gordon, *Marshall* 152). Educated in Canada and England, he received his Ph.D. from the University of Cambridge in 1942 and took on several academic appointments before settling at St. Michael's College at the University of Toronto, where he established the Centre for Culture and Technology in 1963. During his career, he lectured extensively on the international circuit, collected eight honorary doctorate degrees, and produced over ten monographs (many with collaborators), for which he received multiple awards. His first published book, *The Mechanical Bride: Folklore of Industrial Man* (1951), a collection of "exhibits" about the culture industry, put him on the map. He received widespread attention with *The Gutenberg Galaxy: The Making of Typographic Man* (1962) and *Understanding Media: The Extensions of Man* (1964), the latter of which is his most renowned work and introduces the guiding principle "the medium is the message." He became so influential worldwide that "his name entered the French language as *mcluhanisme*, a synonym for the world of pop culture" (McLuhan, "Playboy" 233).

The neologism is apt: McLuhan can be aligned with French theorists like Guy Debord, **Jean Baudrillard**, and especially Gilles Deleuze and Félix Guattari. While Deleuze and Guattari wrote "rhizomes," McLuhan wrote "probes," investigative swoops into the media environment that favored exploration over explanation and foregrounded "the *process* rather than the completed product of discovery" (236). As with cyberpunk narratives, McLuhan's innovative style is immersive, oblique, and compels readers to make their own connections. His prose is not exceedingly neologistic, but he loved wordplay and pastiche—James Joyce's *Finnegan's Wake* (1939) is a chronic touchstone that he unpacks in *War and Peace in the Global Village* (1968)—and occasionally he adopted contemporary slang terms such as "cool" for media (like television) to indicate the conflicting states of detachment and involvement that accompany the experience of watching it.

McLuhan's intellectual foundation also aligns him with cyberpunk; specifically, cyberpunk authors built upon the subversive precepts of New Wave sf,[1] which drew from modernist art and literature. So too did McLuhan draw from the literary inventions of the modernists, namely Joyce, but also T.S. Eliot, Ezra Pound, Wyndham Lewis, and others. He admired Edgar Allan Poe and cited "A Descent into the Maelstrom" as a model for his conception of the media torrent. The works of New Criticism founder I.A. Richards and English author and scholar G.K. Chesterton were central building blocks for the young McLuhan. Harold Innis's theses about the effects of media technologies enabled him to develop the "economy of the human sensorium" that ripened in *Understanding Media* (Gordon, *Marshall* 150). He once said that he "derived all my knowledge of media from people like Flaubert and Rimbaud and Baudelaire," who posited that "style is not a way of expressing something. It's a way of seeing, of knowing"

(McLuhan, "The Medium" 92–93). Joyce in particular endorsed this perspective in *Finnegans Wake*, "the greatest guide to the media ever devised on this planet" (McLuhan, "Open" 152).

Despite the success of *Understanding Media*, the book was ironically *misunderstood* by many readers, including its editors and the publisher, McGraw-Hill, who forced McLuhan to streamline his mosaic style and make the text more accessible. They did not grasp how "McLuhan's preference for a prose style that explores instead of explaining is inseparable from the theme summarized in *the medium is the message*" (Gordon, Introduction 10). This maxim, which asserts that users are shaped more by the form rather than the content of media, sets the tone for his entire methodology, forcing readers to rethink the affective electronic environment that contains and inoculates them like a screen-lit Petri dish; he teases the maxim out further in the punning follow-up to *Understanding Media*, *The Medium Is the Massage* (1967). McLuhan makes a crucial distinction between "hot" versus "cool." Whereas hot, high-definition media (e.g., cinema, radio, print, photography) contain a surplus of information and require little participation by users, cool, low-definition media (e.g., television, telephone, speech, cartoons) contain relatively little data and demand greater involvement. Of the technologies he probes, television dominates his thought. The twenty-first century has seen television transform into a cinematic (and thus hot) medium, but in the twentieth century, there was a clear division. In McLuhan's view, the pictorial, highly visual texture of movies makes viewers into the camera; the two-dimensional, tactile nature of television, on the other hand, makes them into screens.

Other foundational themes in McLuhan's canon seem tailor-made for cyberpunk and sf in general. Most conspicuous is the thesis that all technology extends from the human body, ranging from low technologies like speech (i.e., *uttering* equals *outering*) and clothing ("our extended skin") to high technologies like computers, "constant points of reference for cyberpunk" and, for McLuhan, extensions of the human nervous system (Sterling xiii). Technology amplifies the human, but it also amputates us, as any "medium gives power through extension but immobilizes and paralyzes what it extends [...] The central nervous system reacts to the pressure and disorientation of the amputation by blocking perception" (McLuhan, *Understanding* xviii). Another relevant theme is the global village, a product of electronic implosion wherein specialism, individualism, and fragmentation have reversed and dissolved into a collective (but not necessarily objective) identity. Today we see the global village most conspicuously

105

in the internet, a cyberpunk extrapolation that McLuhan foretold *before* cyberpunk. He was not an sf scholar, *per se*—sf studies was in its infancy in the 1950s and 1960s—but he often cited the genre and associated his ideas with it, beginning with *The Mechanical Bride*, which "he decided [...] was science fiction with comic strips and ads cast as characters" (Gordon, *Marshall* 156).

For the most part, McLuhan represents himself as a passive observer, merely defining the contours of media affect. Periodically, he cannot help being more of an activist in his attempts to cultivate an awareness of the cultural landscape and prevent electronic media from falling prey to a recurrent cyberpunk trope: body and mind invasion (Sterling xiii). "I'm not advocating *anything*," he emphasized in 1969, "I'm merely probing and predicting trends" (McLuhan, "Playboy" 264). In 1966, however, he explained that "I am resolutely opposed to all innovation, all change, but I am determined to understand what's happening because I don't choose just to sit and let the juggernaut roll over me [...] Anything I talk about is almost certainly to be something I'm resolutely against" (McLuhan, "Predicting" 102). Sometimes his anxiety was palpable, and on occasion he could not resist expressing apocalyptic misgivings about the future. Part of this compulsion had to do with him being a devout Catholic, something that is often lost in retrospect. Religion deeply informs his worldview; he may have been a "tuned-in media guru" (Pooley 2016), but he was also a conservatively pragmatic and spiritual man whose perception of media technology was intertwined with his personal beliefs.

In the final decade of his life, McLuhan's health steadily deteriorated. He survived a brain tumor, but his work ethic never wavered, and he remained largely functional until he died of a stroke in 1980. McLuhan's later monographs build on his previous ideas while introducing fresh probes, although his *modus operandi* to "train our physical senses and raise them to a new level of sensitivity" was the same in his first book as it was in his last, posthumously published book, *The Global Village: Transformation in World Life and the Media in the 21st Century* (1989) (Gordon, *Marshall* 237). Other notable works include *Culture Is Our Business* (1970), which revisits the vagaries of the culture industry, and *From Cliché to Archetype* (1970), which, as the title suggests, examines the absurdist interplay between rhetorical clichés and the technology of archetypes. McLuhan developed a keen interest in structuralism during this period. It did not renovate his outlook or approach, but it impacted his notion that effects precede causes as well as his concern with "figure/ground," a favorite probe in which every figure (a recognizable element in a given context) has a ground (an invisible environment) that can become the figure (and vice versa). Such playful but purposeful machinations epitomize McLuhan's entire career and came to a head in the 1970s.

Throughout his lifetime, McLuhan's detractors outweighed his supporters, and he was misread more often than he was understood. Critics were ultimately resistant to his rhizomatic method of inquiry and his fixation on technoculture. In other words, he was too experimental and too science fictional to be taken seriously by both academic and popular readerships, who struggled to navigate his emphasis on style as a means of perception and expression. Some *mcluhanisms* are still frowned upon even though reality is increasingly more science fictional than much sf. In fact, McLuhan makes perfect sense according to the dominant logic of cyberpunk, which dictates that *schizophrenia is a normative condition*, a thesis asserted with hysterical redundancy by William S. Burroughs in *Naked Lunch* (1959) and the cut-up novels that influenced so many cyberpunk authors.

See also: **Jean Baudrillard, Alvin and Heidi Toffler**

Note

1 For added details, see Latham.

Works Cited

Gordon, W. Terrence. Introduction. *Understanding Media*, by Marshall McLuhan, 2nd ed., Ginko, 2017, pp. 9–16.

———. *Marshall McLuhan: Escape into Understanding*. Stoddart, 1997.

Latham, Rob. "'A Rare State of Ferment': SF Controversies from the New Wave to Cyberpunk." *Beyond Cyberpunk: New Critical Perspectives*, edited by Graham J. Murphy and Sherryl Vint, Routledge, 2010, pp. 29–45.

McLuhan, Marshall. "Open-Mind Surgery." *Understanding Me: Lectures and Interviews*, edited by Stephanie McLuhan and David Staines, The MIT P, 2003, pp. 147–57.

———. "Playboy Interview." *Essential McLuhan*, edited by Eric McLuhan and Frank Zingrone, Basic, 1995, pp. 233–69.

———. "Predicting Communication via the Internet." *Understanding Me: Lectures and Interviews*, edited by Stephanie McLuhan and David Staines, The MIT P, 2003, pp. 98–102.

———. "The End of the Work Ethic." *Understanding Me: Lectures and Interviews*, edited by Stephanie McLuhan and David Staines, The MIT P, 2003, pp. 187–205.

———. *Understanding Media: The Extensions of Man*. 2nd ed., Ginko, 2017.

Pooley, Jefferson. "How to Become a Famous Media Scholar: The Case of Marshall McLuhan." *Los Angeles Review of Books*, December 20, 2016, https://lareviewofbooks.org/article/become-famous-media-scholar-case-marshall-mcluhan.

Sterling, Bruce. Preface. *Mirrorshades: The Cyberpunk Anthology*, edited by Bruce Sterling, Ace, pp. ix–xvi.

D. Harlan Wilson

SYD MEAD (1933–2019)

US designer and concept artist.

Syd Mead's career spanned multiple decades, media, and countries and connected the worlds of commercial design, art, and science fiction (sf). A graduate of the Art Center School of Los Angeles (now the Art Center College of Design, Pasadena) in 1959, Mead was first and foremost known as an industrial designer and concept artist whose work was marked by speculative and futuristic sensibilities. Mead initially worked for the Ford Motor Company and other industrial corporations as a commercial designer before launching his own company, Syd Mead Inc., in 1970. Mead illustrated and often envisioned a range of products from everyday objects to interiors to cars, but he also liked unconventional commissions, including a bar in a museum (Parsons 89). Parallel to his commercial work, Mead was an accomplished artist. In 1993, his digital set of fifty art pieces with interface screens became one of the first CD-ROMs released in Japan. He was recognized in a gallery circuit: the exhibition *Cavalcade to the Crimson Castle* featured 114 original paintings and illustrations and had a three-month showing at the Center for the Arts in San Francisco in 1996, while his exhibit *Progressions* debuted at the Forest Lawn Gallery of Fine Arts in Glendale, California, in 2012 and subsequently traveled to galleries nationwide.

The self-identified 'visual futurist' entered the world of sf as a production illustrator with *Star Trek: The Motion Picture* (Wise 1979), designing V'Ger, the intruding entity of the film. His sf designs also include the Russian spaceship in *2010: The Year We Make Contact* (Hyams 1984), the *Sulaco* warship in *Aliens* (Cameron 1986), the time machine launch vehicle in *Timecop* (Hyams 1994), the mask-making cabinet in *Mission: Impossible III* (Abrams 2006), and the interior of the orbital in *Elysium* (Blomkamp 2013). More consequentially for cyberpunk culture, Mead also worked on two instrumentally important cyberpunk movies—*TRON* (Lisberger 1982) and *Blade Runner* (Scott 1982)—while also designing the memory playback deck (and contributing trode designs) that is part of the SQUID device in *Strange*

Days (Bigelow 1995), and in *Johnny Mnemonic* (Longo 1995) designing the cabinet that was supposed to hold Johnny's severed head, which was never used in the film, and Jones the dolphin with his mechanical augmentations. Mead's more direct relationship with cyberpunk, however, appears to rest on two visual clusters: the vision of the city and the visualization of virtual reality.

Mead's iconic contribution to Steven Lisberger's *TRON* is the light cycles, whose races remain among the most memorable scenes of the film (as well as of the 2012 sequel, *TRON: Legacy* [Kosinski]). Motorcycles were always among Mead's favorite objects, but his designs for *TRON* have proven particularly durable, influencing the signature vehicle in the cyberpunk mainstay *Akira* (Ōtomo 1988), which came out six years later (Barder), as well as a range of machines from Christopher Nolan's Batman movies to *G.I. Joe: Retaliation* (Chu 2013). In *TRON*, Mead was nominally only responsible for vehicle designs, with **Moebius [Jean Giraud]** supervising the main sets and costumes and Peter Lloyd the environments. In reality, the three often swapped duties, with Mead designing some of the terrain of the virtual world (Patterson 814) and the clothing pattern on *TRON* (Mead 201). It is not quite clear how much of what can be seen in the film is Mead's design (in his career, he authored relatively few images of virtual spaces), but the color-coded geometric representation of in-film data systems may have impacted **William Gibson** when he was working on *Neuromancer* (1984)[1] and possibly other early depictions of cyberspace.

Mead's most recognized and lauded contribution to cyberpunk is, of course, *Blade Runner*, which has furnished the mode with the totemic location: a seemingly permanently nocturnal city whose corporate neon-laden verticality is imbricated with chaotic multicultural street-level anarchy. Like in *TRON*, it is also not entirely clear how much exactly Mead contributed to the movie. Over time, his name has become emblematic of it and certainly remains, at least in popular opinion, much more recognizable than the names of the special photographic effects supervisor Douglas Trumbull and the director of photography Jordan Cronenweth. At the time, though, Mead might have been seen as less influential, consistently referred to as a 'visual consultant'; according to Lawrence G. Paull, the production designer was "brought in to design cars, and he did a good job" (Sammon 33). Similarly, *The Blade Runner Sketchbook* attaches his name to cars, parking meters, water hydrants, and Deckard's infamous pistol (Scroggy). It was only after the film's release that his contribution as a 'visual futurist'—as the credits name him—became inextricable from the film's reputation.

Mead's ideas were definitely formative in the creation of *Blade Runner*'s 2019 Los Angeles, but there, too, his contribution is dispersed. The tangible influence of *Metropolis* (Lang 1927) on *Blade Runner* came via **Ridley Scott**, like the oft-cited design of the inside of Deckard's apartment, styled after Frank Lloyd Wright's Ennis Brown House. Interestingly, the concept art which has trickled out in Mead's albums and exhibitions over the years shows city panoramas not exactly consistent with what can be seen on the screen. Apart from the two pyramids visible in the opening shots, Mead's concept drawings are far more monumental and vertiginous (Penell 14–15, 24–25), the effect he achieved by taking "the two world trade towers in New York City and the New York street proportions as a today's model, and expand[ing] everything vertically about two and a half times." He also made "the bases of the buildings sloping to cover about six city blocks, on the premise that you needed more ground access to the building mass" (Abohela et al.).

His street-level designs are much more recognizable. The signature sidewalk Chinese diner in one of the first scenes is his creation entirely, as are designs of older buildings retro-fitted with pipes and transformers to make them usable. In visualizing them, Mead was inspired by "[p]laces like Cuba, South East Asia, India, where the technical infrastructure is forced to work beyond the point where it's new" (Zolotoev), aiming at "an exotic, technological interpretation of a Third World kind of country" (Deutelbaum 66). This description uncannily presages the later diagnoses of cyberpunk as a mode that "has a tendency of appropriating other cultural tropes and imagery (particularly from Japan) as window dressing for its narrative goals" (McFarlane, Murphy, and Schmeink 2). Mead expanded on the logic of this visual vocabulary in one of his interviews:

> Things are retro-fitted after the fact of the original manufacture because the old, consumer-based technology wasn't keeping up with demand. Things have to work on a day-to-day basis and you do whatever is necessary to make it work. So you let go of the style and it becomes pure function. The whole visual philosophy of the film is based on this social idea.
>
> (Abohela et al.)

Again, this quality certainly resonates with William Gibson's oft-cited line from "Burning Chrome" (1982): "The street finds its own use for things" (186).

Mead's designs for *Blade Runner* are thus essential in communicating one of the central qualities of the film as well as of the cyberpunk aesthetic at large: the collapse of time and space in which the global flows create layers of accumulated progress (Deutelbaum 67). Interestingly, this collapse is primarily visual, since the film's narrative retro loyalties do little to further cyberpunk's omnipresent imbrications. And while *Blade Runner*'s narrative adds a voice to the discussion of the personhood of technological subjects, something that can certainly pass for a cyberpunk trope, it was Mead's vision of 2019 Los Angeles, along with his later commissions, that has since colonized—foreclosed even—urban imagination across sf audiovisual media. From film and television to short film and digital graphics, to video games, there are very few futuristic visions of the city which do not evoke, consciously or subliminally, the images of Los Angeles from *Blade Runner*.

If the cyberpunk city is Mead's single most important contribution to the mode's sensibility, it also aptly encapsulates the contradictions inherent in treating him as a cyberpunk visionary, since it stands in direct contrast to many of his other creations. The tenor of his work can be argued to be at odds with that of visual cyberpunk. While the latter's visions resonate with dark overtones and dystopic speculation, Mead's work was predominantly and unabashedly optimistic. From his design work, deeply rooted in mid-century American modernism, to his 1977 contribution to the *documenta 6* (Zeisberg), a renowned exhibition of contemporary art, to his conceptual work on *Tomorrowland* (Bird 2015), Mead's futures were informed by a seemingly sincere belief in technology-driven progress, literally and metaphorically relying on bright colors. How much of Mead's visual optimism was necessitated by his public persona of a futurist commissioned by corporate clients and how much simply reflected his Golden Age outlook is difficult to assess. There is, however, a certain irony in the fact that his non-cyberpunk designs can be interpreted as driven by the same species of racialized and class-hierarchical techno-modernity that William Gibson targeted in "The Gernsback Continuum," published in 1981, while *Blade Runner* was already in production. Mead's oeuvre thus straddles two contradictory impulses in speculative envisioning. The shining city and the dystopian metropolis, with all their accouterments and consequences, never truly reconcile in his work. While cyberpunk aficionados love to claim him as their own, in the grander scheme of work Mead was very much a happy utopian.

See also: **William Gibson, Moebius [Jean Giraud], Ridley Scott**

Note

1 See Gibson's "Tron nostalgia" tweet of July 11, 2009.

Works Cited

@*GreatDismal.* "Tron Nostalgia: When I Was Writing Neuromancer, That Was ★the★ Bleeding-Edge Digital Aesthetic. Those Sparse Green Lines! Pong, Meet Case." *Twitter,* July 11, 2009, https://twitter.com/ GreatDismal/status/2580137381.

Abohela, Islam, Amr Al-Gohary, and Khaled Dewidar. *Significance of Future Architecture in Science Fiction Films.* 2007. *ResearchGate,* https://www. researchgate.net/publication/306000011_Significance_of_Future_ Architecture_in_Science_Fiction_Films.

Barder, Ollie. "Katsuhiro Otomo On Creating *Akira* and Designing the Coolest Bike in All of Manga and Anime." *Forbes,* May 26, 2017, https://www. forbes.com/sites/ olliebarder/ 2017/05/26/ katsuhiro-otomo-on-creating- akira-and-designing-the-coolest-bike-in-all-of-manga-and-anime/.

Deutelbaum, Marshall. "Memory/Visual Design: The Remembered Sights of *Blade Runner.*" *Literature/Film Quarterly,* vol. 17, no. 1, 1989, pp. 66–72.

Gibson, William. "Burning Chrome." *Burning Chrome.* Ace, 1986, pp. 168–91.

McFarlane, Anna, Graham J. Murphy, and Lars Schmeink. "Cyberpunk as Cultural Formation." *The Routledge Companion to Cyberpunk Culture,* edited by Anna McFarlane, Graham J. Murphy, and Lars Schmeink, Routledge, 2020, pp. 1–3.

Mead, Syd. "Designing the Future." *Omni's Screen Flights, Screen Fantasies: The Future According to the Cinema,* edited by Danny Peary, Doubleday/ Dolphin, 1984, pp. 199–213.

Parsons, Margaret. "Still Separate ... but Equal?" *The Moving Image: The Journal of the Association of Moving Image Archivists,* vol. 12, no. 1, 2012, pp. 89–91. *JSTOR,* doi: 10.5749/movingimage.12.1.0089.

Patterson, Richard. "The Making of *TRON.*" *American Cinematographer,* vol. 63, no. 8, 1982, pp. 792–95, 813–19.

Penell, Markus. *Syd Mead: Future Cities.* O & O Depot, 2019, https:// web.archive.org/web/20200601221406/https://www.bmiaa.com/ syd-mead-future-cities-at-oo-depot-berlin/.

Sammon, Paul M. "The Making of *Blade Runner.*" *Cinefantastique,* vol. 12, no. 5–6, 1982, pp. 20–47.

Scroggy, David. *Blade Runner Sketchbook.* Blue Dolphin Enterprises, 1982.

Zeisberg, Alexander. "#12 A Self-Driving Car at Documenta 6." *Documenta Archiv,* July 2017, https://www.documenta-archiv.de/en/aktuell/docarts/ 940/12-a-self-driving-car-at-documenta-6.

Zolotoev, Timur. "'A Complete Remake of What We Consider Normal': *Blade Runner* Designer on the Future of Design." *Strelka Mag,* November 2017, https://strelkamag.com/en/article/syd-mead-blade-runner.

Paweł Frelik

MISHA [NOGHA/CHOCHOLAK] (1955–)

Métis / Cree author, editor, poet, and musician.

Misha has had (and continues to have) a fascinating, eclectic career. She has published the nonfiction chapbook *Dr. Ihoka's Cure* (1993) and more recently the nonfiction piece "The Thunderbird's Path" (2016) for *Lightspeed Magazine*'s special issue *People of Colo(u)r Destroy Science Fiction!*. She also has several collections of fiction and prose poems, including *Prayers of Steel* (1988), *Ke-Qua-Hawk-As* (1994), and *Magpies & Tigers* (2007), the first two titles initially published as chapbooks and later collected as *Walk the Red Road: Collected Fiction* (2013). Several of her poems and stories have been used as libretti for musical compositions, most notably an arrangement of her story "Tsuki Mangetsu" (1988), which won the 1989 *Prix d'Italia*. Misha has also published over thirty short stories: "Chippoke na Gomi" (1989) is reprinted in *The Wesleyan Anthology of Science Fiction* and the poems "Wire Movement #9" (1983) and "Wire for Two Tims" (1983) appear in Larry McCaffery's *Storming the Reality Studio: A Casebook of Cyberpunk & Postmodern Science Fiction*. She even writes Indigenous remixes of the literary western, including two contributions to Cynthia Ward's collections *Lost Trails: Forgotten Tales of the Weird West* (2015) and *Lost Trails 2* (2016) and a forthcoming magical realist western titled *Yellowjacket*. Arguably, however, Misha is best known for her acclaimed cyberpunk novel *Red Spider White Web* (1990), which won the 1990 ReaderCon Award, was a finalist for the 1991 Arthur C. Clarke Award, and an excerpt of which appears in *Walking the Clouds: An Anthology of Indigenous Science Fiction*, Grace Dillon's (Anishinaabe) foundational anthology of Indigenous futurisms. *Red Spider White Web* marks Misha as an important figure for both Indigenous futurisms and Indigenous cyberpunk, and according to her website Misha has plans to write a sequel titled *The Bell Factory*.

Red Spider White Web (like many of Misha's fictions) is set in a world filled with nuclear radiation, toxic waste, trash, and pollutants, and her protagonists are subjected to medical experimentation, environmentally induced illness, and sexual violence. In this vein, Misha's fiction differs from most cyberpunk of the late-1980s by focusing on ecological and feminist themes, eschewing the masculinist fantasies that were ascribed to print cyberpunk's earliest wave. Critics such as Nicola Nixon, Karen Cadora, and, more recently, Carlen Lavigne, Lisa Yaszek, and Patricia Melzer have commented on print cyberpunk's initial heteronormative conservatism. "Early cyberpunk," Melzer writes, "has a tendency to 'plug-in' conservative, occasionally reactionary, heteronormative gender and sexual notions into a narrative frame that explores intersections of technology and embodiment" (292). As a result, Mary Catherine Harper situates Misha alongside **Pat Cadigan**, Laura J. Mixon, Lisa Mason, and Sue Thomas as "feminist-oriented cyborg writers" in the cyberpunk movement precisely for her focus on embodiment, particularly commoditized feminized bodies (399). At the same time, early cyberpunk has a track record of reproducing and reifying whiteness by making racial identities largely "obsolescent, as if cyberspace is not a racially coded environment" (Lavender 310). Corinna Lenhardt therefore connects Misha's interest in vulnerable bodies to Indigenous histories of colonialism, medical abuse, and sexual violence, suggesting that by writing a character who "survives, endures, and resists actively against the annihilating oppression of the hegemonic rulers and art colonizers" (347) of a bleak world, Misha both deconstructs the raced and gendered binaries which inform the work of many of her cyberpunk contemporaries and creates a space for 'survivance.' Survivance is Anishinaabe writer Gerald Vizenor's neologism for Indigenous survival and resistance. For Vizenor, "survivance creates a sense of native presence over absence, nihility, and victimry" (1). By foregrounding survivance in cyberpunk, Misha emphasizes the physical, economic, and social precarity entailed by the creation of posthuman bodies without presenting these characters as victims whose absence paves the way for a technological future that they have no stake in. In sum, Misha has a unique perspective on cyberpunk's fascination with the posthuman, always returning to a posthuman body that is vulnerable, disabled, queer, and non-white. Or, as Elyce Helford describes it, this is "everything cyberpunk should have been but wasn't" (cited in *The Wesleyan Anthology of Science Fiction*, 630).

Like much of her prose and poetry, *Red Spider White Web* is very vivid and visceral. As she explains in an interview with Marc Laidlaw, "I wanted [*Red Spider White Web*] to be a book for brain and viscera. The kennings, alliterations and assonances and metaphors and sounds colors smells tastes feelings, living through all six senses." Misha's background as a poet and a musician are clearly reflected in the lyricism of her writing, such as when *Red Spider White Web* opens with the fragmented point of view of a serial killer following his victim: "His circuit is a skull juggler, He's a factory guard who stalks the silent chemical night. Eye guard translucent aquariums of red spiders.

Arachnid fury. Hai shimasu! The towers. The tower spiders. Insect elegance hums. Static treachery. Splashy soshing smelt. Chotto! Kadiskadiskadish. Smelt in season" (11). This fragmented lyrical language captures Misha's style of cyberpunk posthumanism, navigating between a world of environmental waste, technological augmentation, and shamanistic animality, demonstrating the violent actions of human characters are always presupposed by the violence of the world itself, particularly the structural violence of environmental racism, capitalism, and colonialism. She really puts the "meat" into "meat-space" and in so doing the digital life of computer hackers that is common in much cyberpunk is, at most, a background element in a cyberpunk world formed from "splashy soshing smelt."

Misha also transforms cyberpunk's punk attitude into a trickster performance. This is particularly apparent in the values of *Red Spider White Web*'s artist community, who live in the garbage-strewn wasteland of "Ded Tek" outside of the centralized commercial dome cities of "Mickey-san," the novel's analog for the Disney corporation. As Sherryl Vint argues, the novel "takes as its central theme the struggle by art and artists to survive in the familiar cyberpunk landscape of multinational capital, network culture, corporate governance, and economic crisis" (95–96). The protagonist of *Red Spider White Web*, the part-wolverine Indigenous woman Kumo, most clearly embodies this artistic outsider perspective. Kumo compares herself to a number of nonhuman Cree and Japanese trickster figures—"Speel-yi [...] Kw-qua-hawk-as, Tanuki, Kitsune" (94)—as she creates violent and beautiful holograms from fragments of discarded technology, offering a unique spin on **William Gibson**'s cyberpunk adage that "the street finds its own uses for things" (186). In addition, Kumo's history as a part-wolverine genetic hybrid and her salvaged art both speak to the novel's anti-capitalist politics. In a discussion of her story "The Stone Badger" (1991), Misha describes the thematic resonances she sees between anti-capitalist art and Cree and Métis storytelling, particularly stories about the cannibal figure of the Windigo:

> The Windigo is a creature who is essentially a skeleton of ice. To me, he is the epitome of the corporate world. He keeps gobbling up everything in sight—people, trees, animals, rocks—and his hunger is never satiated [...] In the tales, only a weasel, a badger, or a wolverine can kill a Windigo by climbing down its throat and chewing up its icy heart.
>
> (Laidlaw)

While the Windigo may be absent from *Red Spider White Web*, the novel plays out a similar trickster story by pitting a technologically augmented wolverine woman against the insatiable corporate control exerted by the Mickey-san corporation.

This artistic struggle against multinational capital and Kumo's oppositional trickster art also characterizes Misha's own publishing history. Misha got her start as a writer publishing experimental flash-fiction in the 'zine *Factsheet Five*. Most of her chapbooks and collections are published by the small press Wordcraft of Oregon, which operates as an independent, local press for Oregon artists seeking an alternative to larger commercial publishing houses. While this means that some of her early work is now out of print and very difficult to find, her collaborations with Wordcraft demonstrate the value she places on radical, underground science fiction artistic communities. In addition to her own writing, Misha was the fiction editor for *New Pathways into Science Fiction and Fantasy* for several years (under her modified name Michelle Chocholak), as well as a regular contributor for interviews and reviews. Misha had a strong impact on the magazine's direction, attracting several cyberpunk writers such as Paul Di Filippo, K.W. Jeter, and Bruce Sterling, along with cyberpunk illustrations by Tim MacNamara (under the pseudonym "Ferret") and Matt Howarth. She describes her editing philosophy as consciously anti-commercial, asking writers, "what story did you have in the bottom of the drawer that you really wanted to be published that everyone rejected?" (Laidlaw). Her review column "Points of Impact" appeared in *New Pathways*, *Ice River*, and *Science Fiction Eye*. A tongue-in-cheek commentary on reviews that merely summarize a book without adding anything of substance, "Points of Impact" consisted of photographs of Misha destroying books in different ways, including, once, by introducing a paperback to a live wolf.

In sum, Misha has had an enduring influence on cyberpunk culture. In her editing work she created connections between formally experimental sf, cyberpunk, and visual art. As cyberpunk is increasingly popularized through highly visual film and game texts, Misha's viscerally lyrical writing showcases how important poetry and prose can be for the mode; for example, we can see her influence in the recent development of Indigenous cyberpunk through works like Brian Hudson's (Cherokee) short story "Digital Medicine" (2016) and Joshua Whitehead's (Oji-Cree) poetry collection *Full-Metal Indigiqueer: the Pro(1,0)zoa* (2017). In a cultural mode associated with digital frontiers, Misha continues to redirect cyberpunk's posthuman politics toward the original frontiers—occupied native land—finding survivance in even the most bleakly dystopian futures.

See also: **Pat Cadigan, William Gibson**

Works Cited

Cadora, Karen. "Feminist Cyberpunk." *Science Fiction Studies*, vol. 22, no. 3, 1995, pp. 357–72.

Dillon, Grace, editor. *Walking the Clouds: An Anthology of Indigenous Science Fiction*. U of Arizona P, 2012.

Evans, Arthur B. et al., editor. *The Wesleyan Anthology of Science Fiction*. Wesleyan UP, 2010.

Gibson, William. "Burning Chrome." *Burning Chrome*. Ace, 1986, pp. 168–91.

Harper, Mary Catherine. "Incurably Alien Other: A Case for Feminist Cyborg Writers." *Science Fiction Studies*, vol. 22, no. 3, 1995, pp. 399–420.

Laidlaw, Marc. "Interview: Misha Nogha and the Weird." *Weird Fiction Review*, November 20, 2012, weirdfictionreview.com/2012/11/interview-misha-nogha-and-the-weird/.

Lavender III, Isiah. "Critical Race Theory." *The Routledge Companion to Cyberpunk Culture*, edited by Anna McFarlane, Graham J. Murphy, and Lars Schmeink, Routledge, 2020, pp. 308–16.

Lenhardt, Corinna. "Indigenous Futurisms." *The Routledge Companion to Cyberpunk Culture*, edited by Anna McFarlane, Graham J. Murphy, and Lars Schmeink, Routledge, 2020, pp. 344–52.

Lavigne, Carlen. *Cyberpunk Women, Feminism and Science Fiction*. McFarland & Company, Inc., 2013.

Melzer, Patricia. "Cyborg Feminism." *The Routledge Companion to Cyberpunk Culture*, edited by Anna McFarlane, Graham J. Murphy, and Lars Schmeink, Routledge, 2020, pp. 291–99.

Misha. *Red Spider White Web*. Wordcraft of Oregon, 1999.

Nixon, Nicola. "Cyberpunk: Preparing the Ground for Revolution or Keeping the Boys Satisfied?" *Science Fiction Studies*, vol. 19, no. 2, 1992, pp. 219–35.

Vint, Sherryl. "'The Mainstream Finds its Own Uses for Things': Cyberpunk and Commodification." *Beyond Cyberpunk: New Critical Perspectives*, edited by Graham J. Murphy and Sherryl Vint, Routledge, 2010, pp. 95–115.

Vizenor, Gerald. "Aesthetics of Survivance: Literary Theory and Practice." *Survivance: Narratives of Native Presence*, edited by Gerald Vizenor, U Nebraska P, 2008, pp. 1–23.

Yaszek, Lisa. "Feminist Cyberpunk." *The Routledge Companion to Cyberpunk Culture*, edited by Anna McFarlane, Graham J. Murphy, and Lars Schmeink, Routledge, 2020, pp. 32–40.

Stina Attebery

MOEBIUS [JEAN GIRAUD] (1938–2012)

French cartoonist, artist, and writer.

Jean Giraud—a.k.a. Moebius—was born in France in 1938 and started drawing comics in the late 1950s for a variety of French comics magazines. Under his real name, he found success in 1963 with the western series *Blueberry*, written by Jean-Michel Charlier and published in *Pilote* magazine. Although he worked on *Blueberry* for forty years, Giraud had also been interested in science fiction (sf) since childhood; thus, throughout the 1960s he provided numerous covers and inside illustrations for French sf publishers (Opta, Club du Livre d'Anticipation). In a 1970 interview, he still described the idea of drawing an entire sf comic story as daunting (Moliterni and Giraud 7), and focused on drawing one or two *Blueberry* albums a year. He overcame this reluctance in the following years, and started experimenting graphically and narratively, both in *Pilote* and in *L'Écho des savanes*, a publication started by a trio of *Pilote* artists in 1972 under the influence of American underground comix. To differentiate this body of work from *Blueberry*, he revived the pseudonym Moebius, which he had used briefly in the early 1960s.

While Giraud continued drawing, then scripting successful westerns, including several *Blueberry* spinoffs, Moebius became closely associated with sf. *The Horny Goof* (*Le Bandard Fou*; 1974) was his first full-fledged sf story (some of his early comics in *Hara-Kiri* had contained horror and sf allusions), a gleefully obscene and parodic book hewing to the aesthetics of the transgressive underground comix of the time. Later in the same year, Moebius became one of the founders of *Métal Hurlant*, an adult-themed sf comic magazine with high production values, which quickly became the cutting edge of the genre in visual culture and was read and admired across Europe and in the United States, even by non-Francophone readers. The three artists among the magazine's founders—Moebius, Phillippe Druillet, and Jean-Pierre Dionnet—were all avid consumers of sf, and *Métal Hurlant*, as well as the adult French comics scene in general, was deeply influenced by American sf. However, not unlike what was happening in underground comix Moebius and this larger retinue of visionaries did not want to mimic sf conventions; for example, the futures depicted in *Métal Hurlant*'s space opera parodies were often worn down, with decaying technology that frequently took on organic features. When the publisher of *National Lampoon* started publishing a localized version of *Métal Hurlant* in the United States in 1977 (rebranded as *Heavy Metal*), the American version initially relied almost entirely on French material, while other local versions of *Métal Hurlant* started appearing across Europe, exposing this cutting-edge French aesthetic to a global audience In all these variants, Moebius and his visual artistry were the stars of the publication, making him one of the few truly international stars of comics in the late 1970s.

Although Moebius contributed several major sf series to early *Métal Hurlant*—*Arzach* (1975), *The Hermetic Garage* (1976–79), and numerous vignettes—his most influential work of that period is arguably "The Long Tomorrow," a 16-page short story written by Dan O'Bannon, published in two parts in *Métal Hurlant* #7 and #8 (1976), followed by its republishing in *Heavy Metal* #4 and #5 a year later. Moebius had met O'Bannon while the two of them were working on Alejandro Jodorowsky's mid-1970s failed adaptation of Frank Herbert's *Dune* (1965). In "The Long Tomorrow," O'Bannon had written and sketched a compact sf neo-noir/hard-boiled detective plot, complete with first-person narration and a treacherous femme fatale. Like much of what appeared in *Métal Hurlant*, the story verges on parody, and its use of noir conventions is so strictly predictable as to become humorous. However, Moebius turned O'Bannon's words into a fully realized vision of a decaying multi-level city in which hovercars and rocket launch pads coexist with low-level punks and oppressive automated law enforcement. Although the narrative structure and some of the fashion elements anchor the story in the mid-twentieth century, the decaying subway and the graffitied bars more closely resemble the damaged infrastructure of late-1970s metropolises. The city as depicted by Moebius was unobstructed by the limitations of audiovisual special effects, from the Elysian setting of the upper-class to the last decaying subterranean bar, nearly 200 levels below. "The Long Tomorrow" echoes Thierry Smolderen's reading of *Blueberry*: "Instead of simplifying space, as is traditionally done in comics, to leave more room for the figures in the foreground, [Giraud/Moebius] loses himself in his own backgrounds: each brushstroke becomes a microscopic story" (Groesteen and Ciment 12). These microscopic stories, here told with a nib rather than a brush, are everywhere: for instance, a tiny droid, seen in one panel and a few millimeters high, was sufficiently detailed to provide the design for the imperial droid in the opening sequence of *The Empire Strikes Back* (Kershner 1980) (Heileman). In addition, the unnamed city of "The Long Tomorrow" is full of flying cars, robots, and shapeshifting aliens, the texture of every object, the signs and the all-too contemporary squalor realizing a fusion which Bruce Sterling later described in his Preface to *Mirrorshades: The Cyberpunk Anthology* (1986) as a key to the cyberpunk mode: "the underground world of pop culture, visionary fluidity, and street-level anarchy" (xii).

While "The Long Tomorrow" was never officially adapted, its direct influence was quickly felt in cyberpunk's formative years. For example, American film director **Ridley Scott** instructed his design team for *Blade Runner* (1982) to take inspiration from the short story (cited in Lauzrika), and the visual lineage between the two cities is visible in architectural details, in some of the most vertical passages of the films, and in the conflation of 1950s fashion with 1970s street scenes. If Scott Bukatman is correct that "[c]yberpunk provided *the* image of the future in the 1980s" and the "aesthetic of cyberpunk was almost defined by *Blade Runner*" (58; 50), then *Blade Runner's* visual aesthetic was most certainly defined by Moebius. Meanwhile, in his introduction to the graphic novel adaptation of *Neuromancer*, released on Marvel Comics' imprint Epic Comics in 1989, **William Gibson** mentioned how the French artists of *Heavy Metal* influenced "the way *Neuromancer*-the-novel 'looks'" by offering a sharply different visual approach from "anything [he] was seeing on the covers of SF paperbacks or magazines" (5). Gibson is certainly referring to Moebius and "The Long Tomorrow" because on another occasion, in an interview celebrating the 10th anniversary of *Blade Runner*, Gibson remarks that he "was having lunch with Ridley [Scott] and when the conversation turned to inspiration, we were both very clear about our debt to the *Métal Hurlant* school of the '70s—Moebius and the others" (cited in Loud).

In addition to "The Long Tomorrow," Moebius and Chilean director Alejandro Jodorowsky (of the infamous *Dune* adaptation failure) started publishing *The Incal* (1980–88) in *Métal Hurlant*, with a translation in a *Heavy Metal* special graphic novel the same year. Though the series spans a variety of sf subgenres, the first volume closely resembles "The Long Tomorrow" and opens with a similar hard-boiled detective caught in impenetrable machinations and in the implacable power structure of a sprawling vertical city. Compared to the compact "The Long Tomorrow," *The Incal* gradually broadens the scope of the narrative over six volumes, exploring the sewers and the elite quarters at length, before tackling an entire mystical galactic war. The first volumes are also notable for their more sustained attention to the media, presented alternatively as a sycophant to the aristocracy and as peddlers of ultra-violent entertainment. At the same time, while *The Incal* straddles the emergence of the cyberpunk movement in many of its thematic and visual tropes, it does gradually move away from its focus on technology and urban sprawl in favor of a grander and more symbolic vision, imbued with religion and messianism.

Moebius's work is also visible in Steven Lisberger's *TRON* (1983), for which he storyboarded the nascent film. He shared the design work with **Syd Mead**, who would go on to be the main designer for *Blade Runner*, and while some of the iconic visuals of the films were designed by Mead (e.g., the light cycles), Moebius's work is visible throughout: in the costumes, vehicles and buildings, helping shape a memorable vision of what was yet to be called cyberspace. Nevertheless, Moebius moved away from his major contributions to cyberpunk by the time *TRON* was released in theaters. By 1983, he was openly embracing a "crystalline" style in his visuals (Groesteen and Ciment 38–41), aiming for clarity and sparseness, and gradually shedding the proliferating backgrounds which had made him so crucial in shaping visual sf since the mid-1970s. His next series, *The Aedena Cycle* (1983–2001), initially took the form of a pastoral mystical parable, and although it eventually returns to a highly stylized totalitarian city, it makes no pretense to describe a plausible near-future as in his earlier work.

While Moebius may have moved away from cyberpunk motifs in his later work, the influence of his cyberpunk-oriented material is unmistakable. For example, Moebius exerted a strong influence on **Katsuhiro Ōtomo** during the late-1970s before the famed Japanese manga artist began to draw *Akira* (1982–90). Though Ōtomo's style was already well defined at that point, the gritty vision of Neo-Tokyo in *Akira* bears a strong resemblance to Moebius's decaying cities, and in a text published upon Moebius's death, Ōtomo specifically mentions "The Long Tomorrow" as a source of inspiration (Ransom). The early urban episodes in *Akira* also serve as the basis for Ōtomo's *Akira* anime (1998), which helped popularize this visual aesthetic worldwide. In the United States, *Akira* and Moebius's complete works were published roughly at the same time by Marvel's Epic Comics, with Moebius contributing a pin-up illustration to the last issue of Ōtomo's comic-book edition. We can also see Moebius's influence in the depictions of urban life in Frank Miller and Geoff Darrow's *Hard-Boiled* (1990–92) and Frank Miller and Lynn Varley's *Ronin* (1983–84), while **Warren Ellis** and

Darick Robertson acknowledged their debt to Moebius by invit-
ing him to draw three covers (#49–51) of their cyberpunk opus
Transmetropolitan (1997–2002).

Celebrated worldwide as an artist whose influence far exceeds the
realm of comic books, Moebius passed away in 2012. Though his most
significant contributions to the cyberpunk mode date back to a half-
a-decade of groundbreaking work—from "The Long Tomorrow" to
The Incal—his influence remains perceptible to this day, evidenced
most recently in the repetition of Moebius's visual aesthetic in Netflix's
Altered Carbon (2018–2020) and the animated *Altered Carbon: Resleeved*
(2020), both of which are adaptations of **Richard K. Morgan**'s
Takeshi Kovacs novels (2002–05), as well as CD Projekt's *Cyberpunk
2077* video game (2020). Moebius's vision from the late-1970s has
thus helped shape and define the 'looks' of cyberpunk across media
for over four decades.

See also: **Warren Ellis, William Gibson, Syd Mead, Richard K.
Morgan, Katsuhiro Ōtomo, Ridley Scott**

Works Cited

Bukatman, Scott. *Blade Runner.* 2nd ed., Palgrave Macmillan/BFI, 2012.

Groensteen, Thierry and Gilles Ciment. *Trait de génie: Giraud-Moebius.* Centre
national de la Bande dessinée et de l'image, 2000.

Gibson, William. Introduction. *Neuromancer—The Graphic Novel.* Epic
Comics, 1989, p. 5.

Heileman, Michael. "The Mœbius Probe." *Kitbashed. The Origins of Star
Wars*, 2015, https://kitbashed.com/blog/moebius.

de Lauzirika, Charles. *Dangerous Days: Making Blade Runner.* Blade Runner
Partnership, Lauzirika Motion Picture Company, Warner Home Video,
2007.

Loud, Lance. "*Blade Runner.*" Video Vérité, n.d., videoverite.tv/pages/
llwritingbladerunner.html.

Moebius and Numa Sadoul. *Mœbius, entretiens avec Numa Sadoul.* Casterman,
1991.

Moliterni, Claude and Giraud, Jean 'Moebius.' Interview de Gir. *Phénix*, vol.
14, 1970, pp. 2–15.

Ransom, Ko. "Akira's Katsuhiro Otomo Remembers French Artist
Moebius." *Anime News Network*, September 4, 2012, https://www.
animenewsnetwork.com/interest/2012-04-09/akira-katsuhiro-otomo-
remembers-french-artist-moebius.

Sterling, Bruce. Preface. *Mirrorshades: The Cyberpunk Anthology*, edited by
Bruce Sterling, Ace, 1986, pp. ix–xvi.

Nicolas Labarre

JANELLE MONÁE [ROBINSON] (1985–)

American singer-songwriter, rapper, record producer, activist, actress, and author.

Janelle Monáe is noteworthy for her Afrofuturistic concept albums and accompanying music videos, which she describes as "emotion pictures," in which she explores the figure of the android to represent the oppressed Other. She first entered the music scene with her self-financed demo album *The Audition* (2003), although it was not until her EP *Metropolis: The Chase Suite* (2007) that she gained major public recognition. Inspired by Fritz Lang and Thea von Harbou's 1927 film of the same name, the *Metropolis* EP introduces Monáe's alter-ego, Cindi Mayweather, an android rebel from the future who figures prominently throughout her work. Mayweather (and the surrounding narrative) infuses both Monáe's debut full-length album *The ArchAndroid: Suites II and III* (2010) and the highly acclaimed *The Electric Lady: Suites IV and V* (2013), the latter featuring guest appearances by her mentor Prince, as well as Erykah Badu and Esperanza Spalding. Her award-nominated *Dirty Computer* (2018)—both the LP and the visual emotion picture—envisions a cyberpunk reality in which individuals are oppressed by the police state for being 'different' (i.e., dirty computers), which is coded as non-compliant according to a set of heteronormative and white socio-political structures. In 2020 she released "Turntables," a music video/emotion picture as part of the Amazon Studios' bipartisan voter registration campaign. Monáe is also known as an actress and is slated to release her short story collection *The Memory Librarian: And Other Stories of Dirty Computer* in mid-2022.

Monáe incorporates science-fictionality as a storytelling mode across all of what she calls her "space ships" (cited in English & Kim 218)—i.e., songs, concept albums, emotion pictures and music videos, stage performances, and fashion. This allows her to express her views on current social and political matters. Although more commonly associated with Afrofuturism and Black queer futurity than cyberpunk, Monáe has repeatedly incorporated cyberpunk tropes and motifs. Importantly, Monáe is continuously reframing the traditional understanding of cyberpunk by enriching it with three components integral to her oeuvre— Blackness, sexuality, and gender—and in so doing, she draws the audience's attention to those elements which have so far been underrepresented in "masculinist cyberpunk" (Cadora 357).[1]

Monáe's first three concept albums feature her Cindi Mayweather alter-ego from the year 2719. Cindi is an indentured android who has fallen desperately in love with a human (Anthony Greendown) and has been "scheduled for immediate disassembly" because of her insubordination. As a rebellious and revolutionary outsider who functions as an advocate for the ostracized and marginalized, Cindi is "a cyber-girl without a face, a heart, or a mind" ("Violet Stars Happy Hunting!" from *Metropolis: The Chase Suite*, 2007). This time-traveling messianic figure intends to free the city from the Great Divide, "a secret society which has been using time travel to suppress freedom and love throughout the ages" (Monáe). Along with her "dangerous accomplice" Badoula Oblongata (Erykah Badu), Cindi is a member of a group of rebels called Wondaland, named after The Wondaland Arts Society, Monáe's Atlanta-based studio/artist collective record label. Monáe and Badu's "Q.U.E.E.N."—"Q": queer community; "U": untouchables; "E": emigrants; "E": the excommunicated; and "N": those labeled as negroid (Benjamin)—is the vocal anthem of this "gang." Importantly, these marginalized groups resemble the "anti-heroes" and "punks" (criminals, outcasts, and hackers) common to cyberpunk.[2]

In *Dirty Computer*, Monáe develops the character of Jane 57821, who is considered a "dirty computer" because she refuses to conform to the policies of a dystopian state. One of her "sins" is her relationship with both the male character, Ché (Jayson Aaron), and the female character, Zen (Tessa Thompson). As *Dirty Computer* (and her wider oeuvre) demonstrates, a major theme in Monáe's work is forbidden love, either between two races (with androids representing the Other) or genders (Jane is having an intimate relationship with both a man and a woman), a theme that has taken on greater resonance since Monáe revealed in 2018 that she identifies as pansexual (Spanos). Nevertheless, Jane 57821 undergoes a punishing memory wipe, setting up the context for the individual music videos that were released alongside the LP: "Django Jane," "PYNK," "Crazy, Classic, Life," "Screwed," and the Prince-inflected "Make Me Feel." As Christine Capetola writes, Monáe is

> [t]aking cues from the disco-inspired genres of house and techno, Prince and other black pop stars in the 1980s [who] were intimately engaged in exploring these lines of tension between (wo)man and machine. In *Dirty Computer*, "Make Me Feel" is a moment of not only referencing Prince's sound but also of thinking along with him about the differences, if any, between humans and machines.

(249)

Finally, *Dirty Computer* suggests the protagonist Jane 57821 is a projection of Monáe's future self, since 'Jane' can be read as a modification of 'Janelle' while both Cindi and Jane hold the same serial number, suggesting *Dirty Computer* is a prequel to the Metropolis Saga.

Given her worry that certain groups might continue to be oppressed in the future, particularly in *Dirty Computer*'s totalitarian society, Janelle Monáe is an inimitable contributor to the framework of Black queer cyberpunk. As a pansexual spokesperson celebrating diverse sexualities, Monáe embraces the label "freak" and her refusal to perform her socially ascribed gender role is manifested through fashion choices (she routinely wears a black and white tuxedo) as well as her pompadour, Monáe's signature hairstyle. Her attires are frequently future-oriented, masculine or unisex with a classic twist alluding to the fashion of the Jim Crow era. Monáe also pays homage to her working-class roots by donning uniforms. They may be regarded as her own way of (re) gaining control over her body and proving that uniforms, traditionally associated with depriving a person of their individuality, can function as a tool for self-expression. Monáe pairs fashion with her dance abilities, skills that are deployed as a disruptive tool to the oppressive systems that constrain the 'dirty computers' of the world. As a hacker of female fashion whose resistance is in part focused on the power of dance to destabilize heteronormative structures, Monáe restates and re-organizes her body and its meaning and acquires multiple forms, not only as an artist but also as a "queer Black woman in America" (Spanos). Thus, where multiple cyberpunk narratives imagine a color-blind vision of the future,[3] Monáe envisions the world inhabited by non-white and non-binary individuals who continue to face stigmatization. In so doing, Monáe never fails to reflect cyberpunk's potential to portray the contemporary political climate, embodied in *Dirty Computer*'s "progressive edge" (Vernallis 251) as the album resonates with America's socio-political climate and the ways in which people of color and the LGBTQ+ community are oppressed by the state, particularly during President Trump's administration (2016–20).

Monáe's mission to tell stories that foreground "the racialized dimensions of cyberpunk's explorations of the overlaps between 'human' and 'machine'" (Capetola 246) is achieved not only by means of narrative tools but also through her visual aesthetic that makes significant contributions to cyberpunk's audiovisual component. For example, "Many Moons" is both her first music video and a futuristic short film that lays the foundation for her later work. Or "Suite II Overture" not only bears resemblance to sf (and fantasy) scores, but it accounts for an orchestrated introduction to *The ArchAndroid* and was used in the accompanying cinematic album trailer with the entire city of Metropolis sitting on Monáe's head. The premiere of *The Electric Lady* was preceded by the release of an sf trailer titled "Cindi Mayweather: Ministry of the Droids" in which the audience learns that surveillance drones are looking for the rebellious android-fugitive. Monáe also uses glitch and noise as distinctive markers of discontinuity, effectively imitating the non-linearity of the disrupted and additive character of her storytelling; thus, "I Like That" visually resembles a dream with disrupted signal, potentially simulating interrupted sleep, while "Dance Apocalyptic" features noise and glitch to imitate broken signals in the television coverage. Finally, *Dirty Computer* visually bridges cyberpunk's obsession with neon[4] and a queer gaze with 'bisexual lighting': different pink, blue, and purple tones permeate her music videos and emotion pictures, originating in "The Electric Lady" and "Prime Time" (feat. Miguel), but reaching its apotheosis in *Dirty Computer*.

In closing, Janelle Monáe is an outstanding concept and transmedia artist bringing the perspective of a non-binary individual of color to contemporary cyberpunk. She shows that neither race nor sexuality nor gender are topics that can be avoided when exploring the broad contours of cyberpunk culture. Thus, Monáe "creates her own black, queer, and feminist version of cyberpunk through interfacing her body and musical technology" (Capetola 246). Her artistic activity, auditory imagery, and thematic preoccupations enrich cyberpunk with her perspectives on feminism, race, and queerness, and her imaging of the future through a Black cultural lens grounds Monáe as not only the key figure in (Afro)cyberpunk media but a true revolutionary within and beyond cyberpunk culture.

See also: **Steven Barnes, Samuel R. Delany, Nalo Hopkinson**

Notes

1 In addition to Cadora, see also Nixon, Lavigne, and Yaszek for details about "masculinist cyberpunk."
2 During the "Cybernetic Chantdown" that concludes "Many Moons," Monáe enumerates other names and associations stigmatized in American society: crack whore, misfit, tomboy, weirdo, and those with bad hair. Interestingly, some of them are used to reference Black women, a group largely underrepresented in cyberpunk narratives.
3 See Lavender III for details on cyberpunk and color-blindness.
4 See Pawel Frelik's "Incarnations of Light" for a sustained analysis of cyberpunk and neon.

Works Cited

Benjamin, Jeff. "Janelle Monae Says 'Q.U.E.E.N.' Is for the 'Ostracized & Marginalized.'" *Fuse*, September 19, 2013, https://fuse.tv/videos/2013/09/janelle-monae-queen-interview.

Cadora, Karen. "Feminist Cyberpunk." *Science Fiction Studies*, vol. 22, no. 3, 1995, pp. 357–72.

Capetola, Christine. "Janelle Monáe: Dirty Computer (Case Study)." *The Routledge Companion to Cyberpunk Culture*, edited by Anna McFarlane, Graham J. Murphy, and Lars Schmeink, Routledge, 2020, pp. 245–51.

English, Daylanne K. and Alvin Kim. "Now We Want Our Funk Cut: Janelle Monáe's Neo-Afrofuturism." *American Studies*, vol. 52, no. 4, 2013, pp. 217–30.

Frelik, Pawel. "'Silhouettes of Strange Illuminated Mannequins': Cyberpunk's Incarnations of Light." *Cyberpunk and Visual Culture*, edited by Graham J. Murphy and Lars Schmeink, Routledge, 2018, pp. 80–99.

Lavender III, Isiah. "Critical Race Theory." *The Routledge Companion to Cyberpunk Culture*, edited by Anna McFarlane, Graham J. Murphy, and Lars Schmeink, Routledge, 2020, pp. 308–16.

Lavigne, Carlen. *Cyberpunk Women, Feminism and Science Fiction: A Critical Study*. McFarland & Company, Inc., 2013.

Monáe, Janelle. Liner Notes for *The ArchAndroid*. Big Beat Records, 2011.

Nixon, Nicola. "Cyberpunk: Preparing the Ground for Revolution or Keeping the Boys Satisfied?" *Science Fiction Studies*, vol. 19, no. 2, 1992, pp. 219–35.

Spanos, Brittany. "Janelle Monáe Frees Herself." *Rolling Stone*, April 26, 2018, https://www.rollingstone.com/music/music-features/janelle-monae-frees-herself-629204/.

Vernallis, Carol, et al. "Janelle Monáe's Dirty Computer Music Video/Film: A Collective Reading." *Journal of the Society for American Music*, vol. 13, no. 2, 2019, pp. 250–71.

Yaszek, Lisa. "Feminist Cyberpunk" *The Routledge Companion to Cyberpunk Culture*, edited by Anna McFarlane, Graham J. Murphy, and Lars Schmeink, Routledge, 2020, pp. 32–40.

Lidia Kniaź-Hunek

RICHARD K. MORGAN (1965–)

British science fiction, fantasy, comic book, and video game author.

Richard K. Morgan has amassed an impressive corpus of work since his literary debut with *Altered Carbon* (2002): he has published nine novels, a handful of comic book projects (including two volumes of Marvel's *Black Widow*; 2005–06), and helped write two science fiction (sf) video games (*Crysis 2* [Crytek; 2011] and *Syndicate*

[Starbreeze Studios; 2012]). He has won the Philip K. Dick Award (*Altered Carbon*), the John W. Campbell Memorial Award (*Market Forces*; 2004), and the Arthur C. Clarke Award (*Black Man/Th1rte3n*; 2007), but he is most recognizable for his Takeshi Kovacs novels (*Altered Carbon*, *Broken Angels* [2003], *Woken Furies* [2005]), particularly following their adaptation by Netflix (*Altered Carbon*; 2018–20) and the spin-off anime *Altered Carbon: Resleeved* (2020). Except for his fantasy trilogy, A Land Fit for Heroes (*The Steel Remains* [2008]; *The Cold Commands* [2011]; *The Dark Defiles*, [2014]), Morgan has earned a reputation as a hard sf writer of fast-paced thrillers, drawing explicitly on hard-boiled detective motifs common to some cyberpunk fiction. Manipulating and reaffirming those motifs, however, have helped define Morgan as an important, contradictory, and problematic voice in cyberpunk culture.

Morgan's fiction, particularly the Takeshi Kovacs trilogy, tends toward violent machismo and political authoritarianism, typically incorporated through his choice of hypermasculine protagonists closely aligned (or formerly aligned) with military powers. A prime example is the ex-military special forces agent Takeshi Kovacs, who is an elite posthuman weapon known as an Envoy, raised and trained to solve problems with violence. Similarly, *Black Man* features physically upgraded 'Thirteens' who are aggressive military assets confined to 'reservations' or exiled to Mars, at least until they escape and are hunted down by the hypermasculine (and genetically engineered) Carl Marsalis. Finally, *Thin Air* is set in the same universe as *Black Man* and Hakan Veil is an equally violent protagonist as Kovacs or Marsalis, although as a 'hybernoid' he must spend four months of every year in cryogenic suspension. In typical cyberpunk fashion, these protagonists are often rootless, and Morgan emphasizes their isolation. For example, after having been uploaded to a new body—a 'sleeve'—after 250 years offline, *Altered Carbon*'s Kovacs is detached from both his environment and his original skin. This detachment breeds cynicism, and while Kovacs is often placed in situations encouraging him to stand up for (or avenge) others, his experience and emotions take priority and he does not bond with those he helps (Frelik, "Woken" 179).

In many of his novels, Morgan is clearly incorporating and reproducing the noir stylings that fueled much early cyberpunk; in fact, Morgan admits he has "ransacked the genre" (Bullock 2014), but he also borrows from military and political fictions for inspiration. Nevertheless, he remains recognizably indebted to cyberpunk in his commitment to cyberpunk aesthetics and construction of human subjectivity (Frelik, "Woken" 173–74). At the same time, the use of such tropes as implantable wetware and interplanetary travel emphasizes the sociological and economic issues of his worlds. For example, his protagonists are intimately familiar with systems of government and corporate control—the former often absent in the first wave of print cyberpunk—and experience first-hand how omnipresent authoritarian powers assert dominance, often through military force. His protagonists' connections to government-sponsored military action, albeit often in service to corporate interests, differ from the purely corporate and private power struggles most common to cyberpunk, struggles that often ignore or disempower government authority. In addition, despite arguments that Morgan's novels depict the wider population exhibiting an acute political apathy (Bullock 2014) or a critique of unrealistic idealism fueling revolutionary groups, novels such as *Woken Furies* exhibit an optimism toward those counter-politics aimed directly at the authoritarian figures in his novels (Frelik, "Woken" 182). While cyberpunk aesthetics saturate his work, Morgan also focuses on enduring governmental and/or authoritarian powers that diversify cyberpunk's political focus. In other words, Morgan deploys cyberpunk's noir aesthetics to focus on both the poor conditions of those exploited by financial inequality and those centralized political forces actively repressing mass political change to reaffirm the socio-economic status quo.[1]

Morgan's fictions are not without controversy and, in some cases, contradictions. For example, despite the bullets and blood that dominate his writing, he quizzically maintains he is "not a fan of violence," except in entertainment (Flood). He claims the violence in his fictions is about the wasted potential of human behavior and encourages his audience to step away from self-identification with characters who pay terrible costs for their actions. Violence should be sickening (Bullock), but in an ironic fashion it seems his popularity rests upon his audience not getting the memo. After all, while Morgan's protagonists may be addicted to violence, their successes often depend on it, which complicates Morgan's contradictory criticism of the process.

Morgan's seeming glorification of hypermasculinity has also proven problematic. On the one hand, his novels break at times from the "relative paucity of strong female characters in [early] cyberpunk" (Nixon 222); for example, the Kovacs books depict women at the head of 'viable' alternative politics (Frelik, "Woken" 182) while *Thin Air* locates women in high criminal and governmental strata. On the other hand, the depicted hypermasculinity seemingly reasserts cyberpunk as a "boys club" (Cadora 357) that hearkens back to the mode's 1980s-era foundational texts—i.e., **William Gibson, Bruce**

Sterling, **Rudy Rucker**, **Lewis Shiner**, and others—that have been the topic of feminist criticism. Morgan's male-centric perspective decentralizes women's overall importance, seemingly ignoring the diversification that was undertaken by 1990s-era feminist cyberpunk, including **Marge Piercy**, **Melissa Scott**, and **Pat Cadigan**. As a result, Morgan's hypermasculine cyborgs are a "dystopian counter-image" to what **Donna J. Haraway** describes as the "ironic feminist myth of the cyborg" (Heise-von der Lippe 268–69). Case in point: patriarchal systems are common in the Takeshi Kovacs series, and while women have risen to positions of power, excess attention is still given to the sexual capital of women and violence against female-coded sex workers. Any liberatory potential in Morgan's storyworlds is undermined by stereotypically gendered violence. In this way, Morgan reinstates "the alienation, isolation, and nihilism typically associated with masculinist cyberpunk" (Yaszek 32) and, in his undeniable ability to tell an exciting story, he risks tethering cyberpunk to the heteronormative, hypermasculine narrative framework of yesteryear.

Despite the above problems, Morgan's explorations of fragmented selves align in some ways with similar concerns in feminist cyberpunk (Cadora 368), particularly around the importance of biological corporeality. In the Kovacs books, there may appear to be a separation of mind and body: consciousness is digitally recorded, stored, uploaded, and downloaded as implantable stacks while physical bodies that are replaceable and purchasable (itself an economic issue Morgan returns to time and again) are reduced to nothing more than 'sleeves.' Yet, as Paweł Frelik argues, 'stack' and 'sleeve' are intertwined and "a mutually exclusive duality is invalidated in favor of a complex feedback system: body and mind are intimately imbricated" ("Woken" 186). In feminist cyberpunk, Cadora celebrates how bodiless existence remains entwined with "reminders of what it means to be embodied humans" (368), and while Morgan clearly lacks the feminist political intentionality in his work, he appears to have inherited this basic premise: addiction, hypersensitivity to physical stimulation (*Thin Air*), or the need for (recorded) consciousness to be grounded in some kind of physical form (whether 'stacks' or 'sleeves') are constant reminders that these storyworlds are not transhumanist utopias modeled after some fantasy of a Cartesian split between 'mind' and 'body'; instead, corporeality perpetually asserts itself upon Morgan's protagonists. In other words, even when the mind is realized entirely externally to the body, the body is not an 'empty' sleeve simply waiting to be worn, but it carries its own traits, which affect the subjectivity of the accompanying mind (Frelik, "Woken" 186).

While my focus has not been on Netflix's *Altered Carbon*, the streaming series sheds light on an interesting problem applicable to Morgan's fiction; namely, Takeshi Kovacs is of Japanese and Hungarian descent, but his consciousness occupies any number of sleeves throughout the print series and switches bodies in both seasons of the Netflix adaptation. Therefore, Joel Kinnaman played the character in Season 1 while Anthony Mackie took on the role in Season 2, leading to questions about Hollywood 'white washing' the character in the first season. Or, in Season 1, Detective Kristin Ortega (Martha Higareda) has her deceased grandmother 'spun up' to temporarily occupy a heavily tattooed, leather-clad, bearded white man. Comparable questions are applicable to Morgan's fiction: what does race, gender, etc. mean in a seemingly transhumanist future where anyone can occupy any type of sleeve (provided they can afford it)? While it may be tempting to conclude the Kovacs novels construct race and ethnicity as mental data, not physical heritage (Frelik, "Woken" 177), Kovacs frequently draws attention to inconsistencies between stack and sleeve ethnicities in himself and others, thus portraying racial heritage as an inescapable fact of every person and something deeply embedded. Meanwhile, the ability to transfer into sleeves offers interesting opportunities to explore non-binary identities and fluid sexualities, but they are often missed in Morgan's work. In fact, he has claimed in a series of tweets and blog-posts[2] that there is no distinction between sex and gender, and that these characteristics are clear and unchangeable facts assignable at birth. This commitment to (mis)understandings of lived realities helps align Morgan's texts even more forcibly to the masculinist heteronormativity of pre-1990s cyberpunk, which still attracts a notable audience.

In the end, Morgan's contributions to a broader cyberpunk culture have helped popularize what some may consider the best of cyberpunk—but others may consider the worst. On the one hand, Morgan's work is significant in its focus on the role of government structures and authorities in hyper-mediated worlds, a role that has been routinely overlooked in cyberpunk,[3] while also advancing criticism of control systems (and the concomitant exploitation) in place around the body, considerations that must be undertaken as cyberpunk not only increasingly crosses media into TV and tabletop role playing games but also shapes the contours of our quotidian reality. At the same time, Morgan's work must be approached carefully and critically to avoid reaffirming its more problematic assumptions and prejudices. Morgan does not wish to dictate what messages his audiences take from his work (Bullock), but given both the complex, at-times contradictory, messaging in his works and his immense popularity, the opportunities to engage with the material as vectors toward better understanding the good, the bad, and the ugly of cyberpunk culture are immeasurable and, in this manner, Morgan is undoubtedly a key figure in cyberpunk culture.

See also: **Pat Cadigan, William Gibson, Donna J. Haraway, Marge Piercy, Rudy Rucker, Melissa Scott, Lewis Shiner, Bruce Sterling**

Notes

1 Morgan acknowledges that he often returns to the concept of grand ideals abandoned by the self-interested neoliberal emphasis on profit (Alegre 86).
2 See Morgan's blog post "The Trouble with Twitter 2: 2020 Vision" for a summary of his stance
3 For more details, see Paweł Frelik's keynote speech "Takeshi Was Here: Viral Revelations, Globalized Power, and Cyberpunk Myopia" for the Cyberpunk Culture Conference 2020 (CPCC 20).

Works Cited

Alegre, Sara Martín. "Martian Politics and the Hard-Boiled Anti-Hero: Richard Morgan's *Thin Air.*" *Revista Hélice*, vol. 4, no.11, pp. 84–95.

Bullock, Saxon. "From The Vault: Richard Morgan Interview (2002)." *Saxon Bullock*, April 18, 2014, http://www.saxonbullock.com/2014/04/never-mind-the-cyberpunks-an-interview-with-richard-morgan-2002/.

Cadora, Karen. "Feminist Cyberpunk." *Science Fiction Studies*, vol. 22, no. 3, 1995, pp. 357–72.

Flood, Alison. "Altered Carbon author Richard Morgan: 'There's no limit to my capacity for Violence.'" *The Guardian*, February 13, 2018, https://www.theguardian.com/books/2018/feb/13/altered-carbon-author-richard-morgan-violence-netflix.

Frelik, Paweł. "Takeshi Was Here: Viral Revelations, Globalized Power, and Cyberpunk Myopia." Cyberpunk Culture Conference, July 9, 2020, http://cyberpunkculture.com/cpcc20/archive-cpcc20/timetable/%c2%a7keynote-pawel-frelik/.

———. "Woken Carbon: The Return of the Human in Richard K. Morgan's Takeshi Kovacs Trilogy." *Beyond Cyberpunk: New Critical Perspectives*, edited by Graham J. Murphy and Sherryl Vint, Routledge, 2010, pp. 173–90.

Heise-von der Lippe, Anya. "Gothicism." *The Routledge Companion to Cyberpunk Culture*, edited by Anna McFarlane, Graham J. Murphy, and Lars Schmeink, Routledge, 2020, pp. 264–72.

Morgan, Richard K. "The Trouble with Twitter 2: 2020 Vision." Richard K. Morgan, January 2020, https://www.richardkmorgan.com/2020/01/the-trouble-with-twitter-2-2020-vision/.

Nixon, Nicola. "Cyberpunk: Preparing the Ground for Revolution or Keeping the Boys Satisfied?" *Science Fiction Studies*, vol. 19, no. 2, 1992, pp. 219–35.

Yaszek, Lisa. "Feminist Cyberpunk." *The Routledge Companion to Cyberpunk Culture*, edited by Anna McFarlane, Graham J. Murphy, and Lars Schmeink, Routledge, 2020, pp. 32–40.

Adam Edwards

ANNALEE NEWITZ (1969–)

American author and journalist.

Annalee Newitz is the author of two novels, *Autonomous* (2017) and *The Future of Another Timeline* (2019), a chapbook *Old Media* (2019), and twelve short stories. Newitz also writes non-fiction, including *Pretend We're Dead: Capitalist Monsters in American Pop Culture* (2015), based on their Ph.D. dissertation,[1] and is a co-founder of *Bad Subjects*, a San Francisco-based research collective located at UC Berkley, and *Other* magazine. They[2] have also been co-founder and editor-in-chief of *io9*, the internet science and science fiction blog, and became the tech culture editor for *Ars Technica* in 2015. Newitz, who won a Knight Science Journalism Fellowship from MIT, has also published in multiple print and online venues. *Autonomous*, their debut novel, was nominated for the Tiptree/Otherwise, Nebula, Locus, Campbell Memorial Award, and the Kurd Laßwitz Award, and won the Lambda Literary Award for best science fiction, fantasy, or horror novel.

Newitz's non-fiction and fiction tackle such cyberpunk concepts as human relationships to virtual technologies, the effects of technology in making the planet less livable, the dominance of neoliberal corporate culture with its commitment to economic policies that increase inequality, and the dangers of climate change and environmental destruction. For example, both *Autonomous* and *Scatter, Adapt, and Remember: How Humans Will Survive a Mass Extinction* (2016) reimagine locally sustainable cities coupled with the possibility of human survival through both adaptability and technology. Newitz makes the claim in *Scatter* that Saskatoon (a Canadian prairie city with a population of roughly 330,000) provides a model for how cities will need to be redesigned to maximize ecosystem survival:

> Humanity's future depends on our ability to build better cities, which are robust against disaster and sustainable within their

environments. That means dense cities, but ones whose populations aren't at the megalopolis level of Tokyo or New York. So a small city, surrounded by well-managed agricultural regions, might be our best bet. We also need a way to deal with pandemics, which spread like wildfire in cities.

Pandemics obviously mean vaccines and medications and recent COVID-19 models show that inequality in health systems condemns millions of city-dwellers to unnecessary infection and death. Therefore, one of *Autonomous*'s two protagonists, the patent pirate Jack (Judith) Chen, has dedicated her life to making cheap copies of expensive patented medications available to the millions who otherwise have no access to legal drugs. The novel begins when Jack discovers that one of her pirated drugs is harming people, not because she's replicated it badly but because the flaw is in the original design. Zacuity makes it possible for people to be more productive and to enjoy tedious, repetitive jobs—but it can trigger a kind of OCD in which they're unable to stop working, even if it kills them. *Autonomous* uses Zacuity to express the correlation between lack of work autonomy and subsequent illness and death. Despite cyberpunk's emphasis on outcast or underclass protagonists, Newitz's focus on work autonomy, or lack thereof, is somewhat unique in bringing an additional critique to bear on the economic and class issues of her imagined society.

This lack of work autonomy is highlighted when Paladin, the novel's other protagonist, a military bot, is assigned by the International Property Coalition (IPC) to work with the previously indentured human, Eliasz, to hunt Jack down, retrieve the pirated medications, and kill Jack and her associates. Paladin and Eliasz are as much the victims of overblown corporate capitalism as everyone else. This is a world in which everything has been commodified, including human life. Both Eliasz and another character in the novel, Threezed, were born without sufficient wealth to purchase enfranchisement, which has replaced "citizenship" as the concept to which human rights and freedoms are tied. As a result, they were forced to sell themselves or, in Threezed's case, were illegally sold as children into a system of indentured labor. Threezed's indenture includes sexual abuse by various owners, while Eliasz's deeply internalized homophobia and his obsession with Paladin's 'gender' speak to a similarly unpleasant and non-autonomous background. *Autonomous* provides a devastating critique of how capitalism has torqued and deformed the individual's relationship both to work and to other people.

Anti-capitalist critique directed at corporations and neoliberal globalization is common to cyberpunk and, indeed, arises in some of cyberpunk's precursors, such as John Brunner's *Shockwave Rider* (1975), in which corporate interests have overridden human desires and habits to the extent that corporate employees rent children to enable the utmost degree of obedient mobility and reality TV shows depict parents encouraging children in lethal contests for the sake of entertainment. **William Gibson**'s *Neuromancer* (1984) depicts corporations and the people who run them largely as evil, manipulative, and purely interested in their own power and profits. While *Autonomous* similarly reflects questions of the posthuman and the relationship between humans and AI, it also presupposes a future in which genders and sexualities are more fluid and widespread than contemporary practices suggest, echoing feminist and queer cyberpunk of the past three decades.[3] While Jack is female and has sexual relationships with both men and women, other characters have different reactions to forms of gendered and sexual alterity. Eliasz struggles to come to terms with his desire for Paladin, whom he initially genders as male. However, when he discovers that Paladin's brain came from a female soldier, Eliasz immediately and joyfully regenders Paladin. Eliasz's sexual relationship with Paladin is based on Eliasz's anthropomorphization of her essentially genderless state and his commitment to a homophobic gender binary.[4] Questions of gender and sexuality are most clearly spelled out in Paladin's sections of the novel, in part because Paladin comes to these issues as a *naif*. Gender is not a meaningful concept to Paladin, although Paladin is compliant with being gendered (that is, arbitrarily assigned a gender first on the basis of size and function and then on the basis of Eliasz's fear of homosexuality). The most Paladin can do is to allow Eliasz to gender her; Paladin cannot achieve a sense of gender, nor does she want one.

As a military bot, Paladin must research what sort of relationship Eliasz wants with her and what sort of relationship she wants with Eliasz. What's important for Paladin is that she gains her autonomy and control over her own programming, so that her feelings for Eliasz are her own code, not something someone else has written into her responses. "Nobody could find out what she was thinking, unless she allowed it. The key to autonomy, she realized, was more than root access on the programs that shaped her desires. It was a sense of privacy" (299). For Paladin, it's about owning her own thoughts. At the same time, Newitz rewrites the "boys' club" identity of early cyberpunk not only by introducing women as autonomous characters, but also by questioning conservative discourses of sex and gender that much male-written cyberpunk has left uninterrogated.

The issue of autonomy is at the very heart of *Autonomous*. Medea, a human-appearing bot brought up as the daughter of two research scientists, is the first bot professor at her university. She notes that "a lot of roboticists believe that successful autonomous bots need kinship ties, and a period of childhood where they can experiment with different identities." Paladin's first few months of service work as a kind of childhood in which both the IPC's demands and Eliasz's inchoate desires create a kind of experimental space for Paladin; her relationship with Eliasz provides her with her most basic kinship tie. Threezed and Eliasz, however, both demonstrate the trauma created when human children are denied what Medea's parents want to give all bots; in fact, bots have the legal right to purchase their own autonomy after sufficient service, while humans have a harder time with the affective components of moving from slavery to freedom and childhood to adulthood. In this respect, Newitz's characters and her very detailed future world replicate gender theorist Judith Butler's work on the importance of cultural intelligibility and recognition; insofar as queer and trans people fall outside of the network of cultural intelligibility, their lives are precarious and sometimes unlivable. *Autonomous* is filled with humans and bots whose lives are made precarious by the corporate capitalism that limits their freedom to live and work.

Building on the complicated questions about sex and gender that I can only gesture toward in this short overview, Newitz's second novel, *The Future of Another Timeline*, depicts a quite literal battle of the sexes. Moving between 2022, the 1990s, 1893, and the ancient Ordovician Era, Newitz's characters battle to use five ancient Time Machines to alter the past and control present and future. *Future* pits members of a secret history-changing cabal called the Daughters of Harriet (named after Senator Harriet Tubman) and the antagonistic Comstockers (named after Anthony Comstock, the US Postal Inspector who crusaded against allowing information about birth control or abortion) whose mission is to create a world in which women are forever subservient to the men who control women's sexuality and reproduction. Thus, each group becomes increasingly desperate to locate and reverse each other's temporal edits. In one instance, the Daughters successfully revert a history in which one of the Daughters, a trans woman, is murdered outside a gay bar by the Comstockers. While the Comstockers appear to consist solely of straight (presumably white) men, the Daughters are a more diverse lot, including a lesbian couple and a nonbinary person. They also have allies in different eras and places, while the Comstockers appear to be more isolated within their ideological certainties.

Questions of livability are still central in *Future*, particularly as the Comstockers desire to create a world barely livable for women and not at all livable for LGBTQ+ people. The awfulness of their desire for complete control of women is illustrated when the Daughters meet a future "queen," a woman who has no hands since they're not necessary for reproduction. *Future* might be described as a boldly pyrotechnical novel, with an obsession with riot grrrls, music, and murder. There are ways in which this novel also literalizes aspects of Newitz's appeal to "scatter, adapt, and remember." The Daughters do have to scatter in both time and space to survive; they must adapt not only to constantly changing conditions, but to constantly changing presents and pasts as competing timeline edits take precedence. And, finally, the act of remembering is how the Daughters record their changes to the past and locate antagonistic reversions. The murder of Berenice, Enid's trans lover, is part of a dedicated attempt to edit trans women out of history, while rendering ciswomen slaves to men, but the Daughters are only aware of it because protagonist Tess escaped the timeline edit and remembered Berenice. The future the Daughters are determined to bring about will be a very queer time and space, but not one which can be guaranteed since, unlike the Comstockers, the Daughters are not planning to destroy the Machines to safeguard their particular edited version of human history. While it would be a stretch to call *Future* cyberpunk, it addresses some specific themes in cyberpunk culture, such as the creation of futures that are controlled by small cabals of (usually corporate) men and are barely livable for anyone else, but it does so while focusing on the lives of the excluded, notably women, queer people, trans people, and the working class.

A common thread throughout Newitz's work is that while new technologies make life survivable, but distinctly not utopian, it remains possible to be optimistic about humanity's potential to survive what has been called the Sixth Mass Extinction. After researching previous mass extinctions and talking to people working on a broad range of ideas to make the future more sustainable and survivable, Newitz writes, "I emerged [...] with the belief that humanity has a lot more than a fighting chance at making it for another million years" (*Scatter*).

Regarding the potential influence of sf on policymakers, Newitz says, "We're having these wacky surreal futures and we wouldn't have been as prepared for them if we had not been reading really strange science fiction" ("Policy"). In the sense that one might consider cyberpunk as a whole to be "really strange science fiction," Newitz's work contributes to the mode's evolution away from its boys and their toys infancy (a simplification, since women like **Pat Cadigan** and **Melissa Scott** were influential even in cyberpunk's early days, as was the work of **Joanna Russ**). Indeed, we might consider Newitz's work to effectively marry Russ's trenchant critiques of contemporary sexual and gender mores to cyberpunk's analyses of the ways in which corporate cultures—and their antagonists—use and are shaped by technologies, particularly virtual technologies, thus producing not only a new and more inclusive version of cyberpunk but possibly a more optimistic one in terms of humanity's future.

See also: **Pat Cadigan, William Gibson, Janelle Monáe, Joanna Russ, Melissa Scott**

Notes

1 Annalee Newitz earned a PhD in 1991 in English and American Studies from the University of California, Berkley.
2 Newitz adopted 'they/their' pronouns in 2019.
3 For details, see Yaszek, Melzer, and Pearson.
4 This chapter follows the novel's changing use of pronouns for Paladin.

Works Cited

Melzer, Patricia. "Cyborg Feminism." *The Routledge Companion to Cyberpunk Culture*, edited by Anna McFarlane, Graham J. Murphy, and Lars Schmeink, Routledge, 2020, pp. 291–99.

Newitz, Annalee. *Autonomous*. Tor, 2017. Ebook.

———. *The Future of Another Timeline*. Tor, 2019. Ebook.

Newitz, Annalee and Sarah Villeneuve. "Policy is Just Hard Science Fiction: An Interview with Annalee Newitz." *Brookfield Institute*, July 17, 2020, https://brookfieldinstitute.ca/policy-is-just-hard-science-fiction/.

Pearson, Wendy Gay. "Queer Theory." *The Routledge Companion to Cyberpunk Culture*, edited by Anna McFarlane, Graham J. Murphy, and Lars Schmeink, Routledge, 2020, pp. 300–07.

Yaszek, Lisa. "Feminist Cyberpunk." *The Routledge Companion to Cyberpunk Culture*, edited by Anna McFarlane, Graham J. Murphy, and Lars Schmeink, Routledge, 2020, pp. 32–40.

Wendy Gay Pearson

MAMORU OSHII (1951–)

Japanese film and animation director.

Mamoru Oshii has been working in the Japanese animation industry since 1977, where he started as a storyboard artist and technical director. His breakthrough was as the chief director for the first half of the television series *Urusei Yatsura* (1981–86), as well as working on storyboards and scripts for certain episodes. His work on the series led to him directing the first two theatrical films based on the series, *Only You* (1983) and *Beautiful Dreamer* (1984), the latter of which allowed Oshii to develop his signature thematic and visual styles, which include the presence of ruins, animals (especially birds, fish, and dogs), an emphasis on the duality of dreams/reality, allusions to religion and myth, the foregrounding of military hardware/robots/cyborg technology, and a caution against surveillance and systems of control (Ruh 7–10). Oshii continued to develop his directorial skills on projects like *Dallos* (1983–84), *Angel's Egg* (1985), and film versions of the *Mobile Police Patlabor* tv series (1988–89), *Patlabor: The Movie* (1989) and *Patlabor 2: The Movie* (1993), but he is probably best known for his 1995 film *Ghost in the Shell*, which was influential for subsequent cyberpunk themes and aesthetics. If it is the case that "the green digital rain" that permeates the digital reality of **Lana and Lilly Wachowski**'s *The Matrix* (1999), an aesthetic that "has become visually synonymous with the control of 'reality' by technological systems" (McFarlane, Murphy, and Schmeink 1), then it is important to note that this visual motif (among others) originated with *Ghost in the Shell*. Oshii also directed a sequel to the film called *Innocence* and was credited with "story concept" for the second season of the *Ghost in the Shell: Stand Alone Complex* television series. Although he is more well-known for his anime films, Oshii has also worked in live-action film since 1987 and has written manga (Japanese comics), novels, and a substantial number of books of film and cultural criticism. Cyberpunk has given Oshii the opportunity to explore many of his core themes in a different manner than some of his other works. The thematic emphasis on control, surveillance, and rebellion, so common to cyberpunk media, is present throughout Oshii's works, and to understand this consistency it is helpful to examine how Oshii's personal history intersected with that of post-World War II Japan.

Mamoru Oshii was born in Tokyo in 1951, exactly one month before the signing of the Security Treaty between the United States and Japan. Due to Article 9 of the US-authored constitution that had been signed four years earlier in the wake of WWII, Japan had been effectively "disarmed" and therefore relied on America for external defense. Although the Security Treaty was signed without much difficulty, the situation proved different in 1960 with the Treaty of Mutual Cooperation and Security between the United States and Japan, usually called Anpo by its Japanese abbreviation. Oshii was too young to be involved with treaty protests, but it wasn't the last time demonstrators against militarization and Americanization occupied Japan's streets. Protests may have temporarily declined throughout the 1960s, but they increased toward the end of the decade, including opposition over the escalation of the war in Vietnam and the takeover of farmers' lands to accommodate the construction of Narita Airport, known as the Sanrizuka Struggle. As a secondary school student, Oshii became part of these protest movements that would come to influence the rebellious, countercultural stances of the characters in his later works.

Following high school, Oshii attended Tokyo Gakugei University, after which he had a short stint working in radio, then joined the animation company Tatsunoko Production, where he worked on humorous titles such as *Time Bokan* (1975–83). Oshii then followed his mentor Hisayuki Toriumi to Studio Pierrot, where he worked on *Urusei Yatsura* and his visual ideas gained a fuller and more sustained expression. His attraction to military hardware is evident from the first episode (for which he was credited with storyboards and technical direction) where he introduces mechanical flourishes into situations from which they were absent in the original manga, such as tanks, aircraft, and alien ships all depicted in carefully crafted detail.[1] The two *Patlabor* films, featuring a Tokyo police unit using giant robots to fight crime, allowed Oshii to further his exploration of the interface of human and machine.

These experiences are the foundation for Oshii's cyberpunk masterpiece *Ghost in the Shell*, an anime adaptation of **Masumune Shirow**'s manga of the same name (1989–90). In the film, cyborg Motoko Kusanagi fights on behalf of government agency Section 9 to combat cyberterrorism. In the process, Kusanagi questions what it means to be alive, as she is theoretically a mechanical body with a biological brain, but this is something that she cannot resolve for herself. As Joon Yang Kim puts it, "Kusanagi's ontological dilemma questions the rules and limitations for cyborgs that humans define in order to more securely identify themselves by establishing 'others'" (184). Her crisis comes to a head when she encounters the Puppet Master, a former government cyberweapon that was created online but has now gained sentience. In the end, she accepts the Puppet Master's offer to "merge," creating a new lifeform that is a melding of both of them.

Oshii directed a *Ghost in the Shell* sequel called *Innocence* (a.k.a. *Ghost in the Shell 2: Innocence*, 2004), but since Kusanagi has merged with the Puppet Master at the end of *Ghost in the Shell* to become a new entity and has slipped the bonds of the physical to journey into a 'net that is "vast and infinite," she makes only a few select appearances in the sequel, although her presence pervades all of the action. *Innocence* questions where we can (or should) draw the lines between humanity, animality, and artificial life and, in so doing, also "features some of the most spectacular examples of lucent imagery. The very first frame of the film shows a towering skyscraper located in the center of a gridded urban sprawl and glowing with the almost blinding golden light" (Frelik 90). At the same time, *Innocence* is far more literate and reference-heavy than the first film, including allusions to Villiers de l'Isle-Adam's *Tomorrow's Eve* (*L'Eve Future*, 1886), Raymond Roussel's *Locus Solus* (1914), and cyborg philosopher **Donna J. Haraway**.

Oshii's *Ghost in the Shell* has been described as "marking the mainstream introduction and critical consolidation of cyberpunk anime as a respected and acclaimed visual form in the west and constituting an important contribution to cyberpunk culture" (de la Iglesia and Schmeink 162). On both thematic and visual levels, *Ghost in the Shell* was clearly indebted to previous cyberpunk works, notably the visual aesthetics popularized in **Ridley Scott**'s *Blade Runner* (1982) whose influence is "very obvious" (Napier 105). Moving forward, however, the anime has had an immeasurable influence on all cyberpunk media in its wake; in fact, it can be argued that all media afterwards are in dialogue with *Ghost in the Shell* to a greater or lesser degree. As previously noted, it was a key touchstone for *The Matrix*, which in turn created its own ripples of influence.

Similarly, Oshii's animated short film "Je t'aime" (2010), which was actually a music video for the song "Satellite of Love" by the Japanese rock group GLAY, features a lone basset hound (a favorite breed of Oshii's) wandering through a recognizable Tokyo completely devoid of people. The dog eventually encounters a cybernetic being at the Kaminarimon gate in Asakusa. Through the wordless short, the two survivors seem to arrive at a mutual misunderstanding, which ends in a tragedy and the dog is once more left on its own, perhaps underlining the difficulty in communicating across divides of species and technology.

Although not all of Oshii's works can be called "cyberpunk," they touch on Oshii's themes of dreams, technology, and surveillance (including *Urusei Yatsura* or more recent films like *Nowhere Girl* [*Tokyo Mukokseki Shoujo*, 2015]), and a common thread is questioning the reality of what the characters onscreen are experiencing. In this vein, one of his more serious works is *Avalon* (2000), released between the two *Ghost in the Shell* features. *Avalon* uses the premise of people playing an illegal virtual reality game to highlight themes of "the disillusionment of youth, the attraction of immersive war-game simulations, technological addiction and the dangers of virtual reality" (Brown 133). *Avalon* presents the audience with an ontological question that remains unanswered: what is the game? and what is reality? *Avalon* is also an exploration of the ways in which we are watched and controlled, even when we think we have broken free. As **N. Katherine Hayles** explains in a manner applicable to *Avalon*:

> [a]lthough death has (perhaps) been divested of its preeminent position as the ultimate trauma, it is revealed as covering over the actual traumatic experience, which is nothing other than the discovery that reality itself is generated by code [...] reality and simulation no longer constitute mutually exclusive realms but now interpenetrate one another.
>
> (152)

Avalon also marks a jumping-off point for several other live-action projects set in and around the same virtual world, which in turn connects to many of his other works. For example, the short films "Assault Girl" (2007) and "Assault Girl 2" (2008), which were parts of two separate omnibus films Oshii was supervising, led to the feature *Assault Girls* (2009), which was explicitly set in a variation of the world of Avalon (Ruh 235–40). As in *Avalon*, Oshii's thesis in *Assault Girls* is that people have fled to this virtual world because the "real world" has lost the spirit and conflict they need to feel alive. Some takes on this setting of *Avalon*, such as the "micro-series" *Sand Whale and Me* (2017), are more absurdist and comedic, connecting back to the humorous anime on which he got his start and demonstrating that there is room for levity even in Oshii's cyberpunk worlds.

See also: **Donna J. Haraway, N. Katherine Hayles, Sogo Ishii, Katsuhiro Ōtomo, Ridley Scott, Masamune Shirow, Lana and Lilly Wachowski**

Note

1 Appropriately, he later authored a book with the title *Mechaphilia* (2004).

Works Cited

Brown, Steven T. *Tokyo Cyberpunk: Posthumanism in Japanese Visual Culture.* Palgrave Macmillan, 2010.

de la Iglesia, Martin and Lars Schmeink. "*Akira* and *Ghost in the Shell* (Case Study)." *The Routledge Companion to Cyberpunk Culture*, edited by Anna McFarlane, Graham J. Murphy, and Lars Schmeink, Routledge, 2020, pp. 162–68.

Frelik, Pawel. "'Silhouettes of Strange Illuminated Mannequins': Cyberpunk's Incarnations of Light." *Cyberpunk and Visual Culture*, edited by Graham J. Murphy and Lars Schmeink, Routledge, 2018, pp. 80–99.

Hayles, N. Katherine. "Traumas of Code." *Critical Inquiry*, vol. 33, no. 1, 2006, pp. 136–57.

Kim, Joon Yang. "The East Asian Posthuman Prometheus: Animated Mechanical 'Others.'" *Pervasive Animation*, edited by Susan Buchan, Routledge, 2013, pp. 172–93.

McFarlane, Anna, Graham J. Murphy, Lars Schmeink. "Cyberpunk as Cultural Formation." *The Routledge Companion to Cyberpunk Culture*, edited by Anna McFarlane, Graham J. Murphy, and Lars Schmeink, Routledge, 2018, pp. 1–3.

Napier, Susan J. *Anime from Akira to Princess Mononoke: Experiencing Contemporary Japanese Animation.* Palgrave, 2000.

Ruh, Brian. *Stray Dog of Anime: The Films of Mamoru Oshii.* 2nd ed., Palgrave Macmillan, 2014.

Brian Ruh

KATSUHIRO ŌTOMO (1954–)

Japanese manga artist, illustrator, screenwriter, and film director.

Katsuhiro Ōtomo is best known internationally as the creator of the anime *Akira* (1988), but in Japan he first established his name as a *mangaka* (manga creator), beginning with a one-shot manga titled "A Gun Report" (Jūsei, 1973), a manga adaptation of French writer Prosper Mérimée's "Mateo Falcone" (1829). It was published in a special edition of *Manga Action* (*Manga Akushon Zōkan*), a *seinen* (young adult and adult male) manga magazine. Ōtomo became widely known with his serial science fiction (sf) manga *Dōmu: A Child's Dream* (*Dōmu*, 1980–81), a murder mystery set in contemporary suburban Tokyo featuring an old man and a child, both of whom possess extrasensory powers. With its publication in book format in 1983, Ōtomo won the Japanese Science Fiction Grand Prize (*Nihon SF Taishō*), equivalent to the industry's Nebula Award. Ōtomo began to serialize *Akira*, his best-known sf manga, in *Young Magazine*, which ran from 1982 until 1990 and eventually totaled over 2,300 pages—*Akira* was later collected and published in six volumes. Meanwhile, he had become involved in filmmaking, participating in the production of the anime film *Harmagedon: Genma Wars* (*Genma Taisen*; Rintarō 1983) as a character designer and later directing his anime masterpiece *Akira*, which earned him worldwide critical attention. In 2004, he followed *Akira* with his second feature film *Steamboy*, a steampunk anime that depicts an alternate nineteenth-century England where humanity enjoys marvelous steam-powered technology. Ōtomo directed his first live-action movie *Mushishi* in 2006, based on Yuki Urushibara's manga of the same name. Today he is a highly acclaimed *mangaka* and film director who has received several domestic and international awards, including Japan's Medal of Honor with Purple Ribbon in 2013 and the Grand Prix lifetime achievement award at the Angoulême International Comics Festival in 2015.

Before his professional debut, Ōtomo submitted his manga to *COM*, a magazine founded in 1967 by the influential *mangaka* Osamu Tezuka to cater to the maturing manga readership of the 1960s. In this magazine, several important authors, like Shōtaro Ishinomori (*Cyborg 009*), Shinji Nagashima (*Fūten*), and Tezuka, serialized innovative works for young adult and adult manga readers who were no longer satisfied with childish manga stories. Indeed, throughout the 1960s, manga grew out of its status as children's entertainment and developed into a medium of artistic self-expression. Such progress was made under the banner of *gekiga* (literally "dramatic picture"), a body of Japanese comics that attracted college students and adult readers. Ōtomo's earlier works—such as "Boogie Woogie Waltz" (1974) and "Mirror" (1976)—preserve vestiges of *gekiga*'s characteristic dark themes, naturalistic and often gritty drawing styles, and focus on characters who are lowlifes or live on the fringes of society.

Ōtomo's drawing style was also inspired by western New Wave cinema, pop art and illustration (Tadanori Yokoo, Yoshitarō Isaka, and Peter Max), and, most prominently, contemporaneous French comics. Ōtomo is particularly influenced by French comics artist **Moebius [Jean Giraud]**'s work in such magazines as *Métal Hurlant*, a visionary who also influenced Hollywood filmmakers George Lucas and **Ridley Scott** and literary cyberpunk auteur **William Gibson**. Ōtomo came across the translated works of Moebius in sf and subculture magazines in the 1970s, including the Japanese edition of *Starlog*, and Ōtomo's sf manga shorts, such as "Flower" (1979) and "Don Quijote" (1979), bear Moebius's direct influence. Ōtomo describes Moebius's drawing style as "calm, distant, and intelligent" with "even lines," unlike *gekiga*'s then-popular "energetic and thick" lines ("Manga no" 19).

As a result of this influence, Ōtomo is renowned as an artist who gave the stagnating drawing style of manga a renewal. His sophisticated drawing style is distinct from both the Tezuka-inspired, rounded character designs prevalent in postwar manga and the *gekiga*-inspired naturalistic drawing style characterized by thick and coarse lines. His stylistic innovation was in combining evenly drawn, sober linework and *gekiga*'s naturalistic depictions of graphic violence and destruction. This combination forms the essence of Ōtomo's signature style, most manifest in his highly acclaimed sf titles *Fire-Ball* (1980), *Domu*, and *Akira*, with their elaborate designs for "mecha" and buildings, realized in meticulously complex three-dimensional projections, and subjective motion-lines that viscerally communicate the speed of moving vehicles and projectiles.

While Ōtomo's *Akira* is renowned as the definitive landmark in Japanese cyberpunk, he was unaware of the rise of cyberpunk in the United States: he began serializing *Akira* in 1982, just before "cyberpunk" truly gained traction in America's sf scene. As a result, Ōtomo incorporated the concepts and tropes of extrasensory powers, UFOs, paranormal phenomena, and eschatology, all of which were fads in the subcultural media (i.e., popular novels, magazines, movies, TV programs, etc.) of 1970s Japan, known at the time as the "Occultism Fad" (*Okaruto būmu*). In *Akira*, he weaves these (and other) topics together, including youth biker gangs (*bōsōzoku*),[1] biogenetics, and political and military intrigue. Specifically, *Akira*'s storyline develops around the protagonist Kaneda, a teenage biker gang leader, and his buddy/rival Tetsuo. Their accidental encounter with an enigmatic boy with psychokinetic abilities throws them into a world of military conspiracy, political machinations, and revolutionary action, all of which leads them to the hidden secret of the project—or entity—named "Akira" that is allegedly responsible for the destruction of Tokyo over three decades earlier. Thematically, *Akira* addresses the young boys' angst, trauma, and revolt against ossified social and power structures, represented by the modern military and political institutions controlled by the adults in the story, as well as the terror of a new technoscience that defies human control.

Akira's postapocalyptic setting invites a reading of the story as an allegory for Tokyo/Japan's postwar history, including its complicity with U.S. militarism, a sense of socio-political impasse (after the decline of the political movements of the 1960s), and the rise of a rebellious younger generation with new sensibilities and expectations of social reality. The opening of the original Japanese manga is set in the year 2019, 38 years after the detonation of a "new type of bomb" (*shin-gata bakudan*)—the exact term initially used in Japan for the atomic bomb dropped in Hiroshima—that signaled the outbreak of World War III, setting the series up as a "historically grounded engagement" with the "trauma of the atomic bomb" (Lamarre 132). In addition, the future city is called "Neo-Tokyo" and it is still in the process of recovering from the devastation while preparing for another Tokyo Olympics (after the first in 1964). All the while, chaotic anti-government demonstrations take place in the background, further suggesting *Akira* is a re-enactment of Japan's postwar history.

The anime *Akira* was released in 1988 while the manga was still being serialized. It became an instant hit in Japan and overseas, marking a watershed moment in the reception of Japanese anime to western spectators. The production team increased the number of images displayed each second from the standard employed by other traditionally cell-animated Japanese productions to achieve smoother movement and a more dynamic visual sensation. Ōtomo also employed unique, innovative visual techniques to make speed, violence, and destruction more visceral via the swift switching of different (subjective) perspectives, allowing the viewer to "experience" the pronounced speed and destruction. Analyzing the visual techniques in the film, Marc Steinberg argues that the anime "puts the spectator in the position of the object of destruction," thereby creating a sense of being the "victim and controller" simultaneously (17). Similarly, Susan Napier addresses the motif of the metamorphosis of the male adolescent body and claims that the foregrounding of the uncontrollability of youthful bodies and energy is set against the "unmoving structure of power and authority" (41). Finally, Christopher Bolton argues that the endings of the anime and the serialized manga give a sense of a "promising utopian evocation of revolution" in which the youth can "exert their agency without exercising the totalitarian control of adult authorities" (55), though Bolton also points out that Ōtomo offers another ending ("epilogue") to the story. In this alternative ending, added when *Akira* was republished in book format, Tetsuo and his group attempt to build a new state named the "Great Tokyo Empire Akira" (*Dai Tokyo Teikoku Akira*), which suggests their revolution takes a more "conservative and nationalistic" turn (55).

After *Akira's* success, Ōtomo was involved in a series of anime projects. For example, he took on the role of executive director for *Memories* (1995), a feature-length sf anthology of three short anime pieces. Ōtomo directed the closing piece "Cannon Fodder" (Taihō no Machi), a surrealistic work evocative of Eastern European animation rather than Japanese anime. *Memories* is a war fantasy piece that tells the story of a boy who lives in a walled city engaged in constant warfare against an unknown enemy. The plot is simple, narrating the ritualistic process of maintaining and firing the city's enormous cannons over the course of one day, with all citizen activities, from family life to factory labor to education, regulated by the authoritarian war regime solely in service of this one militaristic function. Ōtomo's second large-budget anime film, *Steamboy*, thematically addresses the human greed for power and technological advancement. Like *Akira*, *Steamboy* focuses on its young protagonist's idealism and revolt for freedom and peace against adults' deployment of technology in service of control, all set against the backdrop of the British Empire. The film's topics invite a reading of the "steam ball," a key object in the plot, as nuclear technology. Although Ōtomo spent almost ten years on this project, employing "more than 180,000 drawings and 400 CG cuts" (Sony Pictures), the international reviews and responses were lukewarm. Nonetheless, *Steamboy* is Ōtomo's homage to steampunk, notably in the film's aesthetic and gadget design, as well as to Osamu Tezuka's *Astroboy* with its similar title (Schilling).

More recently, Ōtomo has been active in the anime industry as a film director, scriptwriter, and character designer. In 2013, he worked on a multimedia project of four anime shorts and a video game called *Short Peace*, for which he directed "Combustible," a short anime film about firefighters in the Edo Period. This short won the Media Arts Award from the Japanese government's Agency for Cultural Affairs. He also worked on a promotional project for Nisshin Cup Noodles' 35th anniversary in 2006. For this, Ōtomo served as the character designer for a seven-part OVA (original video animation) series titled *Freedom*. It is reported that Ōtomo has been working on his third feature-length anime *Orbital Era*. While not much is currently known about the project, a teaser clip hosted by its official website shows a boy on a space colony along with a floating image of a slowly spinning skateboard in outer space, reminiscent of *Akira*'s mixture of futuristic technoscience with the youth subcultures of the streets. In this manner, Ōtomo seems to be continuing the expansion of (post-)cyberpunk imagination in his oeuvre and continuing to help expand our understanding of cyberpunk and cyberpunk culture.

See also: **William Gibson, Moebius [Jean Giraud], Ridley Scott**

Note

1 As a homage, players of CD Projekt's *Cyberpunk 2077* can purchase the Kusanagi CT-3X, a motorcycle modelled after *Akira*'s motorbikes.

Works Cited

Bolton, Christopher. *Interpreting Anime*. U of Minnesota P, 2018.

Lamarre, Thomas. "Born of Trauma: *Akira* and Capitalist Modes of Destruction." *Positions: East Asia Cultures Critique*, vol. 16, no. 1, 2008, pp. 131–56.

Napier, Susan J. *Anime from Akira to Howl's Moving Castle: Experiencing Contemporary Japanese Animation*. Palgrave Macmillan, 2005.

Ōtomo, Katsuhiro. *Domu: A Child's Dream*. Dark Horse Comics, 2001.

———. "Manga no chihei hirogatta: Mebiusu-san o itamu" [An Obituary for Moebius]. Asahi Shimbun, April 12, 2012, p. 19.

Schilling, Mark. "The master behind the otaku." *The Japan Times*, June 14, 2004, https://www.japantimes.co.jp/culture/2004/07/14/films/film-reviews/the-master-behind-the-otaku.

Sony Pictures. *Steamboy*, web.archive.org/web/20100125153659/ http://www.sonypictures.com/homevideo/steamboy/title-navigation-3.html.

Steinberg, Marc. "The Trajectory of Apocalypse: Pleasure and Destruction in *Akira* and *Evangelion*." *East Asia Forum*, vols. 8 and 9, 1999 and 2000, Joint Center for Asia Pacific Studies, pp. 1–31.

Shige (CJ) Suzuki

MARGE PIERCY (1936–)

US author and poet.

Marge Piercy's two forays into speculative fiction are unique and distinctive landmarks for multiple genres, and touchstones for feminist approaches to those genres. As a prolific poet, Piercy might seem an unlikely candidate as a key cyberpunk figure, but *Woman on the Edge of Time* (1976) and *He, She and It* (1991)—also known as *Body of Glass*—bookend the period usually regarded as cyberpunk's first wave, and their central concerns trace the mode's cultural shifts, from dystopian science fiction (sf) to post-cyberpunk.[1] *Woman on the Edge of Time* constituted a feminist intervention in utopian sf, and predated **William Gibson**'s earliest cyberpunk by seven years, yet shares the mode's central concerns, offering glimpses of cyberpunk *avant la lettre*. *He, She, and It* shares and extends those concerns with conscious cyberpunk references. Both books therefore explore cyberpunk's core interests in the problematics of embodiment, virtual worlds created within narrative worlds, networked subjectivities, dystopian futures, and technological or information-based life forms—and both books adapt and deploy these concerns to critique the narratives of mastery and control that undergird so many cyberpunk (and cyberpunk influenced) narratives.

Woman on the Edge of Time stands between earlier utopian fiction of a more didactic nature, and later "open-ended" (Somay and Pilmus 26) versions that integrate the idea of utopia into socio-political collective action, an open-endedness that Tom Moylan has identified as a central tenet of the "critical utopia." *Woman on the Edge of Time* is clearly a feminist text, presenting the travails of Consuelo "Connie" Ramos, a middle-aged Chicana woman forcibly committed to a state psychiatric facility. The facility and its contemporary reality are set in sharp contrast with an alternate future in a town known as Mattapoisett that Connie explores over the course of the novel. Akin to a tour guide, Luciente acquaints Connie with this positive feminist "eutopian" (Kessler 311) community, where the elimination of gendered socio-economic distinctions has brought about a more equitable society—even if it takes repeated visits before Connie is able to accept it. The novel offers a second counterpoint too, an alternate reality to Mattapoisett, introduced when Connie finds herself in a nightmarish version of New York City animated by rampant commodification and dehumanization. A contract-prostitute named Gildina provides a brief verbal tour of this nightmare future, against which residents of Mattapoisett are fighting. Here the novel offers a preview of a cyberpunk dystopia, with violently sexual virtual worlds presented for consumption by the wealthy, while the poor serve as living organ banks.

A robust body of scholarship on *Woman on the Edge of Time* addresses the chief cultural and ideological strands of the book, emphasizing the alternate eutopia and dystopia that Connie's experiences illuminate, the connections between Connie's actions and the realization of either of these possible futures, the positioning of gender and gendered bodies as central to social experience and civic participation, and the role of science in defining the monstrous or mad, among other topics. These approaches have rightly tended to regard the novel as sf (or as a 'critical utopia'), but in the emphasis on embodiment, and technologies for surveillance and control of mind and body, it can also be read as a feminist precursor to cyberpunk, particularly via its connections to the themes and ideas in Piercy's subsequent post-cyberpunk novel, *He, She, and It*, and to themes that reappear in the 1990s feminist cyberpunk oeuvre—as well as the feminist cyborg theory of **Donna J. Haraway**. The central threat to Connie, and others committed to state psychiatric care in this novel, is an invasive cybernetic control system being piloted by a cadre of self-serving scientists, designed to render the patients' emotional and cognitive activity more amenable to outside control. Here, Piercy envisions cybernetic integration as neurological rape and subjection, not the enhanced cyborgs common to cyberpunk texts that would emerge a decade later, a violation of corporeal boundaries presented as *contemporary* dystopian reality and not some future dystopian state.

Woman on the Edge of Time often appears in critical works on ground-breaking feminist sf texts, alongside **Joanna Russ**'s *The Female Man* (1975), which has been identified as a cyberpunk precursor,[2] as well as Ursula K. Le Guin's *The Dispossessed* (1974) and Sally Miller Gearhart's *The Wanderground* (1979), but the novel also embodies a tension inherent within cyberpunk and especially post-cyberpunk stories, between such possibilities for subjection and control within realms of techno-scientific innovation, and the possibilities for radical rupture. One of the novel's central speculations—indeed, its central motif—remains enigmatic: the ability to "send" or "catch" across time receives little scientifically speculative (let alone cybernetic or technical) explanation and seems more psychic than mechanical.[3] It appears to have limits but is treated more like a miraculous expression of human potential than a product of *techne*. Indeed, the narrative does not offer much more than circumstantial evidence regarding Connie's visits to the future (beyond a temporary escape from the mental institute that works only if Luciente is 'real' and helping Connie). In this, it closely parallels the neo-spiritual elements in **Lana and Lilly Wachowski**'s ongoing Matrix sequence (1999–2003, 2021), the uncanny psychic feats in Tad Williams's Otherland series (1996–2001), the monstrous stroke in **Pat Cadigan**'s *Synners* (1991), the ambiguously techno-magical Asherah virus in **Neal Stephenson**'s *Snow Crash* (1992), and the angelic visitations in Lyda Morehouse's AngeLINK series (2001–04, 2011), among others.[4] In its proto-cyberpunk form, *Woman on the Edge of Time* highlights the way cyberpunk has found and shifted its footing among the fault lines between traditional constructions of sf, literary utopias, and perhaps even fantasy.

While *Woman on the Edge of Time* has only prescient cyberpunk elements, *He, She, and It* responds more directly to cyberpunk's cultural formations, exploring the machine-human hybridity advanced in Donna J. Haraway's cyborg theories while appropriating and critiquing the technological domains sketched out by William Gibson (Booker). *He, She, and It* features a sprawling continental mega-city, the Glop, set against sheltered enclaves dominated by multinational corporations, alongside which villages akin to Piercy's earlier Mattapoisett eke out a precarious existence, surviving by balancing the needs of the multinationals and using this economic advantage to avoid absorption into the Glop. The dystopian New York City of *Woman on the Edge of Time* has come near to reality in *He, She, and It*: citizens of the multinationals experience a degree of personal and bodily control similar to what Gildina describes in the earlier novel, something Shira Shipman discovers when her husband decides to edit her out of his and his son's life. She returns home to Tikva, an independent Jewish village, where she discovers the two elders Malkah and Avram have created the multinationals' holy grail of research: an artificial person. The story of Yod, the cyborg, unfolds alongside Malkah's retelling of how Rabbi Judah Lowe created the golem (named Joseph) in seventeenth-century Prague.

Just as *Woman on the Edge of Time* creates a complex interaction between technoscientific culture and the natural world, questioning their opposition and the assignment of gendered values to each, *He, She and It* creates a dialogue between cyberpunk and mysticism, a tradition usually addressed as a progenitor of fantasy. Piercy does more than juxtapose the twin stories—Malkah tells the golem's story not to her granddaughter Shira, but to Yod, and it forms an important part of his social programming, a model upon which he can base his engagement with the world, and which allows him to develop a deepening relationship with Shira. In a key moment, as Yod declares his love for Shira within their world's virtual space, their virtual-sexual encounter seems to force the simulation to exceed its programming.

Although many sf narratives embrace this kind of fantastical intrusion, Piercy uses the trope explicitly to link cyberpunk virtual worlds and artificial life with a Jewish mystical tradition. Whereas early cyberpunk built its sleek surfaces and near-future projections on leaps ahead from present-day technologies, *He, She, and It* turns its gaze deeper into the past, tracing cyberpunk-related interests and impulses to much earlier origins than the twentieth century.

Piercy does not, however, allow the reader to envision an expressly posthuman future populated by artificial life. Like the golem, Yod fulfills the function Avram intended, and dies defending Shira and Tikva. Rather than Yod, the cybernetic way forward finds clearer socio-political representation in the compact forged between Tikva and the neo-unionist Glop organizations, and a clearer embodiment in the heavily augmented Nili, a visitor from a post-apocalyptic Middle East. Introduced as a traveling (and sexual) partner with Shira's mother Riva, Nili serves as a re-appropriation of the woman-warrior trope, more empowering than Gibson's Molly Millions. Where Yod embodies a depleted masculinity, strength and attention without machismo or misogyny, Nili is, like Shira and Malkah, a mother, and "real [...] all the way through," and "whatever [she] did, she did thoroughly, and with full intention" (485)—a clearer way forward than the aporia inherent in a sentient weapon (539).

By the time *He, She, and It* was published, the dystopian future glimpsed in *Woman on the Edge of Time* had slouched much nearer to reality. Piercy's return to speculative fiction fifteen years after *Woman on the Edge of Time*, and the epistemic turn toward a deeper history via the golem story and its attendant philosophical excursions, seem intended to offer new ways to resist that future. Both novels conclude with self-sacrifice, with Connie sacrificing herself and her future—and the lives of her manipulative doctors—in an effort to secure Luciente's world, and with Yod's death in the final struggle against the multinationals. But Shira, Tikva, Nili's people, and the freedom fighters from the Glop remain living communities, able to enter into a future of their own making. Like other feminist cyberpunk and post-cyberpunk texts, *He, She and It* works to mobilize communitarian rather than individualist forces in order to offer a more optimistic (albeit guardedly so) vision of their deployment: less a dichotomy of eutopia and dystopia than a continuum of social and technological agency.

See also: **Pat Cadigan, William Gibson, Donna J. Haraway, Joanna Russ, Neal Stephenson, Lana and Lilly Wachowski**

Notes

1 For details on 'post-cyberpunk,' see Kilgore; Murphy.
2 See Delany for added details.
3 For added consideration, see Burling.
4 Not counting *The Animatrix* (2003) or various webcomics and other tie-ins, the Matrix franchise consists of *The Matrix* (1999); *The Matrix Reloaded* (2003), *The Matrix Revolutions (2003),* and the forthcoming *The Matrix Resurrections* (2021).Tad Williams's Otherland series: *City of Golden Shadow* (1996), *River of Blue Fire* (1998), *Mountain of Black Glass* (1999), and *Sea of Silver Light* (2001). Lyda Morehouse's AngeLINK series: *Archangel Protocol* (2001), *Fallen Host* (2002), *Messiah Node* (2003), *Apocalypse Array* (2004), and the prequel *Resurrection Code* (2011).

Works Cited

Booker, M. Keith. "Woman on the Edge of a Genre: The Feminist Dystopias of Marge Piercy." *Science Fiction Studies*, vol. 21, no. 3, 1994, pp. 337–50.
Burling, William J. "Reading Time: The Ideology of Time Travel in Science Fiction." *KronoScope: Journal for the Study of Time*, vol. 6, no. 1, 2006, pp. 5–30, doi: 10.1163/156852406777505255.

Delany, Samuel. "'Some *Real* Mothers …' The *SF Eye* Interview." *Silent Interviews: On Language, Race, Sex, Science Fiction, and Some Comics.* Wesleyan UP, 1994, pp. 164–85.

Kessler, Carol Farley. "*Woman on the Edge of Time*: A Novel 'to Be of Use.'" *Extrapolation*, vol. 28, no. 4, 1987, pp. 310–18, doi: 10.3828/extr.1987.28.4.310.

Kilgore, Christopher D. "Post-Cyberpunk." *The Routledge Companion to Cyberpunk Culture*, edited by Anna McFarlane, Graham J. Murphy, and Lars Schmeink, Routledge, 2020, pp. 48–56.

Moylan, Tom. *Demand the Impossible: Science Fiction and the Utopian Imagination.* Methuen, 1986.

Murphy, Graham J. "Cyberpunk and Post-Cyberpunk." *The Cambridge History of Science Fiction*, edited by Gerry Canavan and Eric Carl Link, Cambridge UP, 2018, pp. 519–36.

Piercy, Marge. *He, She and It.* Random House, 1991.

———. *Woman on the Edge of Time.* Ballantine, 1976.

Somay, Bülent and Robert M. Pilmus. "Towards an Open-Ended Utopia." *Science Fiction Studies*, vol. 11, no. 1, 1984, pp. 25–38.

Christopher D. Kilgore

SADIE PLANT (1964–)

British philosopher and author.

Sadie Plant holds a Ph.D. in Philosophy from the University of Manchester and is considered one of the leading thinkers in the cultural criticism of technology. She has contributed to cyberpunk culture with a feminist critique of technological patriarchy, defined in relation to human transfer into cyber-reality. Her work includes three critical books and numerous book chapters, journal papers, magazine entries, exhibition comments, and conference addresses. In 1995, she and Nick Land co-founded the Cybernetic Culture Research Unit (CCRU) in the Department of New Technology at Warwick University, which she directed until 1997 when she left academia. In her role as "a self-proclaimed cyberfeminist who has been described as the most interesting woman in Britain" (Treneman), Plant has also lectured at the universities of Birmingham and Manchester. She is most notably acclaimed for recognizing technology's potential for women's liberation, and for coining the term 'cyberfeminism.'

Plant's writings engage with various aspects of 'new technoculture' to deal with gender hierarchy in modern technocracies. Her work challenges male visions of technological progression, historically and conceptually revisiting existing imaginaries of cyber-science and cyber-reality. Plant's *Zeros + Ones: Digital Women + The New Technoculture* (1997)—considered "a brilliant and terrifically sustained cyberfeminist rant" and "the best and most original book on the history of ubiquitous computation" ("A Loom with a View")—discloses connections between the cyborg nature of femininity and the masculine encoding of automation. Mapping the history of cybernetics through the story of Ada Lovelace, the nineteenth-century mathematician famous for her work on the Analytical Engine and computer programming, Plant unravels and undercuts the myth of women's inability to think technologically.

Plant's diagnoses are often deeply metaphorical. They also entail notions and coinages that are themselves meta-criticism for naming the mashes of techno and bio environments. Her writing is considered abstract, fragmented, collage-like, and meticulously researched. It became a major inspiration for the current generation of feminist criticism, recently incarnated by *xenofeminism*—"a labour of bricolage, synthesizing cyberfeminism, posthumanism, accelerationism, neorationalism, materialist feminism, and so on—in an attempt to forge a project suited to contemporary political conditions [...] a project for which the future remains open as a site of radical recomposition" (Hester, *Xenofeminism* 1, 152), and whose impact on cyberpunk is still unfolding.

A focal point of Plant's philosophy is the liberating potential of cyberspace and the role of computers in women's emancipation. She specifically reenchants technology-related cultural myths as well as reclaiming high tech for the feminine. "There was this notion," she explains in an interview, "that there was something inherently male about the Net and that you really did have to be a boy nerd to deal with it. I started off simply trying to ditch this notion of it all being masculine and quite by accident I found all these fascinating characters—such as Ada—who really did tell a very interesting story" (cited in Treneman). Thus, Plant's cybertheory and historiographies overlap with arguments around cyberpunk, leveled by science fiction (sf) feminist theorists[1] who, dubbing cyberpunk a fiction "written for the most part by a small number of white middle-class men" (Hollinger 207), aptly defied the genre's representational accountability.

Plant also amplifies the voices of the 1990s feminist wave in cyberpunk fiction—e.g., **Pat Cadigan**, **Marge Piercy**, Laura J. Mixon, **Melissa Scott**, and others—who signaled a need for narratives and epistemologies free from the masculinist outlook that were able to reflect on human techno-environments away from patriarchal terms. Although a lot of her ideas echo concerns blamed on early cyberpunk, including hypermasculinized representation, reactionary worldview, obeisance to authority, and ignorance of sexual politics, Plant uses cyberpunk as a point of reference rather than object of critique. Authors she most often mentions include **J. G. Ballard**, **William Gibson**, Greg Bear, Pat Cadigan, and Octavia Butler. These references seem less interested in the nuances of the development of cyberpunk as a literary genre and more in the conceptual vocabulary the genre (and those authors) provide for the metaphorization of technologized reality outside fiction. Nonetheless, she taps into the revolutionary (and experimental) potential claimed by cyberpunk female authors who, in Plant's view, transform techno-environments from "space for men" into "the integrated circuit" ("Beyond the Screens" 14). "From the perspective of a socialist or humanist feminist," Plant writes, "[cyberpunk] fictions are dystopian visions of future gone wrong; a world for which the revolution never happened. While cyberpunk is often detested for this realism, an increasing number of feminist critics see the possibilities of cyberpunk" ("Beyond the Screens" 15). To Plant, the hope for cyberpunk lies in "the fact that more women are writing cyberpunk fiction" and, paraphrasing Joan Gordon's words "[i]f science fiction can show what it means to be female in the world toward which we hurtle, I want to read it" ("Beyond the Screens" 15).

As a cyberpunk philosopher *par excellence*, Plant is both inspired by cyberpunk imaginaries as well as inspiring many (even if not directly).[2] Her critical exploration of human relationships with cyberspace uses the abstract of high tech to unveil the traps of social organization in a manner characteristic of cyberpunk fiction. Like many cyberpunk writers, Plant delineates technocracies without criticizing technologies; her critique is aimed at technology-facilitated forms of social control. The gendering of labor (woman as a machine), the mechanization of reproduction (womb versus fertility technologies), and the automatization of communication (the media technologies as discourse) are central to her writing. Plant's philosophy proclaims the ever-advancing alienation of social and cultural systems, and solutions to this situation include counter alienations, which is the topic of her two books *The Most Radical Gesture: The Situationist Movement in a Postmodern Age* (1992) and *Writing on Drugs* (1999). The latter discusses the transformative potency of "the virtual" analyzed in relation to the role of psychoactive substances for a creative process.

Drugs as a metaphor for cyberspatial experience is a solid feature of cyberpunk narratives whose characters often shove a big needle into their skull to move between dimensions, epitomized in **Lana and Lilly Wachowski**'s *The Matrix* (1999). In his Preface to *Mirrorshades:*

The Cyberpunk Anthology (1986), **Bruce Sterling** dubs drugs "definitive high-tech products" (xiii) linking them with hallucinatory media (e.g., computers)[3] that initiated the era of cyberdelic escapism and what Graham St. John describes as the "turn on, boot up, jack in" culture (142). Plant's book expands this perspective by tracing the drug routines of Coleridge (opium), Freud (cocaine), Michaux (mescaline), Burroughs (you name it), and other authors who have pursued realities that both destroy and create the self against the structured reality. "To write on drugs," Plant observes, "is to plunge into a world where nothing is as simple or as stable as it seems. Everything about it shimmers and mutates as you try to hold its gaze. Facts and figures dance around each other; lines of inquiry scatter like expensive dust" (*Writing* 248). The book recounts how narcotics have always triggered new perceptions and brought to the fore alternative planes. Long before VR systems—which have also affected our states, moods, and perspectives, and which have been a significant 'influence' on our understanding of matter—psychoactive substances unpacked the neuro-chemical potential of our minds in ways that restructured human thinking about reality; they helped to reposition a human mind in the stiff structures of human flesh.

The role of cyberspace in this context is shown in the potential of an intangible (dematerialized) and displaced body. Considered a womb for weaving one's own subjectivity, cyberspace is a plane for the emancipated transgression of self (Plant, "The Future Looms" 46). This womb renders both *hysteria* and *matrix*; it is "matter, both the mother and the material," which Gibson's *Neuromancer* called "the nonspace": "neither something nor nothing" (Plant, "On the Matrix" 333). Based on the paradox of veiled appearances (from behind the screen) and displayed operations (global reach), cyberspace is an all-encompassing and un-categorizing channel for communication and performance. More importantly, it grants the liberating "absence of penis and its power"— an argument, which became core to the cyberfeminist stance.

A keystone of Plant's criticism, cyberfeminism renders the use of high-tech professions and environments (traditionally associated with men) for advancing the feminist agenda through self-representation by means of "growing expertise in navigating the internet, producing webpages, electronic zines and blogs" (Whelehan xvi). Proposed by Plant in 1991, the term "cyberfeminism" signifies "information technology as a fluid attack, an onslaught on human agency and the solidity of identity" ("Beyond the Screens" 13). "Cyberfeminism," Plant explains, "is simply an acknowledgement that patriarchy is doomed" ("Beyond the Screens" 13), and that gender-based differences in digital discourse are giving in to re-appropriations of the masculinized new information and communication technologies. Although regarded by Plant as "an alien invasion, a program which is already running beyond the human" rather than "a political project" ("Beyond the Screens" 13), cyberfeminism has gained the status of a movement. It became notorious for initiatives such as "A Cyberfeminist Manifesto for the 21st Century," a billboard project by Australian feminist collective VNS Matrix that outlines the abjection and virality of networked femininity.

A huge inspiration for the movement, and for Plant herself, was Donna Haraway's "A Cyborg Manifesto." Using Haraway's woman-cyborg metaphor, Plant revisits the hegemonies that predispose female biological and intellectual faculties. According to Plant, to be a subject, that is, to "gain full membership of the species," women must incessantly prove their efficiency and usability in conditions whereby male is a unitary "1" and female is the absent "0" (*Zeros + Ones* 58). Standing up against such binaries, Plant traces the ontological overlaps of womanhood and machinery, alluding to the masculine nature of the technological environment represented by zeros and ones. She identifies the preconditioning of femininity and the historical ways of circumventing it. More importantly, she points to the programming of both women and machines toward service, obedience, and intelligent assistance aimed at freeing men from overwhelming or dull tasks that exploit women's predisposition to organize, manage, store, prepare, facilitate, and multi-task, and which have eventually earned them a way to taking over men's jobs ("Conference Presentation").

An avid cyberpunk feminist, Plant preaches the emergence of a geek-girl: she-programmer, female coder, woman-hacker. This trope of cyberpositivity (Plant and Land, "Cyberpositive") infests cyberpunk imagery and revolutionizes old "feminine mystiques," putting the cyborg over the goddess (to paraphrase Haraway), exerting deep structural changes in systemic thinking about femininity. Those changes span from linguistics to neurobiology—the former relating to the web as a space for algorithmic poetics begetting new idioms of womanhood; the latter to disorder in matter (the intangible), in substance (quantum), in space (the limitless), as well as their psychological energies. All those problems, as first rehearsed in cyberpunk fiction, have been part of the "visionary intensity" (Sterling xiv) that stirs social practice toward the posthuman condition.

See also: **Pat Cadigan, Donna J. Haraway, Marge Piercy, Melissa Scott, Lana and Lilly Wachowski**

Notes

1 For details see also Nixon, Cadora, Leblanc, and Yaszek.
2 Plant's influence (to greater or lesser degrees) can be found in Elizabeth Bear's *Carnival* (2006), Annalee Newitz's *Autonomous* (2017), Shelly Jackson's post-2000 narrative experiments, and the hypertext work of Carolyn Guertin.
3 It is also no coincidence that Timothy Leary, an advocate for psychedelic drugs, should have written "Cyberpunk: The Individual as Reality Pilot" for the cyberpunk Special Issue of *Mississippi Review* (vol. 16, no. 2/3, 1988), which became the foundation for Larry McCaffery's *Storming the Reality Studio: A Casebook of Cyberpunk and Postmodern Fiction.*

Works Cited

"A loom with a view." *The Irish Times.* October 9, 1997. https://www.irishtimes.com/culture/a-loom-with-a-view-1.113972.
Graham, St. John. *Technomad: Global Raving Countercultures.* Equinox, 2009.
Hester, Helen. *Xenofeminism.* Polity, 2018.
Hollinger, Veronica. "Cybernetic Deconstructions." *Storming the Reality Studio: A Casebook of Cyberpunk and Postmodern Science Fiction*, edited by Larry McCaffery, Duke UP, 1991, pp. 203–2018.
Plant, Sadie. "Beyond the Screens: Film, Cyberpunk and Cyberfeminism." *Variant*, vol. 14, no. 1, 1993, pp. 12–17.
———. "The Future Looms: Weaving Women and Cybernetics." *Body & Society*, vol. 3–4, no. 1, 1995, pp. 45–64.
———. *The Most Radical Gesture: The Situationist Movement in a Postmodern Age.* Routledge, 1992.
———. "On the Matrix: Cyberfeminist Simulations." *The Cybercultures Reader*, edited by David Bell and Barbara M. Kennedy, Routledge, 2001, pp. 326–36.
———. "Seduced and Abandoned: The Body in the Virtual World—The Feminine Cyberspace." Institute of Contemporary Arts (London), March 11–13, 1994, https://www.youtube.com/watch?v=doL9mRMEUGw&t=1795s, [00:00–29:15].
———. *Writing on Drugs.* Faber, 1999.
———. *Zeros + Ones. Digital Women + The New Technoculture.* Fourth Estate, 1997.
Plant, Sadie and Nick Land. "Cyberpositive." *Accelerate. The Accelerationist Reader*, edited by Robin MacKay and Armen Avenessian, Urbanomic/MerveVerlag, 2014, pp. 301–13.
Sterling, Bruce. Preface. *Mirrorshades: The Cyberpunk Anthology*, edited by Bruce Sterling, Ace, 1986, pp. ix–xvi.
Treneman, Ann. "Interview: Sadie Plant: IT girl for the 21st century." *Independent*, October 12, 1997, https://www.independent.co.uk/life-style/interview-sadie-plant-it-girl-for-the-21st-century-1235380.html.
Whelehan, Imelda. Foreword. *Third Wave Feminism: A Critical Exploration*, edited by Stacy Gillis, Gillian Howie, and Rebecca Munford, Palgrave Macmillan, 2007, pp. xv–xx.

Ania Malinowska

MICHAEL ALYN 'MAXIMUM MIKE' PONDSMITH (1954–)

US game designer.

Mike Pondsmith is widely known as the world-builder and a co-designer of CD Projekt Red's (CDPR's) *Cyberpunk 2077* (2020), an action role-playing video game set in a near future based on over three decades of published game content from Pondsmith's company R. Talsorian Games (RTG). His instrumental role in creating *Cyberpunk* (1988), among other tabletop role-playing games (TRPGs) cannot be overstated. *Cyberpunk* helped establish the aesthetic and mechanical basis for all future cyberpunk game franchises, including *Shadowrun* (1989–), *Deus Ex* (2000–), *SLA Industries* (1993), and *Invisible, Inc.* (2015). *Cyberpunk 2020* (1990), the best-known edition of his TRPG, is set in Night City, an American dystopian metropolis that features cyber-equipped, street-savvy mercenaries ("edgerunners") who stylishly break into secure facilities to extract valuable goods. These edge-runners are "survivors in a tough, grim world, faced with life and death choices [...The] quintessential *Cyberpunk* character is a rebel with a cause" (Pondsmith et al. 3). Pondsmith envisioned the TRPG prose and game mechanics required for players to successfully run their *own* cyberpunk stories and established the boundaries, norms, values, and verbs of most successor cyberpunk game titles. *Cyberpunk 2077* took his work to a far greater audience and, despite its well-publicized release issues, represented a significant development in cyberpunk culture.

Pondsmith designed his first game by age eleven, an untitled hyper-space travel game modeled on chess, but it was when he was at the University of California Davis in the 1970s that he met Greg Worth, who introduced him to hobbyist wargaming and, later, *Chainmail*—the precursor to *Dungeons & Dragons*. Playing in the "seedy" Strip area of town, Pondsmith sported "mirrorshades, a ratty army jacket, motorcycle boots and carried a six-inch knife" (Purchese 2017) to dissuade trouble. Pondsmith's graphic design degree landed him his first real job: artist and typesetter at California Pacific, which manufactured boxes for early video games such as *Ultima* (1980).

Slightly past the midway point of the 1970s, Pondsmith stumbled upon Marc Miller's science fiction (sf) TRPG *Traveller* (1977), sold at the time in a slick black box containing multiple books. "If Marc Miller had never written *Traveller*," Pondsmith confesses, "I would have never become a game designer" (cited in Lowder 331).

Pondsmith was immediately attracted to *Traveller*'s character creation system. *Traveller* characters were not novices out on their first adventure; rather, unlike *D&D*, these characters were experienced veterans with biographical depth and a breadth of skills. He was also impressed by the simplicity of the rules and the tools the game provided to build one's own starships, star systems, planets, and alien cultures. *Traveller* introduced Pondsmith to the act of creating "house rules" for the game—i.e., a set of agreed-upon rules for a particular TRPG that are only in play with a particular gamemaster or player group—and these experiences would shape Pondsmith's later work. For example, his first TRPG creation was the spacefaring *Imperial Star* (1982), which led him to a series of epiphanies. "A designer has to think in a much larger *meta*," he commented. "[What pieces] am I going to give to [the players]? [...] *Imperial Star* was a learning experience where I figured out how these pieces work" ("Storytime" 2020).

While the early 1980s signaled the emergence of both literary and cinematic cyberpunk, Pondsmith was instead fixated on the new giant robot designs rolling out of Japan. His first commercial game was inspired by the wildly popular giant mecha anime *Mobile Suit Gundam* (1979–80), entitled *Mekton* (1984). Building on his previous game experience, Pondsmith made it so the player could build and hold battles with giant humanoid spaceships. He was not the only one with giant robots in mind. Riding on the wave of mecha euphoria sparked by the 1985 TV release of *RoboTech* and such competing games as *BattleDroids* (1984), which would become the popular *BattleTech* (1985), and *MechWarrior* (1986) franchises, *Mekton* sold well enough to at least cover the costs of a comedy TRPG *Teenagers from Outer Space* (1987). More important, Pondsmith used borrowed money to found RTG, now regarded as the first Black-owned TRPG company.

In a manner reminiscent of *Traveller*, *Cyberpunk* (1988) was packaged in a stylish box containing several slick black books that promised imaginative gameplay spread over not only the main game but also such early supplements as *Rockerboy*, *Soldier of Fortune*, and *Hardwired*, all published in 1989. The "role-playing game of the dark future," *Cyberpunk 2013* (as it eventually came to be known) laid out the epic characters and world that would be further popularized across the franchise, including *Cyberpunk 2077*: Night City, edgerunning, Johnny Silverhand, Morgan Blackhand, Rache Bartmoss, and Spider Murphy. *Cyberpunk 2020* (1990) updated the rules for character creation, combat, and netrunning (or hacking) and marked the evolution from a box set into a standalone rulebook, reflecting a new era of TRPG publishing around so-called "splatbooks," or supplemental rules and adventures packaged in books with flashy covers made to attract core fans. Although *Cyberpunk* was the core of RTG's product line, Pondsmith released alternative, more experimental products as well: the surrealist sf game *Dream Park* (1992), the youth rebellion game *CyberGeneration* (1993), and the breakthrough steampunk TRPG *Castle Falkenstein* (1994). While *Cyberpunk 2020* became central to the cultural iconography of cyberpunk sf and gaming, Pondsmith continued to evolve and refused to remain defined by his best-known creation or the cyberpunk mode more generally.

As president of the Game Manufacturing Association (GAMA) in the early 1990s, Pondsmith was clearly an established TRPG industry figure. *Cyberpunk 2020* was licensed into the collectible card game *Netrunner* (1996), which evolved its own parallel cyberpunk universe and fandom over the next 25 years. Meanwhile, Pondsmith tapped Ben Wright and David Ackerman to create the TRPG *Bubblegum Crisis* (1996) based on the cyberpunk anime, which sparked discussions with Hero Games about releasing a shared TRPG system called *Fuzion*. *Fuzion* was a free, generic game system released over the Internet, one of the first of its kind, and it primarily supported action-oriented anime play. Wright, Ackerman, and Pondsmith, among others, sought to create a universal TRPG system that would be instantly intuitive to younger generations, who were interested in customizing their characters and less interested in watching them suffer and die, as with earlier games.

By the late 1990s, the TRPG industry—with its boxes, licenses, and splatbooks—had largely imploded, and during this stressful time Pondsmith took a job with Microsoft to develop video games for the early Xbox console. Titles included *MechCommander 2* (2001)—in which he played a cameo part as Steel—*Blood Wake* (2001), and *Crimson Skies* (2003). Pondsmith's enthusiasm for a cyberpunk renaissance, thanks to the commercial and cultural success of **Lana and Lilly Wachowski**'s *The Matrix* (1999), led him to pitch a *Matrix* game for Microsoft, but it would never be greenlighted. He left Microsoft in 2004 for Monolith Productions to work on *The Matrix Online* (2005) a massive multiplayer online role-playing game (MMORPG) based on the *Matrix* movies. RTG continued to re-release back-catalog product, but a new edition of *Cyberpunk*—*Cyberpunk 3.0* (2005)—fell flat among fans and critics alike. Pondsmith took a job as a game design instructor at DigiPen in the late 2000s, and his son, Cody, became increasingly central to RTG's continued development. Cody joined Lisa Pondsmith, Mike's longtime wife and collaborator, in creating *The Witcher* "pen and paper RPG" (2018) with CDPR. This deal owed its existence to CDPR, whose Polish lead developers were huge fans of *Cyberpunk 2020* and had already announced in 2012 the planned release of *Cyberpunk 2077*, granting RTG the rights to develop its already-popular *Witcher* intellectual property within the TRPG market. Fans intuited that CDPR's intricate worldbuilding, attention to detail in character and quest design, and engaging combat systems evident in *The Witcher* games would enchant Pondsmith's *Cyberpunk 2020* universe. When a 2019 trailer revealed cyberpunk icon and *Matrix* franchise star Keanu Reeves in the role of Silverhand, the videogame's fanbase expanded exponentially. Pondsmith continued to fly to Poland semi-annually to consult on the primary details of the *Cyberpunk 2077* game, and in so doing divided his work between a TRPG designer and a video game designer and consultant. Despite numerous, even maddening, delays, *Cyberpunk 2077* was released in December 2020, while RTG released *Cyberpunk Red* (2020) to coincide with the videogame, an adaptation and re-release of the *Cyberpunk* TRPG with a coherent timeline leading to the time period depicted in *Cyberpunk* 2077. Although Pondsmith commented that *Cyberpunk Red* "almost killed [the employees of RTG]" and that the release of *Cyberpunk 2077* was coupled with widespread coverage of its bugs and playability issues (particularly on console play), R. Talsorian employees confirm *Cyberpunk Red* continues to receive healthy product support and is selling well.

Pondsmith's contributions to cyberpunk include popularizing the term within gaming circles, inspiring many other product lines, such as *Shadowrun* and *Netrunner*, and maintaining a richly detailed, thoughtfully extrapolated storyworld for his *Cyberpunk* universe. Along with his wife, son, and RTG in general, Pondsmith has become synonymous with *Cyberpunk 2020*, a game that provided an entry point into a broader cyberpunk mode given over to gun violence and mega-corporate dominance, albeit with stylish technology and cyberware. Undoubtedly, millions will now associate him with *Cyberpunk 2077* (for better or for worse) in part because Pondsmith has made numerous public appearances playing the role of franchise creator to promote the newest iteration of the *Cyberpunk* universe, while also continuing to have substantial input on the overall look and feel of the videogame. He has joined the ranks of other TRPG designers who became videogame superstars: **Warren Spector** and Greg Costikyan. *Cyberpunk Red* will also help maintain the franchise's visibility in the hobby game world and continues to quietly uphold the *Traveller* mechanics and game tools. As a Black American game designer, however, Pondsmith also recognizes the roles of wealth disparity, structural inequality, and racist backlash, all of which are features of a cyberpunk universe. For example, he has emphasized in a 2020 RTG press release that *Cyberpunk* was a "warning, not an aspiration." And, against the backdrop of Black Lives Matter and the brutalization of protesters nationwide, Pondsmith turned to his gamer audience: "It's time to wake up; to face down the people who want in the end, to enslave all of us." In sum, Pondsmith created a player-friendly cyberpunk universe to reflect and expand upon gritty, crime-saturated urban existence, and although it was never intended to predict our collective fate—"Even though I wrote a dystopian dark future about the world called *Cyberpunk 2020*, I am not going to take responsibility for what's going on right now" (cited in Pax)—the ongoing popularity of Pondsmith's creative work demonstrates that *Cyberpunk* (and cyberpunk) perhaps has more cultural relevance today than ever before.

See also: **Warren Spector, Lana and Lilly Wachowski**

Works Cited

Lowder, James, editor. *Hobby Games: The 100 Best*. Green Ronin, 2007.
Pondsmith, Mike. "Mike Pondsmith: Cops and Racists." *R. Talsorian Games*. Blog, June 12, 2020, https://rtalsoriangames.com/2020/06/12/mike-pondsmith-cops-and-racists/.
———, et al. *Cyberpunk 2020: The Roleplaying Game of the Dark Future*. R. Talsorian Games, 1990.
———. *Mekton*. R. Talsorian Games, 1984.
———. "Storytime with Cyberpunk Creator Mike Pondsmith." *YouTube*, uploaded by PAX Online, 2020, http://www.youtube.com/watch?v=MMBJtQzzkBg.
Purchese, Robert. "Making Cyberpunk: When Mike Pondsmith Met CD Projekt Red." *Eurogamer*, July 13, 2017, https://www.eurogamer.net/articles/2017-07-12-making-cyberpunk-when-mike-pondsmith-met-cd-projekt-red.

Evan Torner

THOMAS PYNCHON (1937–)

US author

In his Preface to *Mirrorshades: The Cyberpunk Anthology* (1986), **Bruce Sterling** outlined the literary and cultural influences that had helped form the cyberpunk ethos, from **J.G. Ballard** to **Alvin and Heidi Toffler**, the hacker underground to hip-hop music. But he reserved a "special admiration for a writer whose integration of technology and literature remains unsurpassed: Thomas Pynchon" (x). In a 1986 interview with Larry McCaffery, **William Gibson** referred to Pynchon as his "mythic hero," whose work—especially the 1973 novel *Gravity's Rainbow*—prompted his interest in "a certain mutant pop culture imagery" fused with "esoteric historical and scientific information." McCaffrey included an excerpt from Pynchon's *The Crying of Lot 49* (1965) in his definitive anthology *Storming the Reality Studio: A Casebook of Cyberpunk and Postmodern Fiction* (1991), where he and Richard Kadrey also described *Gravity's Rainbow* as "the best cyberpunk ever written by a guy who didn't even know he was writing it" (21).

The excerpt from *The Crying of Lot 49* featured in McCaffrey's casebook is a brief scene wherein the protagonist, Oedipa Maas, experiences an epiphany in which the geography of a California suburb, with its "ordered swirl of houses and streets," reminds her of a printed circuit card in a transistor radio: both patterned layouts seem to suggest "a hieroglyphic sense of concealed meaning, of an intent to communicate" (Pynchon, *Crying* 24). The passage is quintessential Pynchon, depicting the imbrication of the human world with technological systems, a sinister cybernetic enmeshment characteristic of postwar technocracy. Pynchon knew that technocracy intimately, having worked as a technical writer for Boeing after leaving college; indeed, few modern authors can match Pynchon's technical expertise, and his novels are filled with deft deployments of scientific concepts and rich explorations of the history of technology. His first novel, *V.* (1963) features a lengthy subplot in which a young engineer, before joining the Yoyodyne Corporation (a satirical swipe at Boeing), studies atmospheric radio signals that, like Oedipa's suburb/circuit board, seem to proffer cryptic messages. This character reappears in Pynchon's magnum opus, *Gravity's Rainbow*, spouting a kind of "electro-mysticism," whose sacred trinity is "the cathode, the anode, and the holy grid" (404).

As these examples suggest, Pynchon's novels are units in an evolving mosaic, with characters and ideas recurring from book to book, and with an overarching focus on the tempos and trajectories of western technoscience as it comes to grasp and command the world. This focus helps to explain his popularity among the cyberpunks, and within the science fiction (sf) field more generally,[1] but there is also a pronounced Gothic strain to his technocultural imaginings. Pynchon's novels trade on a powerful charge of paranoia, a sense that the modern world is governed by malign and inscrutable forces—secret societies, sinister cults, evil conspiracies spinning like a muffled clockwork behind the scenes. His fictive universe is radically Manichean, split between agencies of light and darkness, and increasingly weighted to the advantage of the latter faction; the typical Pynchon plot pits an amiable everyman (or woman) against some vast, ungraspable network whose designs on the world, while obscure, are decidedly not benevolent.

Gravity's Rainbow remains his classic treatment of this theme, a novel in which a disorganized counterculture of losers and oddballs, centering on protagonist Tyrone Slothrop, does battle with a faceless "They," which may not be a conscious entity at all but rather a mindless, mechanized nexus of "structures favoring death. Death converted into more death. Perfecting its reign" (167). The explosion of high-tech research sparked off by World War II, which the novel details with a dazzling erudition, is shown to have a hidden occult agenda, driven "by something that needed the energy burst of war" to fulfill "*the planetary mission* yes perhaps centuries in the unrolling [...] waiting for its Kabbalists and new alchemists to discover the Key, teach the mysteries to others" (521). The main narrative agent in the text is a sadistic Gestapo officer obsessed with the V-2 rocket, an instrumentality of destruction that has invaded and remade his psyche and sexuality, the "great airless arc" of its supersonic flight "a clear allusion to certain lusts that drive the planet [...] and Those who use her—over its peak and down, plunging, burning, toward a terminal orgasm" (223). The cybernetic processes of feedback and automated control that guide the rocket come to govern the lives of those living in its terrible shadow, and the novel is filled with delirious imagery of an increasingly cyborgized existence, of characters haplessly enmeshed with the soft machinery of twentieth-century techno-capitalism, from scientific bureaucracy to Pavlovian mind control.

In cleverly metafictive fashion, Pynchon shows how this sinister technocracy differs radically from the gleaming high-tech future prophesied by the early sf pulps, wherein the rocket offered a promise of escape and transcendence, not a sophisticated mechanism of terror and death. As Slothrop descends into an underground V-2 factory, he experiences a hallucinatory vision of a futuristic "Rocket City," replete with "dioramas on the theme 'The Promise of Space Travel'"; yet, "[s]trangely, these are not the symmetries we were programmed to expect, not the fins, the streamlined corners, pylons, or simple solid geometries of the official version at all" (297), but rather a brutal and overlit fascist utopia. This fiercely satirical passage likely inspired Gibson's "The Gernsback Continuum" (1981), wherein the "spray-paint pulp utopias" of sf illustrator Frank R. Paul screen a core of technocratic violence: "The Thirties dreamed white marble and slipstream chrome, immortal crystal and burnished bronze, but the rockets on the covers of the Gernsback pulps had fallen on London in the dead of night, screaming" (32)—a clear echo of *Gravity's Rainbow*'s famous opening line: "A screaming comes across the sky" (3).

But while there are obvious parallels between Pynchon's vision of dystopian modernity and that of the cyberpunks, there are also significant differences. Like Pynchon, cyberpunk authors have been drawn to weird alternative histories of modern technoscience, where the fringe and the mainstream converge, and where—in Gibson's evocative formulation—"the street finds its own uses for things" ("Burning" 195). For both, high-tech objects, from the V-2 to the computer, take on charged, fetishistic meanings, at once cultic and erotic, whether it be Slothrop "dowsing" for rockets with his erect penis (490) or Case, in *Neuromancer*, "pornographic[ally]" stroking the keys of his Ono-Sendai console (47). The cyberpunks share with Pynchon a gearhead fascination for the wayward, anarchic energies of technical invention, but whereas Pynchon is a genuine anarchist who delights in exploding readerly desires for linear storytelling as much as he does in subverting established sociopolitical order, the cyberpunks are better described as libertarian in their leanings, skeptical of institutional orthodoxies but committed, as befits their genre roots, to cohesive plotting and an abiding, if occasionally ambivalent, technological optimism.

While the cyberpunks might be dubious about specific applications of technical expertise, such as the attempt by corrupt elites to use artificial intelligence to cement their hegemony (as in *Neuromancer*), they are not suspicious of technological rationality itself, as Pynchon often is. Certainly, the likes of Gibson and Sterling would never feel prompted to ask, as Pynchon did in a 1984 essay, "Is It Okay to be a Luddite?" Their divergent attitudes toward technology can be seen in their respective stabs at steampunk retrofuturism: Gibson and Sterling's *The Difference Engine* (1990) and Pynchon's *Against the Day* (2006), both of which evoke a Victorian era transformed by anachronistic technologies. But while Gibson and Sterling playfully trace an alternative path of technological progress, they do not reject progress itself, do not see secular modernity as a dire process whereby "unshaped freedom [is] rationalized into movement only in straight lines and right angles," a systematic "reduction of choices, until the final turn through the final gate that led to the killing-floor" (Pynchon, *Against* 10). Like *Gravity's Rainbow*, *Against the Day* sharply satirizes science fiction's confidence in the technological future as a naïve faith fit only for "simpletons [...] gawking at your Wonders of Science, expecting as your entitlement all the Blessings of Progress," which have, like the V-2 rocket, ushered in only a "history of Hell" (554–55).

Pynchon's key differences with the cyberpunks are most visible in his own attempt at a quasi-cyberpunk novel, *Bleeding Edge* (2013). Set during the dot-com crash in the days leading up to 9/11, the novel offers a gallery of satirical portraits of the denizens of Silicon Alley in New York: greedy venture capitalists rub shoulders with dreamy nerds, while Russian mobsters vie with scheming federal agents to advance their corrupt interests amidst the cascading catastrophes. *Bleeding Edge* is highly reminiscent of Gibson's Blue Ant trilogy,[2] following an intrepid female protagonist, fraud investigator Maxine Tarnow, as she puzzles out the agenda of tech billionaire Gabriel Ice and his shadowy start-up company, hashslingrz, with some dubious video footage (à la *Pattern Recognition*) providing a crucial McGuffin. The plot, as usual for Pynchon, is infernally complicated, but the thematic terrain is quite familiar to seasoned readers of the author: a technological landscape seething with conspiracies and paranoia, populated by an assortment of oddballs and crooks.

As the story progresses, Maxine becomes increasingly embroiled with a rogue website called DeepArcher (read: departure), hidden away from surface internet traffic in the "Deep Web." Like a Rorschach blot, DeepArcher means different things to different users: it is either an alluring techno-utopia shielded from the crass commercialism of the World Wide Web or a baleful harbinger of the erasure of "meatspace" in favor of virtuality. Unlike Gibson's console cowboys, who prefer the seeming freedom of cyberspace to the clear constraints of the mortal body, Maxine resists the "vortex taking her farther [...] into the virtual world" (429). In a key scene, her father warns her about the Cold War/militarist origins of the internet in the Pentagon's Defense Advanced Research Projects Agency (DARPA): "As it kept growing, it never stopped carrying in its heart a bitter-cold death wish for the planet [...] Call it freedom, it's based on control [...] Take the next step, connect it to these cell phones, you've got a total Web of surveillance, inescapable" (420). Readers of the novel, armed with such smartphones, are clearly meant to find this prophecy chilling; certainly, it tempers Maxine's fascination for the engrossing power of DeepArcher.

In *Bleeding Edge*, Pynchon demystifies and rejects the transcendence-through-virtuality proffered in so many cyberpunk texts, opting instead for a heartful embrace of mundane, meat-bound existence. This deep streak of Luddism, which has run through his work from the beginning, is linked to an earth-centered mysticism imbibed from the youth counterculture, whose influence on the author was immense (as can be seen especially in his novel *Vineland* [1990]). The cyberpunk writer he resembles most in this regard is **Rudy Rucker**, whose techno-utopianism is tempered by a folksy sensibility borrowed from the 1950s Beats and 1960s hippies. The more hardboiled postures of Gibson and Sterling seem a world away, by contrast. In a 2019 essay, Pascal Rioux-Couillard identified *Gravity's Rainbow* as "the missing link between hippie alternative mythology and cyberpunk disenchanted materialism," which perhaps explains the abiding fondness for it evident among so many cyberpunk authors.

See also: **J.G. Ballard, William Gibson, Rudy Rucker, Bruce Sterling, Alvin and Heidi Toffler**

Notes

1 *Gravity's Rainbow* was nominated for a Nebula Award by the Science Fiction Writers of America.
2 *Pattern Recognition* (2003); *Spook Country* (2007); *Zero History* (2010).

Works Cited

Rioux-Couillard, Pascal. "Is Cyberpunk a Sentient Light Bulb?" *Neon Dystopia*, January 9, 2019, https://www.neondystopia.com/cyberpunk-books-fiction/is-cyberpunk-a-sentient-light-bulb-a-review-of-gravitys-rainbow-by-thomas-pynchon/.

Gibson, William. "Burning Chrome." *Burning Chrome*. Arbor House, 1986, pp. 176–200.

———. "The Gernsback Continuum." *Burning Chrome*. Arbor House, 1986, pp. 28–40.

———. *Neuromancer*. Ace, 1984.

McCaffery, Larry. "An Interview with William Gibson." *The Cyberpunk Project*, 1986, http://project.cyberpunk.ru/idb/gibson_interview.html.

McCaffery, Larry and Richard Kadrey. "Cyberpunk 101: A Schematic Guide to *Storming the Reality Studio*." *Storming the Reality Studio: A Casebook of Cyberpunk and Postmodern Fiction*, edited by Larry McCaffery, Duke UP, 1991, pp. 17–29.

Pynchon, Thomas. *Against the Day*. Penguin, 2006.

———. *Bleeding Edge*. Penguin, 2013.

———. *The Crying of Lot 49*. Harper & Row, 1990.

———. *Gravity's Rainbow*. Penguin, 1987.

Sterling, Bruce. Preface. *Mirrorshades: The Cyberpunk Anthology*, edited by Bruce Sterling, Ace, 1986, pp. ix–xvi.

Rob Latham

RUDY [RUDOLF VON BITTER] RUCKER (1946–)

US author, mathematician, and computer programmer.

Rudy Rucker has published over twenty novels, eight short story collections, an autobiography, and ten works of nonfiction, many focusing on advanced mathematics (his Ph.D. specialization), higher dimensions, and computer programming. He published his first short story, "The Miracle" (1962), in the amateur magazine *The Pegasus* and his first novel was *Spacetime Donuts* (1981), although two-thirds of it had been previously published in *Unearth* in 1978 before the magazine folded. Rucker was one of the core Movement figures who, along with **William Gibson**, **Bruce Sterling**, **Lewis Shiner**, and John Shirley, were eventually branded as the original cyberpunks, and *Spacetime Donuts* provides an example of Rucker's relationship to cyberpunk which would reach its apotheosis in the Ware tetralogy, comprised of *Software* (1982), *Wetware* (1988), *Freeware* (1997), and *Realware* (2000), as well as *Postsingular* (2007) and its sequel *Hylozoic* (2008).

Spacetime Donuts is set in a dystopian world in which Dreamers use sockets in the back of their heads to plug themselves into the virtual heaven of the Phizwhiz, "a vast network of linked computers and robots [… that] always knew what the Users wanted" (1). In his autobiography *Nested Scrolls* (2011), Rucker is quick to point out the similarities between this and Gibson's console cowboys jacking into cyberspace in *Neuromancer* (1984), and to align his anarchic characters with the punk aesthetic: "In proto-cyberpunk fashion, my characters in *Spacetime Donuts* take drugs, have sex, listen to rock and roll, and are enemies of the establishment." However, *Spacetime Donuts* is less focused on virtual reality than its exploration of 'circular scale'—the theory that the universe is recursively folded into its own atoms—as Rucker's characters shrink so much that they find themselves on planet Earth again, inside the atoms of the world they started from. *Spacetime Donuts* therefore anticipates Rucker's focus not only on thought experiments based on advanced mathematics and higher dimensions that shape almost all his fiction, but also his notion of transrealism in which science fictional tropes are mixed with elements drawn from the author's lived experience ("Transrealist Manifesto").

Rucker tends to avoid the high tech/low life dichotomy and the noir-derived style adopted by much cyberpunk. The Philip K. Dick Award-winning *Software* is an early exploration of uploading one's consciousness into robotic bodies, and the play between its title and that of its sequel *Wetware* (which also won the Philip K. Dick Award) makes clear the parallels between the human brain and the computer, going so far as to imply interchangeability. For the human characters in the Ware books, there is no functional difference between robot brains running on computer code software or human brains running on the wetware of the nervous system. However, Rucker does not approach this subject with techno-utopianism, evidenced in *Software*'s Dickian paranoia about mind uploading; the process of mapping the full chemical contents and neural pathways of the human brain requires it to be destroyed in the process, so it is ambiguous whether the robot contains a copy of the human's consciousness or the original transferred into a new vessel. Cobb Anderson, the aging inventor of the robot boppers, faces this dilemma when the boppers, who have gained self-awareness, want to repay him with immortality: "Cobb Anderson's brain had been dissected, but the software that made up his mind had been preserved. The idea of 'self' is, after all, just another idea, a symbol in the software" (149). The uploaded Cobb is happy to accept his identity, but Sta-Hi Mooney, a drug-addled dropout who witnesses the destruction of Cobb's body, believes otherwise: "[W]hether you know it or not, Cobb Anderson is *dead*. I saw him die, and if you think you're him, you're just fooling yourself" (167). Although the novel never explicitly resolves the mystery around Cobb's ontological status, the novel leaves no doubt that uploaded Cobb is some kind of 'person.'

The 'personhood' status is mirrored in the boppers, Rucker's charming lunar-based robots. Cobb realizes that "[w]e cannot build an intelligent robot [...] But we can cause one to evolve" (84). Rather than programming intelligent self-aware robots, Cobb creates the conditions whereby artificial intelligences (AI) are faced with competition, randomization, and "a sort of [...] sexual reproduction, where two programs could merge" (84). The resulting boppers become contemptuous of the "Asimov priorities" (32) that make robots subservient to humans and revolt, whereupon they are exiled to the moon. *Software*'s twin threads—the evolution of AI and the uploading of human consciousness—dovetail in *Wetware*, in which the boppers figure out how to combine human DNA with the bopper software code to "merge bopperdom into the vast information network that is organic life on Earth" (33). In the story, Della Taze is impregnated with the altered code, giving birth to the first meatbop, Manchile, who attempts to impregnate as many human women as possible with meatbop offspring. Meanwhile, the corporation ISDN fights back against the boppers by recruiting Mooney to release chipmold, a fungus that feeds off the energy gradient in the boppers' silicon chips, which merges with the boppers to produce shape-shifting robot-fungi known as "mouldies."

Wetware further destabilizes the barrier between human and robot introduced in *Software* through the figures of the meatbops (a.k.a. meaties), who are humans with half their brains replaced by machines so the boppers can control them, and the mouldies born out of the melding of the chipmold and the boppers. While *Wetware* contains more traditional cyberpunk elements, such as the strange drug, Merge, which melts people together, Mooney's job as a private detective, the sinister corporation ISDN, and the character of Max Yukawa, who Rucker based on "[his] notion of Bill Gibson—a reclusive mastermind with a thin, strangely flexible head" (*Nested Scrolls*)—it (and *Software*) is testament to Rucker's penchant for gonzo humor, derived from the Beat writers and sf humorists (such as Robert Sheckley). Thus, building on this gonzo humor, *Freeware* and *Realware* complicate the arc of the series with mouldie-human sexual relations, the arrival of aliens coded as radio signals, and finally the introduction of the alla, a device that gives the user power of mind over matter. Rucker calls the underlying theme of the series "the process of expanding the range of things that we might regard as being patterns of information" (*Nested Scrolls*).

Rucker's cyberpunk themes and motifs are also evident in *Postsingular* and *Hylozoic*. In the case of the former, *Postsingular* was written as a contrarian response to sf's fixation on the technological Singularity—"I was mildly annoyed by the hype, and I liked the idea of leapfrogging past it" (*Nested Scrolls*)—and tells the story of tech corporation ExaExa releasing nanomachines called orphids that cover the surface of the Earth to form a network via quantum entanglement, which allows intelligence amplification and superhuman AI. The orphids "[learn] to directly interface with people's bodies and brains" (60), so that people can connect to the orphidnet without an interface and travel between neighboring quantum universes. *Postsingular* focuses on street punks Jayjay, Thuy, Sonic, and Kittie, who must collaborate with autistic child Chu and beings from a higher dimension to prevent disgraced ExaExa CEO Jeff Luty from releasing nants, nanomachines that will devour the entire planet and replace it with a digital copy. At the end of the novel, Jayjay and Thuy succeed in unrolling the eighth dimension, which allows everyone to "use a cosmic vanishing point for a universal Web server" (274), which increases the computational power of the world without destroying it. Its sequel *Hylozoic* is set in a world where "human-level artificial intelligence is ubiquitous" and "every object is conscious and alive" (*Nested Scrolls*). The orphidnet functions as an augmented reality overlay, somewhere between traditional cyberpunk representations of cyberspace and real-life interactions with the internet via smart devices. "The orphidnet is all around you," Ond, an ExaExa tech developer, proclaims. "Anyone can dip into it at any time. It'll be teaming with artificial intelligences soon, and I'm predicting they'll like helping people" (62). *Postsingular* is very much aligned with classic cyberpunk in its explorations of the media-saturated world of the internet. Case in point: orphidnet is populated by aggressive personalized ads, which must be stopped by "filter dog" (102) antivirus AI programs. The characters also get involved with *Founders*, an "orphidnet reality soap opera" (111) in which anyone can watch the minutiae of the everyday lives of Nektar Lundquist and her circle of friends, with Jayjay and Thuy becoming celebrities and main characters on the show by the time of *Hylozoic*. Rucker's transrealism is in evidence as Thuy attempts to write a "metanovel," an orphidnet-enhanced multimedia literature project based on her own life. "We're alchemists," Thuy says, "transmuting our lives into myth and fable" (145). In a world where reality is extraordinary, mundane everyday life becomes something to be celebrated and cherished.

Rucker's knowledge of advanced mathematics and his experiences in the world of computer programming have led to Rob Latham declaring him "the resident poet of Silicon Valley, capturing brilliantly the schizoid paradoxes of its techno-hippie ethos" (3). His Beat-derived humor, his enthusiasm, and his interest in drawing from his own life are important and influential to cyberpunk and its evolution. While not everyone agrees with this assessment,[1] and the depiction of female characters in the Ware novels leaves much to be desired, *Postsingular* and *Hylozoic* show that Rucker's views on technology and corporations have developed and become more nuanced over the years, pushing beyond 1980s-era cyberpunk and infusing a broader cyberpunk culture. For example, in *Postsingular* the character of Jeff Luty, ExaExa's disgraced founder, believes in the Singularity, fears death, and is plagued by disgust toward the corporeal body, all of which lead him to want to destroy the world and rebuild it as a nant simulation. In this characterization, Rucker offers a biting critique of tech corporations and the techno-utopianism of Silicon Valley, something lacking from *Wetware*'s portrayal of ISDN as an agent of chaos and change. In addition, Luty exerts his influence by buying politicians and manipulating the media, particularly by pandering to the far right and its apocalyptic urges. Rucker's portrayal of Luty as paranoid, manipulative, and willing to kowtow to the far right reads as prophetic given the role of social media and the rise of the alt-right and its conspiracy theory/QAnon(sense) view of 'reality,' the spread of populism (culminating in the 2016 election of Donald J. Trump and the Brexit vote), and the waves of pro-Trump followers who, fueled by the Big Lie that the 2020 election was rigged and fraudulent, participated in a terrorist insurrection against Washington's Capitol building on January 6, 2021 to somehow overthrow the democratic system and keep Trump in power. Rucker's work therefore shows he is not only a unique contributor to literary sf but also a broader demonstration of how cyberpunk can be "instrumental to decoding the complexities of our technocultural age" (McFarlane, Murphy, and Schmeink 2).

See also: **Philip K. Dick, William Gibson, Hans Moravec, Lewis Shiner, Bruce Sterling**

Note

1 As an example, see Schroeder's "Inheriting Chaos."

Works Cited

Latham, Rob. "Long Live Gonzo: An Introduction to Rudy Rucker." *Journal of the Fantastic in the Arts*, vol. 6, no. 1, 2005, pp. 3–5.

McFarlane, Anna, Graham J. Murphy, and Lars Schmeink. "Cyberpunk as Cultural Formation." *The Routledge Companion to Cyberpunk Culture*, edited by Anna McFarlane, Graham J. Murphy, and Lars Schmeink, Routledge, 2020, pp. 1–3.

Rucker, Rudy. *Freeware*. Avon Books, 1997.

———. *Hylozoic*. Tor, 2009.

———. *Nested Scrolls: The Autobiography of Rudolf von Bitter Rucker*. PS Publishing, 2011, http://www.rudyrucker.com/nestedscrolls/sample/nestedscrolls.html.

———. *Postsingular*. Tor, 2007.

———. *Realware*. EOS, 2000.

———. *Software*. Penguin, 1985.

———. *Spacetime Donuts*. Ace, 1981.

———. "A Transrealist Manifesto." *The Bulletin of Science Fiction Writers of America*, #82, Winter, 1983.

———. *Wetware*. New English Library, 1989.

Schroeder, Randy. "Inheriting Chaos: Burroughs, Pynchon, Sterling, Rucker." *Extrapolation*, vol. 43, no. 1, 2002, pp. 89–97.

Jonathan Thornton

JOANNA RUSS (1937–2011)

US author, critic, essayist, feminist theorist.

Joanna Russ is among the most celebrated feminist science fiction (sf) writers, and her work constitutes one of the sources of cyberpunk. Apart from her most well-known work, *The Female Man* (1975), Russ published seven novels and over seventy short stories, some of which she collected in *Alyx* (1976), *The Adventures of Alyx* (1983), *The Zanzibar Cat* (1983), and *The Hidden Side of the Moon* (1987). Russ was also a prolific sf critic and feminist scholar with two monographs and three collections of her essays and reviews, the most influential being *How to Suppress Women's Writing* (1983) and *To Write Like a Woman* (1995). Overall, she was a major force in moving sf toward literary and social experimentation in the 1960s and 1970s as well as standing at the forefront of both a feminist recalibration of sf and the emergence of a critical utopian tradition,[1] much of which helped influence, if not produce, the cyberpunk emergence of the 1980s. Her fiction has received the Pilgrim Award, the Hugo Award, the Nebula Award, and the Locus Award, and she was inducted into the Science Fiction Hall of Fame in 2013 (see Jones).

Russ wrote what can be called 'proto-cyberpunk' at times, and cyberpunk writers took one of her signature feminist characters, Alice-Jael Reasoner from *The Female Man*, as a model for the female cyborg figure. This is notable in the clear affinities between Jael and **William Gibson**'s Molly Millions, the cyborg assassin of "Johnny Mnemonic" (1981), *Neuromancer* (1984), and *Mona Lisa Overdrive* (1988). **Samuel R. Delany**, for example, remarks on the similarities between the characters: "Both of them have retractable claws in their fingers. Both of them wear black. Both enjoy their sex with men. And there's a similar harshness in their attitudes" (173). Delany takes it one step further to remark not only on all that "Gibson's Molly owes to Russ' Jael," but he also concludes Gibson "is constantly rewriting Russ and [Ursula K.] Le Guin" (173). In fact, beyond the confines of the original 1980s Movement, traces of Jael can be seen in such iconic cyberpunk (or cyberpunk-influenced) characters as Ripley in **Ridley Scott**'s *Alien* (1979), Trinity in **Lana and Lilly Wachowski**'s *The Matrix* (1999), and Alice in *Resident Evil* (Anderson 2002). Yet while it is true that Russ's key legacy for cyberpunk crystallizes in Jael, there is much more in her oeuvre that is relevant to the development of cyberpunk, and which makes this character possible in the first place.

The cyborg, whose existence undermines the opposition between life and machine and the gender binary, is central to cyberpunk at large (Leblanc) and the main conduit linking feminist sf to the genre (Yaszek 33), including in speculative theory like **Donna J. Haraway**'s iconic "A Manifesto for Cyborgs." Haraway acknowledges *The Female Man* as inspiration for her cyborg theory (*Modest_Witness* 70; "Manifesto" 44 fn 27), although several scholars—following Nicola Nixon's critique of cyberpunk's masculinist perspective (1992)—have commented on cyberpunk's demotion of this powerfully disruptive figure to a hyper-sexualized object of male sexual desire. For example, Stacy Gillis compares the female cyborg to the *femme fatale* in *film noir*, arguing that the cyborg's hybridity adds complexity to the figure, yet cyberpunk's treatment of the figure hobbles its revolutionary potential (Gillis 14); similarly, Patricia Melzer argues that while feminist cyberpunk precursors, such as *The Female Man* or **James Tiptree, Jr.**'s "The Girl Who Was Plugged In" (1973), already engage with the human-machine interface, male authors and cultural critics have rarely acknowledged their contribution (see Melzer 295). Nonetheless, for Russ, the cyborg is always a hyper-sexualized *femme fatale*—a woman both literally fatal for men and hungry for sex—and no context can deprive her of her revolutionary potential, even if she dons a latex suit.

Always committed to a critique of power structures, especially those grounded in gender, Russ's work moves from her early, proto-feminist fiction to explicitly feminist and later critically feminist work, each development reflecting on and transforming earlier engagements with the correlations between technology and social inequity in her writing (Cortiel 228). In her proto-feminist phase that is thoroughly part of 1960s and early 1970s New Wave sf, Russ produced work that emerges from a materialist critique of capitalism. Having studied English at Cornell and playwriting and dramatic literature at the Yale School of Drama, Russ never abandoned an early proclivity for science, so writing sf was consistent with her interests; similarly, exploring materialist feminism followed logically from her early short stories. It is in these stories and her first two novels (*Picnic on Paradise* [1968]; *And Chaos Died* [1970]) that Russ experimented with socially exceptional characters—Alyx; Jay Vedh—that are significant predecessors to Jael, not because they are cyborgs, but because much like the cyborg they embody distinct anti-binary disturbances in their binary worlds.

The sword-and-sorcery heroine Alyx makes her first appearance in "The Adventuress" (1967, later collected as "Bluestocking") as she navigates a patriarchal world whose myth of creation shapes the first man from "the sixth finger of the left hand of the first woman" (*Adventures* 9). Alyx reappears in four more stories,[2] collected with *Picnic on Paradise* first as *Alyx* (1973) and, later, as *The Adventures of*

Alyx. The titular character possesses three characteristics that put pressure on standard female characters in sf and fantasy, even if they aren't explicitly feminist. First, she is sexually active with men, but also radically independent from them. Second, she is a version of the *femme fatale* that expresses, as Jason P. Vest puts it, aggression and anger as "womanly violence" (157) that is largely directed against men. And finally, she forms meaningful relationships primarily with other women, particularly younger women whom she mentors. For example, in *Picnic on Paradise* Alyx is a trans-temporal military agent in a far-future interplanetary war who is tasked with guiding a small party of rich civilians to safety on the planet Paradise, a winter tourist resort. While Alyx relates most intensely to other women, she is not concerned with anything resembling a "women's cause" (this is something later short stories and novels will add); yet, despite being the only non-cyborg on Paradise, Alyx creates a distinct dissonance with her world's gendered relationships that connects her to Jael.

Similarly non-binary, Jay Vedh, the protagonist of *And Chaos Died*, is male and refers to himself as "homosexual" (17), but his performance destabilizes such gender/sexual categories. Thus, although he insists that he only desires men, he indulges in passionate sex with a female character and derives sexual pleasure from observing a woman masturbate (Cortiel 159). He thus shares with Jael more than the sound of the letter J: an ambiguous sex/gender performance as well as a distinct proclivity for sexuality that deviates from normalized patterns of desire.

When Jael appears in *The Female Man*, she is as violent, street-smart, and disruptive as both Alyx and Jay, in part because she has bodily modifications that turn her into a lethal weapon in her near-future conflict between Womanland and Manland. Like Alyx, Jael interacts meaningfully mostly with other women, particularly when Jael reaches across temporal and spatial borders to contact the 'J' women of alternate Earths: Jeannine, Joanna, and Janet. Russ also frames Jael's sexuality in ways designed to heighten the gothic discomfort produced by her cyber-modified body: she profoundly dislikes men and trains herself to be an efficient killer of men in her war against patriarchy, particularly when she uses her talons to bloodily kill the Boss-man (all while showing restraint when she decides not to use her teeth to rip out his larynx). At the same time, Jael desires a male body, but not heteronormativity's debilitating politics: she owns an android named Davy, who has the body of a blue-eyed Adonis and not much of a mind. Jael takes the dominant role when she nonchalantly has sex with Davy while Joanna and Jeannine look on in horror—and Janet (who comes from the utopia Whileaway) is overcome with boredom (189–92). While Jael modified her body to kill men, and she does not hesitate to do just that when it serves her broader goals, she is a feminist cyborg, and the meaning of her embodiment depends on other women watching her (including the implied readers). Even her pleasure with the (engineered) male body is more spectacle than joy. Yet Alice-Jael Reasoner is not an isolated figure—her name reveals her lineage: the biblical Jael's distinction comes from driving a spike through a sleeping enemy's head in the words of another woman, Deborah's song of victory (Judges 5: 24–27). Jael combines the tradition of such female warrior figures with that of the uncontainable—i.e., both mad and wise—woman. She is a messy, uncomfortable, and ultimately tragic figure—she never gets to enter the utopian world she fights for.

At the same time, unlike Alyx, Jael is most emphatically an ordinary woman, there is nothing supernatural about her. Like the three other genetically identical characters in *The Female Man*—Janet, Joanna, and Jeannine—Jael is an average woman, mediocre in her world. Their respective universes (and genre affiliations) shape each of the women into a completely different phenotype. This is one of the central tenets of Russ's feminism. Yes, the "womanly violence" becomes more systematically political and the characters' relationships to other women become more openly sexual in her later fiction, but more radical than that, as Russ puts it in her last novel *On Strike Against God* (1980), the point is to "Make the world safe for mediocrity" (81). A mediocre woman who has turned herself into a weapon against "Manland," Jael's opposition to the patriarchy is represented as far from exceptional; she embodies the rage of ordinary women in the 1970s. In that sense, Jael is an everywoman, and the violent, sexual challenge to the patriarchy that she represents can be found everywhere.

Jael's legacy lived on in Russ's subsequent protagonists. She appears in a spin-off story to *The Female Man*, "Gleepsite" (1971), that shows, according to Gwyneth Jones, a world "after the Manland/ Womanland conflict" (53) in *The Female Man*. Certainly, the main character looks a lot like Jael, except that she has bat wings, and the world she appears in is a feminist dystopia without a utopian counterpart. Because *The Female Man* was finished in 1969 but not published until 1975, the short story is the first incarnation of this character in published form.

Russ's later fiction, *We Who Are About To …* (1977), *The Two of Them* (1978), and particularly the short story cycle *Extra(Ordinary)*

People (1984), delivers protagonists who dwell in crisis even as they contemplate utopia. Revolution emerges as both a necessary and impossible foundation for utopia—and Russ's later novels keep contradictions intact through a sustained voice of irony that works quite in line with Haraway's "ironic political myth faithful to feminism, socialism, and materialism" ("Manifesto" 7). Jael and Russ's whole cast of "extra(ordinary)" characters inform the female cyborgs of cyberpunk and their deviance explodes the very foundation of normative heterosexuality—the absolute gender binary—wherever they appear.

See also: **William Gibson, Donna J. Haraway, N. Katherine Hayles, Marge Piercy, Ridley Scott, James Tiptree, Jr., Lana and Lilly Wachowski**

Notes

1 See Tom Moylan's *Demand the Impossible: Science Fiction and the Utopian Imagination* for details on Russ's alignment with the 'critical utopia.'
2 "I Thought She Was Afeared Till She Stroked My Beard (1967; known alternately as "I Gave Her Sack and Sherry"); "The Barbarian" (1968); "Picnic on Paradise" (1968): and "The Second Inquisition" (1970).

Works Cited

Cortiel, Jeanne. *Demand My Writing: Joanna Russ/Feminism/Science Fiction.* Liverpool UP, 1999.

Delany, Samuel R. "'Some *Real* Mothers …' The *SF Eye* Interview." *Silent Interviews: On Language, Race, Sex, Science Fiction.* Wesleyan UP, 1994, pp. 164–85.

Gillis, Stacy. "The (Post)Feminist Politics of Cyberpunk." *Gothic Studies*, vol. 9, no. 2, 2007, pp. 7–19.

Haraway, Donna J. "A Manifesto for Cyborgs: Science, Technology, and Socialist Feminism in the 1980s." *The Haraway Reader.* Routledge, 2004, pp. 7–45.

———. *Modest_Witness@ Second_Millennium. FemaleMan_Meets_OncoMouse: Feminism and Technoscience.* Routledge, 1997.

Jones, Gwyneth. *Joanna Russ.* U of Illinois P, 2019.

Leblanc, Lauraine "Razor girls: genre and gender in cyberpunk fiction." *Women and Language*, vol. 20, no. 1, 1997, pp. 71–76.

Melzer, Patricia. "Cyborg Feminism." *The Routledge Companion to Cyberpunk Culture*, edited by Anna McFarlane, Graham J. Murphy, and Lars Schmeink, Routledge, 2020, pp. 291–99.

Nixon, Nicola. "Cyberpunk: Preparing the Ground for Revolution or Keeping the Boys Satisfied?" *Science Fiction Studies*, vol. 19, no. 2, 1992, pp. 219–35.

Russ, Joanna. *The Adventures of Alyx*. The Women's Press, 1985.
———. *And Chaos Died*. 1970. Berkley, 1979.
———. *The Female Man*. 1975. Orion-Gollanz, 2010.
———. *On Strike Against God*. The Crossing Press, 1980
Vest, Jason P. "Violent Women, Womanly Violence: Joanna Russ's Femmes Fatales." *On Joanna Russ*, edited by Farah Mendlesohn, Wesleyan UP, 2009, pp. 157–67.
Yaszek, Lisa. "Feminist Cyberpunk." *The Routledge Companion to Cyberpunk Culture*, edited by Anna McFarlane, Graham J. Murphy, and Lars Schmeink, Routledge, 2020, pp. 32–40.

Jeanne Cortiel

MELISSA SCOTT (1960–)

US author.

Melissa Scott's novel *The Game Beyond* (1984) was the start of a career that has spanned forty-nine books: twenty-nine as the sole author and twenty written in collaboration with such figures as Lisa A. Barnett, Amy Griswold, and Jo Graham, to name a few. Scott has been nominated twenty-nine times for a variety of literary awards and has won ten times, including the John W. Campbell (now Astounding) Award in 1986 for Best New Writer. Most of her awards come from groups celebrating innovative literature about gender and sexuality, such as the James Tiptree, Jr. (now Otherwise) Award, the Gaylactic Spectrum Award, and the Lambda Award for *Trouble and Her Friends* (1994), *Shadow Man* (1995), *Point of Dreams* (2001), and *Death by Silver* (2013). While Scott has written space opera, fantasy-mystery, and feminist sf, the novel most discussed as relevant for cyberpunk culture is *Trouble and Her Friends*.

Trouble and Her Friends is a novel best understood within the broader context of cyberpunk's evolution, particularly around immediate resistance to its colonizing the imagination from feminist fans and scholars alike. In his Preface to *Mirrorshades: The Cyberpunk Anthology* (1986), **Bruce Sterling** provided a list of cyberpunk's inspirational—and entirely male!—predecessors, including Harlan Ellison, **Samuel R. Delany**, Norman Spinrad, Michael Moorcock, J.G. Ballard, Olaf Stapledon, H.G. Wells, Larry Niven, Poul Anderson, and Robert A. Heinlein (x). Then, in his Preface to **William Gibson**'s *Burning Chrome* (1986), Sterling argues that Gibson's work (and cyberpunk generally) presented new visions of the present and future which superseded all previous work in science fiction (sf), proving "galvanic, helping to wake the genre from its dogmatic slumbers" (ix). In response,

Jeanne Gomoll published "An Open Letter to Joanna Russ" in the feminist fanzine *Aurora* (Winter 1986/87), arguing that Sterling's erasure of 1970s feminist sf added to the techniques that **Joanna Russ** had identified in *How to Suppress Women's Writing* (1983): "They [women authors] wrote it, but they were a fad" (7). It wasn't long before feminist scholars challenged cyberpunk's erasure of 1970s feminist sf and the masculinist claims to radical revolution, notably Nicola Nixon, who argued print cyberpunk "represented a concerted return to the (originary purity) of hard SF rather than creating revolutionary political fictions" and embedded Ronald Reagan's cowboy conservativism (220), while Karen Cadora focused on cyberpunk published by women writers who "began to explore the connections between race, gender, sexuality and cyberspace" in contrast to the 1980s masculinist cyberpunk (371). In so doing, fans and scholars alike helped popularize the growing feminist cyberpunk of the 1990s.[1]

Scott's award-winning *Trouble and Her Friends* is a notable example of that decade's feminist cyberpunk in its subversion of cyberpunk motifs, its exploration of questions around gender and sexuality, and its foregrounding of lesbian hacker protagonists. The novel focuses on two lesbian lovers, Trouble and Cerise, who part because of differences over how to react to the Evans-Tinsdale legislation, an unjust law passed in the United States which criminalizes a controversial technology, the brainworm, used to access the net. Years later, they come together when a cyber-imposter masquerading as Trouble triggers a criminal investigation. Trouble and Cerise are the point of view characters and protagonists but are helped by friends who are their chosen family of queer hackers. The novel title foregrounds this queer community rather than a lone hero. As Graham J. Murphy argues, the old guard of netwalkers who oppose Trouble and her friends and support Evans-Tinsdale are all straight men, but Trouble's friends include gay men who care for her and Cerise and who help them both throughout the novel (41). In this manner, *Trouble and Her Friends* can be read as an explicit rebuttal of masculinist cyberpunk that had been dominating (and, in many ways, is still a formidable presence in) this sf subgenre.

Trouble also troubles gender stereotypes as well as stereotypes about sexuality in a rare representation of girl gangs.[2] For example, when Cerise encounters a group of "dollie-girls" on the street, she reacts to an attack with violence to save herself. She knows from her own experience in just such a gang why the girls are so angry: they have "indentured themselves" to get implants to get corporate jobs only finding out "too late, they always found out too late, that they didn't automatically get the training or the bioware that would let them walk the nets" as Cerise and the others do (24). Cerise escaped her gang but still identifies strongly with the young women from her corporate position, a job she was forced to take when she was caught hacking to avoid imprisonment under Evans-Tindale.

Trouble and Her Friends has proven instrumental in not only providing a feminist response to masculinist cyberpunk but also expanding the concept of "cyberpunk" from the original white masculinist print genre to a "cultural formation" or multi-media "mode" (McFarlane, Murphy, and Schmeink 2). Recent scholarship on *Trouble* draws on gender, feminist, and intersectional theories to identify undeniably important elements in her fiction: lesbian protagonists, queer communities, a sense of embodiment that challenges the mind/body duality, and attention paid to hierarchies of gender, sexuality, class, and ethnicity, elements that comment on the contemporary politics of the late twentieth century.[3] I've already cited Murphy's "Penetrating the Body-Plus-Virtualisation in Melissa Scott's *Trouble and Her Friends*," a strong and persuasive argument for the uniqueness of Scott's challenge to cyberpunk's tropes because of her "exploration of the post/human politics of cyberspace, the stating of the body-plus-virtualisation, and the interrelated functioning of sexuality and corporeal penetration" (40); however, we can also turn to Laura Chernaik's "Difference, the Social and the Spatial: The Fictions of Melissa Scott" for its analysis of not only *Trouble and Her Friends* but also *Dreamships* (1992), *Dreaming Metal* (1997), *The Shapes of Their Hearts* (1998), and *Burning Bright* (1993) to show that the complex demographics of Scott's queer communities in her novels as a whole differ from 1970s separatist lesbian communities. In fact, recent queer theory has expanded definitions of "queerness" to include more than gay and lesbian identities, and Scott's communities and cyberspaces meet Alexander Doty's definition of a "more radical understanding of queer [...] apart from established gender and sexuality categories" (6–7).

What Chernaik describes as Scott's novels creating a "particular way of thinking about cyberspace and the interface of a person with cyberspace" is also addressed in a relatively unique manner in Scott's *Dreamships* duology (*Dreamships* and *Dreaming Metal*) (26). The novels directly challenge cyberpunk's "stock notions: a set of images, drawn from Japanese and other Asian and Southeast Asian cultures [...] and an interest in AI, which is made part of the plot, as well as the milieu" (Chernaik 32) but also cyberpunk's—and Anglophone culture's—ableism. As Analiese Farris notes, cyberpunk (and cyberpunk scholarship) lacks an awareness of disability issues, but one conflict in

Scott's duology is AI/machine rights vs. the human rights of coolies, an underclass of people whose ancestors were brought to the planet Persephone as contract labor. A key aspect of coolie culture is Deaf Culture with its accompanying use of sign language, highlighting that cyberpunk culture has any number of structural inequalities that are ripe for exploration and critique.

This growing scholarly awareness of Scott's role in cyberpunk culture is beginning to encompass her other novels, which fit what Scott identifies as "alternative cyberpunk," fiction which foregrounds and explores the "social criticism" and awareness of social hierarchies which she sees the original cyberpunk as lacking ("Interview").[4] This broader corpus of 'alternative cyberpunk'— *Dreamships, Burning Bright, Dreaming Metal, The Shapes of Their Hearts,* but also *Night Sky Mine* (1996) and *The Jazz* (2000)—combines technology with progressive issues such as "globalization, virtual reality, cyborg culture, environmentalism, religion, motherhood, and queer rights" (Lavigne 2). Therefore, Scott's alternative cyberpunk and the accompanying feminist scholarship is not only part of a larger critique of the self-proclaimed revolutionary 1980s mode of sf that was almost exclusively written by white men espousing a heterosexist punk aesthetic, but also a useful manner of helping create "a narrative vocabulary for the globalized, multinational, interconnected, 'wired' world" (Gomel 366).

In sum, Scott's cyberpunk—alternative or otherwise—combines the technological issues that cyberpunk made (hetero)-sexy in the 1980s with paradigms drawn from intersectional feminist and queer theories and communities to create a progressive alternative not only to the original cyberpunk movement but to the larger genre of sf. Given the backlash against the decolonizing of science fiction by the Sad and Rapid Puppies ("Puppygate"), Scott's contribution (and the contributions of other contemporaries) to that process should not be marginalized; instead, critical attention to her multi-genre body of work would be a strong addition to speculative fiction scholarship and a better understanding of our cyberpunk culture.

See also: **Pat Cadigan, Samuel R. Delany, William Gibson, Marge Piercy, Joanna Russ, Bruce Sterling, James Tiptree, Jr.**

Notes

1 See also Samuel Delany's "'Some *Real* Mothers ...' The *SF Eye* Interview" where he explicitly draws the connections between Gibson's *Neuromancer* (1984) and Joanna Russ' *The Female Man* (1975).

2 The assumption that punks and gang members are male is common. Only recently has scholarship on girl gangs been published (Howell and Griffiths).

3 Schleifer, 1994; Foster 1997; Flanagan and Booth, 2002; Murphy, 2005; Chernaik, 2001; Lavigne, 2013; Marotta, 2014; Melzer, 2020; Yaszek, 2020. The growing scholarship is a strong body of work, but Lavigne notes a correlation between the rise of feminist cyberpunk and the marginalization of the mode in academic scholarship that should concern those of us working in this field (6).

4 I tend to agree with Carlen Lavigne's rhetorical choice to focus on connections rather than genre divisions in *Cyberpunk Women, Feminism and Science Fiction*, the first monograph on cyberpunk women. In this chapter, I use Scott's phrase to discuss her work.

Works Cited

Cadora, Karen. "Feminist Cyberpunk." *Science Fiction Studies*, vol. 22, no. 3, 1995, pp. 357–72.

Chernaik, Laura. "Difference, the Social and the Spatial: The Fictions of Melissa Scott." *Foundation*, vol. 82, 2001, pp. 26–44.

Delany, Samuel. "'Some *Real* Mothers …' The *SF Eye* Interview." *Silent Interviews: On Language, Race, Sex, Science Fiction, and Some Comics*. Wesleyan UP, 1994, pp. 164–85.

Doty, Alexander. *Flaming Classics: Queering the Film Canon*. Routledge, 2000.

Farris, Analise. "Young, Punk, and Disabled: New Worlds for Marginalized Bodies." *Deletion*, May 28, 2018, https://www.deletionscifi.org/episodes/young-punk-and-disabled-new-worlds-for-marginalized-bodies/.

Flanagan, Mary and Austin Booth, editors. *Reload: Rethinking Women + Cyberculture*, The MIT P, 2002.

Foster, Thomas C. "'Trapped by the Body'? Telepresence Technologies and Transgendered Performance in Feminist and Lesbian Rewritings of Cyberpunk Fiction." *Modern Fiction Studies*, vol. 43, no. 3, Fall 1997, pp. 708–742.

Gomel, Elana. "The Cyberworld is (not) Flat: Cyberpunk and Globalization." *The Cambridge History of Postmodern Literature*, edited by Brian McHale and Len Platt, Cambridge UP, 2016, pp. 353–68.

Gomoll, Jeanne. "An Open Letter to Joanna Russ." *Aurora*, vol. 10, no. 1, 1986–87, pp. 7–10.

Howell, James C. and Elizabeth Griffiths. *Gangs in America's Communities*. Sage, 2018.

Lavigne, Carlen. *Cyberpunk Women, Feminism and Science Fiction*. McFarland & Company, Inc., 2013.

McFarlane, Anna, Graham J. Murphy, and Lars Schmeink. "Cyberpunk as Cultural Formation." *The Routledge Companion to Cyberpunk Culture*, edited by Anna McFarlane, Graham J. Murphy, and Lars Schmeink, Routledge, 2020, pp. 1–3.

Marotta, Melanie A. "Acceptance of the Marginalized in Marge Piercy's *He, She, It* [sic] and Melissa Scott's *Trouble and Her Friends*." *Environments in Science Fiction: Essays on Alternative Spaces*, edited by Susan M. Bernardo, McFarland & Company, Inc., 2014, pp. 28–45.

Melzer, Patricia. *Alien Constructions: Science Fiction and Feminist Thought.* U Texas P, 2006.

Murphy, Graham J. "Penetrating the Body-Plus-Virtualisation in Melissa Scott's *Trouble and Her Friends.*" *Foundation*, vol. 34, no. 95, 2005, pp. 40–51.

Nixon, Nicola. "Cyberpunk: Preparing the Ground for Revolution or Keeping the Boys Satisfied?" *Science Fiction Studies*, vol. 19, no. 2, 1992, pp. 219–55.

"Puppygate." *Fanlore*, https://fanlore.org/wiki/Puppygate.

Schleifer, Paul C. "Fear of the 'Other' in Melissa Scott's *Dreamships.*" *Extrapolation*, vol. 35, no. 4, 1994, pp. 312–18.

Scott, Melissa. *Burning Bright.* Tor, 1993.

———. *Dreamships.* Tor, 1992.

———. *Dreaming Metal.* Tor, 1997.

———. Interview with Lyda Morehouse. *Science Fiction Chronicle*, vol. 19, no. 5/6, 1998, pp. 10, 46–47.

———. *The Jazz.* Tor, 2000.

———. *Night Sky Mine.* Tor, 1996.

———. *The Shapes of Their Hearts.* Tor, 1998.

———. *Trouble and Her Friends.* Tor, 1994.

Sterling, Bruce. Preface. *Burning Chrome*, by William Gibson, Ace, 1986, pp. ix–xii.

———. Preface. *Mirrorshades: The Cyberpunk Anthology*, edited by Bruce Sterling, Ace, 1986, pp. ix–xvi.

Robin Anne Reid

RIDLEY SCOTT (1937–)

English film director and producer.

Ridley Scott has directed twenty-seven feature films and countless advertisements and has produced various films and TV series. He has worked in a variety of genres, including thrillers (*Someone to Watch Over Me* [1987]; *Black Rain* [1989]; *Hannibal* [2001]), war movies (*Black Hawk Down* [2001]), fantasy (*Legend* [1985]), the road movie (*Thelma & Louise* [1991]), the gangster film (*American Gangster* [2007]), and such historical epics as *1492: Conquest of Paradise* (1992), *Gladiator* (2000), *Kingdom of Heaven* (2005), and *Exodus: Gods and Kings* (2014). He has been nominated for three Academy Awards for Directing and has received many other awards, including the Best Debut Film Award at the Cannes Film Festival, a Golden Globe, two Emmys, and the Lifetime Achievement Award of the Directors Guild of America. During his career, Scott has had numerous box office hits as well as critical successes and is without doubt one of the best-known living mainstream filmmakers.

Despite Scott's wide range of genres, his two best-known films arguably remain *Alien* (1979) and *Blade Runner* (1982), which are generally considered foundational science fiction (sf) classics, particularly *Blade Runner* whose influence on cyberpunk can hardly be overstated. In the case of the former, *Alien* tells the story of the transport spaceship *Nostromo* invaded by the eponymous alien organism, which kills off the crew one by one. The film culminates in a battle between the creature and the movie's protagonist, Ripley (Sigourney Weaver), a woman who, contrary to genre conventions, is neither scream queen nor damsel in distress, but a tough and determined character who vanquishes the creature.

Thematically, *Alien* features several precursors to cyberpunk, including Mother, the ship's advanced computer system, the character of Science Officer Ash (Ian Holm), who turns out to be an android, and 'the company'—i.e., the British-Japanese conglomerate Weyland-Yutani, an anonymous and ruthlessly profit-oriented enterprise—that orchestrates getting the alien organism to Earth, human casualties notwithstanding. Above all, Scott decided against the clean and shiny aesthetics of earlier space sf, most notably exemplified in Stanley Kubrick's *2001: A Space Odyssey* (1968), and instead opted for a 'used-future' visual aesthetic. The *Nostromo* is an old cargo vessel, built for routine transports and therefore completely functional in its design. Its crew are not the heroic adventurers of cinematic space opera but, instead, are low-paid, blue-collar workers, and the film's emphatically non-glamorous industrial design, its street-level approach to technology, and overall dystopian aura position *Alien* as a forerunner of a distinct cyberpunk aesthetic that emerged only a few years later, particularly in the visual aesthetics that came to define *Blade Runner*.

Blade Runner, an adaptation of **Philip K. Dick**'s *Do Androids Dream of Electric Sheep?* (1968), is set in Los Angeles circa 2019 and depicts Rick Deckard (Harrison Ford) hunting down Nexus-6 replicants, artificial beings who are nearly indistinguishable from humans and who are not ready to accept their four-year lifespan. While tracking down the replicants, Deckard falls in love with Rachael (Sean Young), an advanced replicant prototype who, thanks to artificial memories, is initially unaware that she is not human. The film's treatment of artificial human beings exhibits a cyberpunk sensibility in its blurring of a clear distinction between the human and nonhuman; and, after eliminating two replicants (one is killed by Rachael), and then being saved from death by the group's leader Roy Batty (Rutger Hauer), Deckard comes to a new appreciation of life as he and Rachael flee the city with the suggestion that someone will be sent after them. Famously, the placement of an origami unicorn, coupled with other clues scattered throughout several cuts of the film, provides "strong evidence in *Blade Runner* that Deckard is a replicant, a proposition Scott has confirmed, but Ford has rejected" (Murphy 103).

Blade Runner's tumultuous production—countless script revisions; frictions between Scott and Ford; constant delays in shooting which even led to an interim firing of the director—has become the stuff of Hollywood legend. In addition, the film was a box office disappointment and originally received mixed reviews before gradually turning into a cult classic that has been meticulously analyzed and discussed by its fans. Inextricably linked with *Blade Runner*'s unique career as a sleeper hit are the many versions of the film: the Workprint (1982) version; a 'sneak peek' version shown in San Francisco (1982); the US theatrical release, which included a Ford voiceover and new 'happier' ending comprised of unused footage from *The Shining* (Kubrick 1980); a slightly altered International release; the so-called Director's Cut (1992), which, despite its name, was not overseen by Scott—and the Final Cut which Scott calls his preferred version (Sammon).

The cinematic release of *Blade Runner* predates cyberpunk literature proper: **William Gibson**'s quintessential *Neuromancer* was published two years after the film's release, and Gibson has acknowledged that "I was afraid to watch *Blade Runner* in the theater because I was afraid the movie would be better than what I myself had been able to imagine. In a way, I was right to be afraid, because even the first few minutes were better" (cited in Newitz). Sure enough, the world of *Blade Runner* feels astonishingly close to Gibson's urban Sprawl. In addition to their respective metropolises dominated by all-powerful megacorporations and permeated by Japanese culture, both Scott and Gibson draw on the tradition of hard-boiled crime novels and films. Deckard, a cynical, hard-drinking loner in a Humphrey Bogart trench coat, avowedly echoes the iconic detectives of the 1940s and 1950s film noirs and the voiceover of the US theatrical release is a characteristic film noir element. In addition, they both cite the French comics anthology *Métal Hurlant*—published in the US as *Heavy Metal*—as an important inspiration, especially Dan O'Bannon's "The Long Tomorrow," meticulously illustrated by French comic legend **Moebius [Jean Giraud]** (Gibson, "Introduction"; Robb 34). Finally, "[a]mong *Blade Runner*'s merits is its ability to speak to the early emergence of neoliberal capitalism in the late 1970s and early 1980s: The original *Blade Runner* registered our latent fears about the end of the welfare state, the deregulated plane of unfettered multinational capital, and the dystopia that was set to result in the soon-to-be approaching future" (Flisfeder, "*Blade Runner*" 144).

Blade Runner's main appeal arguably lies in its visual splendor and depiction of a near-future metropolis. Scott and his team—among them visual effects wizard Douglas Trumbull and concept artist **Syd Mead**—take *Alien*'s used-future approach one step further: in this 'retrofitted' future, advanced technology and urban decay coexist, often in the same building or vehicle. *Blade Runner*'s Los Angeles is an inscrutable maze of gigantic buildings and dazzling billboards, omnipresent steam, and permanent rain. *Blade Runner* exemplifies Scott's great talent in creating extremely rich, multi-layered, and evocative images that "produce an inexhaustible complexity, an infinity of surfaces to be encountered and explored" (Bukatman 8). *Blade Runner*'s Los Angeles is a morbid beauty with a sense of tangibility, and everything shown on screen has a haptic quality with a scenery that, if not necessarily realistic, feels real, which in part explains why Scott's urban vision is indistinguishable from many of today's megapolises (Halden). In addition, *Blade Runner*'s audio-visual richness, enhanced by the work of Greek composer Vangelis, has turned *Blade Runner* into more than just a film, but rather "a story-world made up of branching, possible narratives" (Brooker 86). According to Matt Hills, "*Blade Runner* may well be the ultimate 'thick text'" (26), while Matthew Flisfeder sees it as a paradigmatic example of a postmodern film (*Postmodern*).

Scott's sf films certainly display a cyberpunk sensibility, which also holds true for his 1984 commercial to promote the release of the Apple Macintosh personal computer. The ad, which today is often listed among the greatest commercials ever made, was aired during the Super Bowl and is set in a dystopian world clearly alluding to George Orwell's influential dystopia *Nineteen Eighty-Four* (1949). It features English athlete Anya Major personifying the coming Macintosh computer, her white shirt adorned with its image. She throws a hammer against a huge screen displaying a Big Brother-like ruler, a testament to the freeing power of the computer that often accompanied print cyberpunk. Cyberpunk themes also feature in the television series *Raised by Wolves* (2020–), created by Aaron Guzikowski and executive produced by Scott and whose first two episodes Scott directed. The story is again set in a dystopian future and deals with the porous border between humans and androids. Finally, Scott was executive producer on *Blade Runner 2049* (Villeneuve 2017), the long-anticipated sequel to *Blade Runner* that, unfortunately, proved to be a box office failure, and for a number of reasons its indebtedness to the original *Blade Runner* may have been a drain on *Blade Runner 2049*, not its draw (Murphy 105).

In the end, *Alien* and to a much larger extent, *Blade Runner* remain instrumental to cyberpunk's development, particularly in its cinematic offerings. "*Blade Runner*," Andrew M. Butler writes, "helped cement cyberpunk's visual iconography with the seemingly never-ending cityscape, continuous rain and night, neon lighting, and teeming crowds" (121); or, put succinctly, it is hard to disagree with Scott Bukatman's assessment that "[c]yberpunk provided *the* image of the future in the 1980s" and the "aesthetic of cyberpunk was almost defined by *Blade Runner*" (58; 50). By this logic, cyberpunk's visual aesthetic was, if not defined by Scott, then most certainly visualized and firmly engrained in the director's cinematic storyworlds.

See also: **Philip K. Dick, William Gibson, Syd Mead, Moebius [Jean Giraud]**

Works Cited

Brooker, Will. "All Our Variant Futures: The Many Narratives of *Blade Runner: The Final Cut*." *Popular Communication*, vol. 7, no. 2, 2009, pp. 79–91, doi: 10.1080/ 15405700802659056.

Bukatman, Scott. *Blade Runner*. BFI, 1997.

Butler, Andrew M. "Early Cyberpunk Film." *The Routledge Companion to Cyberpunk Culture*, edited by Anna McFarlane, Graham J. Murphy, and Lars Schmeink, Routledge, 2020, pp. 119–27.

Flisfeder, Matthew. "*Blade Runner 2049* (Case Study)." *The Routledge Companion to Cyberpunk Culture*, edited by Anna McFarlane, Graham J. Murphy, and Lars Schmeink, Routledge, 2020, pp. 144–50.

———. *Postmodern Theory and Blade Runner*. Bloomsbury Academic, 2017.

Gibson, William. Introduction. *William Gibson's Neuromancer: The Graphic Novel*, Vol. 1, edited by Tom de Haven and Bruce Jensen, Berkley Books/ Epic Comics, 1989, p. 5.

Halden, Grace. "Photography and Digital Art." *The Routledge Companion to Cyberpunk Culture*, edited by Anna McFarlane, Graham J. Murphy, and Lars Schmeink, Routledge, 2020, pp. 216–27.

Hills, Matt. "From 'Multiverse' to 'Abramsverse': *Blade Runner, Star Trek*, Multiplicity, and the Authorizing of Cult/SF Worlds." *Science Fiction Double Feature: The Science Fiction Film as Cult Text*, edited by J. P. Telotte and Gerald Duchovnay, Liverpool UP, 2005. pp. 21–37, doi: 10.5949/ liverpool/9781781381830.003.0002.

Murphy, Graham J. "Cyberpunk's Masculinist Legacy: Puppetry, Labour, and *ménage a trois* in *Blade Runner 2049*." *Science Fiction Film and Television*, vol. 13, no. 1, 2020, pp. 97–106.

Newitz, Annalee. "How did William Gibson really feel about *Blade Runner*?" *Gizmodo*, July 24, 2013, https://io9.gizmodo.com/how-did-william-gibson-really-feel-about-blade-runner-89647232.

Robb, Brian J. *Ridley Scott.* Pocket Essentials, 2001.
Sammon, Paul Michael. *Future Noir: The Making of Blade Runner.* Gollancz, 2007.

Simon Spiegel

LEWIS SHINER (1950–)

US author and columnist.

Lewis Shiner started his career writing short stories in a variety of genres: his first publication, "Tinker's Damn" (1977), is an android love story published in a "badly butchered" form ("Life") in *Galileo* (October 1977), followed by such tales as the first Dan Sloane mystery "Deep Without Pity" (1980), the surrealistic western "Kings of the Afternoon" (1980), the swamp horror of "Blood Relations" (1981), the horror-tinged 'witchcraft' of "Brujo" (1982), the 'kid meets aliens' "Promises" (1982), the dark humor of "Plague" (1983), and the time travel narratives "Snowbirds" (1982) and "Twilight Time" (1984). It is in this early period that Shiner first met **Bruce Sterling** at the Turkey City Writer's Workshop in Austin, Texas. The workshop proved fruitful for both authors' careers: joined later by John Shirley, **Rudy Rucker**, and **William Gibson**, Shiner and Sterling became two of the formative voices of cyberpunk's earliest literary wave when it was still known as the 'Movement.' Under his pseudonym 'Sue Denim,' Shiner posted a handful of editorials and reviews to Sterling's fanzine *Cheap Truth* (1983–86) and helped Sterling (in his *nom du plume* Vincent Omniaveritas) rail against the sf establishment that needed replacing by a younger generation of rock-inspired writers, at one point writing that "[t]he SF revolution is crying out for literacy, imagination, and humanity" while describing established sf authors as "voices of repression": Robert A. Heinlein offered "senile babblings," Larry Niven embodied "California vapidity," and Kim Stanley Robinson wrote with "moist-eyed urgency" (*Cheap Truth* #10). At the same time he was writing for *Cheap Truth*, however, Shiner was already starting to bristle against the cyberpunk label that was gaining traction, evident in the transition from his debut novel *Frontera* (1984) to his follow-up *Deserted Cities of the Heart* (1988) and his overt rejection of cyberpunk by the early-1990s.

An overhaul of the earlier (and unpublished) stories "And Then Palestrina" and "Soldier, Sailor," the latter eventually published in

Nine Hard Questions about the Nature of the Universe (1990), *Frontera* depicts a run-down Martian colony populated by stranded survivors abandoned by an Earth scarred by devastating socio-political conflicts and global economic collapse. Ultra-powerful corporations (or Japanese *zaibatsus*) Pulsystems and Aeroflot run Earth and have reignited the space race in a desperate bid to return to Mars, ostensibly to find out what happened to Frontera Base and the abandoned settlers who have been presumed dead for nearly a decade. In reality, the competing corporations are trying to take ownership of a cutting-edge transporter and antimatter fuel that has been developed by the Martian settlers' mutated children, an unprecedented technological leap that promises to open the frontiers of space to corporate expansion. Pulsystems is the first to launch this dangerous mission, and the four-person crew includes: Commander Reese, a former inhabitant of Frontera Base who has personal reasons for returning to Mars; Takahashi, a Pulsystems 'company man' whose allegiances are always suspect; Lena, a woman desperate enough to risk her life to avoid returning to a life of economic scarcity; and, Kane, a damaged corporate soldier (and nephew to Pulsystems' CEO) who not only learns he has implanted wetware and programming that turns him into his uncle's puppet but is also suffering from mysterious visions of hero quests that convince him he is entangled in a much larger monomyth he calls the 'Pattern.' While Shiner describes the Martian future as akin to "a shopping mall in decay: cramped, faded, lived-in" (90), he also expertly crafts the intimate connections between people, particularly the tensions among Molly, Reese's daughter who only has fragmented memories of her father, Sarah (a.k.a. Verb), Molly's mutated daughter whose brilliance is the fuel driving the transporter technology, and Curtis, Molly's estranged husband and Verb's father, the Frontera 'leader' willing to do anything to secure Frontera's future. The novel ends in a surprisingly hopeful fashion with the foundations of a new Frontera Base and the first steps toward terraforming the planet.

In his Author's Note to *Frontera*, Shiner explicitly thanks both Gibson and Sterling "for making me see what it was I really wanted to do." This influence is evident in the novel's depictions of multinational corporations, wetware cyborgs, and the dried-out husk of a drained future, elements that became the dominant tropes for the cyberpunk movement. At the same time, Shiner was never comfortable with the cyberpunk label: he remarks in his autobiography that he "never really felt that the label fit me," but admits "I was willing to take all the notoriety it could bring me." Nevertheless, Rucker recounts that following a 1985 cyberpunk panel that turned openly hostile, Shiner allegedly asked, "So I guess cyberpunk is dead now?" (*Nested Scrolls*). While Shiner may have been asking a legitimate question, he continued to capitalize on cyberpunk's popularity: Sterling's edited collection *Mirrorshades: The Cyberpunk Anthology* (1986) features Shiner's posthuman mermaid story "Till Human Voices Wake Us" (1984) and his collaboration with Sterling on "Mozart in Mirrorshades" (1986), the latter a rollicking tale about corporate greed, time travel, and alternate or 'stub' realities that has influenced Gibson's recent work with *The Peripheral* (2014), *Archangel* (2016–17), and *Agency* (2020).

Shiner's later story "The Gene Drain" (1989) is explicitly cyberpunk with its depictions of cyborg attachments turned into fashion accessories, programmable personas, and an artificial intelligence whose malfunction aboard a failed generation starship results in the descendants of the original crew returning to an alien Earth hundreds of years after their ancestors' initial launch. The gulf between the two branches of posthumans is vast: the returnees are 'Carsinagins,' devotees to an illogical messianic religion cobbled together from religious texts, video clips from *The Tonight Show starring Johnny Carson*, and other random digital detritus, while the technology supporting the posthuman cyborgs living on Earth (as the character DNS explains) has taken "over completely from nature. Less than one percent of our population would be viable without some kind of hardware support [...] [a]nd the technology that's holding it all together is shoddy!" While "The Gene Drain" is somewhat humorous, it is also a darkly satirical tale addressing western civilization's dependence on technology in a future that is as decayed, battered, and disappointingly stale as the Martian colony in *Frontera*.

Shiner's second novel, *Deserted Cities of the Heart*, grew from altered versions previously published as "Deserted Cities of the Heart" (1984), "Cabracan" (1986), "Rebels" (1987), and "Americans" (1987). The story follows four main characters who find themselves caught in the complexities of Mexico's political quagmire circa the 1980s: Eddie, a former rocker who has gone missing; Lindsey, Eddie's estranged wife; Thomas, Eddie's brother who not-so-secretly loves Lindsey; and, Carmichael, a feature writer for *Rolling Stone* looking for his next big break. A clue behind Eddie's disappearance leads Lindsey and Thomas into the Mexican interior where they stumble upon not only Eddie but a group of revolutionary freedom fighters working to free Mexico from the corruptions of a corporatized government. At the same time, Carmichael pursues a story that leads him to a private American army working illegally in Mexico. Funded by the proceeds from the Iran-Contra scandal that tainted Ronald Reagan's second term as US president, these soldiers are focused on destabilizing the political climate and eliminating the small band of revolutionaries holed up in some Mayan ruins, the same group of revolutionaries that has taken hostage Eddie, Thomas, and Lindsey, as well as Oscar, their chopper pilot, and Chan Ma'ax, a Mayan tribal leader. Having worked a decade earlier as an anthropologist/ archaeologist on the Mayan site as part of his dissertation, Thomas feels profoundly connected to the history behind these ruins. Eddie, however, is more focused on feeding his drug addiction and begins traveling into the past after ingesting the mysterious properties of a 'magic mushroom,' an experience that Thomas, Lindsey, and the others chalk up to a drug hallucination until Eddie is trapped in the past and Thomas, at the behest of Chan Ma'ax, follows to rescue his brother.

Deserted Cities of the Heart is vastly different from *Frontera*—its drug-induced alternate realities resonate more closely with Shiner's Philip K. Dickian story "Stuff of Dreams" (1981) than any explicitly cyberpunk tale—but Robert Donahoo and Chuck Etheridge remark that in both Shiner novels "the collapse of governments has given corporations total freedom, and [Shiner] explores the human cost of an economic system that takes literally the longings of Ronald Reagan and Margaret Thatcher for total laissez-faire" (184); in addition, both novels feature a cyclical pattern of decline and rejuvenation, although *Deserted Cities of the Heart* "focuses more on adaptation to and acceptance of the pattern than on individual re-creation of heroism" (188). Finally, Shiner's second novel features cosmetic nods to cyberpunk: there are references to 'mirrorshades' and the use of Ilya Prigogine's 'dissipative structures' evoke Sterling's use of Prigogine in his Shaper-Mechanist stories, notably *Schismatrix* (1985).

In the end, *Deserted Cities of the Heart* shows Shiner consciously distancing himself from the cyberpunk tropes he helped popularize; however, following the publication of the "The Gene Drain" a year after *Deserted Cities of the Heart*, Shiner made the divorce official in two separate publications. "[O]ther writers," Shiner lamented in "Confessions of an Ex-Cyberpunk" for *The New York Times* (1991), "had turned the form into formula: implant wetware (biological computer chips), government by multinational corporations, street-wise, leather-jacketed, amphetamine-loving protagonists and decayed orbital colonies." Shiner doubled-down on his grievances in "Inside the Movement: Past, Present and Future" (1992): cyberpunk had become a commodified label used "to sell everything from comics to board games to specialty magazines for keyboard players" and what had once been revolutionary had now become largely "sci-fiberpunk" (17). While Shiner is mostly dismissive of post-Movement cyberpunk—he claims he doesn't "see anything dangerous or threatening about cyberpunk in its current incarnation" ("Confessions")—he grudgingly acknowledged cyberpunk "was escaping, virus-like, into the mainstream, where it continues to thrive" ("Confessions"). At the same time, he also expressed his hope that cyberpunk will present "new paradigms, [work] against prejudice and limited worldviews" and "find a voice with the energy and wisdom and humor to speak to these times" ("Inside" 25). In the end, while sci-fiberpunk may still be a clichéd *poseur*, cyberpunk's evolution as a cultural formation positions it as perhaps the most important "means of engaging with our twenty-first century technocultural age" (McFarlane et al. 3), and, in that vein, Shiner's importance as a figure in cyberpunk culture, even reluctantly so, is no less important.

See also: **William Gibson, Rudy Rucker, Bruce Sterling**

Works Cited

Donahoo, Robert and Chuck Etheridge. "Lewis Shiner and the 'Good' Anarchist." *Fiction 2000: Cyberpunk and the Future of Narrative*, edited by George Slusser and Tom Shippey, U of Georgia P, 1992, pp. 183–90.

McFarlane, Anna, Graham J. Murphy, and Lars Schmeink. "Cyberpunk as Cultural Formation." *The Routledge Companion to Cyberpunk Culture*, edited by Anna McFarlane, Graham J. Murphy, and Lars Schmeink, Routledge, 2020, pp. 1–3.

Rucker, Rudy. *Nested Scrolls: The Autobiography of Rudolf von Bitter Rucker*. PS Publishing, 2011, http://www.rudyrucker.com/nestedscrolls/sample/nestedscrolls.html.

Shiner, Lewis. "Confessions of an Ex-Cyberpunk." *The New York Times*, January 7, 1991, https://www.nytimes.com/1991/01/07/opinion/confessions-of-an-excyberpunk.html.

———. *Deserted Cities of the Heart*. Bantam, 1988.

———. *Frontera*. Subterranean Press, 2008.

———. "Inside the Movement: Past, Present and Future." *Fiction 2000: Cyberpunk and the Future of Narrative*, edited by George Slusser and Tom Shippey, U of Georgia P, 1992, pp. 17–25.

———. "Life as We Know It." *Fiction Liberation Front*. 2019, https://www.lewisshiner.com/autobio.html.

———. "The Gene Drain." *Fiction Liberation Front*. 1989, https://www.fictionliberationfront.net/.

Shiner, Lewis (as Sue Denim). Editorial. *Cheap Truth*, #10. Totse.com, May 1, 2020, totseans.com/totse/en/ego/on_line_zines/cheap10.html.

Graham J. Murphy

MASAMUNE SHIROW (1961–)

Japanese manga artist.

Masamune Shirō (born Masanori Ōta), anglicized as Masamune Shirow, has authored multiple science fiction (sf) and fantasy manga since the mid-1980s that align with cyberpunk's key literary and visual tenets. His major works include *Black Magic* (self-published 1983, re-published 1985), *Appleseed* (1985–89), *Dominion* (1985–86), *Dominion Conflict One: No More Noise* (1992–93), *Ghost in the Shell* (*Kōkaku Kidōtai*, 1989–90), *Ghost in the Shell 1.5: Human Processing Error* (1991–96), *Ghost in the Shell 2: Man-Machine Interface* (1997), and *Orion* (*Senjutsu Chōkōkaku Orion*, 1990–91). He has also published many serialized art books that act as themed illustration compendiums, including *Intron Depot* (1992–), which sometimes features cyberpunk-like technologies.

Shirow is widely regarded as one of Japan's key innovators of cyberpunk aesthetics and themes during the 1980s and 1990s, especially for his depictions of synthetic or cyborgian characters, centralized artificial intelligence (AI) supercomputers, militarized police, and cyber networks. His most famous contributions, *Appleseed* and *Ghost in the Shell*, are acclaimed works of cyberpunk graphic literature that have launched successful, long-running transmedia franchises consisting of OVAs (Original Video Animation—a form of low budget straight-to-video anime), theatrical feature-length anime films, anime TV series, and video games. In 1986, Shirow's work on *Appleseed* earned him a Seiun Award, which is Japan's most prestigious awards body for sf literature. Most of Shirow's major works have been widely translated, published, and re-published, making him one of the most well-known manga artists of his generation.

Along with **Katsuhiro Ōtomo**'s prestigious cyberpunk manga *Akira* (1982–90), and its famous 1988 anime adaptation, Shirow's *Ghost in the Shell* was instrumental in shaping Japan's international, cyberpunk-inflected pop culture image during the 1990s. Set in a "highly information-intensive" future Japan (Shirow, *Ghost* 5) where human consciousness (i.e., the "ghost") can exist within a cybernetic body (the "shell"), *Ghost in the Shell* follows the investigations of a counter-cybercrime unit from the mysterious government department Public Security Section 9, led in the field by the fearless "full-body prosthesis" operative Major Motoko Kusanagi. The manga's mix of dynamic cyberpunk action and dense sf worldbuilding has played an important role in popularizing the series (and the broader medium) with an audience outside Japan. While Shirow does not see *Ghost in* *the Shell* as an original development of the cyberpunk mode, writing, "It's rather light cyberpunk ripping off the aesthetic, and much of it is just 'monkey see, monkey do' imitation" (cited in Ruh 404) *Ghost in the Shell* has grown in influence; as a result, it has become one of Japan's most revered and iconic cyberpunk properties. This reputation has been solidified by its even more influential anime feature adaptation (Oshii 1995), as well as the release of a major live-action Hollywood adaptation in 2017, making it the first Japanese cyberpunk manga to receive such treatment, although this accomplishment has been undercut by the controversy surrounding its casting of white American actress Scarlet Johansson as Kusanagi.

Ghost in the Shell's influence can be seen in several other Hollywood sf productions, most notably **Lana and Lilly Wachowski**'s Matrix film series (1999–2003, 2021). In fact, despite the Wachowskis' acknowledgment of the anime's influence on the development of their film, controversy reportedly "blew up over the resemblance of certain scenes and images" when *The Matrix* was released in March 1999 (Hughes 113). Similarly, Andrew Osmond points out that film director Neill Blomkamp modeled his titular robot protagonist in *Chappie* (2015) on *Appleseed*'s iconic cyborg character Briareos, including the distinctive "insectile head and rabbit-shaped ears" (46). These are only two examples that show Shirow's visuals are among the most well-traveled in cyberpunk, having been subject to numerous transnational replications through adaptation, homage, or inspirational borrowings.

Ironically, many adaptations and media spinoffs of Shirow's corpus are arguably more famous than their source material, such as the *Ghost in the Shell* anime, or the *Appleseed* computer-animated feature (Aramaki 2004). As a result, it is perhaps easy to overlook the qualities and quirks of Shirow's original manga and their connections and contributions to cyberpunk. For example, Shirow has been described as "a brilliant artist with an opaque and mysterious style of storytelling" (Schodt 319), an assessment that is hard to deny given his narratives are often chaotic, episodic, and as densely produced as his visuals, which routinely depict complex and highly detailed technologized societies. It is this vivid attention to detail toward technology and its role in (near) future city-states that ultimately solidifies his status as a cyberpunk visionary.

At the same time, it is misleading to categorize Shirow's work as belonging to the hard-boiled sf that informs early cyberpunk texts: his work is often playful in its mixing of genre tropes, iconography, and aesthetics. For example, *Black Magic*, his first major work, takes place in an advanced technocratic society governed by the super-computer Nemesis. While this may read like typical cyberpunk, this society exists on an inhabitable Venus millions of years in the past as opposed to a far-future reminiscent of **Bruce Sterling's** Schismatrix series (1982–85).[1] The manga's protagonist, Duna Typhon, a special "bioroid" (synthetic human) protector who operates on the fringes of this technocracy, can perform sorcery and is shown utilizing magical artifacts, which is more in line with high fantasy or even cyberpunk-themed games[2] than print or cinematic cyberpunk. Likewise, *Orion* offers a similar blend of sf and fantasy, mixing cybernetic technologies with ancient Japanese mysticism. Meanwhile, *Dominion* is far more lighthearted than its ecologically dystopian setting would suggest. The story takes place in a post-apocalyptic metropolis where the air is no longer breathable without the assistance of an oxygen mask. It portrays its protagonists—a squad of militarized law enforcers called the "Tank Police"—as a likable group of loose cannons who inconsequentially cause huge swathes of collateral damage while in pursuit of the city's professional criminals. Shirow's mangas are also typically more tonally eccentric when compared to their better-known adaptations, or even to the contemporaneous work of other cyberpunk manga artists such as Ōtomo or Yukito Kishiro (creator of *Gunnm*, a.k.a. *Battle Angel Alita*, 1990–95). Shirow's playful cyberpunk worlds can feature "*chibi*-style" caricatures, a drawing technique that momentarily "depicts a character as having a small, chubby body with an oversized head" for cute or comedic effect (Suzuki 114), evident in *Appleseed* and *Ghost in the Shell*, or metareferential in-jokes, such as the hidden messages in *Dominion* that call the reader to purchase the latest volume of *Appleseed* (*Dominion* 69). In sum, Shirow's work demonstrates that highly urbanized cyberpunk dystopias policed by militarized law enforcement need not be devoid of humor or mischief.

Conversely, Shirow's work often grapples with many of cyberpunk's most philosophical themes, including the nature of (post)human existence, AI and the politics of technocracy, the ethics of biotechnology, human–machine relations, multiculturalism, globalism, and the environment. This aspect of Shirow's work often survives (if not thrives in) the adaptation process, such as the film versions of *Ghost in the Shell* and *Ghost in the Shell 2: Innocence* (Oshii 2004), whose ruminations on the cybernetic programmability of identity, memory, and the soul are amplified and have become a staple of the franchise. In Shirow's work, "technology is viewed from a realistic, human scale, and explores how scientific developments impinge on the social, economic, and political fabric of a world not too distant from our own" (Evans and Ridout 38). This evokes the bottom-up, "low-life and high tech" (Sterling 4) approach favored by North American cyberpunk writers such as

William Gibson and Bruce Sterling, and has also been used to partly explain Shirow's popularity within the nascent American manga market of the 1990s (Schodt 319).

Although Shirow was able to successfully cultivate an overseas fanbase, his work set itself apart from other media within the burgeoning cyberpunk canon (including literature, cinema, and comics) through what is perhaps his most recognizable storytelling motif: his use of female protagonists. As David Hughes writes, "Shirow has two main visual interests—lovingly detailed, often insectoid, robotics or machinery, and long-limbed, boyish girls, preferably with guns" (103). His preference toward tomboyish female characters to anchor his cyberpunk narratives was done at a time when "[t]he protagonists of [American] cyberpunk novels [were] nearly always male. When women [did] appear, they hardly ever transcend[ed] feminine stereotypes" (Cadora 357–58). Much has been written on cyberpunk's deep-seated masculinism,[3] but Shirow's heroines resist the stereotyping described by Karen Cadora because they are often skilled and proactive operatives in the military-industrial complexes of their respective cyberpunk worlds, such as ESWAT (Extra Special Weapons and Tactics) member Deunan Knute (*Appleseed*) and "Tank Police" officer Leona Ozaki (*Dominion*). Both characters deftly navigate their respective male-dominated environments in a manner that appears pro-feminist.

It is Major Kusanagi from *Ghost in the Shell*, however, that proves to be Shirow's most enduring and complex creation, and perhaps remains one of cyberpunk's most formidable female characters. Her level of recognition matches (if not exceeds) such North American cyberpunk characters as Molly Millions from William Gibson's "Johnny Mnemonic" (1981) or Sprawl trilogy (*Neuromancer*, 1984; *Count Zero*, 1986; *Mona Lisa Overdrive*, 1988) and Trinity from the Wachowskis' *Matrix* franchise. However, Kusanagi's depiction in the original manga differs from her better-known on-screen incarnations. Shirow's original design emphasized Kusanagi's youth, femininity, and sexuality, which was redesigned "to look far more mature and masculine" (Osmond 55) in subsequent adaptations. So, while Kusanagi is very much the driving force in the manga, appearing completely self-actualized in all facets of her life (and lacking the existential anomie of Oshii's anime version), she is often portrayed in a way that serves an adolescent male gaze (the manga's primary readership at the time), which problematizes any claims of Shirow's cyberpunk being feminist. A virtual reality lesbian threesome involving Kusanagi (which was censored from foreign-language reprints, and later removed by Shirow himself) is an especially explicit example of the adolescent sexual fantasies that imbue much of Shirow's work—a tendency that can be traced back to his earliest amateur contributions in self-published manga magazines such as *Atlas* in the early 1980s, which feature numerous tough yet eroticized young women.

Nevertheless, Shirow's recurring use of female protagonists helped galvanize an entire subgenre of female-driven sf/police procedural manga and anime that tap into cyberpunk themes, having been described as the "[u]ndisputed master manipulator of this popular scenario" (Evans 9). Examples include Kia Asamiya's manga *Silent Möbius* (1989–99), the *Bubblegum Crisis* OVA series (1987–91)—plus its spinoff *A.D. Police Files* (1990)—and, more recently, the anime series *Ergo Proxy* (2006) and *Psycho-Pass* (since 2012). As such, Shirow's untamed imagination and its impact on cyberpunk, both in Japan and overseas, is incontestable.

See also: **William Gibson, Mamoru Oshii, Katsuhiro Ōtomo, Bruce Sterling, Shinya Tsukamoto, Lana and Lilly Wachowski**

Notes

1 "Swarm" (1982); "Spider-Rose" (1982); "Cicada Queen" (1983); "Sunken Gardens" (1984); "Twenty Evocations" (1984); *Schismatrix* (1985).
2 For details about the use of magic in such cyberpunk-themed games as *Shadowrun* (FASA 1989), see Carbonell.
3 In addition to Cadora, see Melzer, Nixon, or Yaszek.

Works Cited

Cadora, Karen. "Feminist Cyberpunk." *Science Fiction Studies*, vol. 22, no. 3, 1995, pp. 357–72.

Carbonell, Curtis D. "Tabletop Roleplaying Games." *The Routledge Companion to Cyberpunk Culture*, edited by Anna McFarlane, Graham J. Murphy, and Lars Schmeink, Routledge, 2020, pp. 200–08.

Evans, Peter J. "Police Stories." *Manga Mania*, vol. 1, no. 8, 1994, pp. 8–11.

Evans, Peter J. and Cefn Ridout. "Future Tense." *Manga Mania*, vol. 1, no. 8, 1994, pp. 36–38.

Hughes, David. *Comic Book Movies*. Virgin Books, 2007.

Melzer, Patricia. "Cyborg Feminism." *The Routledge Companion to Cyberpunk Culture*, edited by Anna McFarlane, Graham J. Murphy, and Lars Schmeink, Routledge, 2020, pp. 291–99.

Nixon, Nicola. "Cyberpunk: Preparing the Ground for Revolution or Keeping the Boys Satisfied?" *Science Fiction Studies*, vol. 19, no. 2, 1992, pp. 219–35.

Osmond, Andrew. *Ghost in the Shell*. Arrow Books, 2017.

Ruh, Brian. "Japan as Cyberpunk Exoticism." *The Routledge Companion to Cyberpunk Culture*, edited by Anna McFarlane, Graham J. Murphy, and Lars Schmeink, Routledge, 2020 pp. 401–07.

Schodt, Frederik L. *Dreamland Japan: Writings on Modern Manga*. Stone Bridge
P, 2011.

Shirow, Masamune. *Dominion*. Translated by Dana Lewis, Frederik L. Schodt,
Toren Smith, and Duane Johnson, Dark Horse Manga, 2007.

———. *Ghost in the Shell*. Translated by Frederik L. Schodt and Toren Smith,
Kodansha Ltd, 2009.

Sterling, Bruce. Preface. *Burning Chrome*, by William Gibson, Gollancz, 2016,
pp. 1–4.

Suzuki, Shige (CJ). "Manga." *The Routledge Companion to Cyberpunk Culture*,
edited by Anna McFarlane, Graham J. Murphy, and Lars Schmeink,
Routledge, 2020, pp. 107–118.

Yaszek, Lisa. "Feminist Cyberpunk." *The Routledge Companion to Cyberpunk
Culture*, edited by Anna McFarlane, Graham J. Murphy, and Lars Schmeink,
Routledge, 2020 pp. 32–40.

Mark Player

WARREN SPECTOR (1955–)

US game designer and producer.

Warren Spector started his career writing for a variety of table-top
roleplaying games (TRPGs) and became an influential editor for TSR,
Inc. on games such as *Bullwinkle and Rocky Role-Playing Party Game*
(1988) and *The Uncanny X-Men Boxed Set* (1990). His career shift
to videogames occurred in 1989 when he worked as a producer for
Origin Systems (1989–96) and Electronic Arts (1992–96) on franchises
like Ultima, Wing Commander, and System Shock, among others, followed by a short period at Looking Glass Studios (1996–97) and seven
years at Ion Storm (1997–2004), where he developed the first installment of the Deus Ex franchise. In 2004, Spector founded Junction
Point Studios, which became a subsidiary of Disney Interactive
Studios in 2007. He left the studio in 2013 to become program director and senior lecturer at the University of Texas at Austin until 2016,
when he joined OtherSide Entertainment as creative director. Spector
has received such honors as a Lifetime Achievement Award at the
12th Annual Game Developers Choice Awards (2011), the Honorary
Award for Lifetime Achievement from the Fun and Serious Games
Conference (2016), and an Honorary Doctorate by Columbia College
of Chicago (2012).

Spector's work as a producer on *System Shock* (Looking Glass
Studios/Origin Systems 1994) resulted in a first-person shooter videogame (FPS) that combines combat, exploration, and puzzle-solving
features. The player embodies a nameless hacker sent to a space station

controlled by SHODAN, a malevolent artificial intelligence (AI) who plans to take control of Earth by uploading herself into its computer networks. To thwart her plans, the player must defeat robots, mutants, and cyborgs controlled by SHODAN and break through her defenses in cyberspace to destroy her. It is important to note that in addition to the cyberpunk motifs of hackers, AIs, and virtual domains, and while referencing cyberpunk's grid-like representation of cyberspace, *System Shock* extended video game depictions of "cyberspace itself into three dimensions, offering a vertiginous wireframe realm without obvious 'up' or 'down,' through which characters can move" (Johnson 143). The game kept "certain standard forms of movement and physical behavior from the 'real' world and overlay an architecture of space with a cyberspace aesthetic," creating a "convergence of (in-game) physical and virtual worlds [that] is even more pronounced in more recent games" (Johnson 145).

Having been approached by Ion Storm "to make the game of [his] dreams" (Wawro), Spector's *Deus Ex* (2000) is a ground-breaking game that, as Steven Joyce argues, uses "a hybridization of genres that parallels cyberpunk's blend of science fiction, noir, and post-modernism" (156). As the first installment of a larger video game franchise, *Deus Ex* is set in a dystopian society at the brink of chaos and plagued by a lethal virus. It is a "cyberpunk pastiche in which fears of unchecked capitalism exist alongside Illuminati conspiracies, Area 51, and the Knights Templar as products of paranoid fantasy" (Johnson 156), a game whose narrative "constructs a maze of political, economic, and social futures—based in the pros and cons of transhumanism—that players must navigate" (Schmeink 39). Aside from the narrative scaffolding, Spector's aim with *Deus Ex* (and *System Shock*) was to capture in video games the sense of immersion procured by TRPGs. He therefore added TRPGs mechanics in *Deus Ex*, such as character customization, skill points to enhance abilities, interaction with non-player characters ("NPCs"), and inventory management, all while combining these features with those from first-person shooters, stealth, and adventure games. This immersion therefore services the broader function of highlighting how "the way players have freedom only within clearly defined limits is symptomatic of how individuals are policed in the information age" (Joyce 169).

Jenna Ng and Jamie Macdonald outline the intimate histories of cyberpunk and video games: "[C]yberpunk has had an unsurprisingly profound and widespread influence on video games [… whose] aesthetics frequently draw inspiration from quintessential cyberpunk texts" (174). At the same time, "[c]yberpunk themes and conventions [...] also influence the narrative and gameplay elements of many video games" (Ng and Macdonald 174). To this point, both *System Shock* and *Deus Ex* show some of the most recognizable traits attributed to cyberpunk: alternation between material space and cyberspace (*System Shock*); sentient artificial intelligence as autonomous characters (SHODAN in *System Shock*; Icarus/Daedalus in *Deus Ex*); global-scale narratives that blend high-technology, hardboiled detective genre, apocalyptic tropes, and conspiracy theories (*Deus Ex*); hackers as protagonists (*System Shock*); nano-augmented and genetically engineered agents with posthuman capacities (neural interface in *System Shock*; nano-augmentation in *Deus Ex*); neo-noir aesthetics made visible in grim urban landscapes (*Deus Ex*), etc.

Beyond the surface details of *System Shock* and *Deus Ex*, cyberpunk's essence is embodied in Spector's game design, philosophy, and innovations. Specifically, Spector believes video games must provide nuanced and meaningful moral choices to the player, and that games must show the consequences of these choices ("Another"). In this vein, *Deus Ex* asks the player "[w]hat's the nature of humanity—at what point in a world of human augmentation do we stop being human and start being [...] something else?" (Spector, "Narrative"). *Deus Ex* therefore forces players to choose among three ways to articulate power and social organization as a consequence of new technology: destroy global communications and cause "a technological dark age in which people have genuine free will" (Spector, "Narrative"); opt for the status quo and let a shadowy elite rule the world; or merge with an artificial sentient being and become posthuman to give birth to a world where "an all-seeing AI can gift us with total connectivity and, one hopes, the empathy that arises from universal connection, at the cost of giving up our freedom" (Spector, "Narrative"). As Lars Schmeink argues, the openness of the ending meant "that the meaning-making process and the ethical positions of the game were not fixed but rather needed the player's collaborative participation" (38). Similarly, Joyce writes:

> Within an elaborate but limited space, players are given wide freedom to achieve specific goals [...] The gameplay thus converges on a question that is central to cyberpunk: How much free choice do individuals have over technology they didn't create and can't hope to replicate without the vast industrial forces that made it possible in the first place?
>
> (158)

In addition to creating these 'morality systems' for his games, Spector is also known as the "Godfather of the immersive sim genre" (Baker), namely a category of games in which "instead of feeling like you're just manipulating a digital puppet, you feel like you're immersing yourself in another world" (Spector, cited in Baker). In other words, according to Spector, developers must avoid breaking players' sense of immersion. The aim is to "remove the barriers to belief, so that players are not constantly being reminded that they're playing a game" (Spector, "Postmortem"). One way to handle this issue is by offering environments to players that explicitly respond to their decisions and actions with clear consequences. In *Deus Ex*, the world is reactive to players' actions (e.g., killing or helping NPCs), even when those actions seem trivial; for example, missions and dialogues with NPCs change based on players' behaviors. To provide immersive sims, designers must also let players freely explore open environments instead of providing a linear, so-called 'railroaded' gameplay. This is one of the reasons for the success of *System Shock*. Finally, rules must be designed in a way that allows emergent behaviors from the players (namely, unanticipated actions and a variety of solutions in order to solve puzzles) and *Deus Ex* permits this as its "goals can be accomplished through stealth, careful planning, undercover work or conversation, through the use of unbelievably high tech equipment or brute force combat tactics" (Spector, "Postmortem").

The immersivity Spector was emulating in *Deus Ex* fuels his more-recent developments with immersive sims, a field that is perhaps more cyberpunk than any of Spector's previous work. For example, "all games can be understood as systems" (Salen and Zimmerman 63), and when those games are complex systems, such as immersive sims, they encourage unpredictable patterns, or what John H. Holland describes as emergent outcomes.[1] Play may therefore be seen as a complex system; a framework in which emergent outcomes occur that can be understood as a liberty gained by the player despite a definite set of rules, constraints, and feedback loops. By analogy, cyberpunk also sees society as a complex cyber-system and, as Tom Moylan argues, cyberpunk protagonists don't transform the social system they live in; they only survive within the system (81). However, emergence can take the form of punk-like play within the larger systems' control and regulation devices. Or, as **William Gibson** famous says, "the street finds its own uses for things" (186). Therefore, like the player of a video game experiencing emergent play while interacting with the game's mechanics, cyberpunk's protagonists can experience emergence through resistance within a closed and dystopian system.

Finally, Warren Spector's legacy can be found in today's best-selling videogames, which are inspired by immersive sims' core principles he promoted throughout his career. One may think of open-world role-playing or action videogame franchises such as Fallout, The Witcher, Elder Scrolls, and Far Cry (cf. Wright), but also of cyberpunk vide-ogames like the Watch Dogs series or *Cyberpunk 2077* (CD Projekt Red, 2020). In sum, Warren Spector's influence upon cyberpunk culture is immeasurable and extends well beyond the casual use of cyberpunk's clichés and tropes; instead, his work proposes a homology between cyberpunk's core characteristics—i.e., cybernetic controls and punk resistance, or an open-ended discourse on the role played by technology on society—and the videogame mechanics that convey it, which are cyberpunk in essence.

See also: **William Gibson, Mike Pondsmith**

Note

1 Holland explains that a set of rules applied to a set of objects in a system yields unexpected behaviors that exceed the sum of what its parts would be likely to create (13–14).

Works Cited

Baker, Chris. "How Warren Spector Created a Genre, and Set Games Free." *Glixel*, June 2, 2017, http://www.glixel.com/news/how-warren-spector-created-a-genre-and-set-games-free-w485404.

Gibson, William. "Burning Chrome." *Burning Chrome*. Ace, 1987, pp. 168–91.

Holland, John. *Emergence*. Helix Books, 1997.

Johnson, Mark R. "The History of Cyberspace Aesthetics in Video Games." *Cyberpunk and Visual Culture*, edited by Graham J. Murphy and Lars Schmeink, Routledge, 2018, pp. 139–54.

Joyce, Stephen. "Playing for Virtually Real: Cyberpunk Aesthetics and Ethics in *Deus Ex: Human Revolution*." *Cyberpunk and Visual Culture*, edited by Graham J. Murphy and Lars Schmeink, Routledge, 2018, pp. 155–73.

Moylan, Tom. "Global Economy, Local Texts: Utopian/Dystopian Tension in William Gibson's Cyberpunk Trilogy." *Beyond Cyberpunk: New Critical Perspectives*, edited by Graham J. Murphy and Sherryl Vint, Routledge, 2010, pp. 81–94.

Ng, Jenna and Jamie Macdonald. "'We Are Data': The Cyberpunk Imaginary of Data Worlds in *Watch Dogs*." *Cyberpunk and Visual Culture*, edited by Graham J. Murphy and Lars Schmeink, Routledge, 2018, pp. 174–89.

Salen, Katie and Eric Zimmerman. *Rules of Play: Game Design Fundamentals*. The MIT P, 2003.

Schmeink, Lars. "Deus Ex." *100 Greatest Video Game Franchises*, edited by Robert Mejia, Jamie Banks, and Aubrie Adams, Rowman, 2017, pp. 38–39.

Spector, Warren. "Postmortem: Ion Storm's *Deus Ex*." *Gamasutra*, December 6, 2000, https://www.gamasutra.com/view/feature/131523/postmortem_ion_storms_deus_ex.php.

———. "A Narrative Fallacy: It's All About Aristotle." *Gamasutra*, August 3, 2015, https://www.gamasutra.com/blogs/WarrenSpector/20150803/250304/A_Narrative_Fallacy_Its_All_About_Aristotle.php.

———. "Another Narrative Fallacy: Games are About Choice." *Gamasutra*, August 12, 2015, https://www.gamasutra.com/blogs/WarrenSpector/20150812/250785/Another_Narrative_Fallacy_Games_are_About_Choice.php.

Wawro, Alex. "Developing *Deus Ex*: An Oral History." *Gamasutra*, June 23, 2015, https://www.gamasutra.com/view/news/240456/Developing_Deus_Ex_An_oral_history.php.

Wright, Steven T. "Why 'System Shock' Matters." *Glixel*, May 23, 2017, http://www.glixel.com/news/why-system-shock-matters-w483835.

Christophe Duret

STELARC [BORN STELIIOS ARCADIOU] (1946–)

Cypriot-Australian contemporary artist, performer, inventor, and writer.

While literary and cinematic cyberpunk have tended to dominate critical and popular discussions of this artistic mode, expanding more recently into discussions of cyberpunk video games, other no-less-important cultural venues have been instrumental in circulating and popularizing cyberpunk's motifs. One largely undertheorized corner of cyberpunk culture is performance art, and Cypriot-Australian 'cyborg performance artist' Stelarc has been at the forefront of this movement since at least the 1970s with experiments in the limits of corporeality, human–machine interactions, and the concept of virtual presence. In his explorations of alternate anatomical architectures, Stelarc uses robotic prostheses, medical procedures, and technological interfaces, including such installations and performances as *Third Hand* (completed in 1980 in Yokohama), *Suspensions* (various performances between 1980 and 2020), *Exoskeleton* (1997), *Muscle Machine* (2003), *Ear on Arm* (for the first time exhibited in 2008), *Walking Head* (developed between 2001 and 2006), and *Re-wired/Re-mixed: Event for Dismembered Body* (2015).[1] Since 1990 Stelarc has had over 250 exhibitions, performances, and projects ("Performances," n.p.). In 1996 he was named Honorary Professor of Art and Robotics at Carnegie Mellon University (Pittsburgh) and in 2002 was awarded an Honorary Degree of Laws by Monash University (Melbourne). Among Stelarc's most significant awards is the Ars Electronica Hybrid Arts Prize, which he received in 2010 (Herath, Kroos, and Stelarc xiv). Perhaps the most compelling accolades, however, come from cyberpunk originateurs John Shirley and William Gibson: the former remarked that "[a]ll the signposts direct us to him" (cited in Bukatman 260) while the latter, in his Preface to *Stelarc: The Monograph*, extols Stelarc for his absolute visions "of some absolute chimera at the heart of a labyrinth of breathtaking complexity" and artistically exploring "moments of the purest technologically induced cognitive disjunction" (viii).

The global interest in Stelarc's works is connected to their contemporary, transgressive character, and visual aesthetics, all of which echo cyberpunk narratives. His art has had a significant influence on modern artistic paradigms, providing context for the performative tendencies that are present in many human/machine interactions (Kluszczyński 225). For example, many of Stelarc's projects have involved transforming the man (the artist) into the machine by turning the artist into the cyborg via technological augmentations attached to the organs or limbs. Stelarc also addresses the cyberpunk concept of connecting corporeality and virtual space by remote steering, thus leaving the control of his body to external agents: for example, in one performance robotic muscle stimulators were connected to the internet, allowing audience members to control him (Herath 42). As Bukatman writes, Stelarc has "treated the body as an environment which needs to be made more adaptable" (260). Thus, his radical artistic practice of body modifications and his search for art-science connections "implies a re-figuring of the spatialities of the body and its environment as well as the temporalities of communicative practices and bodily performance" (Abrahamsson and Abrahamsson 293). While Stelarc redesigns the obsolete body and searches for the practical implications of the possibilities of connecting with a device/network (Zurbrugg 111), he also problematizes the boundaries of humanity and the influence of alternate experiences that can be inaugurated by media. Stelarc's art can therefore be perceived as a mediation between cyberpunk narratives and cultural discourses about human/technology interactions (Farnell 129).

Stelarc's theories of a body as an evolutionary structure and his preoccupation with human–machine interfaces provide the answers to the philosophical questions about the limits of human physiology (Stelarc, "Prosthetics" 591). While his approach stems from the philosophical and critical works of Marshall McLuhan, Gilles Deleuze and Félix Guattari, Jean Baudrillard, Jean-François Lyotard, and Paul Virilio, Stelarc is searching for practical application and tries to design the way for his works to function effectively within posthuman discourses. In other words, it is the act of performance that generates full understanding of his works, so Stelarc refrains from producing, writing, or expressing any coherent theory summarizing his artistic search. Stelarc can therefore be situated in the current of postmodern multimedia avant-garde: his experiments' speculative nature and explorations of a new aesthetics create the space for techno-creativity and cybernetic installations to be included in contemporary art practice (Zurbrugg 93–110). Stelarc underlines the connections between art and science by interrogating the possibilities of diverse modern technologies, particularly in his works focusing on the artist's (typically his) body; thus, he builds on an understanding of art as body awareness while corporeality becomes a component of a discourse that stresses the post-organic (Kluszczyński 228–40).

One of the main ideas permeating Stelarc's art is the strategy of body modification through technological incorporation. For example, following transhumanists' thoughts about biology as a limitation (cf. More), Stelarc states that the body is a flexible, controllable, and fragile structure, biologically not adequate for our times (Kluszczyński 226); thus, Stelarc underlines that its low efficiency comes from the inability to cope with the complexity of accumulated information. Stelarc's efforts are therefore focused on redesigning the body in a way to obtain modular design.[2] Such an approach also means the body is no longer "an object of desire but an object for designing" (Stelarc, "Prosthetics" 591). Therefore, in a manner akin to cyberpunk's hackers plugging into virtual systems or the enhanced abilities that accompany cybernetic implants, the body's abilities can be expanded upon or thoroughly transformed when it is plugged into the cyber-system or transformed by prosthetic limbs or organs (Zurbrugg 109). In his *Suspension* projects, for example, Stelarc was testing the limits of the skin, suspending himself "from ropes attached to hooks pierced into his skin, highlighting in this way the indeterminacy of the body's boundaries delineated by the skin itself and interrogating its status, role and agency" (Kluszczyński 226). Similarly, Stelarc also touched on issues of shaping relations between art and science: in *Stomach Sculpture* (1993), he underwent an endoscopy to place a piece of artwork in his stomach. Conceptually, with the help of technology, his body was radically transformed into a techno-biological art gallery (Kluszczyński 228). This exploration of the body's biological functions was also the focus of *Third Ear* (also called *Ear on Arm*, 2006–08), when a kidney-shaped silicone implant of an ear was surgically attached to Stelarc's left arm. An attached Bluetooth receiver and microphone allowed Stelarc to communicate through it, even sending surrounding voices to another continent (Abrahamsson and Abrahamsson 294). As Stelarc said, "[t]his additional and enabled EAR ON ARM effectively becomes an Internet organ for the body" ("Ear on Arm").

As *Third Ear* makes clear, one of Stelarc's main exploratory topics, particularly in his performance works of the 1990s, is corporeal immersion in interactive networks, an immersion that postulates the individual is no longer perceived as a separate entity from the communications technology and cybernetic infrastructure (Kluszczyński 229). In such projects as *Ping Body*, first exhibited in 1995, and *Fractal Fresh*, first exhibited in 1996, the audience could remotely control Stelarc's body by activating his movements via the internet (229). In a McLuhanesque fashion vis-à-vis 'the medium is the message,' Stelarc referred to the concept of a global cyborg-system—i.e., the Net—and showed new media as extensions of the human nervous system (230). The conceptualizations of the global network as a somatic challenge (242)—i.e., connecting to the global network is so intense that it challenges the conceptual perception of the artist—has also accompanied Stelarc's more recent projects, such as *Obsolete, Involuntary and Avatar Bodies: Fractal and Phantom Experiences* (2007) (Abrahamsson and Abrahamsson 294).

Finally, Stelarc's aspiration to exteriorize the body with cybernetic prostheses is conceptually fully in line with cyberpunk. He proposes "a refined form of cyborg art," taking on the position of an artist-cyborg that is "a cross between an artwork, a model of a hybrid, and a personal or post-personal construction made of wetware, hardware, software and artware combined" (Kluszczyński 232). Similar to the ideas expressed by Donna Haraway, the artist as cyborg thus transgresses categorial boundaries, is a hybrid between different subject positions. This attitude can be found in the *Third Hand* or *Body on Robot Arm* (2015) performances, in which Stelarc focused on the limits of human–machine connections and transformations by attaching himself to an industrial robot arm and moving according to programmed choreography. In *Third Hand*'s first iteration in Tokyo in 1981, the prosthesis was integrated as a natural body component that was manipulated by the artist's body functions. In further versions of the project, the cyber-arm could be controlled via the internet (Kluszczyński 225). Another performance with cyber-prosthesis was named *Amplified Body*

(1991) and included a presentation of a hybrid human-machine system installation, which flickered according to the electrical impulses of the artist's body, sent from brainwaves, muscles, pulse, and blood flow (Stelarc, "Prosthetics" 591–92).

In his rich portfolio, Stelarc has also employed industrial robots as part of his robotic art, including robotic installations that focused on the movement, communication, and contestation of "traditional concepts of aliveness, embodiment and agency" (Herath 24). For example, *Prosthetic Head* (2003) was a virtual 3D representation of Stelarc's head, while *Walking Head Robot* (2006) extended and applied this into a moving robot. *Prosthetic Head* was answering the audience's questions typed on the attached keyboard, and *Walking Head Robot* was reacting to the presence of the audience, moving in pre-stated sequences while displaying facial mimics. Meanwhile, *Exoskeleton* (2003) was a pneumatically powered, six-legged walking machine, in which Stelarc could move around the exhibition, manipulating it with hands. The idea of a moving exoskeleton was further developed in such Stelarc's projects as *Muscle Machine* (2003) and *Stickman* (2017), which are similar to *Exoskeleton* but differently sized moving machines controlled by the artist's gestures.

In sum, the body from Stelarc's point of view is open for new components, and the focus upon transcending our physical limitations via medical and technological interventions finds Stelarc's performative art at the cutting edge of the transhumanist posthuman. Evolution and procreation are no longer needed; it is the implant technology that creates new species (Stelarc "Prosthetics" 591). However, Stelarc rejects the master–slave dynamic common to many cyberpunk narratives. The cyborg is neither perceived as the Other nor as a stranger among biological human beings; instead, the flesh-and-blood body coupled with advanced technologies "become one operational system" (Herath 42), a truly cyberpunk transhumanist posthuman. In this regard, being open to body interventions and experiments, Stelarc provides a space for new and provocative encounters of human and machine.

See also: **Rosi Braidotti, Donna J. Haraway, Ray Kurzweil, Hans Moravec**

Notes

1 For details, see Herath, Kroos, and Stelarc's *Robots and Art*.
2 Under the term 'modular design,' Stelarc understands the object or an organism built of easily replaceable components. According to him, such design enhances the durability and survival parameters of the structure (biological or artificial).

Works Cited

Abrahamsson, Christian and Sebastian Abrahamsson. "Cultural geographies in practice. In conversation with the body conveniently known as Stelarc." *Cultural geographies*, vol. 14, 2007, pp. 293–308.

Bukatman, Scott. *Terminal Identity: The Virtual Subject in Post-Modern Science Fiction.* Duke UP, 1993.

Farnell, Ross. "In Dialogue with 'Posthuman' Bodies: Interview with Stelarc." *Body & Society*, vol. 5, no. 2–3, 1999, pp. 129–46.

Gibson, William. Foreword. *Stelarc: The Monograph*, edited by Marquard Smith, The MIT P, 2007, pp. vii–viii.

Haraway, Donna. "A Cyborg Manifesto: Science, Technology, and Socialist-Feminism in the Late Twentieth Century." *Simians, Cyborgs and Women: The Reinvention of Nature.* Routledge, 1991, pp. 149–81.

Herath, Damith, Christian Kroos, and Stelarc, editors. *Robots and Art: Exploring an Unlikely Symbiosis.* Springer, 2016.

Kluszczyński, Ryszard. "Stelarc—A Singular Artist." *Meat, Metal & Code: Contestable Chimeras. STELARC*, edited by Ryszard Kluszczyński, Centre for Contemporary Art in Gdańsk, 2014, pp. 224–45.

More, Max. "The Philosophy of Transhumanism." *The Transhumanist Reader: Classical and Contemporary Essays on the Science, Technology, and Philosophy of the Human Future*, edited by Max More and Natasha Vita-More, Wiley-Blackwell, 2013, pp. 3–17.

Smith, Marquard, editor. *Stelarc. The Monograph.* The MIT P, 2005.

Stelarc. "Ear on Arm." *Stelarc.org*, 2020, http://stelarc.org/?catID=20242.

———. "Performances, Projects, & Exhibitions 1990–2020: Stelarc." *Stelarc. org*, 2020, http://stelarc.org/media/pdf/Performances_and_Exhibitions_Stelarc.pdf.

———. "Prosthetics, Robotics and Remote Existence: Postevolutionary Strategies." *Leonardo*, vol. 24, no. 5, 1991, pp. 591–95.

Zurbrugg, Nicholas. "Marinetti, Chopin, Stelarc and the Auratic Intensities of the Postmodern Techno-Body." *Body & Society*, vol. 5, no. 2–3, 1999, pp. 93–115.

Agnieszka Kiejziewicz

NEAL STEPHENSON (1959–)

US author.

Neal Stephenson has published more than a dozen novels under his own name and co-authored several books under the pseudonym 'Stephen Bury' with his uncle, the historian George Jewsbury (also known as J. Frederick George). Stephenson is the son of a professor in electrical engineering and holds a degree in geography minoring in physics, and this academic, scientific background informs his fascination with individuals with specialist skills in coding, engineering, robotics, astrophysics, and/or theoretical mathematics, leading to discussions about how his work bridges the divide between the arts and the sciences (Clayton), or typifies the strengthening links between literature and the academy in the US over the post-war period (McGurl). Stephenson explores the cultures that accrete around such specialties and combines detailed descriptions of real and theoretically possible scientific endeavors. Having settled in Seattle, a center for internet start-ups and tech development, Stephenson has a first-hand view of the ways in which technology and its subcultures shape external environments and this continued engagement with cyberculture has seen him lauded as "one of the most prolific and important figures associated with post-cyberpunk" (Kilgore 48).

Stephenson cemented his place as a significant figure in cyberpunk with *Snow Crash* (1992), a novel that features a matrix-like visualized dataspace, computer hackers, and a nefarious corporate antagonist. *Snow Crash* acts as a rejoinder to **William Gibson**'s conception of cyberspace in *Neuromancer* (1984) and its sequels *Count Zero* (1986) and *Mona Lisa Overdrive* (1988); namely, whereas Gibson's lyrical evocation of that non-space behind the computer screen was imbued with a melancholy, noirish sensibility, *Snow Crash* reimagines the world of data and hackers with a brattish, infectious sense of humor. Cyberspace is not only a site for intrigue and action, but for juvenile fun and social sparring. Stephenson's main character is Hiro Protagonist, a Japanese samurai pizza delivery boy whose frenetic lifestyle in the real world is only matched by his online status as a master hacker. Stephenson's irreverence is no barrier to an engagement with some of those larger themes to which cyberpunk lends itself, namely the question of what it means to live in a quasi-virtual world. The 'Snow Crash' virus can kill a person in real life by infecting them online (among other methods) in a neat blending of metaphors between the biological and the computer virus. However, it is Stephenson's account of how social inequalities in real life might be replicated in online spaces that is most influential. He popularized the term 'avatar' to describe a person's online visual representation and showed a cyberspace where such avatars immediately announce the status of the user through the complexity (or crudity) of the graphics, narrative traits that have been most recently copied in Ernest Cline's *Ready Player One* (2011) and *Ready Player Two* (2020). While his key contribution is the depiction of cyberspace as a realm where real activity takes place, Stephenson's cyberspace also had some influence on the development of social media, inspiring the creators of the popular online space *Second Life* (Maney).

Following *Snow Crash*, Stephenson continued to engage with cyberpunk in imaginative ways that pushed the mode forward: the steampunk imagery of *The Diamond Age: or, A Young Lady's Illustrated Primer* (1995) places it in conversation with William Gibson and Bruce Sterling's *The Difference Engine* (1990), a novel that "translated cyberpunk's obsession with [**Alvin and Heidi Tofflers**'] future shock by projecting the force of technological change into a different epoch" (Murphy 526). However, rather than set his novel in a Victorian Age with anachronistic technology, Stephenson gives us a world in which the Victorian aesthetic is maintained in a private enclave of a future society where space has been almost completely privatized and different groups create their own parallel, intricately conceived societies. The action of the Locus- and Hugo-Award winning novel centers around the titular primer, an artificial intelligence (AI) in the guise of a book. Intended to guide a young aristocrat through her early years, the book instead falls into the hands of Nell, a destitute child, and sets about helping her navigate the violent situations that face her. *The Diamond Age* thus traces the rise of this young woman through the echelons of a divided society, thanks to the guidance of an adaptable, nanotechnological, AI that had been intended for more gentile tasks.

Stephenson's voluminous *Cryptonomicon* (1999) provides an account of encryption and cryptocurrency through two narrative threads: one features Alan Turing and is set circa World War II; the other is set against the backdrop of the internet bubble of the late 1990s. This marked a move for Stephenson from cyberpunk sf to historical fiction, while giving the reader a deep dive into the politics and mathematics of cryptography through detailed explanations of key mathematical concepts. Stephenson would develop his interest in historical sf with his Baroque Cycle (2003–04), a three-volume mash-up[1] of sf and historical fiction, some of which gave the deep history of the situations he had explored in *Cryptonomicon*, and featured the ancestors of some of the characters from that earlier novel. This series was followed by *Anathem* (2008) which gives the science-fictional treatment generally reserved for rocket science to the field of abstract mathematics. The novel is set in a future where the arcane knowledge of mathematics is protected by a small segment of society cloistered in a monk-like community, charged with the custodianship of this knowledge. Stephenson's novels are, at this point, exclusively lengthy tomes worthy of the 'baroque' descriptor and unafraid of intricately detailed descriptions of concepts from abstract mathematics, physics, and other scientific fields.

As the co-founder of the Subutai Corporation, formed to explore new ways of using technology to build multi-author multimedia franchises, Stephenson has worked on transmedia writing projects that aim to reimagine literature for the online environment. He oversaw the collaborative writing project eventually published as *The Mongoliad* (2012), which featured fellow sf author Greg Bear, recognized as one of cyberpunk's founding authors through his inclusion in **Bruce Sterling**'s landmark collection *Mirrorshades: A Cyberpunk Anthology* (1986). Set against the backdrop of the Mongol invasions of the thirteenth century, *The Mongoliad* was released on a digital platform starting in 2010 followed by a print version in 2012. The shared universe of the novel encouraged fans to add to the narrative's epic sweep, with fan stories being published digitally as supplements to the main novels. Stephenson's collaboration with Nicole Golland, *The Rise and Fall of D.O.D.O* (2017), is a result of this enterprise.

In later years, Stephenson's work has continued his fascination with contemporary and futuristic sciences and the cultures that spring up around them. The diptych of *REAMDE* (2011) and *The Fall: Or, Dodge in Hell* (2019) deals with Richard 'Dodge' Forthrast, the developer of a fictional massive multiplayer online role-playing game (MMORPG) called T'Rain. When Dodge dies and is uploaded to a cybernetic afterlife of the kind imagined by contemporary transhumanists, his skills as a video game developer shape the new afterlife, giving him the status of a god. While *The Fall* becomes a kind of high-fantasy quest story, the theme of scientific communities is also explored via hard sf in *Seveneves* (2015), which details humanity's exodus from a doomed Earth, the use of the International Space Station to coordinate an escape plan, the establishment of a colony on a fragment of what was once the moon, and the human effort to terraform and repopulate the Earth. *Seveneves* gives detailed accounts of engineering issues and speculative designs for orbital habitations and transport systems, as well as extrapolating a population created via cloning from a small gene pool. Rather than succumb to a kind of transhumanist transcendence based on their futuristic origins, Stephenson peoples his world with deeply human characters who are still driven by history, mythology, sex, and tradition.

Stephenson has put his interest in scientific endeavors to practical use through his work as a technology consultant, and in his calls for a public discussion surrounding the role that writers and artists might have in creating a culture based on scientific progress. His 2011 essay,

"Innovation Starvation," continued a conversation about the role that sf writers might have to play in the development of a society defined by technological change, and Stephenson developed this interest by launching the Hieroglyph Project, which aimed to create sf with the goal of influencing science and technology. Stephenson explains that there are two theories that seek to explain how sf influences scientific progress. The first is the inspiration theory, which argues that people who read sf are more likely to be inspired to take up STEM subjects as their career. The other is through the production of a "plausible, fully thought-out picture of an alternate reality in which some sort of compelling innovation has taken place" ("Innovation Starvation"). To describe such innovations pithily, Stephenson borrows a term from Kim Karkanias of Microsoft Research, the "hieroglyph": "simple, recognizable symbols on whose significance everyone agrees" ("Innovation Starvation"). While Stephenson explicitly states that the mission to consciously produce an sf that might encourage STEM innovation harks back to the Golden Age with its mix of scientific didacticism and sense of wonder, he also credits cyberpunk and specifically Gibson's cyberspace, for shaping the internet and the way it is experienced in contemporary society. The Hieroglyph Project produced the collection *Hieroglyph: Stories and Visions for a Better Future* (2014), which features short stories that engage with real cutting-edge science with the aim of providing scientists and societies with inspirational models for engineering and design.

One potential shortcoming of the Hieroglyph Project's approach is the possibility that using fiction as a tool in service to a distinctly ideological goal puts it at risk of being relegated to the status of a handmaid to STEM subjects, supporting STEM rather than shaping the world on its own terms. As Matthew Snyder points out in his review of the collection, "the innovations that must come from the future will not surface with more gadgetry, gene-splicing, or nanotechnology; it will have to come from the way we arrange our social structures, possessions and relations to objects" (n.p.), an area that requires the kind of innovation found in 'soft sf' which can offer new, utopian, models for (re)structuring communities and societies. Stephenson himself sounds increasingly sympathetic toward this conclusion, having realized that there is a surfeit of ideas and patents for technological innovations, but that these ideas are not necessarily accompanied by an inventor who can also manage a project to the standards of venture capitalists seeking promising investment opportunities, causing systemic risk aversion (Stephenson "Innovation Starvation, the Next Generation"). Stephenson's understanding of this systemic and human aspect of the problem is unsurprising; while his novels indisputably emphasize the importance of science, and of fiction's relationship to science, they are just as interested in the societies and cultures that spring up around scientific ideas and communities, from the seven races in *Seveneves* with their prejudices and founding myths, to the monk-mathematicians of *Anathem*. In sum, Stephenson's passion for STEM subjects and their potential for real-world scientific innovation should never be mistaken for a lack of commitment to the possibilities of fiction in showing those intricate relationships between the sciences and the cultures that birth, nurture, or starve their innovative potential.

See also: **William Gibson, Bruce Sterling, Alvin and Heidi Toffler, Lana and Lilly Wachowski**

Note

1 *Quicksilver* (Volume 1 [2003]); *The Confusion* (Volume II [2004]); *The System of the World* (Volume III [2004]).

Works Cited

Clayton, Jay. "Convergence of the Two Cultures: A Geek's Guide to Contemporary Literature." *American Literature*, vol. 74, no. 4, 2002, pp. 807–31.

Kilgore, Christopher D. "Post-Cyberpunk." *The Routledge Companion to Cyberpunk Culture*, edited by Anna McFarlane, Graham J. Murphy, and Lars Schmeink, Routledge, 2020, pp. 48–55.

Maney, Kevin. "The King of Alter Egos is Surprisingly Humble Guy. Creator of *Second Life*'s Goal? Just To Reach People." *USA Today*, February 5, 2007, http://public.wsu.edu/~fking1/ rosendale_2ndlife.doc.

McGurl, Mark. "The Program Era: Pluralisms of Postwar American Fiction." *Critical Inquiry*, vol. 32, no. 1, 2005, pp. 102–129.

Murphy, Graham J. "Cyberpunk and Post-Cyberpunk." *The Cambridge History of Science Fiction*, edited by Gerry Canavan and Eric Carl Link, Cambridge UP, 2018, pp. 519–36.

Snyder, Matthew. "Saving Spaceship Earth." *Los Angeles Review of Books*, October 22, 2014, https://lareviewofbooks.org/article/saving-spaceship-earth/.

Stephenson, Neal. "Innovation Starvation." *World Policy*, September 27, 2011, http://worldpolicy.org/2011/09/27/innovation-starvation/.

———. "Innovation Starvation, the Next Generation." *Slate.com*, September 29, 2014, https://slate.com/technology/2014/09/neal-stephenson-innovation-starvation-we-have-great-ideas-for-the-future.html.

Anna McFarlane

[MICHAEL] BRUCE STERLING (1954–)

US author, journalist, blogger, and futurist.

Since his science fiction (sf) debut with the story "Man-Made Self" (1976), quickly followed by the *Moby Dick* remix novel *Involution Ocean* (1977), Bruce Sterling has so far published eleven novels (plus one in collaboration with **William Gibson**), over 70 pieces of short fiction (not including dozens of collaborations), and a handful of chapbooks in various media, accruing a number of awards and accolades in the process. He edited the influential *Mirrorshades: The Cyberpunk Anthology* (1986) and served for two years (2014–15) as editor of *Twelve Tomorrows, MIT Technology Review*'s Science Fiction Annual. Sterling has been equally prodigious in his non-fiction work, with dozens of reviews, columns, and critical essays, as well as a handful of non-fiction books. Finally, he was a founding columnist and flagship blogger for *WIRED*, the journal-of-record for cyberculture since the magazine was founded in 1993.

Sterling's prominence in sf came as much through his work as an iconoclastic fanzine critic as through his fiction. The scabrous fanzine *Cheap Truth* (1983–86) that he wrote and edited as Vincent Omniveritas provides perhaps the truest link to cyberpunk's 'punk' element. Mirroring the 'zines produced by the counter-establishment music subcultures of the late-1970s and early-1980s, *Cheap Truth* attempted to tear a rift in sf culture between the supposedly stagnant 'humanism' of the post-New Wave authors and the scrappy attitude of 'the Movement.' The apotheosis and (re)branding of the Movement as *cyberpunk*, however, will always be tied to Sterling's *Mirrorshades: A Cyberpunk Anthology*, even though Gardner Dozois lifted the term from Bruce Bethke's short story "Cyberpunk" (1980) and applied it to Sterling and his *Cheap Truth* ilk well before the anthology's release. *Mirrorshades* collected previously published stories from William Gibson, **Pat Cadigan**, and others (including Sterling) that were branded *cyberpunk* accordingly, although Sterling claimed that the "typical" cyberpunk writer was "a Platonic fiction," a Procrustean bed "where fiendish critics wait to lop us to fit" (Preface ix). Criticizing those "fiendish critics" for their labels, Sterling went on to define cyberpunk as "the definitive product" of the sf zeitgeist, a fusion of the New Wave's (psycho-)social critique with the technological focus of the "hard" tradition (x). He argued that cyberpunk authors were "the first SF generation to grow up […] in a truly science-fictional world" (x) and went on to make an observation that still sounds current:

"Technical culture has gotten out of hand. The advances of the sciences are so deeply radical, so disturbing, upsetting, and revolutionary, that they can no longer be contained. They are surging into culture at large; they are invasive; they are everywhere. The traditional power structure, the traditional institutions, have lost control of the pace of change" (xii).

While Sterling's fiction has never achieved the pop-cultural visibility of Gibson's oeuvre, it has arguably stayed true to cyberpunk's foundational concern: the dialectical tussle between technological change and traditional institutions; indeed, Frederic Jameson claims his own description of cyberpunk as "utopian and driven by [...] a kind of romance of feudal commerce" (221) was aimed more at Sterling's work than Gibson's. Sterling's refusal of an explicit moral positionality on trajectories of sociotechnical change, manifest as a rejection of both optimism and pessimism as useful attitudes to futurity (Raven, "Interview"),[1] might be seen as a philosophy rooted in skepticism: a belief that the only justifiable attitude to the future is a suspension of judgment.

This attitude can be traced through Sterling's fiction, as can his uncanny ability to lock on to new ideas ahead of the sf pack. For example, *Islands in the Net* (1988) featured offshore money-laundering and software piracy long before they became **Neal Stephenson**'s beat in *Snow Crash* (1992); *Heavy Weather* (1994) tackled climate change before anyone had heard the term "Anthropocene," as well as being a rare example of sf that engaged with infrastructural fragility as something more than a plot device; *Holy Fire* (1996) took on the transhumanist trope of technological lifespan extension against a background of youthful artistic ennui in a decadent near-future Europe; and the underrated *Zeitgeist* (2001) concretized the postmodernist notion of consensus reality as a spectacular skein of malleable media narratives which can be steered and influenced by semantic savvy, political clout, globalized flows of dirty capital, or—most frequently—some combination of all three. But perhaps the most influential of Sterling's solo novels is *Schismatrix* (1985), a pioneering work of sf that depicts a long struggle between two posthuman clades, the Mechanists and the Shapers, for control of the solar system. Its crammed prose and eyeball kicks prefigured cyberpunk's literary style, while its ambitious scope and deglamorizing look at posthuman life beyond the gravity well-provided grist for the mill of the 'new space opera' movement.[2] Similarly, *The Difference Engine* (1990), written in collaboration with William Gibson, effectively codified steampunk, thus providing the template for another enduring subgeneric mode.

Sterling's short fiction likewise broke new ground, both in terms of sf itself, and in terms of critical engagement with the unfolding twenty-first century. "Mozart in Mirrorshades" (1985), in collaboration with **Lewis Shiner**, performed an original twist on the alternate history mode by positing that the act of time travel establishes a new timeline, which may then be exploited and colonized by those who control the time-gate—an idea most recently revived by William Gibson for *The Peripheral* (2014) and *Agency* (2020). Meanwhile, stories such as "Green Days in Brunei" (1985) and the Chattanooga sequence of novelettes (*Deep Eddy*, 1993; *Bicycle Repairman*, 1996; *Taklamakan*, 1998) arguably provide a narrative template for climate change-adaptative communities that contemporary solarpunk, still stuck on utopian yearnings, refuses to embrace. We can also trace in Sterling's short fiction his transcendence of the sf literary milieu, on display in his collection *Gothic High-Tech* (2012). By this point, he was fully "disconnected from the economic imperatives of the science fiction novelist" (Raven, "Gothic High-Tech"): only a third of the stories were first published in traditional sf venues, and his increasingly polemical style and allegorical approaches have taken him increasingly beyond sf's modal conventions. Sterling's position as a founding cyberpunk is unarguable, but Sterling has both assembled and transcended the cyberpunk mo(ve)ment, shaping and representing the ethos of cyberculture far more deeply than the neo(n)-noir pastiche of legacy cyberpunk.

Sterling's career beyond sf is marked by a fascination with media and with design, which is perhaps not surprising; after all, the "cyber" in cyberpunk means control, and control necessitates technologies of communication. Sterling's interest, however, is not (only) directed at the abstract or conceptual—he has consistently shown himself to be more interested in the actuality of the technoscientific frontier than the literary-metaphorical. In writing his non-fiction opus *The Hacker Crackdown* (1992), he turned his attention from the anti-heroic romance of the cyberpunk hacker to the more morally fuzzy realm of actual hackers, and went on to co-found the Electronic Frontier Foundation, in recognition that the libertarian freedoms potentially afforded by cybernetic systems would require protection from state authoritarians as much as the "console cowboys" of the digital frontier.

Various influential side-projects have also allowed Sterling to develop his interest in technologies of mediation and the design processes which shape them. With support from Richard Kadrey, Sterling proposed and founded the Dead Media Project in 1995, with a call for assistance in compiling "a book [...] about media that have died on the barbed wire of technological advance" (Sterling and Kadrey); perhaps appropriately, the book never materialized, but a database of submissions from contributors persists on a hand-coded website which (with suitable irony) presents as a moribund medium in its own right. The Viridian Design Movement followed a few years later, and Sterling observed in his manifesto that "contemporary civil society can be led anywhere that looks attractive, glamorous and seductive," and the "best chance for progress is to convince the twenty-first century that the twentieth century's industrial base was crass, gauche, and filthy" (Sterling, *The Last Viridian*). Members of the Viridian Movement formed the influential "bright green" blog (and subsequent book) *Worldchanging* (2006) and are still active in the tech industry as pundits, designers, and futurists. Meanwhile, Sterling's influence and visibility around these themes saw him securing roles as a visiting scholar at various academic establishments, predominantly schools of architecture and design, and publishing his design-theoretical chapbook *Shaping Things* (2006), in which he coined the notion of 'spimes': "manufactured objects whose informational support is so overwhelmingly extensive and rich that they are regarded as material instantiations of an immaterial system" (11). The Viridian Movement ended in 2008 with Sterling claiming that its aim of establishing a technocentric environmentalist discourse had been successfully achieved, noting that "imaginary products" had been "a major theme" of the movement (Sterling, *The Last Viridian*), and gesturing toward a new phase in his work which would develop that theme further.

This new effort has seen Sterling play a crucial role in shaping the practice (and, eventually, the academic discipline) of 'design fiction,' a term credited to Sterling even though he has publicly credited it to Julian Bleecker, claiming only to be its popularizer. Nevertheless, Sterling has defined design fiction as "the deliberate use of diegetic prototypes to suspend disbelief about change" (*Patently Untrue*). While the practice (and theory) has become diverse and schismatic, the core idea is the use of design techniques as a storytelling tool, making (or faking) objects whose form and/or function implies a future in which they might exist. Design fiction might thus be seen as a *détournement* of a much older practice of corporate "vaporware" or marketing through design (e.g., "concept cars," or the fabled Futurama exhibition at the 1939 World's Fair), and/or as a technique from sf cinematic worldbuilding that has been liberated from its original realm of (re)production.

In sum, mirror(shad)ing cyberpunk's assault on the sf status quo, Sterling has been instrumental in retooling the imaginative techniques of futuring central to commercial design into a rebellious and irreverent practice which often serves to deconstruct and critique the capitalistic hegemony from which it initially emerged. Design fiction is not cyberpunk, but it nonetheless manifests the same critical-utopian perspective on futurity which informed cyberpunk, or at least as Sterling shaped it in *Mirrorshades*. It is this gadfly/jester attitude, sometimes comical but simultaneously deadly serious, to the dialectical struggle of technology and institutions—this skeptical suspension of judgment in favour of imaginative experimentation, combined with the assumption that (to paraphrase Gibson) "the street will always find its own use for things," that represents the core of Sterling's thought, as well as his enduring and vital contribution to cyberpunk culture.

See also: **Pat Cadigan, William Gibson, Rudy Rucker, Lewis Shiner, Neal Stephenson**

Notes

1 To put this more plainly, it might be said that in his work, whether fictive or factual, Sterling refuses to moralize on matters of (socio)technological change, and often treats invitations to do so with deflationary scorn.
2 Stories set in the Shaper/Mechanist universe include "Swarm" (1982), "Spider-Rose" (1982), "Cicada Queen" (1983), "Sunken Gardens" (1984), and "Twenty Evocations" (1984), all of which were collected with *Schismatrix* and released as *Schismatrix Plus* (1996).

Works Cited

Gibson, William and Bruce Sterling. *The Difference Engine*. Gollancz, 1990.
Jameson, Fredric. *The Ancients and the Postmoderns*. Verso, 2015.
Raven, Paul Graham. "Interview: Bruce Sterling on Caryatids, Viridian and the Death of Print." *Futurismic.com*, February 11, 2009, http://futurismic.com/2009/02/11/interview-bruce-sterling-on-caryatids-viridian-and-the-death-of-print/.
———. "*Gothic High-Tech* by Bruce Sterling." *Strange Horizons*, December 12, 2012, http://strangehorizons.com/non-fiction/reviews/gothic-high-tech-by-bruce-sterling/.
Sterling, Bruce. *Involution Ocean*. Jove, 1977.
———. *Schismatrix*. Arbor House, 1985.
———. editor. *Mirrorshades: The Cyberpunk Anthology*. Arbor House, 1986.
———. *Islands in the Net*. Arbor House, 1988.
———. *The Hacker Crackdown: Law and Disorder on the Electronic Frontier*. Penguin, 1992.
———. *Heavy Weather*. Millennium, 1994.
———. *Holy Fire*. Orion, 1996.

————. "The Manifesto of January 3, 2000." *ViridianDesign.org*, January 3, 2000, http://www.viridiandesign.org/manifesto.html.

————. *Zeitgeist*. Bantam, 2001.

————. *Shaping Things*. The MIT P, 2005.

————. "The Last Viridian Note." *ViridianDesign.Org*, November 2008, http://www.viridiandesign.org/notes/451-500/the_last_viridian_note. html.

————. "Patently untrue: Fleshy defibrillators and synchronised baseball are changing the future." *Wired UK*, October 11, 2013, https://www.wired. co.uk/article/patently-untrue.

Sterling, Bruce and Richard Kadrey. "The DEAD MEDIA Project: A Modest Proposal and a Public Appeal." *DeadMedia.org*, http://www.deadmedia. org/modest-proposal.html.

Paul Raven

ALLUCQUÈRE ROSANNE 'SANDY' STONE (1936–)

US scholar and artist.

Allucquère Rosanne Stone (a.k.a. Sandy Stone) is a pioneer of transgender studies, transmedia art, and communication technologies studies. She has worked in these fields as a practitioner, theoretician, and educator, most prominently as the founder and director of the Advanced Communication Technologies Laboratory (ACTLab) at the University of Texas, Austin. Her unpublished sf novel, *Ktahmet/ Remember*, is available in fragments on her website, where readers can browse through several chapters in achronological order. Some of her short stories were published in *Galaxy* and *The Magazine of Fantasy and Science Fiction* in the 1970s. She declares that she has held six major jobs, including sound technician, programmer, performance artist, and eventually tenured professor ("Sandy's FAQ"); in terms of a career trajectory she refers to herself as a "discourse surfer" (*War of Desire* 165). This diversity of career paths is reflected in her critical output and pedagogical practice, which converge upon the influence of virtual space and new communication technologies on human embodiment, subjectivity, and community.

It is the intersection of embodiment and technologies that made Stone a crucial influence on cyberpunk-related theory in the 1990s and 2000s. Her article "Will the Real Body Please Stand Up?," first published in Michael Benedikt's edited collection *Cyberspace: First Steps*, and the book *The War of Desire and Technology at the Close of the*

Mechanical Age have been widely cited in debates about the changes human subjectivity undergoes in virtual environments. Stone is an important voice in discussions about the opportunities and threats of technological advancements that result in "decoupling the body and the subject" ("Real Body" 83), taken up by scholars of post- and transhumanism, including in **N. Katherine Hayles**'s *How We Became Posthuman* (1999) and Thomas Foster's *The Souls of Cyberfolk* (2005). The questions and critiques Stone raises vis-à-vis the rhetoric around "decoupling" the body and subject are central to cyberpunk fiction and critical theory, which engage with the tension between devaluing the body (or "meat") in favor of technologically mediated freedom—or what Anders Sandberg has called "morphological free- dom" (56)—in cyberspace or in the form of cyborgization, and the contrary argument that all technologized and mediated communica- tion remains rooted in a racialized, gendered, abled body. It is this alleged disregard for the body that has led some critics to conclude that cyberpunk (or, more specifically, its 1980s-era iteration) is ultimately a conservative genre focused on a white, male, heterosexual perspec- tive (cf. Nixon; Cadora). Stone's studies of cyberpunk's cultural milieu and communities built in and around virtual realities in the 1980s and 1990s posit the complexity of these phenomena: when defining the "virtual age" of the mid-1990s, she claims that "the boundaries between our technologies and ourselves continue to implode; [...] we inexorably become creatures that we cannot even imagine. It is a moment which simultaneously holds immense threat and immense promise" (*War of Desire* 183).

Stone is interested in how communities and "the relationship between sense of self and the body" become virtual when "accus- tomed grounding of social interaction in the physical facticity of human bodies is changing" (*War of Desire* 17). Technological innova- tions have caused the seemingly immutable link between the body and subjectivity to be stretched beyond recognition, and changed the ways in which identity, community, and desire are understood and experienced. Her efforts dovetail with the major concerns of femi- nist cyberpunk fiction, where "[t]echnology is depicted as linking the physical body to virtual/digital spaces that form new realms of experi- ences" (Melzer 296). Among these new realms, Stone is interested in redefining such basic interpersonal structures of feeling as "individual caring, love, and [...] desire," as well as categories of gender and race (*War of Desire* 36, 38). As Stone succinctly puts it, she "[wants] to see how people without bodies make love" (*War of Desire* 38), exploring the unique affordances of communication technologies with regards to creating and satisfying desire.

The War of Desire and Technology is written as an ethnography of cyberspace, using vignettes from the development of information technologies in the 1980s and 1990s to illustrate and analyze crucial paradigm shifts in the field. The case studies reveal the complexities of subjectivity formation in cyberspace, as in the story of a male psychiatrist who created an alternative female persona on CompuServe chat to interact with women as a "woman" (*War of Desire* 70). He was ultimately found out and the women who had corresponded with his female alter ego expressed feelings of deep betrayal. What interests Stone in this situation is that the online persona was not just a bad-faith actor, but in some sense an alternative part of the man's subjectivity, which suggests that technologically mediated communication can influence the experience and perception of gender identity. The other case studies are directly engaged in the history of the early days of the Internet and online communities, with chapters devoted to early message boards and their dissolution (CommuniTree), as well as some of the groundbreaking labs in which new conceptualizations of the uses of online communications and gaming were created (Atari Research Lab). Stone considers these to be critical sites in the development of computing, where they were understood "not only as tools, but also as *arenas for social experience*" and play (*War of Desire* 15). The case studies collectively allow Stone to think through the ways in which desire, embodiment, and subjectivity are experienced and mediated through technology.

Stone's interest in human subjectivity and embodiment under the conditions of cyberspace and advanced communications technologies is rooted in her history of involvement in these fields. The methodology she uses in writing *The War of Desire and Technology* is a creative mix of participatory observation, cultural criticism, and fictionalized writing. "I am not a neutral observer" (37), Stone admits; thus, as an engaged participant, she makes her perspective and investments clear. Specific events in her life often serve as points of departure for more theoretical thinking, from an anecdote about a lecture by Stephen Hawking that leads to an exploration of the blurred lines between human body and assistive technologies, to a discussion of how phone sex operators are an example of a unique use of limited bandwidth in specialized communication. The result is a personal and often humorous account of the early days of computers and online life.

One deeply personal type of embodiment that provides Stone with her privileged insight into how subjectivity changes in the virtual age is that of transgender people: "In cyberspace the transgendered body is the natural body," she writes. "The nets are spaces of transformation, identity factories in which bodies are meaning machines, and transgender [...] is the ground state" (*War of Desire* 180–81). In this sentiment, Stone's two major interests —information technologies and transgender studies—come together, and in "The Empire Strikes Back: A Posttranssexual Manifesto," an essay that has become one of the foundational texts of transgender studies, Stone claims that the concept of transgender and the lived transgender experience can open new avenues in questioning binary categories of gender and sexuality.[1] To emphasize its constructed character, she refers to "transsexual" as a genre, not a gender—i.e., "a set of embodied texts whose potential for *productive* disruption of structured sexualities and spectra of desire has yet to be explored" ("Empire" 165)—and she encourages transgender people to embrace their liminal position ("Empire" 167–68).

The transgender experience can also be theorized using another boundary-crossing figure, the cyborg; for instance, Stone declares the following in the documentary *Gendernauts* (Treut 1999):

> Cyborgs are us. Cyborgs are the creatures that we have become at the close of the mechanical age. Cyborgs are creatures that are made up of many parts, that are only partially together, that are always partial, that are continually in motion and in change, that are pieces of this identity and that identity, that are made up of human and machine, of flesh and mechanics, and electronics, musculature and hydraulics.

Of course, the cyborg is a key figure in cyberpunk and cyberpunk culture and has long been used to comment on the human relationship to technology, but also on non-normative gender expression, sexuality, and feminism (Melzer). Stone's writing on the cyborg is inspired by her mentor **Donna J. Haraway**'s appreciation for the way the hybrid figure blurs the major dichotomies structuring western culture: human and animal, organism and machine, the physical and the nonphysical (Haraway). For Stone, the transgender body and experience becomes synonymous with the cyborg, a condition she believes to be largely universal and indicative of the fragmented, liminal, and blurred subjectivity of those living in the "virtual age" (*War of Desire* 183).

Despite Stone's appreciation of cyberspace as a place of opportunity for oppressed groups, she is far from an unquestioning apologist for leaving the body (or, in some cyberpunk parlance, the "meat") behind. Even as social relations move to virtual modes of communication,

> it is critical to remember that decoupling the body from the subject is an act that is politically fraught. As we enter the era of electronic virtual systems we should be acutely aware of whose agendas we serve. At the close of an era of a particular definition of individuality, consciousness still remains firmly rooted in the physical; the bounded subject is a refractory construct, quite difficult to dislodge.
>
> ("Virtual Systems" 620)

This is a crucial corollary to Stone's enthusiasm for the changes brought by virtual systems. Much like a lot of cyberpunk cultural production invested in interrogating economic, technological, and political systems of power, Stone insists on remaining attentive to the unpredictable consequences of the separation between the body and the self. She emphasizes the limitations of virtual technology, pointing out that no technology on its own can lead to meaningful political change; it is something that needs to be done by "us," embodied people (*War of Desire* 170). Stone is a cyberpunk thinker who remains open to both the liberatory and the oppressive possibilities of the developments of technology, cyborgization and development of virtual space.

See also: **Rosi Braidotti, Donna J. Haraway, N. Katherine Hayles, Shoshana Zuboff**

Note

1   In *War of Desire* and "Empire" Stone uses terminology that is now considered problematic or carries limited meaning in transgender studies (transgendered and transsexual, respectively). When quoting, I use her terms, but in my commentary I prefer "transgender" used as an adjective.

Works Cited

Cadora, Karen. "Feminist Cyberpunk." *Science Fiction Studies*, vol. 22, no. 3, 1995, pp. 357–72.

Foster, Thomas. *The Souls of Cyberfolk: Posthumanism as Vernacular Theory.* U of Minnesota P, 2005.

Gendernauts: A Journey Through Shifting Identities. Directed by Monica Treut, Hyena Films, 1995.

Haraway, Donna J. "A Cyborg Manifesto: Science, Technology, and Socialist-Feminism in the Late Twentieth Century." *Simians, Cyborgs, and Women: The Reinvention of Nature.* Routledge, 1991, pp. 149–81.

Hayles, N. Katherine. *How We Became Posthuman: Virtual Bodies in Cybernetics, Literature, and Informatics.* U of Chicago P, 1999.

Melzer, Patricia. "Cyborg Feminism." *The Routledge Companion to Cyberpunk Culture*, edited by Anna McFarlane, Graham J. Murphy, and Lars Schmeink, Routledge, 2020, pp. 291–99.

Nixon, Nicola. "Cyberpunk: Preparing the Ground for Revolution or Keeping the Boys Satisfied?" *Science Fiction Studies*, vol. 19, no. 2, 1992, pp. 219–35.

Sandberg, Anders. "Morphological Freedom—Why We Not Just Want It, but Need It." *The Transhumanist Reader: Classical and Contemporary Essays on the Science, Technology, and Philosophy of the Human Future*, edited by Max More and Natasha Vita-More, Wiley-Blackwell, 2013, pp. 56–64.

Stone, Allucquère Rosanne. "The *Empire* Strikes Back: A Posttransexual Manifesto." *Camera Obscura*, vol. 10, no. 2, 1992, pp. 150–76, https://doi.org/10.1215/02705346-10-2_29-150.

———. "Sandy's FAQ: Don't die wondering ..." *SandyStone.com.* August 1, 1997, https://www.sandystone.com/faq.shtml.

———. "Virtual Systems." *Zone 6: Incorporations*, edited by Jonathan Crary and Sanford Kwinter, Zone, 1992, pp. 609–21.

———. *The War of Desire and Technology at the Close of the Mechanical Age.* The MIT P, 1995.

———. "Will the Real Body Please Stand Up?" *Cybersexualities: A Reader on Feminist Theory, Cyborgs and Cyberspace*, edited by Jenny Wolmark, Edinburgh UP, 1999, pp. 69–98.

Anna Kurowicka

JAMES TIPTREE, JR. [ALICE BRADLEY SHELDON] (1915–87)

US author.

Alice Sheldon, née Bradley, is predominantly known for writing science fiction (sf) under the pseudonym James Tiptree, Jr., although she also published sf as Raccoona Sheldon and other work as Alice Bradley and Alice Bradley Davey. Tiptree, Jr./Sheldon published 69 sf short stories and novellas between 1967 and 1987, earning numerous awards, among them the 1974 Hugo Award for "The Girl Who Was Plugged In" (1973), the 1977 Hugo for "Houston, Houston, Do You Read?" (1973), and three Nebula Awards: "Love Is the Plan the Plan Is Death" (1973), "Houston, Houston, Do You Read?" (1976), and "The Screwfly Solution" (1977). Tiptree, Jr.'s short fiction has been anthologized in eight collections, including *Her Smoke Rose Up Forever* (1990), and their two novels are *Up the Walls of the World* (1978) and *Brightness Falls from the Air* (1985). Finally, the collection *Meet Me at Infinity* (2000) assembles some of their fiction and previously unpublished non-fiction work (Clute). Alice Sheldon kept a low profile and hid her real identity behind the James Tiptree, Jr./Raccoona Sheldon personae from authors, critics, and fans alike, leading most to assume Tiptree, Jr. was male, at least until sleuthing fans connected Tiptree, Jr.'s remarks about 'his' mother's death to the death of Mary Hastings Bradley whose obituary listed Alice Sheldon as next-of-kin (see Phillips 4).

In her award-winning biography *James Tiptree, Jr.: The Double Life of Alice B. Sheldon*, Julie Phillips documents the many facets of Sheldon's life that surely influenced her later career choices. For example, as a child Alice Bradley accompanied her intellectual and well-to-do parents (lawyer and naturalist Herbert Bradley and travel writer Mary Elizabeth Hastings Bradley) on their travels in Africa and contributed illustrations to her mother's books. As a young woman she became a painter and art critic, eloped and married at the age of 19, divorced six years later, joined the Women's Army Auxiliary Corps, and later worked for the air force as a photo analyst. In 1945 she married again. Together with her second husband, Huntington Sheldon, she joined the CIA as an analyst, then started a chicken farm. In 1957 she returned to university and graduated with a Ph.D. in experimental psychology in 1967 before she turned to writing sf at the age of fifty-two (see Phillips).

One of Tiptree, Jr.'s more influential works is "The Girl Who Was Plugged In," a "proto-cyberpunk" (Simons) narrative that anticipates by a decade the cyberpunk movement. The story is "set in a globalized, corporate-dominated near-future where control of data transfer is the main mechanism of social power and cultural authority," and "with a satire that is at once poignant and scathing," Tiptree, Jr. accentuates "the crucial gap between the gaudy promises of virtual life and the sorry realities of meat-bound existence" (Latham 10–11). In so doing, "The Girl Who Was Plugged In" offers an underlying critical posthumanist questioning of humanism that aligns with feminist theories of embodiment and cyborgization. For example, **Donna J. Haraway**'s "A Cyborg Manifesto" cites Tiptree, Jr. as one of "our storytellers exploring what it means to be embodied in high-tech worlds. They are theorists for cyborgs" (Haraway 310). The importance of "The Girl Who Was Plugged In" for cyberpunk cannot be understated: it draws attention to the romanticization of technology and critiques fanciful visions of the human–machine cyborg as a method of transcending the boundaries set by human embodiment.

The story follows 17-year-old P. Burke, described as "the ugly of the world. A tall monument to pituitary dystrophy. No surgeon would touch her. When she smiles, her jaw—it's half purple—almost bites her left eye out. She's also quite young, but who could care?" (44). Following an attempted suicide, P. Burke is given the opportunity of her lifetime: she can have her consciousness jacked into an automaton named Delphi and take on the coveted role of a media 'god,' worshiped and followed by the mass populace as part of an elaborate marketing program. P. Burke is not disappointed by the procedure:

> Sitting up in bed is the darlingest girl child you've EVER seen. She quivers—porno for angels. She sticks both her little arms straight up, flips her hair, looks around full of sleepy pazazz. Then she can't resist rubbing her hands down over her minibreasts and belly. Because, you see, it's the god-awful P. Burke who is sitting there hugging her perfect girl-body, looking at you out of delighted eyes.
>
> (48)

While P. Burke must disconnect from Delphi for such mundane tasks as eating, sleeping, and tending to her bodily functions, she increasingly identifies as Delphi; nevertheless, P. Burke/Delphi is nothing more than a corporate commodity and, in the end, P. Burke pays with her life for her naivety while Delphi lives on to entice the masses (albeit not as successfully), piloted by a replacement operator in the corporate machinery.

Part of the story's success is the innovative use of narrative voice; specifically, the narrator challenges conventional reader expectations by commenting on P. Burke's transformation at the hands of a corporation that is planning to use her as a remote operator for Delphi. The result shows "our girl, looking—If possible, worse than before. (You thought this was Cinderella transistorized?)" (47). The ironically distanced narrator continues to draw attention to P. Burke's mulish existence as the invisible operator: "who remembers that carcass? Certainly not P. Burke, she hasn't spoken through her own mouth for months. Delphi doesn't even recall dreaming of her when she wakes up" (61). P. Burke's inability to fully merge with Delphi proves a stumbling block to futuristic dreams of escaping human embodiment for a world of perfect high-tech bodies. As **N. Katherine Hayles** argues, our understanding of what it means to be 'human' is influenced by the body we inhabit and our corporeal interactions with the world, the body, "resonant with cultural meanings," existing as a "congealed metaphor, a physical structure whose constraints and possibilities have been formed by an evolutionary history that intelligent machines do not share" (284). In its posthumanist critique, "The Girl Who Was Plugged In" suggests that embodied experiences are both richer and more complicated than simply uploading our minds into perfect techno-bodies in the future that awaits us.

"The Girl Who Was Plugged In," and Tiptree, Jr.'s work more broadly, addresses critical posthumanist questions about what it means to be human in technologically futuristic but politically dystopian contexts. The integrations of frequently non-normatively embodied humans and machines, as well as the use of prosthetic embodiment and cyborgization, continue to generate critical interest and attention, most recently from the perspective of Disability Studies. For example, Lindsey Dolich Felt argues that "The Girl Who Was Plugged In" negates a technological cure narrative and "imagines creative and embodied forms of resistance in technological society that reorient existing definitions of the hacker as well as the disabled body" (5).

At the same time, Tiptree, Jr. anticipated our own concerns over climate change, exploring ecological arguments at a time when ecocriticism was only just emerging as a critical field in the United States, particularly following the success of Rachel Carson's *Silent Spring* (1962). For example, the short story "The Last Flight of Doctor Ain" (1968) depicts a protagonist who is trying to save the Earth, which throughout the story is described as a woman (Gaea) he loves. The story voices concerns about human impact on the planet, and Ain's solution of eradicating humanity by spreading a lethal virus continues to echo not only in contemporary speculative fiction but our global condition (this chapter is being written in the midst of the Covid-19 pandemic). In sum, Tiptree, Jr./Sheldon repeatedly comes back to contemplating (or struggling with) epistemological and ontological philosophical questions about the human condition and critical posthumanism.

Throughout their career, Tiptree, Jr. built friendships with fellow authors like Ursula K. Le Guin, **Joanna Russ**, and **Philip K. Dick** (see Krasnostein and Pierce). The letters to friends, fans, and editors, often signed "Tip," tended to overplay traditionally male-coded interests like guns and hunting (see Phillips 418–19). While clearly transporting feminist ideas ("Houston, Houston, Do You Read?" [1976]) and sharply critiquing the role of women in patriarchal societies ("The Women Men Don't See" [1973]), Tiptree, Jr.'s writing had frequently been read as "ineluctably masculine" and their friend Robert Silverberg even compared Tiptree, Jr.'s "lean, muscular, supple" stories to Hemingway's (Silverberg quoted in Phillips 3). In addition, the fact that the Raccoona Sheldon stories needed written intervention from mentor Tiptree, Jr. to find a publisher seems to prove Sheldon right in choosing a male pseudonym. When the truth about Sheldon was revealed, Silverberg graciously admitted his error (Phillips 418–19). However, the thorough debunking of these gendered assumptions about Tiptree, Jr.'s "masculine" way of writing has wider ramifications, challenging ingrained notions about the connection between an author's biology and their so-called gendered literary style. This has helped (and continues to help) pave the way for women and non-binary authors in sf, even if much early cyberpunk has been interpreted as a step backward (see Melzer). Sheldon continues to be a compelling author given her complex gender identity, sexual orientation (she identified as bisexual), and the constant challenging of cultural assumptions about gender and genre conventions (Latham 11).

While Sheldon remains one of the most influential sf writers thanks to her corpus of work as both James Tiptree, Jr. and Raccoona Sheldon, her legacy has arguably been tainted because of the mysterious circumstances surrounding her and her husband's death. As John Clute writes, it was believed Sheldon's husband of forty years, Huntington Sheldon, had "contracted Alzheimer's Disease in the early 1980s. This seems not to have been true. Whatever the case, in 1987, herself in precarious health, she shot him (in apparent accordance with a pact they had much earlier agreed upon), telephoned his son to tell him what she had done, and then killed herself." While acknowledging Tiptree, Jr.'s influence as a writer who challenged cultural assumptions of disability, disability scholars and activists argued that her potential enactment of a decades-old suicide pact should be reframed as a caregiver murder of her elderly, disabled husband (see Lothian). As a result, the "James Tiptree Jr. Award" for science fiction and fantasy, launched in 1991, was renamed the "Otherwise Award" in October 2019. In the end, while the exact circumstances of the Sheldons' deaths remain unclear, Tiptree, Jr.'s role as a proto-cyberpunk author is unmistakable, evidenced by the inclusion of "The Girl Who Was Plugged In" in **Pat Cadigan**'s *The Ultimate Cyberpunk* (2002) and its routine appearance in online cyberpunk reading lists. Finally, while Tiptree, Jr. certainly laid the foundation for print cyberpunk's emergence in the 1980s, the impact is arguably more keenly felt in the feminist cyberpunk of Cadigan, **Melissa Scott**, **Marge Piercy**, and a host of other feminist authors who emerged in the 1990s to help steer cyberpunk toward broader considerations of embodiment that are 'resonant with cultural meanings.'

See also: **Pat Cadigan, Philip K. Dick, Donna J. Haraway, N. Katherine Hayles, Marge Piercy, Joanna Russ, Melissa Scott**

Works Cited

Clute, John "Tiptree, James, Jr." *The Encyclopedia of Science Fiction*, edited by John Clute et al., May 7, 2020, https://sf-encyclopedia.com/entry/tiptree_james_jr.

Felt, Lindsey Dolich. "Cyberpunk's Other Hackers: The Girls Who Were Plugged In." *Catalyst*, vol. 5, no. 1, 2019, pp. 1–38.

Hayles, N. Katherine. *How We Became Posthuman: Virtual Bodies in Cybernetics, Literature, and Informatics*. U of Chicago P, 1999.

Haraway, Donna. "A Cyborg Manifesto: Science, Technology and Socialist-Feminism in the Late Twentieth Century." *The Cybercultures Reader*, edited by David Bell and Barbara M. Kennedy, Routledge, 2000, pp. 291–324.

Krasnostein, Alisa and Alexandra Pierce, editors. *Letters to Tiptree*. Twelfth Planet P, 2005.

Latham, Rob. "Literary Precursors." *The Routledge Companion to Cyberpunk Culture*, edited by Anna McFarlane, Graham J. Murphy, and Lars Schmeink, Routledge, 2020, pp. 7–14.

Lothian, Alexis. "Alice Sheldon and the Name of the Tiptree Award." *Otherwise Award*, 2019, https://otherwiseaward.org/2019/09/alice-sheldon-and-the-name-of-the-tiptree-award.

Melzer, Patricia. "Cyborg Feminism." *The Routledge Companion to Cyberpunk Culture*, edited by Anna McFarlane, Graham J. Murphy, and Lars Schmeink, Routledge, 2020, pp. 291–99.

Phillips, Julie. *James Tiptree, Jr.: The Secret Life of Alice B. Sheldon*. Picador, 2007.

Schnelbach, Leah. "What James Tiptree Jr. can teach us about the power of the SF community." *Tor.com*, August 24, 2016, https://www.tor.com/2016/08/24/james-tiptree-jr-on-this-day/.

Simons, Fraser. "'The Girl Who Was Plugged In' is Must Read Proto Cyberpunk." *Consuming Cyberpunk*, June 10, 2019, https://consumingcyberpunk.com/blog/2019/6/9/the-girl-who-was-plugged-in.

Steiger, Kay. "The most prescient science fiction author you aren't reading." *Vox*, April 25, 2019, https://www.vox.com/the-highlight/2019/4/18/18282660/james-tiptree-jr-feminist-dystopian-science-fiction.

Tiptree, James Jr. "The Girl Who Was Plugged In." *Her Smoke Rose up Forever*. Orion, 2004, pp. 43–78.

Anya Heise-von der Lippe

ALVIN (1928–2016) AND HEIDI (1929–2019) TOFFLER

US futurists and authors.

In his Preface to *Mirrorshades: The Cyberpunk Anthology* (1986), cyberpunk author and editor **Bruce Sterling** identifies celebrity futurist Alvin Toffler's bestseller *The Third Wave* (1980) as "a bible to many cyberpunks" (xii). Toffler's futurist studies have since been recognized as foundational texts for cyberpunk's distinctive worldview. Unbeknownst to Sterling at the time and many of Toffler's readers to this day, however, is that Alvin Toffler did not write *The Third Wave* alone, or any of the other works attributed solely to him. He co-wrote all of them with his wife Heidi Toffler, whose contributions went uncredited for decades. Heidi Toffler notes in a 2000 interview conducted by Joel Kotkin with Alvin Toffler and herself that it was she who demanded her husband take full credit for their joint work. "Al says he pleaded with Heidi to let him put her name on the books— even as far back as [their 1970 book] *Future Shock*," Kotkin paraphrases the two as saying, "but she insisted it would be bad for business. She felt, and still feels, that mainstream America is not ready for 'strong' women." It wasn't until the publication of the duo's *War and Anti-War: Survival at the Dawn of the 21st Century* (1993) that Heidi Toffler publicly shared authorial credit with Alvin Toffler. From that moment on, Heidi Toffler delivered lectures, participated in interviews, and published in the open alongside her famous husband (Kotkin 110).[1]

The Tofflers wrote and edited thirteen books over the course of five decades, but their most important contributions to both futurist studies and the cyberpunk movement are *Future Shock* (1970) and *The Third Wave* (1980). In these two books (and the numerous articles, lectures, interviews, and other books that followed), the Tofflers foresaw a future that, in retrospect, looks a lot like many fictional cyberpunk worlds: a future where accelerating advances in technology are creating computerized, decentralized, information-saturated societies.

Starting with essays published as early as the mid-1960s, the Tofflers began advancing a line of argument they would pursue for the rest of their lives: that humanity was witnessing the emergence of a post-national computerized global civilization based on "knowledge work" ("Societies at Hyper Speed" 4.17). In the future, the Tofflers foresaw, power is decentralized by high technology and information serves as the coin of the realm. Unfortunately, the future's technological and informational superabundance creates a new problem: "the dizzying disorientation brought on by the premature arrival of the future," a crippling feeling of technocultural alienation and "information overload" called "future shock" that prevents us from both seizing the disruptive opportunities and countering the technological threats of our wired tomorrow (*Future Shock*, 13; 305–26).

The Tofflers' vision of a future where technological advances increasingly shock the global system is credited with inspiring numerous readers ranging from world leaders and Silicon Valley founders to media moguls and science fiction (sf) writers: "J.D. Power cites the Tofflers as mentors. Ted Turner credits the Tofflers' works with inspiring him to start CNN in 1980. And for Steve Case, *The Third Wave* struck like 'a lightning bolt' that created his obsession with cyberspace and ultimately led to his co-founding AOL" ("The Toffler Legacy"). As the Tofflers' official biography (on the Toffler Associates webpage) asserts, their "work influenced politicians, generals, executives, musicians and writers, including former Chinese prime minister Zhao Ziyang, former Soviet leader Mikhail Gorbachev, former House Speaker Newt Gingrich, and some of the most prominent innovators of our time." Across the globe, creators, businesspeople, and politicians treated the Tofflers' insights as a blueprint for the future.

Early cyberpunk authors built imaginary worlds based directly on the future the Tofflers forecast. For example, John Brunner writes on the acknowledgments page of his proto-cyberpunk novel *The Shockwave Rider* (1975), which is about a rogue computer programmer suffering from information overload, that the novel's "'scenario' […] derives in large part from Alvin Toffler's stimulating study *Future Shock*, and in consequence I'm much obliged to him." In his far-future Shaper/Mechanist series—"Swarm" (1982); "Spider-Rose" (1982); "Cicada Queen" (1983); "Sunken Gardens" (1984); "Twenty Evocations" (1984); *Schismatrix* (1985)—Bruce Sterling describes how his sprawling universe evolved after "[n]ew sciences and technologies had shattered whole societies in waves of future shock" (in Goicoechea 29). These are only a few examples of how the Tofflers' shocking future served as a cognitive map for the emergence and expansion of the cyberpunk movement.

Scholars concur that the Tofflers' influence upon cyberpunk, and particularly first-generation print cyberpunk, runs both long and deep. Rob Latham observes that cyberpunk inherited a "fascination with corporate mass-mediatization and 'global integration'[…] derived from the critical and creative work of [William S.] Burroughs, **[Marshall] McLuhan**, and Alvin Toffler" (39; editors' bold). Graham J. Murphy goes further, describing what he calls "cyberpunk's obsession with

Alvin Toffler's future shock" (519). And Damien Broderick sees the Tofflers' "notion of accelerating change" in *Future Shock* as an early entry into the discourse of the technological singularity that informed both futurist studies and the sf of the 1980s and 1990s (279).

Ironically, the Tofflers did not set out to become celebrity futurists whose studies would inspire a generation of forward-looking statespeople, entrepreneurs, and artists. The two met while studying as English majors at New York University in the late 1940s. Trained in Marxist theory, after college they worked first for Henry Wallace's Progressive Party and then for five years as labor organizers and employees of a Cleveland, Ohio fan factory (Nichols 1161; Judis 17; Toffler, *Third Wave* 145). The Tofflers' experience at the factory shaped their understanding of both industrial line work as an outdated mode of production and Marxism as an outmoded theory of economics; instead, they came to suspect the future lay elsewhere. As it turned out, so did their careers: they quit their factory jobs and shifted to journalism, Alvin Toffler writing first for *Labor's Daily* and then *Fortune* magazine while Heidi Toffler worked uncredited as her husband's researcher and editor (Judis 17; Kotkin 110).

As journalists and lapsed Marxists, the Tofflers were drawn to writing about systematic changes in society, evidenced by their *Fortune* piece "A Quantity in Culture" (1961), an extensive description of the many ways that "the character and quality of American society are being drastically changed, in both their public and private aspects, by [a new] mass interest in cultural activities" (127). The Tofflers later published an article under Alvin Toffler's name in the monthly magazine *Horizon*, "The Future as a Way of Life" (1965), in which they identified accelerating change itself as the most recent and greatest systematic change of all to affect society. Here they debuted their future shock thesis, presenting a draft of the vision of a technologically driven, radically changed future that would ultimately become *Future Shock*.

The Tofflers open *Future Shock* with the following pronouncement: "This is a book about what happens to people when they are overwhelmed by change. It is about the ways in which we adapt—or fail to adapt—to the future" (3). The Tofflers derive their concept of future shock from the phenomenon of "culture shock," viewing the future as a strangely transformed and alien place much as an sf writer does (12–13). They organize their journalistic study of the future into six parts: "The Death of Permanence," "Transience," "Novelty," "Diversity," "The Limits of Adaptability," and "Strategies for Survival." In the first five sections, they give examples of different ways that technology drives at a quickening pace new social, cultural, and even biological trends. In the last, they discuss ways to avoid future shock, such as building futurist-oriented programs of education (353–78), "taming technology" through expanded institutional oversight (379–95), and encouraging the reading of sf "as a mind-stretching force for the creation of the habit of anticipation" (376).

The Tofflers developed their future shock thesis into a theory of world history in their 1980 global bestseller *The Third Wave*, concluding that the changes they first identified in *Future Shock* comprised only a part of a "new civilization bursting into being in our midst" (*The Third Wave* 18). The Tofflers describe three "waves" in the history of human civilization: agricultural, industrial, and a third wave "based on diversified, renewable energy sources; on methods of production that make most factory assembly lines obsolete; on new, non-nuclear families; on a novel institution that might be called the 'electronic cottage'; and on radically changed schools and corporations of the future" (26). The bulk of *The Third Wave* is devoted to discussing the many ways that life will be revolutionized for the citizens of the future as technology decentralizes, democratizes, and otherwise reconfigures civilization. The message that early cyberpunk authors took from *The Third Wave* is summed up by Bruce Sterling: "the technical revolution reshaping our society is based not in hierarchy but in decentralization, not in rigidity but in fluidity" (xii). In the Tofflers' vision of tomorrow, cyberpunks found a future ready-made for them to build upon and popularize in their fictions.

The Tofflers never replicated the widespread success of *Future Shock* or *The Third Wave*, although they did publish *Powershift: Knowledge, Wealth, and Violence at the Edge of the 21st Century* (1990), a follow-up in which they explore how knowledge becomes a source of power and wealth in the third wave. The two visionaries continued to publish books and articles, give interviews, and present public lectures about life in the third wave well into the twenty-first century. In 1996, they founded the advisory firm Toffler Associates, whose "goal was, and continues to be, to expand their capacity to guide government and businesses working to transform their organization to be Future Proof®." The duo's biography on the Toffler Associates website sums up their accomplishments:

> The Tofflers bravely forecast many of the realities of contemporary society and politics, including the acceleration of daily life, the decline of the nuclear family, cloning, virtual reality, information overload, and the threat of terrorism. Many of these predictions have come to bear and the central thesis of their work has

proven absolutely true—that a knowledge-based new economy would replace the Industrial Age.

("Toffler Legacy")

Serving as a holy writ to many cyberpunks, the Tofflers' vision of tomorrow has shaped the movement since its formative years, and it continues to shape our collective imaginings about what the future of our knowledge-based economy might hold.

See also: **William Gibson, Marshall McLuhan, Rudy Rucker, Lewis Shiner, Bruce Sterling**

Note

1 Accordingly, throughout this entry I will refer to all works attributed solely to Alvin Toffler in my Works Cited as being co-authored by "the Tofflers."

Works Cited

Broderick, Damien. "Racing Toward the Spike." *Prefiguring Cyberculture: An Intellectual History*, edited by Darren Tofts, Annemarie Jonson, and Alessio Cavallaro, The MIT P, 2002, pp. 278–91.

Brunner, John. *The Shockwave Rider*. Del Rey, 1975.

Goicoechea, Maria. "Bruce Sterling: *Schismatrix Plus* (Case Study)." *The Routledge Companion to Cyberpunk Culture*, edited by Anna McFarlane, Graham J. Murphy, and Lars Schmeink, Routledge, 2020, pp. 24–31.

Judis, John B. "Newt's Not-So-Weird Gurus: In Defense of the Tofflers." *The New Republic*, October 9, 1995, pp. 16–25.

Kotkin, Joel. "The Future is Here!" *Inc.*, December 2000, pp. 108–13.

Latham, Rob. "'A Rare State of Ferment': SF Controversies from the New Wave to Cyberpunk." *Beyond Cyberpunk: New Critical Perspectives*, edited by Graham J. Murphy and Sherryl Vint, Routledge, 2010, pp. 29–45.

Murphy, Graham J. "Cyberpunk and Post-Cyberpunk." *The Cambridge History of Science Fiction*, edited by Gerry Canavan and Eric Carl Link, Cambridge UP, 2018, pp. 519–36.

Nichols, Peter. "Alvin Toffler." *Science Fiction at Large*, edited by Peter Nichols, Harper and Row, 1976, pp. 116.

Sterling, Bruce. Preface. *Mirrorshades: The Cyberpunk Anthology*, edited by Bruce Sterling, Ace, 1986, pp. ix–xvi.

"The Toffler Legacy." https://www.tofflerassociates.com/about/the-toffler-legacy/.

Toffler, Alvin. *Future Shock*. Random House, 1970.

———. "A Quality of Culture." *Fortune*, November 1961, pp. 64, 124–27.

————. "Societies at Hyper-Speed." *The New York Times*, October 31, 1993, pp. 4, 17.

————. *The Third Wave*. William Morrow and Company, 1980.

Doug Davis

SHINYA TSUKAMOTO (1960–)

Japanese director, writer, producer, editor.

Tsukamoto Shinya is the writer-director, and usually the producer, editor, cinematographer, co-star and either art director or production designer, of fourteen feature-length films. Eleven of them are from original ideas, and three are adaptations: *Hiruko the Goblin* (1991), from Daijiro Morohoshi's *Yokai Hunter* manga (1974); *Gemini* (1999), from Edogawa Rampo's "The Twins: A Condemned Criminal's Confession to a Priest" (1924); *Fires on the Plain* (2014), from Shōhei Ōoka's1951 novel. Since the age of fourteen, Tsukamoto has also made a dozen shorts, ranging from one to fifty minutes, including *Tokage* (2003), *Haze* (2005), segments of the anthology films *Female* (2005) and *Venice 70: The Future Reloaded* (2013), and an adaptation of Osamu Dazai's *The Setting Sun* (1947) for the television series *Kaidan Horror Classics* (2010).

In his mid-twenties, Tsukamoto quit as a director of TV adverts to pursue acting, establishing the experimental Kaijyu Theater group with Kei Fujiwara and Tomorô Taguchi, both of whom would star in several of his films. He returned to filmmaking with two shorts, *The Phantom of Regular Size* (1986) and *The Adventure of Denchu-Kozo* (1987), the latter adapted from a Kaijyu stage play; both now look like studies for his debut feature, *Tetsuo: The Iron Man* (1989). His earlier features won awards at sf, horror, and fantasy film festivals around the world; his later, less fantastical work has been equally successful at major international film festivals, notably Venice, Sitges, and Locarno. Tsukamoto is also a film and TV actor and a voice artist for adverts and videogames.

Despite a small-town high-school horror movie (*Hiruko the Goblin*) and occasional historical pictures (*Gemini, Fires on the Plain, Killing* [2018]), Tsukamoto's main concern—shared with cyberpunk, if not always in a cyberpunk idiom—is with intersections of the human body, the contemporary city, and neoliberal globalization. He repeatedly subjects bodies and minds to the stresses of unhomely urban environments, giving disturbing form to the distortions demanded by an

236

economic system antagonistic to human thriving. His mostly noctur-nal neo-noirs—*Tokyo Fist* (1995), *Bullet Ballet* (1998), *A Snake of June* (2002)—trace increasingly weird psychosexual obsessions, overlapping with paranormal horror in *Nightmare Detective* (2006) and *Nightmare Detective 2* (2008). In contrast, the bright, daylight palettes of *Vital* (2004) and *Kotoko* (2011) offer no relief to protagonists struggling with traumatic amnesia and terrifying paranoid delusions. However, Tsukamoto primarily explores these intersections through grotesque excess.

Japanese cyberpunk has long been dominated by comics and ani-mation, such as **Katsuhiro Ōtomo**'s *Akira* (manga 1982–90; anime 1988) and **Masamune Shirow** and **Mamoru Oshii**'s *Ghost in the Shell* (manga 1989–; anime 1995–). If *Tetsuo*, the foundational film of Japanese live-action cyberpunk, has a precursor it is **Sogo Ishii**'s fre-netic early attempts—*Crazy Thunder Road* (1980), *Shuffle* (1981), *Burst City* (1982)—to develop a carnivalesque style appropriate to his tales of punk insurrection. Part of the *jishu eiga* (self-produced films) movement that emerged as Japan's studio system collapsed, Ishii uses a violently whiplashing camera, often perilously close to the action, and rapid editing to produce synesthetic blurs of motion, color, and light. *Tetsuo* retains this chaotic energy, and thus also recalls the loud, violent indus-trial performance art of Survival Research Laboratories. But Tsukamoto tempers it with an artisanal patience and precision that simultaneously positions his work alongside the Cornell boxes and the SRL-inspired Slick Henry of **William Gibson**'s *Count Zero* (1986) and *Mona Lisa Overdrive* (1988). *Tetsuo* develops this cyberpunk tension between pulp trash and avant-garde experimentation by constructing its gleefully gruesome narrative mash-up of sex, violence, home invasion, and *kaiju* smackdown through a painstaking, innovative audio-visual style.

In a derelict factory, a metal fetishist inserts a pipe into his thigh. Maggots infest the wound. He flees into the streets and is hit by a car. The sarariman driver and his girlfriend dump the body in the woods, and then fuck as the corpse watches. Later, an electronic component sprouts from the sarariman's cheek. As he waits for a train, a fellow commuter prods at a semi-organic lump of metal and is infected by the metal fetishist. Her arm becomes machinic. She pursues the sarariman and, as she attacks him, her features merge with those of the metal fetishist. The sarariman kills her, then dreams about a darkly exoticized version of his girlfriend sodomizing him with a phallic pipe that snakes out from her crotch. Awake, his sexual prowess seems enhanced, but even as he and his girlfriend fuck his body undergoes terrifying,

SHINYA TSUKAMOTO

shameful transformations. His penis mutates into an enormous drill. They fight, and she repeatedly knifes him. But she is aroused by the violence and, in the confusion, torn apart by his penis-drill. He continues to mutate. The metal fetishist enters the sarariman's house through the water pipes and erupts through the girlfriend's corpse in quasi-human form. A curious courtship ensues, a titanic battle that culminates in them merging into a battletank. They roll on Tokyo, intent on "rust[ing] the world into the dust of the universe."

Anglophone reviewers (Rayns, Harrington) compared *Tetsuo* to the work of queer avant-garde, underground and indie filmmakers Kenneth Anger, Jack Smith, and Todd Haynes, but tended to identify Tsukamoto most closely with **David Cronenberg**. From the experimental *Stereo* (1969) to his cyberpunk paean to the new flesh, *Videodrome* (1983), Cronenberg's viral narratives, ambivalent body horror, and chilly examinations of phallic libido clearly resonate with *Tetsuo*, but perhaps the more interesting recurring comparison is with David Lynch's decidedly un-cyberpunk *Eraserhead* (1977). Like *Tetsuo*, this "surreally weird" (Harrington) pulp/avant-garde blend unleashes disturbing mutant imagery in a black-and-white post-industrial landscape. Lynch's horrific and ironically nostalgic world is defined by stasis: long takes, repetitive actions, a locked-off camera. But Tsukamoto never pauses. His headlong, pell-mell camera seems incapable of distinguishing characters from their environment or deciding which is more significant. It is as fascinated by the city's abandoned industrial machinery and rotting material infrastructure—pipes, vents, ducts, wiring, tunnels, architectural supports—as it is by the perpetually anxious but psychologically flat characters who pass through these detrital locations. By refusing to segregate the organic from the inorganic, the human from the machine, *Tetsuo* pushes cyborg imagery to an extreme. Unlike Robocop's clean-edged bulk or the Terminator's impervious chromium skeleton, the machines with which characters merge are messy and fleshy, rusting and rotting. This is emphasized by the grain of the 16mm filmstock, which alternates between viscous murk and hyperreal crispness, a contrast of visual textures that yokes together the analog world of material experience and the coming era of digital mediation.

Uninterested in the familiar conventions of narrative structure and continuity editing derived from classical Hollywood's Fordist production-line logic, *Tetsuo* favors aggressive montage. It explodes the illusionistic spacetime of popular cinema through chaotic mosaics of sound and image, of vulnerable bodies and corroding waste. Undercranked sequences race jerkily through the streets, piling jump cut upon jump cut; stop-motion-animated components flurry around actors who must have posed motionless for hours at a stretch; on a thumping industrial punk soundtrack, piledrivers pound relentlessly. These aesthetic choices are representative of cyberpunk's navigation of local and global shifts to the post-Fordist era of neoliberal capital. *Tetsuo*'s distinctive style and narrative spacetime figure postmodern incredulity toward such overarching, explanatory metanarratives as the myth of progress (Lyotard). But they are also determined by the realities of post-studio *jishu eiga* filmmaking and the neoliberal drive to worker precarity: an 18-month, no-budget, indie shoot, mostly in a small apartment where cast and crew also lived.

While cyberpunk's champions often seemed enamored of digital disembodiment and flow, *Tetsuo* ceaselessly reiterates their material underpinnings, its shattered industrial settings prefiguring the e-waste catastrophe. Gibson's *Neuromancer* (1984) teeters on this transition to the immaterial, exploring its possibilities and limitations through, for example, the simstim sequence in which Case passively inhabits Molly's sensorium as she walks through the city. Tsukamoto inverts this so as to explore the sadomasochistic subjectivity of life in the globalized city. In the *Tetsuo* and *Nightmare Detective* films, characters possessed by others are reduced to passengers in their own bodies; in *A Snake of June*, a stalker coerces the modest protagonist—via cell phone and a remote-control vibrator—to act upon her sexual fantasies.

Tsukamoto also explores the tension between embodiment and control through homoerotic depictions of anxious masculinity, troubling doppelgangers (often played by himself), and body-modification practices, including boxing training, piercing, tattooing, cutting, scarification, mastectomies, and amputations. This uncertain erotics of vulnerability and enhancement, damage and transformation, is relentlessly materialist, eschewing the virtual (although *Vital*'s unreal, possibly posthumous, terminal beach resembles the simulated reality in which Case loiters with Linda Lee's avatar, and the *Nightmare Detective* dreamworlds recall the inner worlds of **Pat Cadigan**'s *Mindplayers* [1987]).

Tetsuo II: Body Hammer (1992), shot in color and with a bigger budget, has something more closely resembling a plot: a skinhead cult (played by members of experimental theater group Shinjuku-Ryozanpaku and avant-garde dance troupe Dai-Rakuda-Kan) repeatedly abduct a sarariman's wife and child so as to trigger the massive stress response that will turn him into a deadly cyborg. Extending Tsukamoto's fascination with inhuman urban spaces, *Tetsuo II* includes not only derelict industrial spaces—the shirtless, ripped skinheads work out near a blast furnace with weights fashioned from abandoned machinery—but also Tokyo's glass-fronted yet utterly opaque business district, reflecting emptiness back upon emptiness (Huang). Such unmappable placeless spaces (Augé) recall the bemused, rudderless wandering through the Westin Bonaventure Hotel that Fredric Jameson took as emblematic of the postmodern condition (Jameson). To them, Tsukamoto adds the brutal geometries and serial repetitions of concrete apartment blocks that dwarf, isolate, and engulf the people who trudge by them. These implacable settings hothouse sadomasochistic subjects and behaviors, and violence erupts not from psychology but from economics, from an environment built to maximize profit rather than human fulfillment.

After abandoning preliminary work on a Tarantino-produced *Flying Tetsuo* movie in the late-1990s, Tsukamoto finally returned to the series with the Anglophone *Tetsuo: The Bullet Man* (2009). Flashes of color occasionally burst into its over-saturated black-and-white—like the eruptions of rage that precipitate its protagonist beyond reason, transforming him into an incredible cyborg hulk. It is visually striking, but belated.

Tetsuo's impact on the development of live-action cyberpunk was immediate and international. Japan's *Gunhed* (Masato Harada, 1989) and *Mikadroid: Robokill Beneath Disco Club Layla* (Satoo and Tomoo Haraguchi, 1991) are narratively more coherent but concomitantly mundane. The French *Vibroboy* (Jan Kounen, 1994) and the South Korean *Teenage Hooker Becomes Killing Machine* (Gee-Woong Nam, 2001) deploy Tsukamoto-influenced cyborg imagery with great verve, while the retro-technology and practical effects of Canadian Brandon Cronenberg's violent *Possessor* (2020) seem less indebted to his father's films than to Tsukamoto. Ishii's *Electric Dragon 80.000V* (2001), obsessed with electronic/metallic mutation and boxing, ventures more directly into *Tetsuo* territory. Shozin Fukui, a former assistant of both Ishii and Tsukamoto, features *Tetsuo*-like camerawork, stop-motion animation, scrapyard imagery, and human–machine mutations in the short, *Caterpillar* (1988). His *√964 Pinocchio* (1991)—about an abandoned, malfunctioning cyborg sex slave—develops a more idiosyncratic concern with technological augmentation, and his less manic *Rubber's Lover* (1996) adds BDSM and splatterpunk to the blend. This shift in sensibility would come to dominate live-action cyberpunk. In *Tokyo Gore Police* (Yoshihiro Nishimura 2008) and *The Machine Girl* (Noboru Iguchi 2008), for example, computer-generated splatter supplants the craft of physical effects. This embrace of the digital has deprived live-action Japanese cyberpunk of texture, heft, and critical purchase. Especially in comparison to Tsukamoto, it has become lightweight.

See also: **Pat Cadigan, David Cronenberg, William Gibson, Sogo Ishii, Mamoru Oshii, Katsuhiro Ōtomo, Masamune Shirow**

Works Cited

Augé, Marc. *Non-Places: An Introduction to an Anthropology of Hypermodernity.* Translated by John How, Verso, 1995.

Harrington, Richard. "Tetsuo: The Iron Man." *The Washington Post*, July 24, 1992, https://www.washingtonpost.com/wp-srv/style/longterm/movies/videos/tetsuotheironman.htm.

Huang, Tsung-Yi Michelle. *Walking Between Slums and Skyscrapers: Illusions of Space in Hong Kong, Tokyo, and Shanghai.* Hong Kong UP, 2004.

Jameson, Fredric. *Postmodernism, or, The Cultural Logic of Late Capitalism.* Duke UP, 1991.

Lyotard, Jean-François. *The Postmodern Condition: A Report on Knowledge.* Translated by Geoffrey Bennington, U of Minnesota P, 1984.

Rayns, Tony. "Tokyo Stories." *Sight & Sound*, vol. 1, no. 8, 1991, pp. 12–15.

Mark Bould

VERNOR VINGE (1944–)

US author and professor of mathematics and computer sciences.

Vernor Vinge is an award-winning writer who has published five story collections, eight novels, and two essays. He has won three Hugo awards for Best Novel (*A Fire Upon The Deep* [1993]; *A Deepness In The Sky* [2000]; *Rainbow's End* [2007]), two Hugo awards for Best Novella (*Fast Times At Fairmont High* [2002]; *The Cookie Monster* [2004]), and a Prometheus Special Award for Lifetime Achievement in 2014. Perhaps most famously, Vinge is the inventor and promoter of the idea of the "Singularity," the exponential and uncontrollable development of artificial intelligence (AI) leading to a point of no return. Vinge posits that the Singularity can have unforeseen developments, such as the physical merging of human and AI, which he presented in his essay "The Coming Technological Singularity: How to Survive in the Post-Human Era," at the 1993 VISION-21 Symposium sponsored by the NASA Lewis Research Center and the Ohio Aerospace Institute.

Vinge's status as a major science fiction (sf) writer was established early on with the publication of his novella *True Names* (1981), which later also earned him the 2007 Prometheus Hall of Fame Award. The novella's plot revolves around a group of hackers, the Warlocks, who secretly surf the cyberspatial "Other Plane" to satisfy their own curiosity or need for power. They use pseudonyms and hide their true names to avoid being "owned" by other hackers or national powers. The protagonist is Mr. Slippery, whose real name, Roger Pollack, is discovered by the US government, which makes him an asset at its service. With the help of another hacker, Erythrina, he must discover the identity of the Mailman, a powerful figure who threatens government databases and world security. Half proto-cyberpunk novel, half computer game-like fantasy, *True Names* is a milestone in speculative fiction as it conveys all the topics that will be developed later in the cyberpunk mode: government control, cyber-war and hacking, and even a transhumanist Singularity when a dying Erythrina uploads her mind into cyberspace. The novella is even subtly referenced in **William Gibson**'s cyberpunk defining novel *Neuromancer* (1984) when the hacker Case must learn the 'true name' of the Wintermute AI as part of his mission. Therefore, Vinge not only introduces an iconic description of cyberspace in *True Names*, but also helped develop narrative tropes that became standards of cyberpunk fiction, such as hacker communities sheltering themselves behind anonymity, explorations around transhumanist bodily tran-scendence, the ambivalence of large power structures (whether gov-ernmental or corporate) using AI for their own purposes, and the revolutionary political power of hacking, topics that have since been adapted in varying degrees by the feminist cyberpunk authors of the 1990s, such as **Pat Cadigan** (*Synners* [1991]) or **Melissa Scott** (*Trouble and Her Friends* [1994]), and such 'post-cyberpunk' authors as Charles Platt (*The Silicon Man* [1991]), Charles Stross (*Accelerando* [2005]), and **Cory Doctorow** ("I, Robot" [2005]; "I, Row-boat" [2006]), to name only a few. As a result, *True Name*'s influence on real-world hackers and cryptography activists the Cypherpunks was such that Colin Milburn describes it as "required reading" for the group (376).

   True Names also laid the foundations for Vinge's treatment of AI and integrated technology, two central and recurring elements in his fiction. For example, the post-cyberpunk story *Rainbow's End* (2007) features AI, portable technology, and politics at the core of the story. The narrative follows a motley crew of hackers in their fight against an evil politician who wants to mind control the world through projected subliminal messages. In the book, Vinge offers an ethical reflection on technological progress, as the Promethean promise of a better, technologically enhanced human life comes with a heavy price for individual freedoms. Or, in his earlier space opera Zone of Thought series (*A Fire Upon The Deep* [1992], *A Deepness*

In The Sky [1999], and *The Children Of The Sky* [2011]) Vinge provides a vivid representation of the Singularity, represented by the
"Beyond," a zone inhabited by god-like disembodied entities that
resonate with transhumanism's visions, popularized by such figures as
Ray Kurzweil, Max More and Natasha Vita-More, Hans Moravec,
and Nick Bostrom.[1]

From cyberspace to augmented reality and the Singularity,[2] Vinge
deploys the technological motifs common to cyberpunk and post-
cyberpunk fiction alongside a conservative-libertarian political stance.
As *True Names*, *Rainbow's End*, and the Zone of Thought series show,
the enemy in Vinge's fiction is usually an entity that has an 'evil' plan
to bring down the existing power structure by misusing a technology
that is otherwise presented as beneficial. In Vinge's novels, political
power, is inherently flawed, and when it becomes over-centralized,
as in the Realtime series (*The Peace War* [1984] and *Marooned in Real
Time* [1986]), it becomes downright dangerous; thus, while technology may be neutral in itself, it is liable to be abused in the name of
power. Power is therefore never seen as a manicheistic incarnation
of good or evil. For example, when a community rallies around the
notion of freedom, as in *True Names*, *The Peace War*, or *Rainbow's End*,
it is not to seize or destroy power by means of revolution and thus
impose a socially equitable society, but rather to counterbalance the
threatening strength of a centralized political entity.

Vinge's stance toward technological progress is undoubtedly posi-
tivist, as is his view on the technological Singularity: "The acceleration of technological progress has been the central feature of this
century. We are on the edge of change comparable to the rise of
human life on Earth. The precise cause of this change is the immi-
nent creation by technology of entities with greater-than-human
intelligence" ("Technological Singularity"). Vinge therefore insists
that the Singularity will be a new age for mankind. In discussing
possible paths leading toward the Singularity, Vinge presents nothing
less than a map to the techno-utopian future—and promoting themes
that have often been discussed in the cyberpunk canon. For example,
he describes "pure artificial intelligence" as the advent of computers becoming "superhuman," autonomous entities beyond the limits of human intelligence, such as Wintermute and Neuromancer
in Gibson's *Neuromancer* or Eunice, the avatar software of his more
recent novel *Agency* (2020). "Intelligence Amplification," on the
other hand, is the technological augmentation of human capacities through AI, opening the way to a future merging of man and

machine, shown (among other narratives) in **Masumune Shirow**'s *Ghost in the Shell* (1996) or *Upgrade* (Whannell 2018), the latter a story about Grey Trace (Logan Marshall-Green), a paralysis victim who learns to control his body through an implanted chip called STEM. Similarly, the "group mind" from *A Fire Upon the Deep* refers to the possibility of humanity working collectively through social networking to attain super intelligence, represented partly in *Anon* (Niccol 2018), a film about digital surveillance via ocular implants and the ubiquity (but also potentiality) of a vast informational network. Vinge has also written and talked about a "digital Gaia" which would happen when all objects and persons can immediately communicate with each other on the planet, creating a huge database where the Earth itself would become the ultimate server. What will emerge is therefore "a world come alive with trillions of tiny devices that know what they are, where they are and how to communicate with their near neighbors, and thus, with anything in the world." As a result, "much of the planetary sensing that is part of the scientific enterprise will be implicit in this new digital Gaia. The Internet will have leaked out, to become coincident with Earth" ("Creativity Machine"). This premise of a digital Gaia is one of the imaginative steps undertaken in Stross's *Accelerando*. Finally, "biomedical improvement" could lead to artificial memory implants in humans and other permanent physical improvements—a staple in cyberpunk, including (but not limited to) Gibson's "Johnny Mnemonic" (1981), **Warren Spector**'s Deus Ex game franchise (2000–16), and **Charlie Brooker**'s *Black Mirror* episode "The Entire History of You" (Welsh 2011).

This positive narrative (or narratives) of humanity's future development through AI and technology has had a tremendous resonance. Vinge's predictions have led him to be invited to numerous scientific events sponsored by NASA and other agencies, and an online teaching program founded by transhumanists Peter Diamond and Ray Kurzweil has taken up the name "Singularity University." For Vinge, the Singularity is seen as a very plausible, if not hopeful, possibility, even if he does recognize the possibilities of a non-ethical use of technological development, which he considers a negative 'side-effect' compared to the gains for mankind:

> There are possibilities for total failures that are credible—where life on earth is destroyed and things like that—but the alternatives are there, and they are every bit as compelling as those the most extremely optimistic philosophers in history have

ever described. In fact, some of the things technology can support are so good that part of what bothers people is the idea of finally being confronted with the reality of getting what we have wanted since the beginning of time. When you finally have the possibility of doing some of these things, you have to look those possibilities in the face and ask, "What did we mean when we said we wanted that?"

(cited in Hewes)

Here, as in all his writings, Vinge offers a much more optimistic future than the dystopian visions that cyberpunk often imagined for the technological developments of AI; as a result, his vision and techno-optimism stand in contrast to the individualistic view that dominates much cyberpunk, or at the very least a particular strain of cyberpunk and post-cyberpunk fictions.

In the end, Vernor Vinge is a key figure of cyberpunk and cyberpunk culture. From *True Names* to his more recent fictions, coupled with his non-fiction and public speeches, Vinge's work vis-à-vis the political implications of cyberspace or the possibilities (and pitfalls) of the coming technological Singularity has considerably expanded the reach of the cyberpunk mode by bringing recognition to the mode's technological interests and adding scientific plausibility. Vinge has therefore managed to create an sf universe that has merged into our own, whether through his influence on other writers' works, or on our collective understanding of technological progress itself.

See also: **Charlton 'Charlie' Brooker, Cory Doctorow, William Gibson, Melissa Scott, Masumune Shirow, Warren Spector**

Notes

1 For details, see Max More and Natasha Vita-More's edited collection *The Transhumanist Reader* (2013).

2 Vinge does offer slightly different approaches to the Singularity in *A Fire Upon the Deep*. For example, in the "Slow Zone" technology and AI are present and are in the process of constant development, but the possibility of the Singularity is still very remote. And, in the "Unthinking Depths" technology is still primitive, and AI hasn't even been discovered yet.

Works Cited

Hewes, Arlington. "How Will We Get To The Technological Singularity?" *Singularity Hub*, July 17, 2012, https://singularityhub.com/2012/07/17/sh-interviews-vernor-vinge-how-will-we-get-to-the-technological-singularity/.

Milburn, Colin. "Activism." *The Routledge Companion to Cyberpunk Culture*, edited by Anna McFarlane, Graham J. Murphy, and Lars Schmeink, Routledge, 2020, pp. 373–81.

Vinge, Vernor. *A Deepness in the Sky*. Tor Books, 1999.

———. *A Fire Upon the Deep*. Tor Books, 1992.

———. *Marooned in Realtime*. Bluejay, 1986.

———. *Rainbow's End*. Tor Books, 2007.

———. *The Children of the Sky*. Tor Books, 2011.

———. "The Creativity Machine." *Nature*, March 22, 2006, https://www.nature.com/articles/440411a.

———. *The Peace War*. Bluejay, 1984.

———. "Technological Singularity." *The Transhumanist Reader: Classical and Contemporary Essays on the Science, Technology, and Philosophy of the Human Future*, edited by Max More and Natasha Vita-More, Wiley, 2013, pp. 365–75.

———. *True Names*. Dell, 1981.

Sébastien Doubinsky

LANA (1965–) AND LILLY (1967–) WACHOWSKI

US film directors, writers, and producers.

With their mainstream début *Bound* (1996), Lana and Lilly Wachowski emerged as dynamic writing, directing, and producing siblings whose imprint upon American filmmaking has been unmistakable. Their legacy was cemented when the release of their second film, *The Matrix* (1999), spawned not only a multimedia narrative universe, but also introduced "bullet time" as a groundbreaking filmmaking visual technique. While most of their films are categorizable as science fiction (sf), and the Matrix franchise has even become a convenient shorthand for cyberpunk in the twenty-first century (Gillis 2), their creative work has explored a variety of styles and genres. However, their films all share a thematic preoccupation with a core idea that aligns cyberpunk sf with queer theory and intersectional feminism: the Wachowskis insistently challenge "the reification of the subject as natural, eternal, and concrete" (Bukatman 311). For example, *Bound* is an abundantly stylish neo-noir thriller that transforms the traditional misogyny of the *femme fatale* figure into a gender-positive lesbian love story. The film's intricate heist plot explores this theme by pitting the two female lovers against a variety of straight men who perpetually underestimate them—on those occasions where they even acknowledge their existence at all.

This anti-essentialist theme fuels *The Matrix* (and subsequent entries in the franchise), where the cyberpunk motif of 'jacking in' to a liberating virtual reality was cleverly inverted: the franchise's central concept hinges on the idea that reality itself is a simulation in which we perform generic and normative identities. Thus, when Neo (Keanu Reeves) takes Morpheus's (Laurence Fishburne) invitation to ingest the red pill (as opposed to the blue pill that offers the acceptance of a life lived in blissful ignorance), he comes to understand the central question of the first film (including its marketing)—i.e., "what is the matrix?" His enlightenment is thereby presented as a liberatory flight that offers him an escape from the stifling constraints of a social hierarchy defined by oppressive white heteronormativity. While the first film's somewhat formulaic Hero's Journey narrative has clearly made it possible to interpret *The Matrix* as a celebration of straight white masculinity,[1] Neo's growth involves discovering his true self in a racially diverse community of queer rebels, and the film's two sequels, *The Matrix Reloaded* (2001) and *The Matrix Revolutions* (2002), invest even more heavily in the liberating power of queerness as a way to explore cyberpunk's distinctive strategies for dealing with "the problem of the subject in the electronic era" (Bukatman 9).

This queerness is evident above all in the sequels' depiction of Zion, the underground rebel community of misfits, deviants, and outcasts who are united by bonds of solidarity rather than those of familial or societal conventions. The rebels have developed alternative hierarchies of leadership, which are—again—striking for their degree of diversity in race, gender expression, age, and ability. Their struggle for liberation hinges not only on Neo's abilities as "The One," but also on their shared strengths as a collective. More than a mere action movie franchise, the Matrix films illustrate the kind of utopian possibility that José Esteban Muñoz described as *queer futurity*: "one in which multiple forms of belonging in difference adhere to a belonging in collectivity" (20).

Nowhere in the franchise is the Wachowskis' dedication to this utopian sense of queer futurity clearer than in the infamous "cave rave" scene in *The Matrix Reloaded*. In the midst of the rousing speech that rebel leader Morpheus gives the citizens of Zion, he speaks these words: "Remember that for one hundred years they have sent their armies to destroy us. And after a century of war, I remember that which matters most: *we are still here!*" The rebels respond with a loud cheer, while we see footage of a majority-Black crowd raising a single fist in defiance, clearly framed as a united "we" that fully disavows a purely identitarian logic (Muñoz 20). The joyous collective rave scene that follows this moment is among the most ecstatic mainstream expressions of a queer futurity that is grounded in desire: "Queer futurity does not underplay desire," Muñoz writes. "In fact it is all about desire, desire for both larger semi-abstractions such as a better world or freedom but also, more immediately, better relations within the social that include better sex and more pleasure" (30). This unconditional embrace of a queer futurity grounded in love, solidarity, and desire gives the franchise a liberatory utopian potential, irrespective of the main plot's primary focus on the heterosexual romance between Neo and Trinity (Carrie-Anne Moss). It lies both in the franchise's restless creativity that spread its storyworld creatively across multiple media platforms (Jenkins 115–16) and in the storyworld's refusal to reproduce conventional or reassuring answers to the complex questions about power, oppression, and utopia that it raises. Both elements are guided by "the ecstatic and horizontal temporality" that queerness offers as the radical alternative to a restrictive and monolithic "straight time" (Muñoz 25).

Although what was ostensibly the final film in the Matrix franchise was released nearly two decades ago, the Wachowskis' cyberpunk storyworld has undergone a recent resurgence. First, there was a 2019 announcement that a fourth film titled *The Matrix Resurrections* was under development.[2] Second, *The Matrix*'s lasting cultural footprint was illustrated yet again when, on May 17, 2020, billionaire entrepreneur and anti-union advocate Elon Musk tweeted the phrase "[t]ake the red pill." While this cryptic reference triggered abundant speculation regarding the tweet's intended meaning, many far-right activists celebrated what they saw as a vindication of their ideology by a hugely influential celebrity. Just over an hour later, Ivanka Trump, then First Daughter of the United States, entered the fray by quote-tweeting Musk's imperative, adding the exclamation "Taken!" Shortly thereafter, writer-director Lilly Wachowski responded publicly to Ivanka's post, tweeting out simply "Fuck both of you."

This minor exchange that briefly "broke the internet" in the final months of the tumultuous Trump presidency obviously testifies to the enduring influence of *The Matrix* and just how thoroughly the film (and the larger franchise) has permeated economic, political, and popular culture. At the same time, the outrage, debate, and confusion surrounding Musk's statement, Ivanka Trump's response, and Lilly Wachowski's pointed reply illustrates the contradictory ways in which the film gains meaning among different audiences over the years: it shows how both the interpretive frameworks we apply to the film and the way various audiences relate to the cyberpunk mode aren't unified or singular but remain deeply contested.

The struggle among opposed groups claiming ownership of this popular franchise can be broken down to the opposition between a particular form of online culture defined by toxic geek masculinity on the one hand, and progressive activists on the other (Salter and Blodgett 3–5). Within the former group's tribal expression of online culture, the term "redpilling" has been adopted as code for a loosely allied network of men's rights activists, straight male gamers, incels, and other misogynist groups associated with the "alt-right." This "redpilled" online community views mainstream culture as increasingly allied with "social justice warriors" to indoctrinate audiences with liberal values. As fostered by communities of predominantly straight and cis-gender white male gamers on online forums like 4chan and Reddit, redpilling constitutes a way of furthering the conspiracy theory that "white (Christian) straight men are under siege and that mainstream institutions are complicit in attacking them" (Greene 67). On the other hand, progressive audiences make up a different interpretive community that has recognized in Neo's choice to take the red pill and join a rebellion against institutional oppression—notably embodied within the film by white men in business suits—a powerful allegory for the transgender experience (VanDerWerff).

A similar logic can be observed within the straight romance plots of *Speed Racer* (2008) and *Jupiter Ascending* (2015), where the Wachowskis provide reassuringly familiar Hollywood frameworks from within which they playfully subvert audience expectations regarding aesthetics, narrative structure, and gender roles. *Speed Racer*, a box office failure that has since developed a devoted cult following, has a generic plot but a radical visual sensibility: where digital visual effects have generally reproduced the normative conventions of Hollywood 'realism,' the Wachowskis instead mounted an eye-melting display of swirling primary colors, physics-defying action, and aggressive cartoonishness that subverted the aesthetic norms of blockbuster filmmaking. And while *Jupiter Ascending* is somewhat less garish in its visual design, it takes every opportunity to embrace camp, reverse gender hierarchies, and destabilize the straight male gaze that dominates Hollywood cinema (Mulvey 8).

In the period between those two productions, the Wachowskis collaborated with German director Tom Tykwer on *Cloud Atlas* (2012), an ambitious 172-minute adaptation of David Mitchell's time-hopping novel of the same name, first published in 2004. Produced independently of the studio system, the film's complexly interwoven narrative structure takes cyberpunk's recurring theme of overlapping and intertwined identity in a radical new direction. Their screenplay combines the novel's clearly separated short narratives into an audacious experiment in continuity editing, within which a small group of actors takes on a variety of roles across the many distinct episodes and historical periods. While the film has been understandably criticized for applying "yellowface" make-up effects to white actors, the film's unusual form constitutes a radical attempt to emphasize how these identities are "rooted in various forms of socially imposed inequality and domination" (Wright 6).[3]

A less elaborate but similarly anti-essentialist approach underlies *Sense8*, the Wachowskis' speculative series that was financed and distributed by Netflix in collaboration with veteran sf showrunner J. Michael Straczynski. The show introduces eight transnational characters who discover that they are all mentally and emotionally linked to each other. These 'sensates' are remarkably diverse in terms of ethnicity, class, sexuality, and gender expression, and the series has a strong focus on the ways in which their personal lives are impacted by the extent to which they deviate from heteronormative straight time. The supernatural connection they share is a potent cyberpunk-derived symbol to express how queerness stands in clear opposition to societies in which "racism, sexism, capitalism, and heteronormativity are structurally organized" to oppress identities that deviate from its norms (Nash 11). The Wachowskis' work on *Sense8* alongside their celebrity activism for queer and antiracist movements therefore shows how these pioneers of cyberpunk cinema continue to apply the liberating power of queerness across their creative output, irrespective of those who attempt to redirect these energies toward their own reactionary goals.

As transgender women who transitioned in the years after the first three Matrix films were released, the Wachowskis have devoted their shared careers as sibling filmmakers to intersectional progressive causes, combining in their work across media positive representations of BIPOC, queer, and trans characters. At the same time, they have sought (and often found) connections to mainstream audiences via feature films, series, and transmedia offshoots with spectacular visual effects and high-concept plots, frequently derived from the cyberpunk mode. While the Matrix franchise has had the greatest impact of all their productions to date, their consistent devotion to its key thematic issues can be easily recognized across their entire oeuvre, in which their affinity for cyberpunk-derived themes and imagery has always been grounded by an explicitly queer perspective.

See also: **Pat Cadigan, William Gibson, Katsuhiro Ōtomo, Melissa Scott, Ridley Scott, Masumune Shirow, Neal Stephenson**

Notes

1 Keanu Reeves, the film star who took on the starring role after the Wachowskis' first choice Will Smith declined, is of mixed racial identity, but can easily pass for white—certainly to the extent that countless white male teenage boys identified strongly with him.
2 Slated for release (at the time of writing this chapter) on December 22nd, 2021.
3 The Wachowskis' co-directed adaptation of *Cloud Atlas* would also be the beginning of an ongoing partnership with David Mitchell, who contributed to *Sense8* and later co-wrote *The Matrix Resurrections* (2021).

Works Cited

Bukatman, Scott. *Terminal Identity: The Virtual Subject in Post-Modern Science Fiction.* Duke UP, 1993.
Gillis, Stacy, editor. *The Matrix Trilogy: Cyberpunk Reloaded.* Wallflower, 2005.
Greene, Viveca S. "'Deplorable' Satire: Alt-Right Memes, White Genocide Tweets, and Redpilling Normies." *Studies in American Humor,* vol. 5, no. 1, 2019, pp. 31–69.
Jenkins, Henry. *Convergence Culture: Where Old and New Media Collide.* New York UP, 2006.
Mulvey, Laura. "Visual Pleasure and Narrative Cinema." *Screen,* vol. 16, no. 3, 1975, pp. 6–18.
Muñoz, José Esteban. *Cruising Utopia: The Then and There of Queer Futurity.* 10th anniversary edition, New York UP, 2009.
Nash, Jennifer C. *Black Feminism Reimagined: After Intersectionality.* Duke UP, 2019.
Salter, Anastasia and Bridget Blodgett. *Toxic Geek Masculinity in Media.* Palgrave Macmillan, 2017.
VanDerWerff, Emily. "How The Matrix Universalized a Trans Experience—And Helped Me Accept My Own." *Vox,* March 30, 2019, https://www.vox.com/culture/2019/3/30/18286436/the-matrix-wachowskis-trans-experience-redpill.
Wright, Erik Olin. *How to Be an Anticapitalist in the Twenty-First Century.* Kindle edition, Verso Books, 2019.

Dan Hassler-Forest

NORBERT WIENER (1894–1964)

US mathematician, philosopher, and author.

Norbert Wiener was the founder of cybernetics, and his work played an essential role in the history of science fiction (sf) in the United States during the twentieth century, providing cyberpunk sf with some of its most central themes. His groundbreaking work on computing and automation, undertaken in such books as *Cybernetics or, Control and Communication in the Animal and the Machine* (1948) and *The Human Use of Human Beings: Cybernetics and Society* (1950), have laid the foundation for cyberculture to develop—without it, cyberpunk would not have been possible.

Wiener was born in 1894. A precocious child, he started higher education at Tufts College at the age of eleven, where he obtained his bachelor's degree in mathematics in just three years. Moving to Harvard and then to Cornell, he earned his master's degree in 1911 and his Ph.D., back at Harvard in 1913. His research into anti-aircraft guns laid the foundation for his work in information theory, and his growing unease with the militarization of science post-World War II was epitomized by his eventual rejection of any government or military funding. Later, Wiener became a professor at the Massachusetts Institute of Technology (MIT) and started to work on the development of machines that served as the basis for modern computers. While he is most renowned for his academic publications, his work is also key in science communication; he helped to form a public discourse on cybernetics, computers, and automation, his *Cybernetics* becoming a "pop culture phenomenon" (Hamilton 412) through mass-market editions. As a facilitator of communication between scientists and the public, his interest in sf played an important role and made him a central inspiration for writers from the Golden Age to the cyberpunks and beyond.

From childhood, Wiener was a reader of scientific magazines and no stranger to H.G. Wells's and Jules Verne's works (cf. Conway and Siegelman). As the field of sf in the United States was starting to grow—with Hugo Gernsback's *Amazing Stories* magazine, first published in 1926 — so-called "gadget science fiction" suggested future inventions by the genius of an individual creator, a view that Wiener's father had pushed on his son, seeing him as a prodigy that could shape the future (Wiener, *Ex-Prodigy*). At MIT, Wiener got in touch with the young John W. Campbell Jr., who was writing sf stories and wanted some advice from his professors (cf. Nevala-Lee). Wiener took the time to help Campbell, who would rise from writer to editor of *Astounding Stories* (1937), thus intimately connecting Wiener with early-Golden Age sf and the tradition of sf writing. In fact, Wiener's relationship with Campbell, Jr. helped prompt the eventual cyberneticist to take a stab at writing fiction as W. Norbert: "The Brain" and "The Miracle of the Broom Closet" were both published in 1952 in *Technical Engineering News*. Wiener also wrote the novel *The Tempter* (1959), which "deals with the disjunction between scientific research and industrial exploitation of a new invention but is not sf" (Clute and Langford).

Wiener's *Cybernetics* positioned information as the elementary unit that allows the calculation and study of systems, a proposition that linked biological, psychological, social systems with physics and mathematics. Building on the work of Warren McCulloch and Walter Pitts, Wiener "explained the mind's subjective process of perception in the new terms of information processing" and created the bridge between the human and the machine "using an electronic scanning mechanism operating at the same frequency as brain waves in the visual cortex" (Conway and Siegelman 179). This view proposed that humans and machines could correspond in a way that they could interchange: "switches corresponded to synapses, wires to nerves, networks to nervous systems, sensors to eyes and ears, an actuator to muscles" (Rid 49). *Cybernetics'* implications would be developed later in *The Human Use of Human Beings*, whose central point was "showing how adopting a cybernetic viewpoint could improve the writing of laws, reveal problems with the Cold War demands for secrecy in science, and point out the dangers and opportunities of the 'Second Industrial Revolution'" (Kline 81).

While Wiener had dabbled in sf, his relationship with the genre grew increasingly ambivalent after the publication of *Cybernetics*; reviews from the sf magazines praised it (Bailey, Ley), while writers like Isaac Asimov, Robert Heinlein, L. Ron Hubbard, and L. Sprague de Camp incorporated its concepts into their stories (Nevala-Lee). However, Wiener's ideas provided Hubbard with some of the conceptual elements of Dianetics (Nevala-Lee), a development that led Wiener to realize that his theories were misunderstood, which opened him up to criticism for his association with sf (Kline). Typically, sf writers saw cybernetics and machine development in necessary correlation to each other, so that it became "the science of robots" (Kline 88), oversimplifying Wiener's theories. In 1952, *Scientific American* launched a special edition featuring an advertisement for Wiener's book side by side with Asimov's *I, Robot* (1950) and Kurt Vonnegut's *Player Piano* (1952) and Vonnegut's novel was heavily

inspired by cybernetics, even featuring Wiener as a character. Wiener
refused to endorse the novel, calling it "mediocre" and no way near "the
caliber of work by his heroes Jules Verne and H.G. Wells" (Kline 90). In
1953, Wiener clearly stated his rejection of contemporary sf.

Wiener's legacy cannot be overstated, particularly as it applies to
those first cyberpunk authors who would start publishing their fiction
nearly twenty years after his death. It may have been "the context of
war which hastened the production of the cybernetic imagination"
(Pfohl 116), but it is arguably cyberpunk fiction and culture that continue to popularize and distribute this "cybernetic imagination" to
a mass-market audience, an imagination that is Wiener's enduring
legacy. For example, in Mark Neale's documentary *No Maps for these
Territories* (2000), **Bruce Sterling** remarks that this cadre of 1980s-
era authors recognized that the advent of increasingly sophisticated
computer systems meant "[t]he boundaries of the human body would
be crossed." Therefore, when Bruce Sterling reflected on the nature
of cyberpunk in his Preface to *Mirrorshades: The Cyberpunk Anthology*
(1986), ruminating that technology itself played a new role as something that was no longer outside but inside, "under our skin; often
inside our minds" (xiii), the famed author and editor was channeling
Wiener, whether knowingly or not. Similarly, the flow of information
in **William Gibson**'s *Neuromancer* (1984) generated a world where
the human was augmented via hardware, the ubiquity of cyborg bodies realizing Wiener's dreams. The blurring between the actual and
the virtual featured in cyberpunk novels, comic books, movies, video
games, and so forth may have originally been a metaphor but has
now become reality. To some extent, this is Wiener's legacy as the
'father' of cybernetics. After all, **N. Katherine Hayles**, writing in
How We Became Posthuman, remarks that "[o]f all the implications
that first-wave cybernetics conveyed, perhaps none was more disturbing and potentially revolutionary than the idea that the boundaries
of the human subject are constructed rather than given" (84). As a
result of framing "control, communication, and information as an
integrated system, cybernetics radically changed how boundaries were
conceived" (84). In sum, "cybernetics intimates that body boundaries are up for grabs" (Hayles 85), and it is this "intimation" that has
been the stock-in-trade of cyberpunk narratives and fuels contemporary cyberpunk culture as corporeal boundaries are routinely crossed,
whether in the literary fictions of William Gibson, Bruce Sterling,
Pat Cadigan, **Melissa Scott**, and **Steven Barnes**, in the recent
visual-acoustic offerings of **Janelle Monáe**, or in the video game

industry that packages the visual iconography of cyberpunk that helps fuel multi-billion dollar corporate profits. The cybernetic reality that Wiener helped usher forth means moral rules no longer bind our cybernetic imagination, if they ever did, as the relationship between our technologies and posthuman selves becomes increasingly ambiguous, perilous, and promising.

Interestingly, while Hayles acknowledges Wiener's central role in the history of cybernetics, she also points to an internal contradiction; namely, while Wiener envisioned "powerful new ways to equate humans and machines, he also spoke up strongly for liberal humanist values" (85). Consequently, Wiener is at odds with the near-limitless implications of cybernetics:

> On the one hand, he used cybernetics to create more effective killing machines [...] applying cybernetics to self-correcting radar tuning, automated anti-aircraft fire, torpedoes, and guided missiles. Yet he also struggled to envision the cybernetic machine in the image of a humanistic self. Placed alongside his human brother (sisters rarely enter this picture), the cybernetic machine was to be designed so that it did not threaten the autonomous, self-regulating subject of liberal humanism. On the contrary, it was to extend that self into the realm of the machine.
>
> (Hayles 86)

This tension is keenly evident in Wiener's legacy, particularly through the first wave of cyberpunk authors and filmmakers whose work throughout the 1980s displays a conservatism that reinscribes the liberal humanist subject—i.e., white, male, straight—at the center of their respective cyberpunk universes, a source of critique advanced to varying degrees by Nicola Nixon, Karen Cadora, Lauraine Leblanc, or, more recently, Carlen Lavigne, Lisa Yaszek, Wendy Gay Pearson, and Patricia Melzer. The feminist and queer cyberpunk of the 1990s offers a foundation for post-millennial cyberpunk culture to overcome the staunch adherence to a liberal humanism embedded in earlier cyberpunk and to realize the full implications of what it means to cross the boundaries of the human body in a move that takes the systems theory of cybernetics to its logical conclusion.

See also: **Steven Barnes, Rosi Braidotti, Pat Cadigan, William Gibson, Donna J. Haraway, N. Katherine Hayles, Janelle Monáe, Melissa Scott, Bruce Sterling**

Works Cited

Bailey, James Osler. *Pilgrims Through Space and Time: Trends and Patterns in Scientific and Utopian Fiction.* Argus Books, 1947.

Cadora, Karen. "Feminist Cyberpunk." *Science Fiction Studies*, vol. 22, no. 3, 1995, pp. 357–72.

Clute, John and David Langford. "Norbert Wiener." *The Encyclopedia of Science Fiction*, August 12, 2018, http://www.sf-encyclopedia.com/entry/wiener_norbert.

Conway, Flo, and Jim Siegelman. *Dark Hero of the Information Age: In Search of Nobert Weiner the Father of Cybernetics.* Basic Books, 2005.

Hamilton, S.N. "The charismatic cultural life of cybernetics: reading Norbert Wiener as visible scientist." *Canadian Journal of Communication*, vol. 42, no. 3, 2017, pp. 407–29.

Hayles, N. Katherine. *How We Became Posthuman: Virtual Bodies in Cybernetics, Literature, and Informatics.* U of Chicago P, 1999.

Kline, Ronald R. *The Cybernetics Moment: Or Why We Call Our Age the Information Age.* Johns Hopkins UP, 2015.

Lavigne, Carlen. *Cyberpunk Women, Feminism and Science Fiction.* McFarland & Company, Inc., 2013.

Leblanc, Lauraine. "Razor girls: Genre and Gender in Cyberpunk Fiction." *Women and Language*, vol. 20, no. 1, 1997, pp. 71–76.

Ley, Willy. Review of *Cybernetics*, by Norbert Wiener. *Astounding Science Fiction*, vol. 41, no. 1, 1948, pp. 153–56.

Melzer, Patricia. "Cyborg Feminism." *The Routledge Companion to Cyberpunk Culture*, edited by Anna McFarlane, Graham J. Murphy, and Lars Schmeink, Routledge, 2020, pp. 291–99.

Nevala-Lee, Alec. *Astounding - John W. Campbell, Isaac Asimov, Robert A. Heinlein, L. Ron Hubbard and the Golden Age of Science Fiction.* Harper Collins, 2018.

Nixon, Nicola. "Cyberpunk: Preparing the Ground for Revolution or Keeping the Boys Satisfied?" *Science Fiction Studies*, vol. 19, no. 2, 1992, pp. 219–35.

No Maps for These Territories. Directed by Mark Neale, 3DD Entertainment, October 4, 2000.

Pearson, Wendy Gay. "Queer Theory." *The Routledge Companion to Cyberpunk Culture*, edited by Anna McFarlane, Graham J. Murphy, and Lars Schmeink, Routledge, 2020, pp. 300–07.

Pfohl, Stephen. "The Cybernetic Delirium of Norbert Wiener." *Digital Delirium*, edited by Arthur and Marilouise Kroker, New World Perspectives, 1997, pp. 114–31.

Rid, Thomas. *Rise of the Machines: A Cybernetic History.* Norton, 2016.

Sterling, Bruce. Preface. *Mirrorshades: The Cyberpunk Anthology*, edited by Bruce Sterling, Ace, 1986, pp. ix–xiv.

Wiener, Norbert. *Ex-Prodigy: My Childhood and Youth.* The MIT P, 1953.

Yaszek, Lisa. "Feminist Cyberpunk." *The Routledge Companion to Cyberpunk Culture*, edited by Anna McFarlane, Graham J. Murphy, and Lars Schmeink, Routledge, 2020, pp. 32–40.

Willian Perpétuo Busch

SHOSHANA ZUBOFF (1951–)

US philosopher, scholar, and academic.

Shoshana Zuboff, Professor Emerita of Harvard Business School, is an academic working across social psychology and critical digital studies. Dealing with recent transformations of capitalism, Zuboff's work offers a window into the perennial cyberpunk themes of digitalization, data surveillance, automation, and individual freedom in a world increasingly dominated by techno-capital. These themes are examined in *In the Age of the Smart Machine: The Future of Work and Power*, although it is the recent *The Age of Surveillance Capitalism: The Fight for a Human Future at the New Frontier of Power* that firmly establishes Zuboff's work as key to cyberpunk culture. Here Zuboff describes "surveillance capitalism" as a "rogue mutation of capitalism," "a parasitic economic logic" which "claims human experience as free raw material for hidden commercial practices of extraction, prediction, and sales" (*Surveillance Capitalism* frontispiece). This brief description signals alignment with cyberpunk and its dystopian extrapolations of a world largely subsumed under capitalist logic.

Zuboff frames the dot-com crash at the turn of the century as a key moment in surveillance capitalism's development. Concerned for its economic viability, Google declared a "state of exception" (*Surveillance Capitalism* 75) and began to use the data collected in Google Search's "reflexive process of continuous learning and improvement" (*Surveillance Capitalism* 68) for a new purpose: monetization via targeted advertising. Recording and analyzing users' search data let Google exploit what Zuboff calls "behavioral surplus," data that allowed Google to predict users' interests and enhance "the profitability of ads for both Google and its advertisers" (*Surveillance Capitalism* 75). The personalized holographic ads of cyberpunk films such as *Minority Report* (Spielberg 2002) or *Blade Runner 2049* (Villeneuve 2017) may have seemed just one step away.

Exploring new ways to monetize its data, Google soon shifted toward "economies of action," targeting users' decisions on the premise that "the surest way to predict behavior is to intervene at its source and shape it" (*Surveillance Capitalism* 200). In this sense, Zuboff gives her key term 'surveillance' a wide ambit. It does not refer merely to secret observation, but to myriad power dynamics within data-intensive society. It extends her earlier concept of the "information panopticon" (*Smart Machine* 322): information systems capable of monitoring and shaping many kinds of user behavior. As Tim Jordan has argued, "cyberspace seems to many to offer greater possibilities for panoptic mechanisms to make more corners of society visible" (200–01)—and with smart devices spreading cyberspace into all aspects of society, there are fewer and fewer unsurveilled corners.

Whereas behavioral economists at least pretend to be concerned for individual autonomy, Zuboff's fieldwork finds that "data scientists trained on economies of action [...] regard it as perfectly normal to master the art and science of the 'digital nudge' for the sake of their company's commercial interests" (*Surveillance Capitalism* 294). Such economies of action are designed around a fundamentally cyborg subject. Our phones and other devices, and the software they run—social media, news, finance, health and wellbeing apps, spyware and other malware—may not *quite* be the remote brain of **James Tiptree Jr.**'s "The Girl Who Was Plugged In" (1974), or the implanted data storage of **William Gibson**'s "Johnny Mnemonic" (1981), but these technologies have become intimate, everyday, even prosthetic. When we try to rip them from our lives, it hurts. It is in these socio-technological networks that economies of action alter and iterate their interventions until the desired user behavior is produced.

Just as worryingly, however, it is less and less the data scientists, or any humans, who are pulling the strings. Cyberpunk fiction has long been fascinated by new categories of things being offered for sale: the portal that won't open without a micropayment; the memories of the perfect vacation that you never really took; the weaponized prosthetics from your friendly local implants parlor. Zuboff's focus is likewise on new areas of social life ("action") becoming colonized by the logic of the market ("economies"). *Economies of action* also echoes economics terms such as *economies of scale* and *economies of scope*. What Zuboff is getting at here is how certain kinds of power lead to other kinds of power, because of the complementary ways they are structured. As a simple example, integrating Google into one aspect of your life lowers the threshold for you to accept it into others, from getting your knowledge on Search, to navigating with Maps, to storing your files on Drive, to buying apps in Play, to someday maybe taking a self-driving Waymo. More subtly, power can accumulate in economies of action in ways that cannot be described in terms of human psychology. Zuboff characterizes this as a shift from 'Big Brother' to 'Big Other.' Her frequent refrain is, "Who decides? Who decides who decides?" (180). The implied answer is often that perhaps no one does. Many behaviors we once decided for ourselves can now be 'decided' by techno-economic processes that leave humans out of the decision-making process. When such processes tailor themselves to your behavior, that doesn't mean they are getting to know you better as you know yourself, nor as other humans—unscrupulous corporate scientists or otherwise—might feasibly know you. Rather, it only means automated processes are converging on the right algorithm to steer your observable behavior "while remaining steadfastly indifferent to the meaning of that experience" (*Surveillance Capitalism* 376–77). The 'Big Other' not only reads us like a book, but also re-writes us into the kind of book it likes to read: that is, not a book written for humans.

In these respects, Zuboff links two prominent cyberpunk themes: surveillance and automation. Her concern is not simply that robots may steal our jobs, but that the entire fabric of society may be reorganized along the lines of inhospitable machine rationality. This grows out of Zuboff's interest in machinic processes displacing and transforming human practices. Working within a critical sociological-philosophical tradition—including Ferdinand Tönnies, Max Weber, and Jürgen Habermas—Zuboff investigates the erosion of human lifeworlds by the practices and technologies of (so-called) rationalization. Zuboff's *In the Age of the Smart Machine* directly addresses automation and the future of work. Ethnography with office workers reveals computerization as a rationalization with a "withering effect on the sociality of the office environment" (139). Jobs where workers once utilized "at least some small measure of their personhood now emphasized their least individually differentiated and most starkly animal capacities" (*Smart Machine* 141). Zuboff's depiction of neoliberal degradation echoes the dehumanized worker drones of *The Matrix* (Wachowskis 1999) or *Sleep Dealer* (Rivera 2008). Similarly, fiction such as Matthew De Abaitua's Seizure trilogy (2007–16) and Malka Older's Centennial Cycle (2016–18) explore the frictions arising from such algorithmic governance. As Surian Soosay writes, imagining the oppressively rationalized environment of a near-future Amazon warehouse, but with wider applicability: "Being human is an inconvenience here" (2017).

Zuboff's analysis is not uncontroversial. For instance, **Cory Doctorow**'s riposte *How to Destroy Surveillance Capitalism* clears room for a more hopeful account of automation. Doctorow, who has frequently explored data surveillance in his writing, questions Zuboff's emphasis on persuasion; specifically, he suggests that when surveillance capitalism appears to verge on mind control, it's probably because we are being taken in by how such technologies are marketed and hyped. "[E]nding the use of automated behavioral modification feels like the plotline of a really cool cyberpunk novel," Doctorow writes, but argues that a more mundane account of surveillance capitalism may be more accurate and useful. First, he suggests, surveillance capitalism has rendered populations as precisely segmented data, which makes us more searchable. For Doctorow, it is important to preserve the distinction between forcing a given individual to do something versus simply finding someone already teetering on the brink, and taking advantage. Second, Doctorow distinguishes between implanting new motives or values and merely sharing false information. He thinks that Zuboff underestimates the latter, especially since digital networks now make it easy to form a "community of people who reinforce one another's false beliefs." Third, each of these forms of power—searching for the already suggestible and spreading disinformation—is amplified by a lack of digital pluralism stemming from "monopolistic dominance over informational systems" (notably by Google). Finally, Doctorow does acknowledge some small amount of what might be called 'mind control'—i.e., "using machine learning, 'dark patterns,' engagement hacking, and other techniques to get us to do things that run counter to our better judgment"—but he is skeptical that this is intensifying; instead, he asks: "what if the voracious appetite [for data] is because data has such a short half-life—because people become inured so quickly to new, data-driven persuasion techniques?"

Zuboff has emerged as a key theorist of contemporary techno-capital, and thus a significant touchstone for cyberpunk culture. Her work invites reflection on how cyberpunk has shaped the reception of, and resistance to, capitalism's dynamics over the last few decades. *The Age of Surveillance Capitalism* is a magisterial and ferocious polemic that somehow remains ambivalent about whether the main problem is the "surveillance" part, or the "capitalism." When earlier phases of capitalism are mentioned in passing, there is a distinctly upbeat tone: "competitive production, profit maximization, productivity, and growth" (*Surveillance Capitalism* 66). Google prior to 2000 is characterized, quite sincerely, as a company treating users as ends-in-themselves. Furthermore, Zuboff's analysis tends to downplay issues of class, gender, and race and how they relate to surveillance capitalism. These are curious oversights, especially given the prominence of the theme of racist bias in contemporary critiques of algorithmic governmentality (cf., for example, Noble; O'Neil), although they mirror much classic cyberpunk's marginalization of those who do not fit the mold of the individual white, male hero.

Moreover, *Surveillance Capitalism*'s criticisms of neoliberalism do not fully anticipate neoliberalism's techno–utopian wing. Defenders of surveillance capitalism happily acknowledge the broken promises of capitalism as it exists, only to claim these promises will be fulfilled *this* time around, using digital platforms instead of old-fashioned markets. Defenders of surveillance capitalism tend to locate it within a broadly cyberpunk imaginary—smart cities, ubiquitous computing, Quantified Self, eXplainable AI, eXtended Reality, neural interfacing, etc.—and are often intent on *transforming* human nature in a transhuman fashion, not dutifully preserving it.

Lastly, one can critique Zuboff's tendency to prolific neologization where perfectly serviceable terms already exist—or one could argue that it is a rhetorical strategy. As any shrewd cyberpunk knows, the street finds its own uses for things, and that may well be the case for names. Zuboff deploys what I call a *neologistic surplus*. In an era of digital discourse, to coin a conceptual term is necessarily to invoke the logic of virality. You're less likely to achieve the reach you want by proffering a single perfect pearl of content, than by playing the odds and grinding numerous good-enough variations. To neologize is not only to name the unnamed, but also to mark discourse with nodes and edges, to construct a speculative scaffold around which discourse may coalesce. I call this process *anticipatory nominalism*.

Zuboff's critique of capitalism is marked by ambivalence, and in choosing her as a key figure of cyberpunk culture, the question arises: How deserving is cyberpunk of its status as the quintessential genre of anti-capitalism? Certainly, cyberpunk often celebrates its own capacity to unlock large-scale truths—to reveal systems, assemblages, multitudes, classes, hyperobjects—via "key figures" who both typify and transcend the logics of late capitalism—hackers, couriers, gumshoes, assassins, entrepreneurs, near-future witches, double or triple agents. Such individuals resonate both with capitalism's continual self-reinvention *and* with emancipatory anti-capitalist practices, and provoke the question: who are they *really* working for? Similarly, Zuboff's desire to speak in a fresh voice, to a broad and perhaps unpredictable audience, is admirable. Yet the single-handed attempt to innovate a set of world-changing tools—and largely sidelining Marxist, feminist, anti-racist, queer, and other critical traditions—may ultimately be self-defeating. As Evgeny Morozov puts it, "If you don't want to talk about capitalism then you'd better keep quiet about surveillance capitalism." Zuboff generates an undeniably gripping narrative, extrapolating a future where only a tiny elite retain any agency whatsoever. Yet, in extrapolating a compelling dystopian future, you always run the risk of minimizing capitalism's dystopian past and present. You run the risk, also, of neglecting capitalism's alternatives.

See also: **Cory Doctorow, William Gibson, James Tiptree, Jr.**

Works Cited

Doctorow, Cory. *Walkaway*. Head of Zeus, 2017.

———. "How to Destroy Surveillance Capitalism." *OneZero*. August 26, 2020, https://onezero.medium.com/how-to-destroy-surveillance-capitalism-8135e6744d59.

Morozov, Evgeny. "Capitalism's New Clothes." *The Baffler*, February 19, 2019, thebaffler.com/latest/capitalisms-new-clothes-morozov.

Jordan, Tim. *Cyberpower: The Culture and Politics of Cyberspace and the Internet*. Routledge, 1999.

Noble, Safiya Umoja. *Algorithms of Oppression: How Search Engines Reinforce Racism*. New York UP, 2018.

O'Neil, Catherine. *Weapons of Math Destruction*. Crown, 2016.

Soosay, Surian. "Portrait of an Amazonian." *Vice.com*, January 6, 2017, www.vice.com/en/article/mg7wgp/portrait-of-an-amazonian.

Zuboff, Shoshana. *In the Age of the Smart Machine: The Future of Work and Power*. Basic, 1988.

———. *The Age of Surveillance Capitalism: The Fight for a Human Future at the New Frontier of Power*. Profile, 2019.

Zuboff, Shoshana and James Maxmin. *The Support Economy: Why Corporations are Failing Individuals and the Next Episode of Capitalism*. Penguin, 2004.

Jo Lindsay Walton

HONORABLE MENTIONS

Anna McFarlane, Graham J. Murphy, and Lars Schmeink

Before turning our focus to more individuals of key influence to cyberpunk culture, we would like to point out that over the past few years this cultural formation has become more and more international, expanding beyond the duality of western and Japanese imaginaries. Instead, cyberpunk flourishes in the works of writers and filmmakers worldwide, its motifs and cultural negotiations integrated in much broader movements of futurist imagination, including (but not limited to) African Futurism, Gulf Futurism, Latinx Futurism, Sino Futurism, and so forth. In *The Routledge Companion to Cyberpunk Culture*, we tried to show "how cyberpunk saturated and adapted itself to diverse cultural localities in alternately familiar, disorienting, and surprising ways that affirm cyberpunk as a global phenomenon" (McFarlane, Murphy, and Schmeink 3), and we would like to refer the reader to the *Companion* to explore the breadth of cyberpunk culture. A cultural formation, however, does not just constitute itself through the grand moments and big splashes, but also needs the smaller changes, the legion of little steps toward new things—that is, cyberpunk culture is in large part influenced by all those working within the field, especially on the margins (geographically or politically), and slowly but steadily pushing to expand its purview. We would be hard-pressed to integrate the works of these cyberpunks into the framework of such a volume as this, as their key influence lies not in their individual impact, but in their connected movement to become part of the cultural formation, to carry it beyond what it has been. To those cyberpunks from outside the mainstream cultural production, to all the writers and filmmakers, artists and musicians, designers and activists, scholars and scientists, that against the hegemonic odds incrementally move the boundaries of cyberpunk culture, this is an honorary mention. You expand the practice of cyberpunk culture; you shift the discourse with every word, scene, image, sound, or material. You are the true cyberpunks.

As befits the Routledge series, this collection is called *Fifty Key Figures in Cyberpunk Culture*; yet, in brainstorming, debating, arguing, and shortlisting our candidates (and finding contributors to write on them), we opted to include this Honorable Mentions section, in part to cheat Routledge's limitations of only choosing fifty figures, but more seriously to shine a spotlight on some of those figures that could possibly have made the final list had this collection been edited by others. Of course, there are bound to be names missing from even this Honorable Mentions list that will help fuel our argument from the Introduction that *Fifty Key Figures in Cyberpunk Culture* is a deliberately problematic text, but in providing some attention to some of the others who have contributed in ways both big and small to the evolution of this mode, we hope readers will gain an even broader insight into cyberpunk culture and its agents. And, of course, this list may provide the impetus for other scholars to take us up on our invitation (or challenge) outlined in the Introduction to edit something akin to *Fifty More Key Figures in Cyberpunk Culture* at some future date.

Kathy Acker (US author; 1947–97) was an experimental writer whose work channeled a kind of anarchist, nihilist feminism. Her novel *Empire of the Senseless* (1988) can be read as a rejoinder to **William Gibson**'s *Neuromancer* (1984) with the character of Molly Millions warped and reworked into a traumatized revenge-seeking cyborg. The novel, told in a series of vignettes that give the work the effect of surreal collage, was excerpted in Larry McCaffery's *Storming the Reality Studio: A Casebook of Cyberpunk and Postmodern Fiction*. Under Acker's pen, dystopian society is brought truly to the point of collapse and the bleak relentlessness of that possibility stands in sharp contrast to the excitement of some of Gibson's individualist male characters who see a broken society as an opportunity to prove themselves through the hustle. Acker's avant-garde style rendered *Neuromancer* relatively realist by comparison and led some to question cyberpunk's much-vaunted postmodern credentials (de Zwaan).

Greg Bear (US author; 1951–) is often identified as one of the inductees to literary cyberpunk's earliest wave, even if he isn't part of that initial core founding of **William Gibson**, **Bruce Sterling**, **Lewis Shiner**, John Shirley, and **Rudy Rucker**. Sterling's inclusion of the story "Petra" (first published in *Omni*, 1982) in the edited collection *Mirrorshades: The Cyberpunk Anthology* (1986) certainly brands Bear as close to the 'Movement' since the story is set in a 'post-apocalyptic' future following an event known as Mortdieu where the rules governing reality are malleable and gargoyles come to life to mate with humans. Meanwhile, in "Blood Music" (1983; *Blood Music*, 1985), biotechnology specialist Vergil Ulam creates (and then injects himself with) a 'biological computer' that evolves to transform not only the human species into a posthuman form but reshapes the very nature of (observable) reality. The story demonstrates the intimacies between cyberpunk and an emergent biopunk in its "biological posthuman motif" (Schmeink 24) and, given that cyberpunk in the 1980s was "anarchistic, libertarian, and self-consciously literary," Bear's work of this period "helped invent the language and conceptual terrain for nanotechnology, so both ["Petra" and "Blood Music"] were considered cyberpunk texts" (Luckhurst 27).

Bruce Bethke (US author; 1955–), author of the short story "Cyberpunk" (1983), is perhaps best known for providing editor Gardner Dozois with the source material for the 'cyberpunk' appellation. "Cyberpunk" follows the character Mikey, who is akin to the computer hackers popularized in contemporaneous cyberpunk stories, and in typical teen angst fashion Mikey uses his skills to rebel against his parents and exploit 'the Net' for his (and his friends') personal gain. Bethke acknowledges that while he created the neologism 'cyberpunk' in a deliberate fashion—"I took a handful of roots—cyber, techno, et al.—mixed them up with a bunch of terms for socially misdirected youth, and tried out various combinations until one just plain sounded right" (Foreword)—he by no means claims to have been the inventor of cyberpunk fiction as a genre of writing. Nevertheless, Bethke's story, written in 1980, was well-circulated prior to its publication three years later and, as John Clute writes, it was "almost certainly inspiring Gardner Dozois's use of the term Cyberpunk to designate the new movement, in an exclamatory fashion ironically distinct from Bethke's own jaundiced view of the 'romance' of Cyberspace." Bethke expanded "Cyberpunk" into a full-length novel that was never published (he claims it is because his publisher wanted him to completely alter the ending) but is available online, and he returned to cyberpunk-inspired form with the 1996 Philip K. Dick Award-winning *Headcrash* (1995), a satirical tale about corporate America, the internet, and a virtual reality experience that is a nascent form of today's social media.

Kathryn Bigelow (US film director; 1951–) added to the cyberpunk cinema tradition, begun with the likes of **Ridley Scott**'s *Blade Runner* (1982), with *Strange Days* (1995). The film draws on some of the visual tropes established by Scott—a neon-streaked, rain-soaked Los Angeles provides the setting for a film in which the SQUID, a device that looks like a jellyfish and attaches to the head via electrodes, allows the 'viewer' to live the recorded experiences of others, or to relive their own memories. Under Bigelow's direction the film brings concerns about the significance of the approaching millennium together with the racial tensions that had recently been stirred up by the beating of Rodney King and the subsequent LA Riots. Bigelow did not return to sf explicitly in her work after this film, but some of the aesthetics and themes of *Strange Days* would return in her war films, particularly *Zero Dark Thirty* (2012), and *Detroit* (2017) (cf. McFarlane).

Stephen Patrick Brown (US editor) is perhaps best known in the sf field for launching (with Daniel J. Steffan) *Science Fiction Eye*, a publication Takayuki Tatsumi describes as "the first cyberpunk journal" (1); however, Brown's involvement in the fledgling movement hearkens to its earliest days, which Brown chronologically unpacks in "Before the Lights Came On: Observations of a Synergy," published in Larry McCaffery's *Storming the Reality Studio: A Casebook of Cyberpunk and Postmodern Fiction*. Brown recounts how his connections (and friendships) among many of cyberpunk's foundational members, his mutual introductions, and his sharing of their draft manuscripts—e.g., **Bruce Sterling** confirmed (as best his recollection) in an e-mail that Brown gave him a draft of **William Gibson**'s "Johnny Mnemonic" (1981) before it was published in *Omni*—helped lay the foundation for their early correspondences which then flourished into a mutual admiration and provided the necessary gravitational pull to unite Gibson, Sterling, John Shirley, **Rudy Rucker**, and **Lewis Shiner** under the eventual 'cyberpunk' label.

John Brunner (UK author; 1934–95) was an instrumental 'proto-cyberpunk' figure whose *The Shockwave Rider* (1975), a novel influenced by the work of **Alvin and Heidi Toffler**, notably *Future Shock*, depicts "an information-driven world where rigid hierarchies are under threat from savvy hackers who use their know-how to decrypt and disseminate subversive knowledge" (Latham 10).

Brunner's *The Shockwave Rider* helped lay the groundwork for literary cyberpunk narratives featuring dystopian futures populated by data hackers, cyberspatial networks, computer viruses, and the seemingly unrestrained power of capitalist megacorporations that emerged full force less than a decade later.

Scott Bukatman (US academic and professor; 1957–) is a well-known cultural theorist with a lengthy history of publications, including monographs (such as 1997's *Blade Runner*, published by the British Film Institute), numerous academic articles in peer-review journals, book chapters, and so forth. As per his contributor biography to *Cyberpunk and Visual Culture*, Bukatman is particularly interested in "how such popular media as film, comics, and animation mediate between new technologies and human perceptual and bodily experience" (xi), a focus on full display in his influential *Terminal Identity: The Virtual Subject in Postmodern Science Fiction*, one of the earliest academic studies of cyberpunk and a nascent cyberculture. *Terminal Identity* helped lay the foundation for cyber studies in general, and it remains as important an exploration of 'terminal identity'—i.e., those complex media(ted) sites where conventional subjectivity is replaced by a subjectivity borne from computer and televisual media—in the 2020s as when it was first published in 1993.

Wendy Carlos (US musician and composer; 1939–) is, in terms of cyberpunk, most prominently known for the score to *TRON* (Lisberger 1982) but is actually a key figure in the establishment of electronic music as a medium. She can be credited with bringing electronic music out of avant-garde obscurity with her record *Switch-On Bach* (1968), which produced Johann Sebastian Bach's music with Moog-synthesizers and broke with the experimental approach to electronic music at the time, rejecting its "alien, hostile listening experience" and opting to promote the new musical medium with "melody, harmony, rhythm" (Carlos). Further, Carlos went on to score soundtracks to speculative fiction films and introduce new techniques. For example, she inaugurated the use of synthesizer-distorted vocals on her score for *A Clockwork Orange* (Kubrick 1971), thus creating a sound effect of the cyborg or machine-inflected voice often used for sf films.

The Cypherpunks (group, privacy rights advocates, activists) were founded as a mailing list in 1992 by Timothy May, Eric Hughes, and John Gilmore and advocated for privacy and cryptography in information technology, stating in their "Cypherpunk Manifesto" that "[p]rivacy is necessary for an open society in the electronic age [...] The Cypherpunks are actively engaged in making the networks safer for privacy" (Hughes 81–83). The group was heavily inspired by cyberpunk, deriving its name from the literary movement and recommending to new members an inspirational reading list that included works such as **Vernor Vinge**'s "True Names" (1981), John Brunner's *The Shockwave Rider* (1975), or **Neal Stephenson**'s *Snow Crash* (1992). Colin Milburn argues that "the cypherpunks were not simply reading sf; they were putting it into practice" (377) by coding software tools and advocating for privacy rights. Most notably, one early contributor of the group later came to fame through what Milburn calls the "most explosive implementations of the cypherpunk vision" (377): Julian Assange created WikiLeaks as a form of cyberpunk activism and with the Cypherpunk Manifesto in mind.

Ellen Datlow (US editor; 1949–) is one of the most important and well-respected editors in the broadly defined field of the 'fantastic.' Datlow's importance for cyberpunk in her behind-the-scenes role cannot be understated, particularly given her central role as associate fiction editor (1979–81) and fiction editor (1981–98) for the science/science fiction magazine *Omni* (including its online format; 1996–98, 2005–) as well as *Sci Fiction* (2000–05) and *Tor.com* (2013–). Under Datlow's mentorship, *Omni* published **William Gibson**'s "Johnny Mnemonic" (1981), "Hinterlands" (1981), "Burning Chrome" (1982), "New Rose Hotel" (1984), "Skinner's Room" (1991), and Gibson collaborations "Red Star, Winter Orbit" (with **Bruce Sterling**, 1983) and "Dogfight" (with Michael Swanwick, 1985), among other stories. Given the centrality of Gibson's role in cyberpunk's formative years, this mode arguably would never have taken the shape that it did had Datlow not provided Gibson with the venue in *Omni* to publish his writings and help fuel literary cyberpunk's first (and foundational) wave.

Candas Jane Dorsey (Canadian author; 1952–) anticipated the feminist criticism of masculinist cyberpunk and the rise of 'feminist cyberpunk' of the early to mid-1990s with her late-1980s short story "(Learning About) Machine Sex" (1988). It follows Angel, a brilliant computer programmer who is also a part-time member of the sex trade, itself a biting commentary on the prostitution of one's body and skills that takes place in both patriarchal and misogynistic industries. The critique continues with Angel's creation of Machine Sex, a sex program that Angel truly doesn't believe will actually come to market: "*That's right*, she told herself, *trying to sell it is all right – because they will never buy it*" (Dorsey 368). Unfortunately, the willingness for the industry to exploit new markets proves Angel wrong and the story ends with a provocative (and distressing) apposition: "A woman and a computer. Which attracts you most? Now you don't have to choose.

Angel has made the choice irrelevant" (368). While "(Learning About) Machine Sex" is generally crowded out by other cyberpunk titles— e.g., it is absent from both Pat Cadigan's *The Ultimate Cyberpunk* (2002) and Victoria Blake's *Cyberpunk: The Big Book of Hardware, Software, Wetware, Revolution and Evolution* (2013)—it is a piercingly effective cyberpunk short story.

Gardner Dozois (US editor, author, and columnist; 1947–2018) is known throughout the broadly defined field of the 'fantastic' for his voluminous work as an editor on *The Year's Best Science Fiction* annual collections, the *Isaac Asimov* anthologies, and dozens and dozens of other series and standalone titles. It was in his editorial "Science Fiction in the Eighties," published in *The Washington Post* (December 30, 1984), that Dozois wrote about a group of ambitious (and 'young') upstarts in the field who were "not satisfied to keep turning out the Same Old Stuff" and, instead, seemed to be interested in "literary risk-taking" which signaled "an exciting time for sf as a genre." Dozois wrote about this group—which included **Bruce Sterling**, **William Gibson**, **Lewis Shiner**, **Pat Cadigan**, and Greg Bear—as "purveyors of bizarre hard-edged, high-tech stuff, who have on occasion been refereed [sic] to as 'cyberpunks.'" The use and popularization of the term 'cyberpunk' (taken from Bruce Bethke's short story of the same name) in a mainstream venue like *The Washington Post* cemented Dozois as responsible (despite his dubious claims that the term had been used earlier) for identifying and perhaps codifying 'cyberpunk' as a label that its authors, notably Sterling, would simultaneously capitalize upon and push back against all while cyberpunk was becoming increasingly popular.

Fredric Jameson (US scholar; 1934–) is currently Knut Schmidt Nielsen Distinguished Professor of Comparative Literature at Duke University. He is a literary scholar and Marxist critic known for his theorization of postmodernism, notably in *Postmodernism, or, The Cultural Logic of Late Capitalism*. His interest in postmodernism brought cyberpunk to Jameson's attention and he was particularly interested in reading William Gibson's work as a specific response to its contemporary cultural conditions. In *Postmodernism*, he provided one of the most oft-quoted summaries of cyberpunk as the "supreme *literary* expression if not of postmodernism, then of late capitalism itself" (418, fn 1). Years later, when Gibson moved into the realm of contemporary realism, while remaining true to cyberpunk styles, Jameson argued that his blend between postmodernist realism and cyberpunk provided a "mapping of the new geopolitical Imaginary" of our globalized and media-saturated times, a "laboratory experiment in which the geographic-cultural light spectrum and bandwidths of the new system are registered" ("Fear and Loathing" 107). As such, Jameson has always been an astute commentator on the linkage between a globalized reality and the cyberpunk imaginary.

Steven M. Lisberger (US film director; 1951–) is perhaps best known for directing *TRON* (1982), a film he co-wrote (to varying degrees) with Bonnie MacBird and Charles S. Haas, featuring music composed by Wendy Carlos ("*TRON*"). While the film may not have been a financial success for Walt Disney Corp., it marks a phenomenal visual breakthrough in its depiction of cyberspace and helped "set the standards for representing game space [that] still resonates in the popular cultural sensibility. With its 90°-angled grid-structure, the overlay of physical and virtual space, and the dark background lit with neon circuitry, *TRON* provided the space beyond the screen with its original blueprint" (Murphy and Schmeink 102). In addition, *TRON* was one of the earliest films to rely extensively on computer-generated imagery (CGI), so much so that its reliance upon computers disqualified the film from an Academy Award nomination for special effects ("*TRON*"). Finally, the visual splendor of Lisberger's *TRON* was exported to local arcades as cross-promotion with coin-operated games released largely concurrently with the film allowed "kids of all ages to flock to the local arcade to relive the cinematic adventures […] or, alternately, play the game and then travel to the theater to witness the video game spectacle on the big screen" (Murphy and Schmeink 102).

Brian McHale (US academic; 1952–) is currently Arts and Humanities Distinguished Professor of English at Ohio State University and most influential for his work on postmodernism, especially in *Postmodernist Fiction* and *Constructing Postmodernism*. In the former, he argued that postmodernist fiction and science fiction were indebted to each other, noticing a "'postmodernization' of science fiction" following the late 1960s (*Postmodernist* 69). In the latter, he identifies sf's "*aesthetic contemporaneity*" (*Constructing* 225) as a genre to present postmodern reality, especially through the aesthetics of cyberpunk. In a chapter titled "POSTcyberMODERNpunkISM," he explores the overlap between the two literary forms before devoting another chapter to constructing "a poetics of cyberpunk" (*Constructing* 243), which to this day remains one of the most comprehensive explorations of cyberpunk motifs and repertoires available to scholars of the literary genre.

Tom Maddox (US author; 1945–) was a prominent figure in literary cyberpunk's original emergence, contributing the short story "Snake-Eyes" (originally published in *Omni*, 1986) to Bruce Sterling's edited collection *Mirrorshades: The Cyberpunk Anthology*

(1986). His novel *Halo* (1991) might be best described as a mixture of the seedy streets and virtual vistas of **William Gibson**'s *Neuromancer* and the extraterrestrial colonies common to **Lewis Shiner**'s *Frontera* (1984) or **Bruce Sterling**'s Schismatrix sequence. John Clute describes *Halo* as "an intense contemplation of the nature of artificial intelligence [...] in a Virtual-Reality [sic] environment." Arguably, Maddox is perhaps better known for his friendship with Gibson: the two collaborated on the "Kill Switch" and "First Person Shooter" episodes of the 1990s television series *The X-Files*; in addition, as per his Acknowledgments at the end of *Neuromancer*, Gibson gives credit to Maddox for coining the term Intrusion Countermeasures Electronics (ICE). Maddox has had an intermittent career as a literary figure in the cyberpunk mode (and sf more broadly), and largely disappeared from view in the 1990s.

Lisa Mason (US author; 1953–) published her debut novel *Arachne* (1990) following the publication of the shorter "Arachne" (1987) in *Omni*. *Arachne* and its sequel *Cyberweb* (1995) are replete with the cyberpunk tropes of the early to mid-1990s, including a female protagonist, artificial intelligence entities, and digital avatars populating a virtual reality matrix. As Lisa Yaszek writes, Mason was one of a handful of authors who emerged in the late-1980s and transitioned into the early-1990s and "pioneered a strain of feminist-friendly cyberpunk" (35). Although Mason has largely drifted from cyberpunk in her writings, this early work retains its strength as a testament to the writing skills and imaginative wonders of a 'feminist cyberpunk' period that took cyberpunk's tropes into directions that had been largely unexplored in the cyberpunk published at the time.

Laura J. Mixon (US author; 1952–) released her debut novel, *Glass Houses* (1992), during what critics such as Karen Cadora have identified as a wave of 'feminist cyberpunk' in the early to mid-1990s. *Glass Houses*, a novel John Clute calls a "remarkable debut," includes the requisite tropes that had grown common to cyberpunk, but stars a lesbian protagonist that enjoins *Glass Houses* with a series of other writings at the time that overtly queer masculinist cyberpunk, including **Melissa Scott**'s *Trouble and Her Friends* (1994) and Mary Rosenblum's *Chimera* (1993). Mixon cleverly fuses biology and technology when the novel's protagonist, Ruby, uploads herself into robotic waldoes, which is "reflected in the doubling of prepositions: Ruby is 'I-Golem' or 'I-Tiger' or 'me-Rachne' when she is linked to them" (Cadora 360), all the while challenging corporeal boundaries that is reminiscent of **Donna J. Haraway**'s work with the cyborg.

Mixon expanded her cyberpunk focus on advanced waldoes and meg-acorporate malfeasance with the linked *Proxies* (1998) and *Burning the Ice* (2002), a duology that also includes a singularity event, interstellar theft, a distant ice world, and bio/cloning technologies.

Hans Moravec (Austrian-Canadian scientist and futurist; 1948–) is mainly known for his scientific work in robotics and his transhu-manist publications, most famously *Mind Children: The Future of Robot and Human Intelligence* and its updated version *Robot: Mere Machine to Transcendent Mind*. He was the first to formulate that robotics and artificial intelligence (AI) design can simulate human reasoning far better than simple sensorimotor functions, thus prompting the phe-nomenon to be called Moravec's Paradox. Regarding cyberpunk, Moravec is most famous for his transhumanism and the argument that human biologies are limited and need to be overcome. In *Mind Children*, Moravec thus argues for a "mind transferral" (115), leaving behind the often evoked 'meat' of the biological and uploading one's mind into a robotic body. In his view, this would trigger a transcend-ence to a posthuman state; we would become "superintelligences with astronomical powers of observation and deduction" (122) and kickstart further scientific progress and posthuman development. Consequently, for many cyberpunk authors, Moravec's visions are the techno-utopian keystone for imagining the singularity and a post-human existence.

Lyda Morehouse (US author; 1967–), who also writes paranormal romances under the pen name Tate Hallaway, released the AngeLINK series of cyberpunk novels: *Archangel Protocol* (2001), *Fallen Host* (2002), *Messiah Node* (2003), *Apocalypse Array* (2004), and the standalone pre-quel *Resurrection Code* (2011). Although not a religious series *per se*, the AngeLINK arc uses angels and fallen angels (devils) in tandem with the dystopian tropes common to cyberpunk to capitalize on the religious, transcendent, and/or utopian imagery often deployed not only in virtual reality narratives but also in the internet's utopian hey-day circa the 1990s. The series, however, is "not evangelically didac-tic" (Murphy 220) and it satirizes organized religion "by targeting the oppressive beliefs, illogical practices, and social inconsistencies of any organized religion that uses rigid moral and ethic[al] codes to foster discrimination, bigotry, political oppression, socially-acceptable iden-tities, and blind fidelity" (Murphy 221). While Morehouse "combines the pleasure she takes in the democratizing nature of the computer with her marked interest in religious issues," (Lavigne 174), as a queer artist the AngeLINK series also aligns with feminist-queer cyberpunk, particularly of the early- to mid-1990s, itself perhaps no surprise given Morehouse's admiration for **Marge Piercy**'s *He, She and It* (*Body of Glass*; 1991) as well as the works of **Melissa Scott**, whose *Trouble and Her Friends* (1994) is a queer rewriting of nearly all of the cyberpunk tropes that had been popularized a decade earlier.

Darick Robertson (US artist; 1967–) is a well-known artist within the comic book industry, having worked for the mainstream presses of DC Comics and Marvel as well as such independent publishers as Eclipse Comics, Valiant Comics, and Malibu Comics, the latter where he met **Warren Ellis** while working on *Ultraforce* (1994–96). Robertson's influence upon cyberpunk is undoubtedly his illustration of Warren Ellis's *Transmetropolitan* (1997–2002). While Robertson by no means originated the visual density of urban cyberpunk comics— for example, the influence of **Moebius [Jean Giraud]** and his illustration of Dan O'Bannon's "The Long Tomorrow" (1976) is evident—his work nevertheless revels in subtle flourishes. For example, Christian Hviid Mortensen notes that Robertson "includes at least one television in almost every panel with a metropolitan street view and the fact that nobody seems to pay attention to the screens indicates they have become part of the visual white noise of the City" (12). Robertson's work on *Transmetropolitan* provides a visual splendor to the seemingly never-ending verticality of an urban sprawl teeming with cybernetically enhanced, disenfranchised hustlers navigating a dense mediascape, a near-future vision that was popularized not only in the works of **William Gibson**, **Pat Cadigan**, and others, but has become *de rigueur* for a particular (and dominant) vision of cyberpunk culture.

Justina Robson (UK author; 1968–), nominated twice for the 2005 Philip K. Dick Award (*Silver Screen* [1999] and *Natural History* [2003]), embodies the narrative potential of what may be called a 'post-cyberpunk' generation of writers; in other words, writers whose utilization of cyberpunk's common tropes proves them resilient and whose "short- and long-form fictions contribute to cyberpunk's thematic arcs" (Kilgore 48). For example, AI entities and nanotechnologies appear through Robson's oeuvre, albeit to greater or lesser degrees, and *Silver Screen* and *Mappa Mundi* (2001) may be aligned with cyberpunk's near-future storyworlds, embodied by **William Gibson** or **Pat Cadigan**, while *Natural History* and its sequel *Living Next Door to the God of Love* (2005) are reminiscent of **Bruce Sterling**'s far-future Schismatrix universe with Robson's depiction of the Unevolved and the Forged. More recently, Robson has taken to writing what may be called 'cyberpunk fantasy'—*Glorious Angels* (2015), *The Switch* (2017), and the Quantum Gravity series (starting with *Keeping it Real* [2006]) —which blends the cyberpunk tropes with magical elements, including dimensional realms populated by cyborgs, elves, elementals, and demonic creatures. As John Clute writes, Robson is "an author of very considerable ingenuity and verve, with a great deal of imaginative muscle to flex."

Mary Rosenblum (US author; 1952–2018) emerged as part of what critics such as Karen Cadora identify as a wave of 'feminist cyberpunk' in the early- to mid-1990s, chiefly on the strengths of her novel *Chimera* (1993). The novel queers many of the tropes popularized by masculinist cyberpunk a decade earlier, including figuring cyberspace not as the feminine matrix needing to be penetrated by predominantly male hackers but, instead, a network of electronic fibers grafted to the corporeal form that "is explicitly identified with the male body" (Cadora 362). Similarly, *Chimera* shows Rosenblum "has no allegiance to the heterosexual paradigm. Several of the main characters who move through cyberspace are lesbian, gay, or bisexual" (Cadora 363), a marked departure from the common, if not rank, heteronormativity that dominated (and, in many respects, continues to dominate) literary and visual cyberpunk.

John Shirley (US author; 1953–) is one of the cadres of authors— see also **William Gibson**, **Bruce Sterling**, **Lewis Shiner**, and **Rudy Rucker**—at the core of literary cyberpunk's earliest days when it was still a loose affiliation dubbed the 'Movement.' Shirley's notable entries include *City Come A-Walkin'* (1980), a story about nightclub owner Stu Cole who, while struggling to keep his dive bar Club Anesthesia financially soluble, is visited by the City, a surreal embodiment of San Franciscans' media(ted) dreams, fears, and desires come to life. John Clute and Chris Williamson see in the novel the common protagonist of Shirley's early fiction, if not Shirley himself who has fronted a number of punk-rock bands: "punk, anarchic, exorbitant, his mind evacuated of normal constraints, [and] death-loving." It is Shirley's A Song Called Youth series—*Eclipse* (1985; an excerpt appeared as "Freezone" in *Mirrorshades: The Cyberpunk Anthology* [1986]), *Eclipse Penumbra* (1988), and *Eclipse Corona* (1990)—that showcases the strides literary cyberpunk was making even in its earliest literary incarnations by featuring a punk-rock driven resistance force battling against a racist, right-wing privatized security force, the destabilization of nation-states, and the resurgence of fascist political governance.

Works Cited

Bethke, Bruce. "Cyberpunk." *Amazing Science Fiction Stories*, vol. 57, no. 4, 1983, pp. 94–105.

———. "Family Matters." *Stupefying Stories*, September 22, 2021, https://stupefyingstories.blogspot.com/2021/09/ family-matters.html.

———. Foreword. "Cyberpunk." *Infinity Plus*, 1997, http://www.infinityplus.co.uk/stories/cpunk.htm/.

"Bio." *Darick Robertson*, n.d., https://darickrobertson.com/temp/bio-temp/.

Brown, Stephen P. "Before the Lights Came On: Observations of a Synergy." *Storming the Reality Studio: A Casebook of Cyberpunk and Postmodern Fiction*, edited by Larry McCaffery, Duke UP, 1991, pp. 173–77.

Cadora, Karen. "Feminist Cyberpunk." *Science Fiction Studies*, vol. 22, no. 3, 1995, pp. 357–72.

Carlos, Wendy. "Switched-On Bach" *Wendycarlos.com*, n.d., http://www.wendycarlos.com/+sob2k.html#history.

Clute, John. "Bethke, Bruce." *The Encyclopedia of Science Fiction*. September 6, 2005, http://www.sf-encyclopedia.com/entry/bethke_bruce.

———. "Maddox, Tom." *The Encyclopedia of Science Fiction*. April, 4 2017, http://www.sf-encyclopedia.com/entry/maddox_tom.

———. "Mixon, Laura J." *The Encyclopedia of Science Fiction*. August 12, 2018, https://www.sf-encyclopedia.com/entry/mixon_laura_j.

———. "Robson, Justina." *The Encyclopedia of Science Fiction*. July 19, 2021. https://www.sf-encyclopedia.com/entry/robson_justina.

Clute, John and Chris Williamson. "Shirley, John." *The Encyclopedia of Science Fiction*. 26 July 2001, https://www.sf-encyclopedia.com/entry/shirley_john.

de Zwaan, Victoria. "Rethinking the Slipstream: Kathy Acker Reads 'Neuromancer'." *Science Fiction Studies,* vol. 24, no. 3, 1997, pp. 459–70.

Dorsey, Candas Jane. "(Learning About) Machine Sex." *Northern Stars: The Anthology of Canadian Science Fiction*, edited by David G. Hartwell and Glenn Grant, Tor, 1994, pp. 354–69.

Dozois, Gardner. "Science Fiction in the Eighties." *The National Post*, December 30, 1984, https://www.washingtonpost.com/archive/entertainment/books/1984/12/30/science-fiction-in-the-eighties/526c3a06-f123–4668–9127–33e33f57e313/?postshare=5611479011076442&tid=ss_mail.

Hughes, Eric. "A Cypherpunk's Manifesto." *Crypto Anarchy, Cyberstates, and Pirate Utopias*, edited by Peter Ludlow, The MIT P, 2001, pp. 81–83.

"Ellen Datlow." *The Internet Speculative Fiction Database*, n.d., http://www.isfdb.org/cgi-bin/ea.cgi?156.

Jameson, Fredric. *Postmodernism, or, The Cultural Logic of Late Capitalism*. Duke UP, 1991.

———. "Fear and Loathing in Globalization." *New Left Review,* vol. 23, September/October, 2003, pp. 105–14.

Kilgore, Christopher D. "Post-Cyberpunk." *The Routledge Companion to Cyberpunk Culture*, edited by Anna McFarlane, Graham J. Murphy, and Lars Schmeink, Routledge, 2020, pp. 48-55.

Latham, Rob. "Literary Precursors." *The Routledge Companion to Cyberpunk Culture*, edited by Anna McFarlane, Graham J. Murphy, and Lars Schmeink, Routledge, 2020, pp. 7–14.

Lavigne, Carlen. *Cyberpunk Women, Feminism and Science Fiction*. McFarland & Company, Inc., 2013.

Luckhurst, Roger. "Greg Bear." *Fifty Key Figures in Science Fiction*, edited by Mark Bould, Andrew M. Butler, Adam Roberts, and Sherryl Vint, Routledge, 2010, pp. 27–32.

McFarlane, Anna. "Cyberpunk and 'Science Fiction Realism' in Kathryn Bigelow's *Strange Days* and *Zero Dark Thirty*." *Cyberpunk and Visual Culture*, edited by Graham J. Murphy and Lars Schmeink, Routledge, 2018, pp. 235–52.

McFarlane, Anna, Graham J. Murphy, and Lars Schmeink. "Cyberpunk as Cultural Formation." *The Routledge Companion to Cyberpunk Culture*, edited by Anna McFarlane, Graham J. Murphy, and Lars Schmeink, Routledge, 2020, pp. 1–3.

McHale, Brian. *Postmodernist Fiction*. Routledge, 1987.

———. *Constructing Postmodernism*. Routledge, 1992.

Milburn, Colin. "Activism." *The Routledge Companion to Cyberpunk Culture*, edited by Anna McFarlane, Graham J. Murphy, and Lars Schmeink, Routledge, 2020, pp. 373–81.

Moravec, Hans. *Mind Children: The Future of Robot and Human Intelligence*. Harvard UP, 1988.

Mortensen, Christian Hviid. "Beyond the Heroics of Gonzo-Journalism in *Transmetropolitan*." *Cyberpunk and Visual Culture*, edited by Graham J. Murphy and Lars Schmeink, Routledge, 2018, pp. 5–20.

Murphy, Graham J. "Angel(LINK) of Harlem: Techno-Spirituality in the Cyberpunk Tradition." *Beyond Cyberpunk: New Critical Perspectives*, edited by Graham J. Murphy and Sherryl Vint, Routledge, 2010, pp. 211–27.

Murphy, Graham J. and Lars Schmeink. "'Tactics of Visualization'; or, From Visual to Virtual Cyberpunk (and Back Again)." *Cyberpunk and Visual Culture*, edited by Graham J. Murphy and Lars Schmeink, Routledge, 2018, pp. 101–04.

Schmeink, Lars. *Biopunk Dystopias: Genetic Engineering, Society, and Science Fiction*. Liverpool UP, 2016.

"Scott Bukatman." Contributor Biography. *Cyberpunk and Visual Culture*, edited by Graham J. Murphy and Lars Schmeink, Routledge, 2018, pp. xi–xiv.

Takayuki, Tatsumi. "The Future of Cyberpunk Criticism: Introduction to Transpacific Cyberpunk." *Arts*, vol. 8, no. 1, March 25, 2019, http://dx.doi.org/10.3390/arts8010040.

"*TRON*." *IMDb* [Internet Movie Database]. n.d., https://www.imdb.com/title/tt0084827/?ref_=fn_al_tt_2.

Yaszek, Lisa. "Feminist Cyberpunk." *The Routledge Companion to Cyberpunk Culture*, edited by Anna McFarlane, Graham J. Murphy, and Lars Schmeink, Routledge, 2020, pp. 32–40.

INDEX

Note: Page numbers followed by "n" refer to end notes.